EARLY SLAVERY
AT THE CAPE OF GOOD HOPE,
1652–1717

Karel Schoeman

EARLY SLAVERY
AT THE CAPE OF GOOD HOPE,
1652–1717

Protea Book House
Pretoria
2007

Karel Schoeman
Early slavery at the Cape of Good Hope, 1652–1717
First edition, first impression 2007

Protea Book House
PO Box 35110, Menlo Park, 0102
1067 Burnett Street, Hatfield, Pretoria
8 Minni Street, Clydesdale, Pretoria
protea@intekom.co.za
www.proteaboekhuis.co.za

Typography and design by Hond CC
Printed and bound by Interpak Books

ISBN 978-1-86919-147-4

Foreword

Awareness of and interest in slavery in the Cape Colony is steadily increasing, but most of the work that has been done on this subject is in Dutch or Afrikaans, and there are only five general surveys in English,* of which the most accessible to the general reader, *Those in Bondage* by Victor de Kock, was published in 1950.

The purpose of this book is to bring together the widely scattered information on the first sixty-odd years of slavery at the Cape and make it available to the general public.

The period covered begins with the arrival of the first white settlers under Jan van Riebeeck in 1652, for it was only seven weeks later that he mentioned the possibility of slave labour, while the first known slave reached the Cape in 1653. The closing date is the year in which the members of the Council of Policy at the Cape admitted to their principals, the Gentlemen XVII in the Netherlands, that the colony had within less than sixty years become committed to and dependent on slave labour.

While this was never the intention, this book in fact to a certain extent complements the collection of slave trials published recently by the Van Riebeeck Society under the title *Trials of slavery* (2005), which with the range of texts transcribed and the extensive editorial matter gives remarkably full coverage to the period 1708–94. Together these two works, though differing in content and purpose,

---

*   Böeseken, *Slaves and free blacks*; De Kock, *Those in bondage*; Ross, *Cape of torments*; Shell, *Children of bondage*; and Worden, *Slavery*; but see also Armstrong and Worden, 'Slaves'.

cover the entire period during which the Cape was governed by the VOC (Dutch East India Company).

While every attempt has been made to keep within the period dealt with, for lack of sufficient information on the early years it has occasionally been necessary to use somewhat later evidence, more specifically from the writings of O.F. Mentzel, who was at the Cape in 1733–41, and even on occasion Lady Anne Barnard, who arrived in 1797. This has been done with due caution, however, for the world of Cape slavery was neither monolithic nor static, in spite of the happy assumption of so many writers on the subject that examples may be plucked arbitrarily and at random from any point between 1652 and 1795, or even 1834.

This study is based on published sources, both primary and secondary, already investigated by me for the book published in Afrikaans as *Armosyn van die Kaap; die wêreld van 'n slavin, 1652–1733* (2001; 2nd ed. 2005). It is, however, a new reworking of these, intended for English-speaking and non-South African readers. As far as the final chapter is concerned, the section on Armozijn van de Caab is a re-presentation of information in the earlier work, with some additional details, while the accounts of Angela van Bengalen and Evert van Guinee are based on the corresponding chapters in my book *Kinders van die Kompanjie* (2006).

As far as possible I have quoted verbatim from contemporary documents, allowing them to tell their own story. In spite of this, however, I have in all honesty towards my readers had to make greater use of words such as 'probably', 'possibly', 'likely', 'seem' and 'appear' than I myself would prefer.

While I have undertaken no archival research for the present book, I have made use of some transcriptions and other copies which happened to be in my possession already: the muster roll of the Company's slaves and convicts (1693) originally transcribed by Dr H.F. Heese; documents relating to Claes van Malabar (1692), Godfried Meijhuisen (1697), Alexander van Bengalen (1699) and the death of Armozijn van de Caab (1733); the reports on the Slave Lodge by

K.J. Slotsboo (1710) and L.M. Thibault (1804); and the lists of clothing distributed to the Company's slaves (1720–21).

I have avoided a statistical presentation, and have tried to refrain from analysis and interpretation for which I am not qualified, leaving the facts to speak for themselves, and providing references as far as possible to more authoritative and academic works in the endnotes.

I would like to express my gratitude to Gerald Groenewald, who with his knowledge of the period concerned and the archival sources relating to it, was always prepared to answer questions and solve problems as they arose, as will be clear from the endnotes; and to Annette Bester and Rothea Pelser of the University of the Free State, who were no less willing to provide photocopies and obtain interlibrary loans respectively. I would further like to thank James Armstrong for help frequently received in the past, and Nigel Worden.

Finally I am grateful to Jill Martin for her firm but tactful editing, and to Nicol Stassen of Protea Book House for agreeing to publish the book.

15 March–27 April 2006   Karel Schoeman

Contents

1. Beginnings (1652–58)

In 1651 the Dutch East India Company (*Verenigde Oostindische Compagnie* or VOC) decided to establish a halfway station at Table Bay for the benefit of its shipping between the Netherlands and the East: here ships would be able to meet, exchange news during the course of the long voyage, have their sick cared for and obtain refreshments. Early the following year a small party under Jan van Riebeeck landed here, and began to erect a fort with earthen ramparts on what was then the shore of the bay (the present Strand Street in Cape Town) and lay out a garden on the banks of the mountain streams where visiting ships had until then obtained their drinking water.

The outpost was a foundation of the Company, which was a largely autonomous commercial body, acting independently of the Dutch state. It was subordinate to the Company's board of directors, known variously as the 'Gentlemen XVII' (*Heren XVII*), 'Council of XVII', 'the XVII' or 'the Lords and Masters', who formed the highest level of government in the VOC, and to the Governor-General and Council of (East) India in Batavia, who ranked immediately below them.[1]

By the end of the first year the pioneer party consisted of 110 men and 15 women and children, all of them white and predominantly from the Netherlands, the north-western portion of the German-speaking area and Scandinavia. They were mostly sailors, soldiers and artisans, and few had any experience of the VOC's extensive trading empire which stretched from the Red Sea to Japan, apart from Van Riebeeck himself, who had served the Company for some years in Batavia (modern Jakarta), Tonkin (the present Vietnam) and Japan. Van Riebeeck was therefore one of the few members of the party who had any personal experience of slavery.

When the Portuguese, having rounded the Cape of Good Hope in 1488, began large-scale seaborne trading with the East, they found there various established systems of bondage and slavery in which slaves were captured by dealers or in warfare, sold themselves or members of their families in times of famine or were held for debt.[2] In India slaves were mostly indigenous to the country, while in the Indonesian archipelago 'large-scale deportations' were common.[3] Most slavery was of the domestic type, and slaves were mainly concentrated in cities.

'Arabian' or Muslim dealers also carried on a lively trade in slaves from the interior of Africa whom they acquired at the various ports along the East Coast. As the Portuguese could not obtain sufficient slaves for their own purposes through the existing channels, this trade was extended by them after they established their colonial capital at Goa on the west coast of India. African slaves were generally referred to by the Muslims as *caffirs* or 'unbelievers', in the sense of 'non-Muslims', and this term was adopted by the Portuguese. During the sixteenth and seventeenth century '*caffirs*' were to be found in all parts of the Portuguese colonial world and beyond, serving not only as house slaves and labourers but also in the Portuguese army and as sailors on Portuguese ships. They are said to have done duty in the army of a Bengali ruler, and there was a black bodyguard at the Chinese court formed of fugitive black slaves from the Portuguese trading colony at Macao.[4]

Dutch trading expeditions financed by individual private companies began visiting Asia in 1595, while the VOC officially received the monopoly in trade east of the Cape of Good Hope from the Dutch States-General on its creation in 1602.[5] Here it gradually established itself, by treaty or conquest, in conveniently situated harbours and on islands from the Red Sea to Japan. In the process it found itself becoming increasingly involved in intra-Asian trade in order to obtain the goods it required for export to Europe, these being spices and pepper at first, which came to be replaced by cotton goods, silks, tea and coffee as the century drew to a close.

As its field of activity was enlarged and its commitments increased, the Company also began to realise the advantages of slave labour, although the Dutch, unlike the Portuguese, had no previous experience of slavery in Europe. It therefore became increasingly involved in the local slave trade, to which it made its own distinctive contribution. Vink refers in this regard to 'an intellectual, theoretical mentalité steeped in Christian humanism mixed with healthy doses of pragmatism', which it grafted on 'preexisting indigenous traditions',[6] while Fox, in simpler phraseology, points out that the VOC 'was the first to introduce impersonal, institutional slave-holding in which a corporation—not an individual—held persons in perpetuity.'[7]

Although the subject of slavery under the VOC, and more especially in Batavia, seems of considerable importance for an understanding of the way in which slavery subsequently developed at the Cape, little research has unfortunately been done on this subject up to now.[8] 'Indeed,' as Vink writes, 'the sufferings of the slaves in Asia occurred mainly in silence, largely ignored by both contemporaries and modern historians.'[9] On the other hand, as Arasaratnam remarks in a passage which Vink quotes:

> The evidence of the slave trade in the Indian Ocean is scanty and periodic, and could reflect the nature of the trade. There are huge gaps in the evidence, which might reflect the spasmodic and periodic nature of the slave trade, but also the sheer lack of information for long stretches of time.[10]

In 1619 the VOC established the city of Batavia (the modern Jakarta) on the island of Java in the Indonesian archipelago as its capital in the East and the centre of its trade. After this development its need for labour became so great that the members of the small population of free whites (freeburghers) which developed under the Company were for a time allowed and encouraged to take part in slave trading. Not only were slaves needed as labourers, however, but the ambitious Governor-General, Jan Pietersz Coen, even saw them as potential colonists. 'There cannot be too many of them gathered in Batavia,' he wrote to the Gentlemen XVII in 1623. 'They should be employed in fruit growing, cattle breeding, in fisheries and various offices and services. How and in what manner time will tell.'[11]

As early as 1616 the XVII discussed the possibility of obtaining slaves from Madagascar, which was not far off the route of its ships between the Cape and the East,[12] but eventually this proved inconvenient and preference was given to markets closer to Batavia. Initially slaves were obtained largely from Bengal in the north-east of India and Aracan (the present Bangladesh), where they were captured in the delta of the Ganges by local pirates and Portuguese renegades in armed vessels. Between 1626 and 1662, according to Vink, 'the Dutch exported with reasonable regularity 150–400 slaves annually from the Arakan-Bengal coast. During the first thirty years of Batavia's existence, Indian and Arakanese slaves provided the main labor force of the company's Asian headquarters.'[13] The earliest slaves at the Cape would also be predominantly from Bengal, but after the area had been incorporated in the Mughal Empire in 1666, the supply of slaves was cut off.

A fairly constant source of slaves was also the Coromandel or east coast of India, where the VOC had established trading posts at an early stage with a view to purchasing the cotton goods it required for its intra-Asian trade. Vink lists a number of booms in the slave trade here caused by local wars and famines, of which those occurring in 1646, 1659–61, 1673–77, 1688 and 1694–96 are of particular relevance to the Cape. During the famine period in 1659–61, 8000 to 10 000 slaves were exported to Ceylon (Sri Lanka), Batavia and

Malacca (Malaka) by the Company.[14] It is also possible, however, that many of the slaves bought in Coromandel had originally been obtained in Aracan and Bengal.

Finally, as far as India is concerned, during the Company's vigorous and successful campaign against the Portuguese in 1658–63, large numbers of captives from the Malabar or west coast of India were also incorporated in its labour force.

From the 1660s, however, relatively more slaves were obtained from the Indonesian archipelago, where they were acquired by local slave dealers from over a wide area through warfare and by means of raiding expeditions, the most important trading centres being Macassar in Celebes (Sulawesi) and Bali.

Macassar, long famous as a centre of local trade, became an especially important source of supply after the defeat of its independent sultanate in 1668 and 1669 and its subjugation by the VOC.[15] The island of Bali is described by Raben as 'extremely fragmented' and 'the stage of prolonged endemic warfare between neighbouring states during the second half of the seventeenth century', to which he adds, 'for decades Lombok was embroiled in a war between the Balinese and the Sumbawese'.[16] Macassar, Bali and Sumbawa ('Bouwa') were to be represented by many slaves at the Cape.

Indonesian slaves were also obtained more incidentally at other places such as Timor and Roti, while the island of Nias, off the west coast of Sumatra, is described as 'a well-known slave supplier'.[17]

'Over the two decades 1663–1682 about which we have an unbroken series of import numbers,' writes Raben, 'a total of 9,809 slaves were imported in Batavia by Indonesian vessels, an average of 490 per year. Almost one quarter came from Bali, more than two-fifths from Makassar, and some twelve per cent from Buton (these figures are probably higher, as many will have been brought to Batavia via ports other than those in their homeland).'[18]

Death rates on the slave ships were often high, due to factors such as inadequate provisions, poor conditions on board and the physical condition of many of the slaves. Of 1300 slaves bought by the Company in Aracan and Bengal in 1625, for example, half died on the voyage to Batavia,[19] and of 2118 shipped from Coromandel during a famine in 1646, 572 died on the way.[20]

Because of high death rates, widespread absconding and a strikingly low rate of reproduction among the VOC's slave population, it was constantly necessary to replenish their numbers, and the steady increase in the size and scope of its activities also increased the demand for slaves.[21] By the middle of the century, however, the most urgent need had passed, and Company slaves were frequently employed in agriculture or lent out to needy freeburghers.[22]

The altered situation is reflected in the increasing carelessness which characterised the Company's records and administration. In 1651, for example, a third of its work force was found to be incapable and 60 individual slaves who could not be traced were simply written off, while in 1660 there were said to be 1420 fewer slaves than given in the official records.[23] By 1678 the Company was having to hire 500 slaves from private slave owners, which cost it 72 000 guilders a year.[24] At the same time Niemeijer also notices a relative improvement in the situation of Company slaves, the men living in families, often with freeborn wives, and sometimes even owning slaves themselves.[25]

The mostly readily available information on the workings of the VOC, here as elsewhere, relates to Batavia, where it operated on the largest scale and had the largest and best-documented establishment. After the capture of Ceylon from the Portuguese, which was completed by 1658, attempts were also made to subjugate and colonise the island, and large numbers of slaves and 'coolies' or hired labourers were brought from the south of India, specifically from the port of Tuticorin, from which the Cape was also to obtain a batch of slaves some time afterwards. Most of the slaves intended for Ceylon seem to have come from Malabar on the west coast of India, however, after it had likewise been captured from the Portuguese.[26]

Initially the Company required slave labour chiefly for constructing fortifications and loading and unloading ships, but as their numbers increased, so did the work assigned to them. C.J. Simons, visiting the Cape as Commissioner in 1710 after some twelve years in the East, summarised the possibilities in an attempt to show local authorities what might be done.

> Also the deportees [*exiles*], and especially the Easterners, could be used to great advantage as woodcutters in the Company's forests, as [in Ceylon] this is done by some 20 such under the supervision of a *schieman* [*boatswain*] and his mate, who also see to the shipping of it; and although the Company's slaves there are not by far so strong and agile as the Madagascar Kaffers [*at the Cape*], the heavy masonry-work (not to be compared with that here) is however also done [by them] under supervision of a European foreman and his [halfcaste] assistant; and moreover they are for the most part also used on the timber-wharf, and in the carpenter's shop, and with the copper-smiths and coopers, and in the arsenal, which has only a European foreman, the ordinary workers being only half-bloods, natives, and Company's slaves (…).[27]

The Company was therefore compelled to keep up an active trade in slaves until the end of its existence, and on a considerable scale. Placing this in a wider contemporary context, Vink remarks, 'The volume of the total Dutch Indian Ocean slave trade was (…) 15–30% of the Atlantic slave trade, slightly smaller than the trans-Saharan slave trade, and one-and-a-half to three times the size of the Swahili and Red Sea coast and the Dutch West India Company slave trades.'[28]

Only a relatively small group of ministers of religion and laymen in the Netherlands questioned the morality of Dutch participation in the slave trade and slavery, but justification was found in Scripture and in historical precedent, and specious arguments were presented in favour of slavery such as the opportunities it provided for converting the heathen.[29] The VOC itself was never inclined to let moral questions interfere with business and profit. While it appointed ministers and sick comforters to look after the spiritual welfare of its employees, and had the children of its own slaves baptised as a matter of routine, missionary work which might endanger its relations with indigenous peoples was discouraged, and it was only in a few specific areas such as Formosa (Taiwan) and Ceylon that any notable evangelisation took place.

As the extent of the Company's slave holdings increased, so too did the problems involved in slave ownership. As early as 1617 the Gentlemen XVII in the Netherlands had forbidden the sale of slaves by Christians to non-Christians,[30] and in 1622 the local authorities tried a case which dealt with the alleged mistreatment of a slave.[31] By the same year complaints were already being heard about the fugitive slaves infesting the jungle immediately surrounding Batavia.[32]

It was likewise in 1622 that the first notable piece of slave legislation was enacted, a *plakkaat* or ordinance with nine articles issued in 1622 which Niemeijer describes as 'the juridical foundation for the slave society of Batavia',[33] although Fox comments that it 'seems to derive less from Roman law than from strict Christian principles'.[34] It followed the same general line as the earlier limitation on slave transactions, but made a finer distinction than hitherto among Christian, 'Moor' (Muslim) and 'heathen' slave owners, and instituted checks on slave transactions. In so doing, remarks Fox, it 'created the basis for a complex book-keeping system to regulate the flow of commodities'.[35]

This legislation was amplified in 1625 by a further ordinance of ten articles, 'most of which,' according to Fox, 'were directed at curtailing the excessively severe and uncontrolled punishment of privately owned slaves and at providing a framework for the obligations of slaves to their masters.'[36]

The ordinances of 1622 and 1625 are described by Fox as 'the basis, and indeed the substance, for the consolidated "Statutes of Batavia"',[37] although the latter were more than just a further piece of legislation on slavery. The Statutes of Batavia were in fact the codification of the laws by which the VOC governed Batavia, promulgated in 1642 under Governor-General Van Diemen, which ten years later would become applicable at the Cape as well, and at the latter place their provisions with regard to slaves would help shape the local manifestations of slavery and attitudes towards it.

Of the 30 unnumbered articles in the Statutes devoted to slaves and slavery under the heading '*Slaeven ofte lyffeygenen*',[38] two are perhaps of special interest. Firstly the slave owners were given permission to make use of '*domestycke straffen*' or 'domestic punishments' on their own authority, although these were not defined and the definitions given to them in practice were to vary widely over the years. The use of handcuffs and chains was forbidden, as was 'torture or other mistreatment'.[39]

Secondly, while slaves who caused injury to their masters verbally were to be scourged and chained, those 'who came to forget themselves to such an extent as to raise their hands against their masters and mistresses', whether armed or not, were to be sentenced to death.

The articles dealing with slavery seem mainly intended to safeguard the position of the slave owners, but there are a number among them which appear to offer some measure of relative security or safeguard to the slaves themselves. Slave transactions were not be concluded in 'drunken gatherings' (although this may also have been administrative precaution); Christian slave owners were to give their slaves religious instruction and have them baptised; owners killing their slaves were to be duly punished, although the form of punishment was not clearly prescribed; slaves who were treated 'unmercifully' were allowed to complain to the authorities if they had 'great and pressing' reasons, but were to be scourged and returned if their complaints were judged to be unfounded; and if a master was through illness or weakness no longer able to support his slaves, the latter might ask to be set free. Provision was also made for the freeing of slaves by their owners.

Much further slave legislation was of course to follow, and 'by a rough count,' according to Fox, 'the Company issued over two hundred ordinances that were directly and immediately pertinent to slaves, plus countless others that affected the condition of slaves indirectly'.[40]

The names used in the heading of that section of the Statutes which dealt with slaves, *slaven* and *lijfeigenen* in modern Dutch, were those most commonly in use at the time: they were in fact synonymous, although *lijfeigene* may also be translated as 'bondsman'. The term *dienstbaarheid* or 'servitude' was sometimes used with reference to the condition of slavery, and slaves were referred to by the circumlocution *dienstbare mensen*, 'servile people' or 'bondspeople'. A slave owner was called a *meester, lijfheer* ('bondsmaster') or *patroon*, the corresponding feminine forms being *meesteres, lijfvrouw* and *patrones*.

Visitors to Goa and other centres of Portuguese settlement during the sixteenth and seventeenth centuries regularly commented on the large retinues of slaves which formed part of everyday life in private households. This was the example followed in due course by other European powers who came to trade and establish colonies in Asia, and also by the small community of private citizens of European origin (freeburghers) in Batavia.[41]

Slaves belonging to private individuals or to Company officials in their personal capacity were used largely for housework and gardening and for looking after children and horses, though they might also be hired out as so-called coolies or artisans. In individual cases a surprising amount of freedom was possible, and they could even, with the approval of their masters, keep shops, receive formal training in a craft, or possess slaves of their own.[42]

While the VOC initially obtained its labour force from Bengal and Aracan, as already mentioned, the private dealers who supplied the Batavian market 'without exception' traded in slaves from the Indonesian archipelago.[43] Harbour records for Batavia, for example, note the arrival there of 65 indigenous ships during the month of March 1653, with a total crew of 647, bringing 49 male and female slaves for sale in addition to a wide variety of other goods.[44]

There were accordingly slaves from both India and Indonesia in the town, and while the slaves manumitted in Batavia in the years 1646–49 came mainly from Bengal, Coromandel and Malabar, more than 11% had their origin in Bali.[45] Niemeijer has subjected similar statistics for a period of a little more than a year in 1652–53 to closer analysis, according to which Chinese and other Asian slave owners in Batavia manumitted mainly slaves from Bali, while the figures for Europeans referred in the first place to slaves from Bengal, Malabar and Coromandel, in that order.[46] This was in other words the situation here at about the time that slavery was instituted at the Cape.

After Bengal had ceased to be a source of slaves for the VOC, slave trading with the Indonesian archipelago gained steadily in importance, and Raben points out the rise in the number of slaves imported in Batavia by Asian ships, mostly from Macassar and Bali, as from 1669, with a peak of 1584 slaves in 1671.[47]

It was as a result of this boom that the slave holdings of both officials and freeburghers in Batavia grew to remarkable proportions, and that slave households came into being among the Dutch which equalled those for which the Portuguese had already become known in Goa. Likewise, when the local market was abundantly supplied, passengers on ships from Batavia took to selling slaves at the Cape on their homeward journey. This trade soon became organised and grew steadily in volume, and the wealthier freeburghers of the Cape were at last able to acquire slave labour for themselves.

By 1679, when the total population of the inner city of Batavia amounted to 17 740, there were 1711 Europeans and 9938 slaves, though by no means all of the latter belonged to white owners.[48] Niemeijer gives the total population for the same year as 32 124 and the figures for the two groups as 2227 and 16 695 respectively, which appears to include the suburbs immediately outside the city walls.[49]

21

Referring to the earlier centre of Dutch administration here, he remarks that the 'naturalness of slavery in Asia and the frequent supply of indigenous slaves made pre-colonial Jacatra a slave society',[50] and in quoting these later figures he likewise describes slavery as 'probably the chief characteristic of Batavian society'.[51]

By 1642 complaints had already been heard about the noise made in or outside churches during services by the slaves who had accompanied their masters,[52] and the Dutch ship's surgeon Nicolaus van de Graaff, who last visited Batavia in 1687, describes with sarcastic disapproval the formal church parade on Sundays where every woman was attended by one or more slaves, 'so that, before the beginning of the sermon or after the service, the entire churchyard in front of and around the church doors is so full of sunshades, male and female slaves, guards and attendants that it is almost impossible to pass, in addition to those waiting outside the churchyard with their carriages in order to take their masters and mistresses home'.[53]

A striking account of a slave household in Batavia at about the same time is given in a letter written in 1689 by Cornelia Johanna van Beveren to relatives in the Netherlands. She was the daughter of a Dutchman of good family who had been helped to obtain a senior post in Batavia, and had recently married Jurriaen Beeck, the locally born son of a wealthy freeburgher merchant. Referring to the extensive grounds of her new home, she remarks that she intended to lay out a garden on one half, 'and the rest remains for the slaves, who are 59 in all and accordingly need a good deal of space'.

> Your Honour has asked me to describe what work 59 slaves do. I will therefore oblige. Three to four boys follow me and my husband when we go out, also the same number of girls, five or six attendants, male and female, stand behind our chairs at table, three boys who play on the double bass, violin and harp while we dine. The remainder of the boys I use for housework, errands, sewing, knitting and similar handiwork; one

takes care of the drink in the pantry, two or three in the kitchen, so that each always has his work. The girls I use for lacemaking, embroidery and plain sewing, three or four look after me, one has to sit in the hallway to receive messages, so that Your Honour has had a summary of the slaves' lives.[54]

Here already one finds the Dutch terms *jongens* and *meiden* ('boys' and 'girls'), commonly used for white servants, applied to slaves, and in a similar situation in South Africa these names would eventually come to be used exclusively for non-whites, irrespective of age.[55]

While the Beecks' household cannot be regarded as altogether typical, it was nonetheless indicative of the way slaves had become status symbols in the colonial world. By the end of the century they formed well over half the population of Batavia, and in Colombo, the capital of Ceylon, a similar situation had developed. Vink describes VOC settlements like these as 'true slave societies, in which slaves played an important part in both luxury and productive capacities, empowering particular groups of elites, deeply influenced cultural developments, and formed a high proportion (over 20–40%) of the total population.'[56]

By the end of the eighteenth century there are references to as many as 200 slaves in a single Batavian household,[57] and by 1816 there were 12 000 slaves in the city and its immediate surroundings, the highest total for a single household being 165.[58] It was not until 1860 that the last slaves in Batavia were officially emancipated,[59] a full generation after emancipation had come into effect at the Cape under British rule. 'In general,' remarks De Haan, however, 'service by slaves was extremely expensive, and extremely bad.'[60]

Another distinctive element in Batavian society of some relevance to later developments at the Cape was that, given the shortage of European women, it was common for European men to have children by local women, who were sometimes acknowledged and even legitimised by their fathers. The children of slave women legally inherited the status of their mother, however, and were slaves themselves, and it was therefore quite possible for a white man to sell off his own illegitimate family.[61]

Racially mixed marriages were less common, but nonetheless occurred and were generally accepted, even in the case of relatively senior officials. In 1639, for example, the Dutch official Adriaen van der Stel was sent to Mauritius as governor with his wife, a daughter of the coloured woman Monica da Costa, who was already pregnant with their first child, a future Governor of the Cape.[62] By 1649 the Gentlemen XVII could express surprise at the number of repatriating officials returning to the Netherlands with coloured wives, mentioning by name men with the rank of Senior Merchant, and examples such as these could be multiplied.[63] In some cases the women concerned were manumitted slaves.

Niemeijer gives statistics for the period 1616–41, reflecting the situation which came into being shortly before the establishment of a settlement by the VOC at the Cape. According to this, of the 801 Dutch men contracting marriage, 347 were married to Dutch wives, 84 to European women of other nationalities, 133 to women from the Indonesian archipelago, 85 to women from India, and 55 to women with names of Portuguese origin. Among a total of 1067 European men of all nationalities, there were 184 marriages to women of Indonesian and 128 to women of Indian origin.[64] In the relatively small colonial world of the VOC interracial marriages were therefore not an unfamiliar phenomenon.

Two further groups in the multiracial population of Batavia also deserve mention.

The so-called 'Mardijkers' (*orang merdéka* or 'free people'), sometimes referred to simply as *zwarten* or 'blacks', were free, coloured Christians of Indian origin, with Portuguese or Dutch names followed by a patronym or toponym: Niemeijer gives examples such as Marcus van Bali and Francisco Pietersz, with 'Susanna van de Kust' (i.e., the Coast of Coromandel) being translated into Susanna da Costa.[65] They formed a small community, totalling little more than 5000 by 1679,[66] but Mardijkers quite frequently found themselves at the Cape when banished there by the authorities for some misdemeanour and were absorbed into the local coloured population. They are sometimes described as the Batavian equivalent of the 'free blacks' at the Cape, but unlike the latter, who were manumitted slaves, they appear always to have been free.

A notable part of the population of Batavia was formed, finally, by a large community of Chinese men with a reputation for hard work who devoted themselves largely to trade and finance.[67] They too were often to find themselves deported to the Cape.

During the earliest months of the VOC's refreshment post at the Cape, before colonisation by whites was decided upon, Jan van Riebeeck on several occasions expressed a wish for colonists from the Mardijker and Chinese communities of Batavia, and in general the ties between Batavia and the Cape were always close. Knowledge of conditions in the East under the VOC is therefore of some importance as regards an understanding of developments at the Cape, and this applies specifically to slavery. Not only were the precepts for slave owning laid down by the Statutes of Batavia followed here, but so too, for want of an alternative, the precedents established over a period of some thirty or forty years in the East. This applies especially to Van Riebeeck himself with his earlier experience of life in the East, and to his immediate successor as Commander, Zacharias Wagenaer, who came to the Cape directly from Batavia with his wife; but all seven men who were in charge of the Cape over the period 1652–78 had lived and worked under the VOC in the East, while Simon van der Stel, who served as Commander and Governor in 1679–99, had grown up there.

As regards the development of early Cape slavery, a special role may well have been played by Wagenaer, who succeeded Van Riebeeck in 1662 and spent more than four years at the Cape, proving himself an active and conscientious Commander. Not only had he served the Company in the East since 1643, but for the greater part of 1661, immediately before his transfer to the Cape, he had occupied the responsible post of *fabriek* or director of public works in Batavia,[68] in which capacity he was in charge of the Company's slave force and responsible for hiring slave or coolie labour for official projects.[69] It is not known what arrangements he made with regard to the slaves at the Cape, apart from providing them with new living quarters, but he may well have established standards which influenced subsequent developments.

It was, however, the form of slavery that existed in Batavia in about the middle of the century that all these men knew, not its full flowering in later decades, and once established at the Cape under their supervision and with their guidance, the institution would continue to develop largely along its own lines as determined by local conditions.

After the retirement of Simon van der Stel in 1699, it would be mainly through isolated individual officials that the Cape would keep in contact with the wider world of slavery under the VOC, such as J.C. d'Ableing, who was Chief of the Company's post at Palembang in Sumatra when he was dismissed for private trading and shortages in his administration, but was reinstated as Secunde or 'Second Person' of the Cape from 1707 until 1710. In addition, contact was kept up through the thousands of repatriating officials who visited the Cape with the return fleet which early each year took the VOC's valuable cargo of trading goods to Europe, and finally, of course, through the hundreds of slaves who over the years were imported to the Cape from the East.

Besides the slave trade of the Indian Ocean, the Dutch were at this time involved on an even larger scale in that of the Atlantic. Here the West India Company (WIC), a parallel organisation to the VOC which had been founded in 1621,[70] had colonies in West Africa, the Caribbean and North America and was briefly in control of the Portuguese colonies of Angola and Brazil as well. Even after it had been ousted from the latter by the middle of the century, it retained a series of forts and trading posts along the Gold and Slave Coasts of Africa, in the area known comprehensively as Guinea, and continued to play an active part in supplying slaves from the interior of Africa to the Americas.

The Atlantic slave trade, which assumed vast proportions and in which various European nations were involved, has been extensively documented,[71] but it was of little significance to the settlement at the Cape, and the information concerning it is unfortunately of no great relevance to slavery in South Africa, apart from its earliest phase under Van Riebeeck.

This then was the general context in which the VOC outpost was established at the Cape.

On 21 April 1652, a fortnight after his arrival, Jan van Riebeeck 'proceeded a good way up the kloof of the Table Mountain, about 2 miles', presumably over Kloof Nek in the direction of Camps Bay, a Dutch mile being variously given as equal to 5 or 7 kilometres. With his customary enthusiasm he 'found everywhere the finest flat clay ground and other beautiful, broad, fertile soil' which might be cultivated by 'industrious Chinese'.[72]

On the 27th, walking out in the direction of the present Mouille Point, he came upon 'the most beautiful land for sowing and for grazing cattle that one could desire' and spoke of the possibilities for cultivation, 'for which we require some married Chinese and other free Mardijckers or even also Hollanders', the earliest suggestion of colonisation by the Dutch.[73] The following day he set out with a party accompanied by armed soldiers in the opposite direction, towards Salt River and the valley of the Liesbeek River, and declared that

> even if there were thousands of Chinese or other tillers they could not take up or cultivate a tenth part of this land. It is moreover so fertile and rich that neither Formosa [*Taiwan*] which I have seen, nor New Netherland [*the present New York and Albany*] which I have heard of, can be compared with it.[74]

These references to 'Chinese or other industrious people or families' were repeated in his official Journal,[75] and it was not until 25 May, seven weeks after his arrival at the Cape, that Van Riebeeck, writing to Batavia, requested 'some slaves for the dirtiest and heaviest work, to take the place of the Dutchmen in fetching stone, &c., to be obtained only at a distance (…)—some slaves from Batavia would therefore be welcome who know how to cut stone and [to help] dig up the soil (…).'[76] At the end of the year the Council of India replied: 'We have not been able to persuade any Chinese to leave their country for such a distant land and with such uncertain prospects. Neither can we at the moment send any slaves, because we require them ourselves.'[77]

The idea of slave labour had taken root, however, and on 2 April 1654, after two years of struggling against the difficulties with an inadequate work force, Van Riebeeck noted in his Journal that 'it would be very much cheaper to have the agricultural work, seal-catching and all the other necessary work done by slaves in return for a plain fare of rice and fish or seal and penguin meat alone and without pay',[78] a suggestion he repeated in his report to the Gentlemen XVII some three weeks later.[79] At the same time he suggested the use of slaves in the silver mines he hoped to discover at the Cape. 'The slaves might also be used for seal killing and agriculture,' he added, 'and their food being cheap while they receive no pay, the costs would be very little. Together with rice they might with little expense be brought in a vessel from Madagascar where they are cheap.'[80]

Early in 1653 the Cape was visited by Martino Martini, a Jesuit missionary working in China who was returning to Europe via Batavia on one of the ships of the return fleet. With this knowledgeable and experienced man Van Riebeeck discussed the possibility of trading with harbours on the south-eastern coast of Africa, 'where much gold, tusks, ebony and fine Caffers or slaves were to be had at cheap rates and easily for Genoa [sic], red cotton, coarse and painted cloths, tobacco, iron, glass beads of all colours, little bells, and salt

(…)'.[81] Here too the name 'Caffers' was used in the original sense of non-Muslims from the interior of Africa, as had already become customary in the East.

In reporting to the XVII on the information obtained from Martini, Van Riebeeck requested permission to undertake a trading expedition to these regions himself, using one of the small vessels kept at the Cape for transport in local waters, conjuring up visions of discovering 'the real Ophir whence Solomon was supplied with gold'.[82]

There seems to have been no official reaction to this, though Van Riebeeck repeated his suggestions the following year, adding to them the prospect of also obtaining rice from Madagascar.[83] As the Gentlemen XVII were very much concerned with profit and increasingly worried about the expense of running the outpost at the Cape, he placed increasing emphasis on the savings which would be brought about by the importation of supplies from Madagascar, and the economic benefits to be achieved by the importation of slaves: 'The Madagascar slaves besides would save wages, and less men might be kept here to save expense for the Company,' he was writing to the XVII by 1655,[84] and elsewhere in the same letter, 'This would enable you to discharge a good number of paid labourers and keep them at agriculture and seal fishing. Some slaves might also be obtained for Batavia at a nominal figure.'[85] In one of his frequent visionary moments he foresaw 'being able to send so many [seal]skins home, and so many slaves to India, that in course of time you may expect better things from this place, [to which the Almighty may give His blessing]'.[86]

In the meantime, however, when the return fleet of 1654 had not touched at the Cape and food supplies were running dangerously low, Van Riebeeck had been forced to undertake an expedition of this nature on his own authority. Frederick Verburgh, who had the rank of Bookkeeper, was sent to St. Helena in the galiot or 'decked boat' *Tulp* in an attempt to overtake the return fleet and obtain supplies,[87] and the galiot *Rode Vos*[88] was despatched to Madagascar on

8 May 1654 with instructions to buy 25 or 30 tons of rice, besides arrack, cadjang (a legume), beans, black and white sugar, wax, and 'some syrup, or otherwise honey, to make beer';

> Besides 30 or 40 slaves, more or less as you may be able to conveniently take on board—among them 10 or 12 slave girls from 12 to 15 or 16 years of age—the men slaves, however, in the range between 16 to 20 and 23 years.[89]

When the *Tulp* returned to the Cape, Verburgh, who had in the meantime been promoted to Secunde or 'second person',[90] was likewise sent off on 3 July,[91] to explore the coast of Africa, investigate the possibilities of trade, and obtain from Madagascar 'as much rice as you can get for your cargo, besides 8 or 10 slaves or more'.[92]

The *Rode Vos* returned to Table Bay on 25 August, having been instructed by the commander of the Dutch outpost on Mauritius that it was unnecessary to call at Madagascar, as a yacht had been sent to the Cape with provisions.[93] The *Tulp* was more welcome when it returned on 12 December,[94] having visited Antongil Bay in the north-east of Madagascar where the Dutch had on previous occasions acquired slaves,[95] and obtained 2 tons of white rice and 5 or 6 tons of paddy (unhusked rice), but no more, it would appear, than 2 or 3 slaves.[96] They had been hospitably received by the 'King' of Antongil, who promised Verburgh 'to have as much rice and as many slaves in readiness as we might want,' as Van Riebeeck reported to Batavia. 'Especially if we decided to leave Hollanders there, for they seem much inclined towards us. Verburgh had promised to return, and they had undertaken to have the rice and slaves in readiness.'[97]

These attempts not having achieved immediate success, Van Riebeeck turned to Batavia in a more determined fashion, and in the winter of 1655 despatched an order for 'some buttons, 20 catty silk, 100 bundles cane, 80 or 100 slaves, [and] 6 or 8 mares for breeding purposes', specifying in an attachment, '80 or 100 slaves, among them 2 or 3 who can make cane matting'.[98] At the same time, however, Verburgh was sent again to 'the great island of Madagascar' in the *Tulp* with provisions for 25 men. 'You are sent purposely to Antongil to greet the King,' his instructions ran, 'and keep the trade alive until we receive further orders from home. You are further to inquire particularly into everything, and also try and get [as many slaves as possible, but] not younger than 15 and not older than 20 or 25 years.'[99]

The galiot set out on 14 August,[100] but was not heard of definitely for more than 18 months. It was only in March 1657 that a French ship returning from Madagascar brought to the Cape four survivors of the expedition,

> which during the night between 1 and 2 December 1655 had been overtaken by a hurricane near the river of Colamboelo, opposite St. Maria [*an island near Antongil Bay*], and had been lost with 40 lasts of rice which had been obtained there;[101] all the men and some of the merchandise had, however, been saved, but all except 11 of them had died of sickness on St. Maria, including the junior merchant Frederick Verburgh, skipper, the assistant Cornelis van Heijningen, and the mate. Six of the 11 men had voluntarily remained with the French and were looking after the salvaged goods.[102]

Even before the departure of the *Tulp*, Van Riebeeck had been writing to the XVII advocating that the Cape should be provided with a larger vessel such as a 'proper yacht or flute ship with 12 or 14 pieces [*cannon*]' for trade with Madagascar on a large scale: 'The galiots are too weak and small for this purpose.'[103] By the time the failure of the *Tulp*'s expedition became known, however, freeburghership had been instituted at the Cape and more purposeful plans were being made to obtain slave labour, so that expeditions to Madagascar were not continued immediately.

While the above developments were taking place, a number of slaves had reached the Cape singly or in small groups, partly through Van Riebeeck's exertions, but mainly by chance. As these men and women can be distinguished individually, it is worthwhile paying some attention to them, for they reveal a good deal about the world of slavery under the VOC and illustrate the wide field from which the Cape's slaves were obtained.[104]

The first return fleet to visit the Cape on its way from Batavia to Europe early in 1653 brought to the settlement its first known slave, the stowaway Abraham: he arrived on board the *Malacca* on 2 March 1653 and was left behind to be returned to his owner, who was stated to be the arrack distiller Cornelius Lichthart.[105] In spite of the difficulties the members of the little settlement had experienced in establishing themselves over the past year, Van Riebeeck was able to provide the ships with cattle and sheep bartered from the Khoikhoi, cabbage, carrots and beetroot from the garden, and milk. Abraham was not sent back to Batavia until 1656, after it had proved impossible to buy him 'for a reasonable sum' from his owner, and Van Riebeeck complained that 'in consequence of ill health the man was unable to earn half his food'.[106]

What makes Abraham's case more interesting is the fact that he appears to have been claimed by 'Sieur Adriaan van der Burgh' and that Van Riebeeck sent to Batavia with him 'a declaration by the slave himself from which it seems that he ran away from Lichthart's house'.[107]

On 14 August 1654 Van Riebeeck mentioned having received from the Dutch Commander on Mauritius 'a certain male and female slave with their children and effects, belonging to an orphan under his care and left by the Junior Merchant Joost van der Woutbeeck, who had requested that the whole should be sent to Batavia.' They were duly forwarded, together with a 'fugitive and recovered slave of the Company to be tried at Batavia'.[108]

In December 1654 Frederick Verburgh brought back from his first expedition to Madagascar the slave woman Eva, aged about 30, with her son Jan Bruyn, a boy of 2 or 3 years old.[109] She was placed in the service of Sergeant Jan van Herwerden, a senior member of the community and particular favourite of Van Riebeeck, whose wife came out to join him in the course of the following year.[110]

A male slave called Anthony was probably brought to the Cape on the same occasion, but first appears in the records on 12 March 1655, when Van Riebeeck notes his having disappeared 'quite suddenly' and the fact that he had possibly been killed by the Khoikhoi, 'the more so as this slave was always fighting with them'.[111]

In June 1655 Rijckloff van Goens,[112] commander of the return fleet on its way to Europe, sent back from St. Helena two stowaway slaves, 'the one called Claes Cat to be delivered to Cornelis van Beest, the other called Josep, to be delivered to the Fiscal at Batavia, who are their owners, which persons you are not to retain, but to send to their masters'.[113]

A list of slaves compiled some years later further includes 'Mary, of Bengal, bought for Riebeeck at Batavia by Jacob Reiniersz, and sent hither.'[114] This refers to a former Secunde at the Cape who had married Van Riebeeck's young cousin, leaving the Cape for Batavia in January 1654,[115] so that Maria van Bengalen probably arrived here with the return fleet of 1655.

According to Blommaert and other published sources, the next addition to the small group of local slaves occurred in November 1655 when Van Riebeeck in his private capacity bought Angela and Domingo van Bengalen from Pieter Kemp, commander of the return ship *Amersfoort*. This was, however, the date of Kemp's visit to the Cape on the outward journey from Europe,[116] and the transaction would seem more likely to have occurred on his return from the East in February–March 1657 as rear-admiral of a return fleet with a cargo valued at 1½ million guilders.[117] Angela van Bengalen, whose age on arrival is unknown, was to spend her long life at the Cape, dying in 1720 as a prominent member of the local 'free black' community.[118] Her companion, according to Upham, was also a woman, in spite of the seemingly masculine name.[119]

In this way the families of Van Riebeeck and Van Herwerden, the most senior of the local officials, were provided with slave labour, and further slaves were added to the household of the former over the next few years. In March 1656 four French ships touched at the Cape on their way to Madagascar in one of the many attempts at colonisation undertaken here by the French during the course of the seventeenth century,[120] and Admiral De la Roche Saint-André presented Van Riebeeck with a slave whose origins are unknown and whose name is not recorded. His death is noted by Van Riebeeck as having occurred on 14 June of the same year,[121] but on his return to the Cape the Frenchman further presented the Commander's wife with three slave girls. They were Cornelia and Lijsbeth, two 'Arabian girls' from Abyssinia (Ethiopia), as Blommaert describes them, aged 10 and 12 respectively, who had presumably been acquired in the flourishing slave trade around the Indian Ocean, and a girl of about 5 who had been sent as a gift by the 'King' of Antongil on Madagascar and was called Kleine Eva by the Dutch.

By the time Rijckloff van Goens visited the Cape as Commissioner on his way back to Batavia early in 1657, the Van Riebeecks were in possession of five young women and girls, who shared three cramped rooms in the Fort, one of which was Van Riebeeck's office, with them, their small children and the Khoi girl Krotoa (Eva) who was living with them to be educated. It was in these circumstances that Krotoa acquired not only Dutch, which was to make her extremely useful to the whites as an interpreter, but also Portuguese, probably from the Bengali slaves, Portuguese being a widely known means of communication in the East.

During his visit, however, Van Goens drew attention to the paragraph in the *Generale Artikelbrief* (General Articles or legal code of the VOC) which stipulated that all gifts received by officials must be turned over to the Governor-General and Council for the benefit of the Company.[122] In accordance with this provision he laid claim to certain of the slaves, whom he distributed on an official basis. His official Instruction to Van Riebeeck, dated 16 April, lists 11 'male and female slaves', which appears to include both those belonging to the Company and those privately owned, and is made up as follows:

4 slave women and 1 male slave at the Commander's; 1 slave at the sergeant's; 1 female slave at the sick visitor's; 1 female slave at the junior merchant's; 1 female slave at the gardener's; 1 Madagascar female slave to sweep the fort; 1 slave at the surgeon's.[123]

The 'male slave at the Commander's' may have been 'Myndert, of Antongil, obtained from the junior merchant Cops', who is mentioned in a list compiled in 1659,[124] although it is not known when he reached the Cape.

Eva, the 'Madagascar female servant' referred to by Van Goens, was later sent to Robben Island in May 1657 to help quarry stone,[125] being described as 'strong enough and able to carry the stones down and pile the same in good order alongside the others, that they may dry the harder'.[126] Here Jan Woutersz, the superintendent of the island, soon complained that she 'does nothing but run about the island, chasing the sheep and driving them from the lands. She needs somebody to look after her and does not heed and cannot understand signs, gestures or thrashings, so that no credit can be gained at this work with such people.'[127] She was brought back to the mainland in March 1658 when Woutersz and his wife, the former slave Catharina van Bengalen, were removed from the island.[128]

At this stage there is also a reference in the official correspondence to a certain Espaniola, described as a 'black French slave or fugitive',[129] who had possibly absconded from one of the visiting French ships and was possibly from Madagascar as well. She was despatched to Robben Island together with Eva.[130]

The muster roll or annual census of 31 May 1657 mentions three 'Batavia female slaves' belonging to the Commander's wife, which probably refers to Angela, Domingo (presuming her to have been female) and Maria van Bengalen. The sick comforter Pieter van der Stael by that time was in possession of 'his own Batavia female slave bought from the gardener', Hendrick Boom, and the surgeon Jan Vetteman had 'one slave of his own'.[131]

The muster roll further lists one Catharina van Paliacatte, 'a black',[132] on Robben Island, who is not mentioned in other early sources, and this raises the question of how many other slaves there may have been at the Cape in the early years whose presence was not recorded. Paliacatte refers to the modern Pulicat, head office of the VOC on the Coromandel or east coast of India.

Finally, on 17 December 1657 the Council of India wrote that they were sending out 'a female slave named Maria of Bengal, sentenced [by the court in this city] in consequence of her thieving propensities to exile on Robben Island during the term of her natural life'.[133] She was a passenger on the *Malacca*, which arrived at the Cape on 6 March of the following year,[134] and must be distinguished from Van Riebeeck's slave of the same name.

As a matter of interest it may be added that the Cape, in a postscript to a letter of 16 January 1658, was similarly informed that they were to expect 'Domingo of Batavia, lately a soldier, sentenced on the 28th August to be shot, but pardoned by us, and sentenced to exile of Robben Island'. He arrived on 18 February on the *Schelvis*, which brought to the Cape rice, beans and cadjang, as well as a cargo of goods for the projected slave trade in Angola and Guinea.[135] The form of his name gives the impression that this is a reference to a former slave;[136] although there is also a later reference to 'an exile from Batavia, named Domingo of Bengal', being sent to Robben Island in July to be 'serviceable'.[137]

The known presence at the Cape of distinct individuals called Maria van Bengalen and Domingo van Bengalen must serve as a warning against confusing people bearing the same common slave names.

While the various accounts do not seem consistent and can by no means be regarded as complete, it would appear that by the end of 1657, shortly before the arrival of the first officially acquired groups of slaves, some 20 odd slaves had been mentioned in some connection in local records. By April 1657 Van Goens found 11 resident slaves here, 3 of whom were men and the remainder women or young girls,[138] and one can only wonder what the situation of these unprotected females was in a community consisting mainly of white males, who were mostly sailors, soldiers and artisans.

As far as the origins of the slaves mentioned during the first five years of the white presence at the Cape are known, the majority were from Bengal, where, together with Coromandel, Batavia purchased most of its slaves at the time, and Madagascar. The reference to 'Batavia female slaves' means no more than that they were obtained from Batavia and does not necessarily indicate their origin, as the two slaves known to be from Bengal were described in the same way.

In addition to these individuals, at least two other women of slave origin are known to have had connections with the Cape during the early years of settlement.

At some stage it had become customary for senior officials of the VOC on repatriating from the East to be accompanied for their own convenience by a number of their personal slaves. In 1636 the Gentlemen XVII in the Netherlands had issued a prohibition on bringing back slaves from Batavia in this way, which was reaffirmed in 1645 and 1657. 'For infringements the punishment was severe,' writes Fox, 'and the only exception allowed was in the case of a suckling child who still needed a wet-nurse, for whom six months' upkeep had to be provided in advance to the Company Treasury in Batavia for her return voyage.'[139]

To this prohibition and its subsequent affirmations no attention seems, however, to have been paid, as was so often the case in the VOC. There is a record, for example, of an 'Indian woman, born on the Coast of Coromandel', who was brought to the Netherlands in

1651 by Arnoldus Heusden, commander of the return fleet that year, and baptised in Delft by the name of Katharine when she was believed to be in danger of death.[140] The Council of India likewise wrote to Van Riebeeck in 1656 that 'some black servants are now leaving [Batavia] with their masters and mistresses. They are to be sent back, unless you are shown our written authority that they may be taken to Holland',[141] while the Gentlemen XVII themselves suggested to him at the same time that, 'as black people are occasionally brought to this country by the higher officers of the Company as servants, and who again return to India, it would not seem strange to us if you were to attempt to persuade them to remain at the Cape and settle there, supporting themselves as Mardijkers'.[142]

It is often stated that as slavery was not acknowledged in the Netherlands, slaves automatically became free on arrival there, but this does not invariably seem to have been the case,[143] and it is also not borne out by all the evidence available in the context of the VOC.[144] By 1776 at any rate slaves who had been brought there were freed automatically only after a year's residence.[145]

This custom of taking slaves to the Netherlands continued, in spite of the formal prohibitions the authorities issued from time to time. In 1689 Samuel Elsevier, future Secunde of the Cape, on returning with his family to the Netherlands from Ceylon where he had been in Company service was, for example, accompanied by an 'East-Indian slave'. In 1693 the 'Indian slave of Mr Samuel Elsevier' was baptised in the small Dutch town of Oirschot and thus described in the baptismal register, where his name was recorded as Adam Matande. He seems to have remained in the service of the family, subsequently accompanying them to The Hague, though presumably no longer as a slave.[146] It is not known whether he was with them when Elsevier came to the Cape in 1697.

After the establishment of the outpost at the Cape, these slaves were often sent back to Batavia on their masters continuing the voyage from Table Bay, and this new possibility quite likely encouraged the custom of taking slaves on board. At the end of 1655 the

Council of India wrote to Van Riebeeck: 'As we cannot well refuse for the comfort of families proceeding home to allow them to take with them some slaves under promise that those who can conveniently spare them at the Cape shall send them back to this country, you will be pleased to see that this is done, and the slaves returned by the first ships to be delivered to [those who are entitled to them] or set at liberty as their owners determine.'[147] As this implies, the repatriating slave owners occasionally manumitted their slaves as a gesture of goodwill.[148]

With the arrival of slaves at the Cape, the multiracial nature of the VOC's trading empire became apparent, even though they formed only a small minority in the little community and were often transient visitors only, and within a few years the first racially mixed marriage took place.

On 15 March 1656 Jasper van den Boogaerde, former Governor of the Moluccas (Melaku in Indonesia), arrived at the Cape as commander of the return fleet, bringing at least two female slaves with him, one of whom accompanied him to the Netherlands and returned with Rijckloff van Goens the following year.[149] He continued his voyage on the 28th, leaving behind a second slave, Catharina van Bengalen, who was due to be sent back to his son-in-law Dirck Sarcerius in Batavia 'with the first married family proceeding thither',[150] but on 11 April Sarcerius himself arrived at the Cape with the second section of the return fleet, having resigned suddenly and dramatically from the Company's service. It was seemingly by Sarcerius that Catharina was now, 'at her own request', set free and allowed to remain at the Cape,[151] and on 26 April she received official permission to marry the Assistant Jan Woutersz, a Dutchman.[152]

The couple had obviously become acquainted during Catharina's brief stay at the Cape, for on 4 April Van Riebeeck had noted in his Journal: 'Rainy weather; N.W. wind as before. In the afternoon the shallops *Robbejacht* and *Peguijn* arrived safely in the roadstead from the Saldanha Bay with a cargo of about 3,000 seal-skins, and the assistant Jan Woutersz with all his men and equipment, as there were no more seals to be caught in the bay.'[153] Marriages of this kind between a white man and a white woman on a passing ship were not uncommon during the early years when there was a great shortage of marriage partners, but this was the first case of a racially mixed marriage at the Cape.

The couple were married by the secretary of the Political Council, as was customary in the absence of a minister, on 21 May, 'in the open Council chamber after the reading of the Sunday service', and the name of the bride was given as 'the honourable maiden, Catarina Anthonis, from Salagon in Bengal, formerly a slave girl in the service of the Hon. Boogaerd' (*'d'eerbare jonge dochter Catarina Antonise., van Salagou* [sic] *in Bengale, gewesene slavinne van d'heer Bogaert'*).[154] With regard to her place of origin, given as 'Zalegon' and 'Celagon' in other sources,[155] one wonders in passing whether this might have been Sirjganj in the modern Bangladesh.

Jan Woutersz from Middelburg had entered the service of the VOC in 1644 as Assistant, this being the lowest rank in the hierarchy of the Company. After having been degraded to cadet, he was in 1653 sent from Batavia to the Cape, where he acted as a substitute for the Bookkeeper Frederick Verburgh and was reinstated as Assistant in 1654 at 20 guilders a year, and his contract with the Company renewed for three years.[156] He seems to have been slightly disabled, for in quoted statements he twice refers to himself as 'cripple Jan' (*'mancke Jan'*).[157]

Although Woutersz appears to have been reasonably well educated, no advantage was taken of this, and he was mostly placed in charge of the groups of men sent to Dassen Island to hunt, kill and skin seals, which even the official records describe as 'difficult, messy and dirty work'.[158] Van Riebeeck's Journal includes numerous letters written by Woutersz from the island, reporting on conditions and requesting further supplies such as '2 large wooden troughs for [seal] oil, a number of empty casks, 50 long, straight clubs, firewood, arrack, meat, rice, 1 leaguer of pegs, bread, oil, vinegar and flaying knives'.[159]

After his marriage Woutersz was still sent out regularly to Dassen Island, but he and his wife would have lived in the Fort, which was the only accommodation available, and quite likely in the main building with the other officials and their families. He is said to have eaten at the Commander's table, together with other officials such as the sick comforter, the upper surgeon and the bookkeeper, and his wife, 'a former slave of the Lord Bogaert', is specifically stated to have had her meals there during his absence,[160] and to have received the same 'honour and respect' as their wives.[161] When she became pregnant it appears also to have been anticipated that she would be assisted by the latter in her confinement, as was customary at the time.[162]

Here difficulties could easily have arisen among the members of the very small group living in close and confined quarters; moreover, the six white women at the Cape at this time, the wives of the Commander, Secunde, sergeant, sick comforter, surgeon and gardener, were all Dutch and as far as is known had no experience of life in the East and probably no previous contact with members of other races.[163] The position of Catharina van Bengalen in their midst is illustrated by the list of 'Women and children' in the muster roll of 1657, which describes her rather unnecessarily as 'The wife of Jan Woutersz, soldier, a black woman',[164] and when he was sent to Saldanha Bay at the end of 1656 to hunt seals, he was permitted to take her with him at the Company's expense.[165]

That there was considerable tension, in the marriage, the white community in the Fort or both, became clear early in 1657 when complaints were voiced about Woutersz's consumption of arrack on Dassen Island, and he was charged with slandering the Commander, Jan van Riebeeck, and his wife. Any challenge to authority was taken seriously by the VOC, and Woutersz was sentenced to make a public retraction, beg forgiveness on his bare knees and have his tongue pierced with an awl, a common punishment for slander at this period, in addition to the loss of rank as an Assistant, and the confiscation of his possessions. He was furthermore to be banished to Robben Island for three years as soon as his wife, who was described as 'far advanced in pregnancy', 'should have recovered from her confinement'.[166]

On the entreaty of all the local white women, and in consideration of his wife's condition, the piercing of Woutersz's tongue and his banishment to Robben Island were revoked, but he was degraded to the rank of common soldier at 12 guilders a month.[167] Two months later, however, after 'beautiful white stone, soft and easily worked', had been discovered on Robben Island, the official Journal noted that 'three paid servants [of the Company] and three exiles and slaves' had been sent out there, 'one as superintendent, one as shepherd and 4 to work at stone cutting, to see what can be accomplished at that work'.[168]

The new superintendent, as it subsequently appears, was Jan Woutersz, who had been partially and dubiously restored to favour by banishment in a responsible post to this bleak and desolate island. It had hitherto served as a sheep run for the Company (a few months later their number was given as 350, and early the following year there were 450),[169] and was beginning its development as penal colony, but was also of some strategic importance, located as it was at the entrance to Table Bay.

The muster roll compiled at the end of May 1657 lists 4 white convicts on the island, together with 'The Chinaman' and Catharina van Paliacatte, who had both been banished to the Cape for life,[170] while the 'Convicts and men in irons' listed a year later had been increased by 4 white men, making a total of 10. Two of the slaves sent out with Woutersz were also women, Eva van Madagascar and Espaniola,[171] so that Catharina van Bengalen, who accompanied her husband with their child, would not have been without some female company.

Some details of the daily life of this little isolated group may be gleaned from the official correspondence. They received supplies from the mainland by boat, and in Woutersz's official Instruction Van Riebeeck stipulated, 'We have allowed you and the other servants full rations of brandy, viz.: every day half a mutsjen. The convicts, however, shall only receive half that quantity. (…) The convicts, male and female slaves, have to be content with birds [*penguins*] instead of meat and pork, which are given you only for the Company's wage earners.'[172] In August Woutersz wrote to the mainland to ask for barley to be supplied to them rather than rice, 'as it goes further when eaten with penguin meat'; adding, 'We also ask for a cock and 2 or 3 hens which we wish to keep here, then the place will look like a country village.'[173] On another occasion he was supplied with 'a length salempouris, 1 pair shoes, 4 lengths negro cloth and 2 lbs. tobacco',[174] salempouris being a cheap cotton cloth from the Coromandel coast often worn by slaves, and 'negro cloth' coarse cotton used for bartering purposes in West Africa.

By March 1658, after Woutersz had been in charge of Robben Island for ten months, Van Riebeeck stated that he was 'behaving as badly as before and is paying no attention to the sheep', as well as neglecting to light beacon fires for the benefit of shipping in the bay. 'Moreover, he is guilty of drunkenness whenever he is able to obtain liquor, either from the rations or by purchase, and completely disregards the repeated instructions concerning various matters issued to him (…).' It was therefore decided to dismiss him for 'dereliction and bad conduct', and Van Riebeeck ordered that he 'with his wife and child is to be brought over to the yacht *Schelvis* in which he is to sail for India via Mauritius as a soldier.'[175] This was done at the end of the month, and with this, Catharina van Bengalen disappears from the local record.

As a matter of interest it may be mentioned that a racially mixed marriage similar to that of Catharina van Bengalen and Jan Woutersz took place at the end of the same year as theirs, involving two passengers on an outward bound ship from the Netherlands who on 29 September 1656 were given official permission to be married at the Cape. They were the junior officer Anthoni Muller and 'a certain young Bengali woman named Domingo Elvingh',[176] about whom nothing more is recorded, but who most likely was a manumitted slave like Catarina Antonis van Salagon.

It was not until two years later, as far as is known, that the next 'mixed' marriage took place here, a few months after the departure of Jan Woutersz and his family for the East, the bride in this case being Maria van Bengalen, a slave resident at the Cape. She was not the woman of that name who had been bought for Van Riebeeck in Batavia and who was still in his possession by 1660,[177] and cannot have been the slave banished from Batavia in 1659, by which time the woman in question here was already married. The records merely state that she had formerly belonged to the chief gardener Hendrick Boom and subsequently to the sick comforter Pieter van der Stael, from whom she had been bought by the freeburgher Jan Sacharias from Amsterdam with the purpose of freeing and marrying her. According to Dr Böeseken, this is the earliest slave transaction for which a record has been found in the Deeds Office.[178] It took place on the same day on which the Council of Policy gave its permission for the marriage, but no price was mentioned, and it may well have been a nominal sale for a token amount.[179]

Sacharias appears in the muster roll for 1656 as a soldier, but he left the service of the Company in October 1657,[180] shortly after the institution of freeburghership at the Cape. By 1658 he was described as 'freeman and resident within this fort, who is serving as cook to the junior merchant, fiscal and assistants',[181] and at the time of his marriage he asked to be appointed as bailiff and messenger, which was done 'with the salary customary at Batavia'.[182] He was 27 years of age.[183]

As regards his wife, she was not as lucky as her predecessor Catharina, who had had senior officials of the Company to vouch for her, and her past appears to have been regarded as dubious. Whereas the former was referred to in the official documents as 'the honourable maiden, Catarina Anthonis', Maria, who was 20 years old, is described merely as 'the young woman Maria, born in Bengal',[184] and in the resolutions of the Council of Policy the word 'honourable' which had originally been written before her name was deleted.[185] At the same time Van Riebeeck added in the margin that the Council had been assured 'that the said Maria not only fully understands the Dutch language but also speaks it, and already has considerable knowledge of Christ according to the Reformed religion'.[186] The couple were married before the Council of Policy after the Sunday service on 21 July 1658.

There is a further stray reference to Maria van Bengalen in Van Riebeeck's Journal shortly after the war with the local Khoikhoi had broken out. In September 1659 he describes how the Khoi interpreter Krotoa and some companions set out for the interior with a message for the Kaapman tribe: 'they called at the redoubt Duijnhoop on their way past and, finding nobody there but the black wife of the free burgher Jan Sacharias, they seized a pair of tongs and an axe and then assaulted her.[187] She called out to Eva, who, she says, refused to come to her aid but only slapped her hand on her thigh and continued on her way.'[188] More precisely, Krotoa turned her back to Maria and slapped her buttock, which is the word used in the original Dutch, as a gesture of contempt.

Duinhoop was a small fort which had been erected in 1654 on a dune near the mouth of the Salt River,[189] but the reason for Maria's presence here is not clear, unless she and her husband were by this time farming in the Liesbeek valley and had taken refuge there from Khoi attacks, as other freeburghers had done.[190] The presence of a pair of tongs and an axe seems to indicate that they were living here at the time.

The next reference to the couple is in April 1660, when they had a child by the name of Maria baptised by a visiting minister after the 'annual Day of Thanksgiving and Prayer' commemorating the arrival of Van Riebeeck's group six years before. On that occasion the officiating minister 'preached on the first arrival of our people here and the bountiful blessings bestowed upon us by Almighty God in all our endeavours'.[191]

In September of the same year Sacharias, described as 'freeman and land messenger', was one of a party of four freemen who undertook a five days' journey beyond the Hottentots-Holland mountains to the east in order to make contact with the Chainoqua, a Khoi tribe rich in cattle with whom the Dutch had only recently become acquainted. They were received hospitably, and two Khoi messengers accompanied them back to the Fort.[192] In January 1661, however, Sacharias was placed on Robben Island as supervisor, the position occupied by Jan Woutersz shortly before. 'He is considered suitable for the post, and has been appointed at a salary of 10 guilders a month and will live there with his black wife, who is a Bengali. He is no farmer in any case.'[193] The last remark seems to confirm the impression that he had tried his hand at farming, but suggests that it had not been a success.

Maria van Bengalen's life on the island would have been similar to that of her predecessor Catharina. It is not clear what female company she had, but when a female slave was sent to the mainland for medical treatment in September, Sacharias was informed by Van Riebeeck that 'we cannot send anyone in her place. You will just have to manage until this one recovers, when she will be sent back to you.'[194] In the winter of 1663, when a slave woman with a child was found on a Portuguese ship captured in the Atlantic Ocean, Van Riebeeck's successor Zacharias Wagenaer, a more humane man, had her conveyed to the island with the regular delivery of food and drink, 'namely brandy for three months but all other edible goods for six months', specifying that she was 'to act as servant and companion to the woman married there who has had to lead a lonely life for so long'.[195] At the same time Sacharias and his wife again had a child baptised by a visiting minister,[196] and there were now 3 men, 2 women and 3 children on the island who would have to be supplied with provisions.[197]

After his visit to the island early in 1664, Wagenaer furthermore ordered a good 'weather-proof' house of locally made bricks and thatch to be erected, and subsequently the Journal regularly records the despatch of masons, as well as materials for repairing the existing buildings,[198] which seems to indicate that these had previously not been in good condition.

By this time people relegated to Robben Island were conveniently out of sight and mind, and Maria van Bengalen is not mentioned again until May 1665, when 'a certain dropsical Bengali woman married to a local Hollander' was tapped and a large quantity of fluid removed.[199] She was described as seriously ill 'and almost unable to move', and died in the early morning of 21 May,[200] aged about 27. Sleigh remarks that hydropsy ('dropsy') could be interpreted as a symptom of the deficiency disease beri-beri which was later to assume serious proportions on the island.[201]

Jan Sacharias was at this time replaced on Robben Island by the surgeon Pieter van Meerhoff. When this decision was taken and for what reasons is not clear, but Van Meerhoff set out for the island with his wife and family three days after the death of Maria van Bengalen.[202] In 1669 Sacharias was re-instated in order to replace an unsatisfactory supervisor,[203] but two years later the Journal, after referring to 'faithless acts (…) in selling sheep to our own and foreign ships', records that he had been brought back to the mainland, 'and not without weighty reasons, in consequence of various fraudulent actions (…), for which the Fiscal will prosecute him'.[204]

So little is known of slaves and ex-slaves that a tentative postscript may perhaps be added here. In 1672 Hubert Hugo visited the Cape on *De Pijl*, on the way to the island of Mauritius, where he had been appointed commander by the VOC. After he had continued his voyage, the German J.C. Hoffmann, who was a member of his party, noted that the quartermaster ('*Speisemeister*') Jacob Jansz de Nijs from Amsterdam had on 4 December been married on board ship to 'a young little girl' (literally translated: '*mit einem jungen Mägdlein*') called Maria Zacharias, whom he described as the daughter of a Dutch sergeant and 'a black Bengali slave woman'.[205] It is not known how soon after the marriage of her parents in 1658 the daughter of Jan Sacharias was born, but it could well be she who accompanied the ship from the Cape, possibly in the company of her father, and was now married at the age of thirteen or fourteen. Shortly afterwards a disparaging reference to the presence of one 'Jan Sagerijasse' as member of Hugo's Council on Mauritius occurs in another source.[206]

It is a striking fact that both men who married ex-slave wives during the early years at the Cape ended on Robben Island. This may be coincidence, but seems less so when one bears in mind that Sacharias's successor Van Meerhoff likewise had a non-white wife, the Khoi interpreter Krotoa, who became an alcoholic while living on the island, if this process had not begun earlier. Quite possibly there were tensions in all three marriages which made it preferable to remove the couples concerned from the small white community in Table Bay, but even if this was the case, it seems likely that the tensions were caused largely by the community itself. As has already been mentioned in the case of Catharina van Bengalen, the latter consisted mainly of people from Northern Europe with little or no experience or even knowledge of the East or of non-European peoples, and a considerable amount of racial prejudice, as was made even clearer in their relations with the Khoikhoi.

By virtue of their manumission and subsequent marriages to whites, Catharina and Maria van Bengalen were nonetheless regarded in principle as members of the white community, whatever degree of acceptance they may have experienced in practice. At the Cape, however, unlike the East, marriage to a non-white woman does not seem to have been looked on favourably by the small white community, at any rate during the early years, and the two men who married ex-slaves also seem not to have been highly regarded, quite apart from their marriages. In the verbose and vehement charge drawn up against him, most likely by Van Riebeeck himself, Woutersz at any rate is stated to have arrived at the Cape as 'a man of little repute' and to have been restored to favour only for want of suitable labourers for the seal-hunting.[207] He is also said to have led a 'debauched life',[208] and to have taken in 'two black women' at the time the *Prinses* (probably the *Prinses Rojaal*) visited the Cape, with a hint of sexual misbehaviour.[209]

It is noteworthy that none of the men who were to become senior officials or the most prominent members of the later freeburgher population had a non-white wife, although a number of wealthy freeburghers made 'mixed' marriages.[210] On the contrary, Frederick Verburgh and Hendrick Lacus, both of whom were to serve as Secunde in due course, were both married during the same period to daughters of Dutch ministers of religion on their way from Europe to Batavia.

The situation of these two former slave women was therefore exceptional, and the lot of the women and girls remaining in a state of slavery, whether in the Fort or as convicts on Robben Island, was far more typical of the period. Apart from this handful of females, however, and the single unidentified 'male slave' mentioned in Van Riebeeck's household by Van Goens, there was by 1657 still no slave labour at the Cape to assist in the manifold tasks undertaken by the Company, and the need increased when freeburghership was introduced early in 1657.

2. The first slave imports (1658)

As early as 13 May 1652, some five weeks after his arrival, Van Riebeeck in writing to the Council of India about the fertility of the Cape had remarked that it would 'not be unserviceable to the Company if under conditions framed by the Company some free men from India or Holland were licensed and permitted to come hither and take up their residences here as subjects of the Company'.[1]

This was only one suggestion among many in Van Riebeeck's enthusiastic and enterprising letters, but at the end of 1654 the Gentlemen XVII, having received a favourable account of Hout Bay from a visiting skipper, themselves wrote to ask his opinion on settling 'a few families' here.[2] To this development he responded with equal enthusiasm and at length in a letter dated 28 April 1655, in which he welcomed the idea of colonisation but recommended the Liesbeek valley near Table Bay as more suitable for settlement than Hout Bay.[3]

Freeburghership was not unknown in the world of the VOC, where there were a number of free communities consisting chiefly of former servants of the Company, most notably in Batavia, Ceylon, and Ambon in the Indonesian archipelago. As their opportunities for trading were strictly limited by the monopolistic Company and they were unable to compete with the local farmers, their opportunities were limited, however, and their most profitable occupation proved to be running taprooms or bars for members of the local white garrisons. Under the WIC, immigrants had been encouraged to settle in Brazil before it was returned to the Portuguese in 1654, and there was at this time a reasonably flourishing colony in New Netherland (North America).

As far as the Cape was concerned, it was envisaged that free-burghers would take over the Company's farming activities, and especially develop wheat farming so as to end the local community's dependence on rice from Batavia. In addition, they would be able to help in the defence of the settlement, so that the garrison could be reduced. From the Company's point of view, Van Riebeeck at this time was particularly anxious not to lose the knowledge and expertise of Company servants whose five-year contracts were due to expire early in 1657 and who would normally return to Europe. While a certain amount of immigration, both organised and incidental, of individuals and families would take place over the years, ex-servants of the Company would provide the greatest number of new freeburghers for the entire VOC period.

Van Riebeeck's plans were approved by the XVII, and on 21 February 1657 the refreshment station at the Cape became a colony with the formal institution of freeburghership.[4]

Initially two groups of men, former employees of the Company whose contracts had expired or been cancelled for the purpose, were settled on plots on land in the Liesbeek valley where they were to farm collectively. The conditions on which they received freedom were soon changed by Rijckloff van Goens during his visit as Commissioner a few months later, and the men were assigned smaller individual farms and encouraged to send for their wives and families from Europe.

Van Riebeeck had already in 1656 begun sowing crops in the Liesbeek valley at the back of Table Mountain, some 15 kilometres from the Fort, where they would be sheltered from the south-easterly winds which regularly devastated the gardens in the Table Valley. While the Table Valley had little to offer apart from its mountain streams and some limited grazing, the valley of the Liesbeek had both in abundance, as well as fertile soil, and firewood both in the ravines of the mountain above it and on the Cape Flats beyond the river. Once the white settlers had entrenched themselves here, it became possible for the whites to survive in their new environment.

The start was slow, and Van Goens, visiting the Cape in April, found there 130 Company servants, who for reasons of economy he reduced to 100, 10 freeburghers, 6 convicts, 11 slaves,[5] 6 white women and 12 children, 145 people in all.[6] From the end of the year, however, the number of freeburghers increased rapidly: by 1658 there were 52, by 1660 70, and in 1660, the year of Van Riebeeck's departure, 93, in spite of the fact that a good few men returned to the Company's service, discouraged by the difficulties experienced, or decamped on passing ships.

Although a number of freeburghers preferred to settle in the immediate vicinity of the Fort, where their humble thatched cottages formed the nucleus of the later Cape Town, it had been specifically intended that they should take up farming. The farmers among them initially worked their small pieces of ground themselves, assisted by *knechten*, white farmhands who were either freemen themselves or else hired from the Company. These labourers were expensive, however, and also proved to be refractory, causing many difficulties, in addition to which the work on land which had never been cultivated proved extremely difficult. The appearance of freeburghers on the scene therefore caused the question of slaves for the Cape to be raised anew.

This had as a matter of fact been anticipated by Van Riebeeck, for among the many points made in his letter of 28 April 1655 had been the thought: 'And the sooner to fix them on their own legs, a good quantity of slaves would be required for them; the latter might be obtained from Madagascar with the yacht as mentioned above, or they might be imported from India [i.e., *Batavia*] and given on credit to the free men until they have means to pay.'[7]

At this time Frederick Verburgh had just been sent on his second voyage to Madagascar, and the provision of a yacht for further trading expeditions was under consideration, and the XVII had shown some understanding of Van Riebeeck's labour problems. 'We can see that you badly require slaves,' they replied the following October, 'especially for the seal fishery, which would save a good deal of wages, slaves only costing their food. [We] will consider the matter further, to find out how to meet your wants in case the seal skins are in good demand and pay well, which the approaching sales will show.'[8]

In the same letter, however, Van Riebeeck had become even more adventurous: 'As the West India Company,' he wrote, 'have lost Brazil and the trade with Angola is [apparently] open to every one, we believe that slaves, rice and ivory may be obtained [very cheaply] at [certain] places, and the yacht mentioned above might be used for the purpose as far as Angola.'[9] In their reply, in which they mentioned incidentally having heard that Madagascan slaves were 'of a very lazy disposition',[10] the XVII took up this idea: 'In the meantime you may inform us whether you think that Angola can be easily reached from the Cape. In that case some slaves might be obtained from there, as it is said that they do not cost much, and as you would require a flute for the purpose, we might send you one.'[11]

Angola had been in Portuguese hands again since 1648, and there was at this time a flourishing slave trade between the Angolan harbour Luanda and the sugar plantations in Brazil, but the truce between the Netherlands and Portugal had expired in 1651 and the situation between the two countries was extremely tense.[12] Moreover, the entire area to the west of the Cape of Good Hope (including, incidentally, Table Bay itself) was officially situated within the charter territory of the WIC,[13] so that it is not clear what lay behind this line of thought.

By October 1656 the possibility of obtaining Angolan slaves had nonetheless taken definite shape, and Van Riebeeck was informed, 'As you are in want of slaves, we intend to fit a vessel out for the purpose, and to be sent to Angola; it may also obtain tusks, hides, rice, &c., in these parts, and bring everything to the Cape. (…) Having performed this voyage, it may be despatched, during the S.E. monsoon, to Cabo Negro and Angola, and should more slaves at reasonable prices be obtained there than you require, you may gradually send the surplus to Batavia with the outward bound vessels.'[14] Elsewhere in the same letter further information is provided: 'The slave vessel abovementioned will be built by the Amsterdam Chamber [of the VOC], and be 120 feet long, 26 feet wide, 11 feet in the hold and 5½ ditto above it, without poop or foredeck. It is to be ready in spring and start for Angola.'[15]

On his way back to the East early in 1657 Van Goens arrived at the Cape Verde islands at the same time as the Director of the WIC on his way to Guinea, with whom he discussed 'the Angola trade'.[16] In his Instruction written at the Cape shortly afterwards he referred to slaves from Angola,[17] and Van Riebeeck himself was hoping that he would be allowed to exchange 40 or 50 Angolan slaves for slaves from the East.[18] In the meantime, however, the plans being made in the Netherlands were growing more ambitious. In correspondence dated March 1657 reference is made not to a single vessel but to two ships, the *Hasselt* and *Maria*, and full instructions in this regard were given to Van Riebeeck which are in their way so revealing that they deserve to be quoted at length.

[The ships] have a larger crew than usual; the surplus number is to be sent to Batavia from the Cape. Sixty or seventy men may remain in the *Hasselt*, and a proportionate number in the *Maria*. (…)

That you may not be at a loss what to do when such a large number of slaves is suddenly brought to you from the West Coast, we have provided you with sufficient provisions shipped in the two yachts. (…)

As a large number of casks will be required to carry water for the slaves, we did not like to send you any empty, but filled them with flour and barley. (…)

You are to order from India some clothing for the slaves; from us you receive some coarse cloth to protect them against the cold.

Eighty or a hundred slaves may be kept by you at the Cape, the rest are to be sent to Batavia with the various ships after having been thoroughly refreshed at the Fort. The best and strongest are to be sent, the weak ones, should there be any, you are to keep back for yourselves.

You are to treat the slaves well and kindly, to make them the better accustomed to and well disposed towards us; they are to be taught all kinds of trades, that in course of time the advantage of such instruction may be beneficial to yourselves, and a large number of Europeans excused. They are also to be taught agriculture, as it would be too great an expense to feed such a lot of people from Holland or India. You are therefore to arrange things so that you have a large quantity of [local] grain on hand when the slaves arrive, in order to feed them and to save the provisions which we have sent you and which you are to forward to India.[19]

The same letter also stated that the ships were 'destined for the slave trade on the coast of Guinea and Angola',[20] and specific reference was made to 'Arder' on the Slave Coast (Allada in modern Benin), which seems a more realistic proposition, as this was where the WIC obtained most of its slaves.

In a subsequent letter it was suggested that the ships might also cruise off the coast of Angola in the hope of capturing Portuguese ships or 'prizes' there.[21]

The *Maria* arrived in Table Bay on 13 July 1657 from the Netherlands with 39 men on board and no deaths en route,[22] followed on 10 August by the *Hasselt* with 151 men, a single death having occurred on the way out.[23] On 3 September they set out together on their slaving expedition,[24] but after they had cruised off Luanda for some time with no success, the *Maria* was sent back to the Cape.[25] Here she was once again despatched to Angola, accompanied by a smaller vessel, the locally built *Robbejachtje*, 'to explore all ports, bays, inlets, rivers, etc., to see whether slaves or other commodities can be obtained for the benefit of the Hon. Company'.[26] She returned on 29 May after a fruitless expedition.[27]

The *Hasselt* meanwhile continued on her way to Guinea; but the first batch of slaves to be brought to the Cape was not to arrive by this ship, for on 26 March the *Wapen van Holland* brought the news that the *Amersfoort*, which had left the Netherlands in October, had on 23 January captured a Portuguese slaving ship in the South Atlantic Ocean 'with 500 male and female slaves on board. The *Amersfoort* had taken off 250 slaves and left the rest in the Portuguese ship, which was old and unserviceable. Some were falling ill and dying owing to the long duration of the voyage.'[28]

As appeared subsequently from the ship's log, the *Amersfoort* had enough water for 'about six weeks', and her crew was placed on a ration of 8 *mutsjes* a day 'and a half *mutsje* of brandy every morning because of the stench caused by the blacks', while the captured slaves were given 4 *mutsjes* each.[29] She reached Table Bay just in time before her water supply ran out, arriving there on 28 March with the 250 slaves she had taken on board reduced by death to 170. The 'List of dead negroes' kept on board and subsequently transcribed and published by Van Rensburg makes depressing reading, though these statistics are not exceptional for a slave ship engaged in the Atlantic trade: '3 negroes died; another one; two deceased; one negro thrown overboard; a negro died; another negro thrown overboard', and so on, few days passing without a similar entry.[30]

Van Riebeeck duly noted the arrival of the survivors, 'of whom many were very ill. The majority of the slaves are young boys and girls, who will be of little use for the next 4 or 5 years. They were also brought ashore to be refreshed and restored to health.'[31] To the Council of India he remarked briefly ten days later, 'The best had died. Of the survivors (many of whom are still dying daily) most are girls and boys (…).'[32]

'This was the first important importation of slaves at the Cape,' as an editorial note to this entry in Van Riebeeck's Journal points out. It at was the same time that Jan Woutersz and his wife Catharina van

Bengalen were removed from Robben Island and sent on to Batavia.

Like most of the slaves exported by the Portuguese from Luanda, the members of this consignment probably came from over a wide region, having been brought to the coast by slave dealers in chained gangs along trade routes stretching deep into Central and Southern Africa.[33] They therefore represented many different tribes, cultures, languages and dialects and had little cohesion as a group. Moreover, they did not keep their own names at the Cape, as did the Guinean slaves who arrived shortly afterwards, but seem without exception to have been given European names or nicknames by the Dutch: Anthony, Jan Meeuw, Christijn, Domingo, Tomaso and Claesje are examples.

Some three weeks after the arrival of the *Amersfoort*, the Journal reported that the sick comforter, Pieter van der Stael, had begun instructing the new arrivals every morning and afternoon.

> To encourage the slaves to attend and to hear or learn the Christian prayers, it is ordered that after school everyone is to receive a small glass of brandy and two inches of tobacco. All their names are to be written down and those who have none, are to be given names, paired or unpaired,[34] young or old. All this is to be done in the presence of the Commander, who will attend for a few days to put everything in proper order and subject these people to proper discipline, signs of which are already apparent.[35]

'This was the first school established in South Africa,' observes a further editorial footnote.

'All slaves are also being properly clothed to protect them against the daily increasing cold,' continues the same Journal entry. 'The strongest have also been put to work so that they may as soon as possible be of service to the settlement.'

Meanwhile the *Hasselt* had pursued its way along the West Coast of Africa.[36] Its instructions were to proceed to Arder or Ardra (Allada), Popo (Grand Popo) and Apa, well-known centres of the slave trade situated close together on the coast of the modern Benin under the same ruler, to which captured slaves were brought by dealers from the interior.[37] By virtue of a special arrangement with the WIC, the ship was allowed to trade here and along the coast to the east- and southward, but not to the west and north-west, nor were the crew allowed to trade in ivory, which was the monopoly of the other company.[38] The *Hasselt* had, however, been particularly recommended to obtain its slaves from Ardra and Popo as they were of the 'best kind', 'reasonably civilised, diligent, sensible and not malicious, but on the contrary very subservient and obedient', and had been warned against buying at trade centres further eastwards, for although the slaves were much cheaper at 20 guilders each (the normal price being 30 to 33 guilders),[39] they were also 'much more obstinate and malicious'.

Full information was further provided on dealings with the 'king' or local chief and the method of conducting the protracted haggling on the beach which was expected to last for two or three months. The ship's officers were urged to obtain 300 slaves, 'no old men or old women, but solely sturdy young men and as few women as possible', though sufficient trade goods for 500 had been provided, consisting of cowrie shells (a common form of currency in West Africa), beads, bracelets, fine coral, iron bars, cotton textiles and fine silks.

While the intention had initially been to make for Ardra, on approaching the ship encountered 'two canoes (...) laden with merchandise, in one of them there was a *molaet* [*mulatto*] who owned the whole, and who stated that he came from the Mina [*the WIC's castle at Elmina*] and was going to Popo; (...) he informed the officers that there were 3 or 4 ships at Ardra, and consequently caused mischief to the trade there; that in consequence of the advice of the *moelaat* the trade was confined to Popo'.[40]

The coast in this area consisted of a labyrinth of lagoons, swamps and marshes, and the interior of rain forest was largely impenetrable to the whites. A modern writer refers evocatively to 'the heat and rains and mists and storms of a tropical climate' and 'the forbidding beauty of the landscape: the line of luminous surf, the strip of white beach, the swathe of bronze mangrove-swamp, the wall of dark forest',[41] but to the whites stationed at the WIC's trading posts along the coast, tropical diseases were often fatal. Slaving ships anchored at some distance from the shore and trading was done on the beach. The people sold there came from a relatively restricted area in the forests of the hinterland, but though they represented a variety of small groups and tribes living in isolation in the forest, they probably shared a common language and culture.[42]

At Popo the *Hasselt* acquired 271 slaves in the course of negotiations which lasted ten weeks, 'among them many old people, and by no means of the best quality'.[43] The price was subsequently calculated at 'between 53 and 54 guilders' each and blamed on the complex bookkeeping system of the VOC by means of which the merchandise sent from Batavia for the purpose had been credited.[44] The ship's officers also complained about the merchandise,

> and stated that it was ample but not properly assorted, which was necessary if the buyers were to conduct the slave trade according to their [own] wishes, instead of taking whatever the inhabitants of those parts wished to be rid of, namely young, old, cripple, lame, etc., while on the contrary if the merchandise were properly assorted, consisting chiefly of cowries, besides further beads and curios, they would be able to trade as they wished and would receive preference above all other traders of whatever nation, for with cowries it was possible to trade and negotiate just as one liked; without them, however, it was practically impossible to obtain any trade, as the (…) officers had seen clearly on this voyage. With the merchandise received, though more than ample, trade would be sluggish and unprofitable, and without the cowries there was the danger that they might have to return

with an empty ship and little profit and even great loss to the Hon. Company.[45]

The *Hasselt* had been specially built and equipped for the transport of slaves, and the conditions must have been considerably better than on the *Amersfoort*, but only a few incidental details are mentioned in the available documentation. The orlop deck of the ship, where the crew normally slept, had for example been left free for the use of the slaves, and the ship's officers were warned against making them travel in the hold 'because of the stench and filth this would cause'. They were advised to lay in supplies of palm oil and malagueta grain (a kind of pepper) to be served with the beans and barley provided for the slaves, and *'millie'*, which probably indicates maize. There is also a reference to them using 'St. Thomas pieces of cloth' to clothe the slaves, this being a reference to the island of São Tomé in the Gulf of Guinea.[46]

'You are to take good care of the health of the slaves,' the Instruction continues specifically,

> as this is of great importance to the Company, and also to take care that they are kept well and properly clean, treating them kindly in order to give them no cause for complaint and thereby justifying them in opposing you and mastering the ship, of which saddening examples have been seen.
>
> Furthermore you will always have to keep good guard and be sure to be on the lookout in order not to be overpowered by them unexpectedly.[47]

The *Hasselt* reached Table Bay on 6 May, almost seven weeks after the *Amersfoort* with its Angolan cargo, with 228 slaves on board, 43 having died en route. It was the beginning of the Cape winter: 'During the day it began to rain fairly heavily,' notes the Journal, 'and the wind increased in force from the N.W.' Van Riebeeck was, however, considerably better satisfied with the quality of this consignment, which he described as 'an exceptionally fine, strong and lively lot'.

Unlike the slaves from Angola, many of those from Guinea seem to have kept their own names, and this gives them a certain limited identity and individuality when they make a brief appearance in the records: Jajenne, Houwj, Gegeima or Cattibou.

While Van Riebeeck was urgently in need of slaves for the Company's work, the needs of the freeburghers had also to be considered, and Van Goens during his visit a year before had left the explicit instruction, 'The burghers to be the first served with slaves from Angola; afterwards the [Company's] servants may get some;[48] some of the best to be selected for the Company's lands, that the garrison may be gradually relieved from field labour and reduced in number as that of the burghers increases.'[49] In April 1658 the XVII likewise stipulated that the burghers were 'allowed to have two or three slaves [each], the amounts for the same to be paid to the Company in produce'.[50]

After the arrival of the slaves from Angola, Van Riebeeck had drawn up a specific scheme dated 11 April, according to which the white establishment was to be reduced to 82, and 75 slaves were to be used in the service of the Company, largely for agricultural purposes. 'With this number the Establishment here can be carried on whilst at all times every effort is made to reduce expenditure, and we intend to sell to the freemen the rest of the slaves, about 40 in number including the sick.'[51] The projected sale apparently took place shortly afterwards, 'at 50, 62½ and 75 guilders according to their age and size, to be employed in agriculture, wood-sawing, fishing, etc.'. On 9 May slaves from Guinea were similarly sold to the freeburghers 'on credit at 100 guilders each'.[52]

According to Van Riebeeck's earliest reports, a total of 398 slaves had been received in all from Angola and Guinea, but a good proportion had to be forwarded to Batavia as instructed, and Van Riebeeck reported reassuringly that 'they are provided daily with refreshments, only so that, being healthy and without scurvy, they may arrive in good health, which God grant!'[53] In despatching a batch of Guinean slaves by the *Hasselt* towards the end of May, however, he was obliged to write:

We intended to send you 140 or 150 slaves by this yacht, but as many have died since and the freemen and others have bought more than 80 for their service, only 102 were left, who, we hope, will arrive in good health, as the skipper has ere this conveyed slaves and taken good care of them. About 107 have remained here for the Company, among them about 60 sick, and well as the old, crippled, lame and lying-in women (*kraam vrouwen*), of whom some are still dying daily, so that we fear that not more than 50 or 60 will remain alive for the Company, besides a good number which [*sic*] may probably still recover and, if sufficiently strong, will be sent on by the next ship.

As regards the nature of the slaves, it seems that the Guinea ones are certainly the biggest and strongest, but those from Angola stand this cold climate better, as the Guinea ones are more and more falling in [*sic*], whilst those from Angola on the other hand are coming on well and have, excepting 37, all been discharged. The rest are all of the Guinea nations, of whom about two-thirds are ill (…).[54]

'The youngest we sent to Batavia,' he added in a letter to the Council if India early in the following year, 'and the oldest, limited to the number fixed by you, we have kept here at the Cape. They are, however, rapidly dying away and have already been reduced to 60, whilst various grey men and women are lying down sick and will also die, so that very little can be done with them (…).'[55] Elsewhere he remarked that male deaths probably predominated among the slaves because 'the men are mostly old and cannot bear this cold climate as well as the younger ones who were sent to Batavia under orders',[56] and among the deserters later that year he mentioned particularly 'an old and sickly couple who could hardly walk without a stick and always pretended that they were incapable of doing anything, so that they are bound to perish'. They were found in the interior near Tygerberg five days later, however, 'so weak and exhausted that they could hardly walk'.[57]

Statistics provided by Van Riebeeck at the end of May 1658 break down the population of the colony as follows: 'garrison 80, sick 15, Dutch women and children 20, healthy and sick slaves of the Hon. Company 98, freemen 51, male and female slaves of freemen and others 89, exiles 7, making a total of 360 persons to be fed'.[58]

According to what is probably the final and authoritative summing up of the developments of 1658, drawn up by Van Riebeeck on 5 March 1659, of the 402 slaves received at the Cape, 172 had been sent on to Batavia as ordered.[59]

The *Amersfoort* had brought 174 Angolan slaves, 92 of whom had gone to Batavia; 32 had died, 7 had absconded and not been recaptured, 24 had been sold to the freeburghers and Company servants, and 19 were in the service of the Company.

Of the 228 slaves brought from Guinea by the *Hasselt*, 80 had been sent to Batavia, being the 'youngest and best', 52 had died, 55 had been sold, and 41 remained for the Company, 'including the old and sick'.

The Company was in possession of 60 Angolan and Guinean slaves (22 men and 38 women), 'besides 2 Arabian "messieurs", 2 Madagascar do., and one boy', whose history is unknown.[60]

A total of 79 slaves were sold to freeburghers and Company servants in their private capacity,[61] and Van Riebeeck himself, who had recently started farming on his own account, is known to have bought 13 slaves on 30 April, 10 May and 31 December 1658. He also indulged in various subsequent transactions with the Company and freeburghers involving both purchase and exchange, and during the early years he was probably the largest slave owner at the Cape. A statement compiled towards the end of 1659 mentions no fewer than 23 individuals from Angola, Guinea, Madagascar, Bengal and Abyssinia owned by him, including Eva and her son Jan Bruyn, Kleine Eva, Cornelia and Lijsbeth, who have all been mentioned already.[62]

In sending his statement to the XVII, Van Riebeeck referred to 'a separate list specifying the slaves and cattle of the freemen and Company's servants',[63] but this, if it has survived, has not been published. It is not clear from the available sources what the individual slave holdings of the freeburghers were, but until the archives of the VOC have been fully studied and analysed some indication may be obtained from random references in the Journal.

By this time the two original large groups had broken up and the men were farming in small partnerships, forming nine companies of agriculturists in all,[64] so that Van Riebeeck based subsequent calculations on '6 slaves for the farm of two owners'.[65] It was only as married men were joined by their wives or the others gradually found brides on passing ships that single farming became general.

From casual references it appears that the free fisherman Maerten Jochumssen owned 2 slaves,[66] Casper Brinckman 4 'Guinea slaves— male and female',[67] and Jan Reijniers likewise 4.[68] The free miller W.C. Mostaert, soon to become one of the most prosperous and prominent of the freeburghers, owned 'male and female slaves', which likewise implies at least 4 in all,[69] while the free sawyer Leendert Cornelisz, living in the forest at the back of Table Mountain, had 12.[70]

The widespread sickness and deaths among the slaves did not make for a promising beginning, nor were the following months much better, for during the night of 2–3 June 1658, some nine weeks after their arrival, 5 male and 2 female Angolan slaves belonging to the Company absconded. Soldiers and Khoikhoi were immediately sent out to find them, 'in order, if possible, to catch some of them and make an example of them before the others to prevent a recurrence', but though some were seen a few weeks later 'on the coast between here and the Saldanha Bay', they were never recaptured.[71]

This started a spate of desertions, involving men and women, individuals and groups, Angolan and Guinean slaves and those belonging to both the Company and the burghers.[72]

In the first place these slaves naturally desired to regain their freedom, but they also seem to have hoped to be able to return overland to their homes, and when absconding they often stole provisions such as rice, clothing, blankets and tobacco for the journey.[73] 'Some of them have even planned to seize a boat which belonged to one of the ships, and which was being used for fishing in the river or near the beach,' Van Riebeeck reported with regard to a group of slaves from Guinea; 'they intended to make off with it, searching for their country by sailing along the coast.'[74]

An extremely important secondary factor in many cases would, however, have been the treatment they received from their new owners.

As far as the Company's slaves were concerned, there was of course some measure of supervision and control, although it may be significant that the official in charge of Robben Island asked that the two slaves working under him be replaced, 'because those who are here would rather be at the Cape, and I can get no work out of them, even if I [beat them to death]'.[75] Even this measure of control, limited though it may have been, was largely lacking in the case of the freeburghers.

It must be remembered that the new slave owners at the Cape for much the greater part had no previous experience of slavery or even of life in a slave-owning society. On the contrary, they were mainly members of the working and peasant classes in Northern Europe, who at home would not even have had white servants, but would have been more likely to have been employed in that capacity themselves. Their knowledge of slavery would have been limited to what they had heard at second hand or even more remotely from travellers or read in travel journals, and with the exception of the senior officials, the early white settlers at the Cape were seldom educated men or in possession of book knowledge. It would seem reasonable to say that the single most important source of such limited knowledge of the institution of slavery they would have had would have come from the Bible. With this work most of them would have been familiar, even if illiterate themselves, at least through church services or the daily prayer services conducted by a sick comforter which were compulsory under the VOC.

Apart from their ignorance and preconceptions with regard to slavery, the first white slave owners under Van Riebeeck also had little if any experience of dealing with non-European races, and in this context it is important to remember that the latter were at this time generally regarded as inferior to Europeans, even by educated men. In letters written over the period 1676–77, for example, the English physician, scientist and scholar Sir William Petty wrote quite typically of the 'considerable' differences

> between the Guiny Negros & the Middle Europeans; and of Negros between those of Guiny and those who live about the Cape of Good Hope [*Khoikhoi*], which last are the most beast-like of all the souls [*sorts?*] of men with whom our travellers are well acquainted. I say that the Europeans do not only differ from the aforementioned Africans in collour (…) but also (…) in naturall manners, & in the internall qualities of their minds.[76]

The slaves for their part had been forcibly removed from their homes and found themselves not only in a strange country but in a completely alien culture. Except to the extent that some of the slaves from Angola may have picked up a certain amount of Portuguese, there was during the first few months also no way in which Africans and Europeans could make themselves mutually intelligible. The situation was therefore marked by fear, resentment, misunderstanding, unwillingness, impatience, incomprehension and, inevitably, the growing use of violence, though certain of the freeburghers whose slaves had disappeared stated in bewilderment that the latter 'had never been treated badly, locked up or beaten by them'.[77]

On 19 June it was thought advisable by the authorities to send the Fiscal and Sergeant round formally 'to all the freemen, in order, as has often been done before, to warn them to treat their slaves properly and not to make them surly by continual beating, thumping and scolding, lest more run away'.[78] This was within the first four months of slaves becoming generally available, and the words 'as has often been done before' are significant.

This warning seems to have had little effect, and by 6 August it was felt necessary to issue an official notice or *plakkaat* in which it was stated 'that some of the freemen still treat their slaves harshly and tyrannically, binding and beating them mercilessly with rods and other scourges', canes of split bamboo and knotted cords being mentioned specifically, and they were admonished to administer 'domestic correction' only, thus applying the Batavian norm to the Cape as well.[79]

Before the end of June enough of the fugitives had been recovered for an example to be made of them, and all the freeburghers together with their slaves were summoned to the Fort to be present: 'all are to be tied to a post in the open and scourged; one is to be branded, whilst two are to be placed in chains, linked to each other, until their masters request that they be set free'.[80] The result was that the reactions of the slaves gradually became more desperate, and there were rumours of plots to kill the whites, while Van Riebeeck recorded slaves stealing and collecting knives, and also stealing a pistol.[81]

On the other hand, fugitives also began to return of their own accord as it became clear to them that escape was no solution to their bondage.[82] Factors contributing to this development were the extremely cold Cape winter, especially to people unaccustomed to this kind of weather; 'so cold,' as Van Riebeeck wrote towards the end of July, 'that in some marshes and pools there was ice the thickness of half a finger',[83] as well as the inhospitable nature of the interior,[84] with its wild animals and shortage of water. A search party sent out fruitlessly beyond Tygerberg after runaway slaves reported that 'everywhere they had seen rhinoceroses and elephants by the hundred, also many elands, harts and steenbuck, etc.'[85] While African slaves might have managed to deal with wild animals if armed, they were also threatened by the apparently instinctive enmity between the Khoikhoi and the *Zwartemans* or 'black men' as they called the slaves.[86]

Van Riebeeck remarked at an early stage that the Khoikhoi 'are very jealous of the slaves and cannot bear them, being always at loggerheads with them'.[87] This had appeared as early as 1655, when the fugitive slave Anthony was believed to have been killed by Khoikhoi, and there was a significant incident on Van Riebeeck's farm on 17 May 1658, barely a week after the sale and distribution of the slaves from Guinea, when the Khoi Chaihantima, who had visited the Fort on behalf the Chainoqua Chief, was assaulted by some freeburghers' slaves in the Liesbeek valley on his way back to the Overberg, in what may well have been a typical encounter.

According to Chaihantima's own account,

he had been assaulted by those at the Bosheuvel because he and some men had come among the plough cattle of these farmers and the slaves had feared that they intended to steal them. One of the Guinea slaves had indicated to him to go away, but as it seemed as if he would not leave the cattle which were in the slave's charge, the latter had called one of his comrades, who had let loose the dog which had overtaken Chaihantima and prevented him from escaping. The slaves rushed at him and would have killed him if our Netherlanders themselves had not liberated the Hottentots.[88]

The fact that this was a time of mounting tension between the white settlers and the local Khoikhoi, which was to lead to open warfare within a year, increased the feelings of apprehension among the scattered and isolated freeburghers, and they were officially ordered 'to be on their guard and to keep their weapons prepared lest they be surprised, and not to go about unarmed'.[89]

It was during this time, incidentally, and in these circumstances, that the young freeburgher Jan Sacharias and the former slave Maria van Bengalen were married.

By the end of August the number of fugitive slaves still at large had reached 28, and it was feared that they could multiply, 'having about a third of their women with them', and so become a serious threat to the small colony.[90] It was therefore announced on 28 August that the blacksmith had been ordered to make enough chains for all the Company slaves, 'except some very old and sickly men, the females and the children', and also to provide the freemen everywhere, on application, with chains for that purpose in order to prevent further desertion.'[91]

This was duly done, but shortly afterwards 14 of the Company's slaves, men and women, were reported to have absconded 'notwithstanding the fact that each had a chain on his leg with an iron ball at the end',[92] while others succeeded in breaking their chains, so that the links had to be made thicker.[93] 'The slaves that are young and strong are very apt to run away,' Van Riebeeck reported to Batavia early in 1659, 'so that we keep [them] in chains, who are accordingly hardly able to do half work.'[94]

By this time the fugitives were also widely scattered and guards had to be posted 'at all places they were likely to pass, as far as Hout Bay and even the Bay False [*False Bay*] to watch out for them night and day. Some were even sent out as far as the Leopard Mountains [*Tygerberg*] and Mountains of Africa [*Drakenstein and Hottentots-Holland*] to search for the remaining 7 women and 3 men, and they had orders not to return until they were relieved by fresh parties',[95] remaining out for ten days at a time.[96] The demands this made on the small white community were of course considerable.

By the beginning of September the freeburghers had asked permission to return some of their slaves to the Company,[97] and on 8 September they formally brought to the Fort 'half of their male and female slaves, (…) as they dared not keep all of them any longer, for it had become quite evident that they were naturally inclined to run away in spite of being well treated':[98] 'preferring to do their work with Dutch servants,' as Van Riebeeck afterwards informed the Council of India.[99]

'The number of Company's slaves here at present,' Van Riebeeck noted on the 30th of the month, 'including those returned to the Company by the freemen for fear of desertion, is only 83, made up of 34 men and 49 women. They are mostly old and useless, and about 30 are mad, ill or crippled, and can be of no particular service. We shall be relieved of this burden, however, as they will soon die off.'[100]

Towards the end of October, when the first spate of desertions seemed to be over, a plot was discovered among the Guinean slaves to kill the white servants on Van Riebeeck's farm, one of the latter actually having been attacked, and make off with the draught oxen: 'none, including the women, were without knives, which they had stolen here and there and collected'. 'It is therefore clear,' Van Riebeeck concluded, 'that the Guinea slaves will have to be more closely guarded as they are strong, daring fellows, while the women are obviously also very brave.'[101]

At the same time, however, Van Riebeeck was sending orders to the freeburghers to bring their scythes and sickles to the Fort to be sharpened with a view to the approaching harvest,[102] and by the end of November, riding out to the Liesbeek valley, he found 'the freemen and also the ensign Jan van Harwarden busily engaged in reaping barley', assisted by a number of visiting seamen with experience of farming.[103] It may be significant that there is no mention of slaves among the harvesters: if any were present, they would have been in chains.

By January 1659, four freeburgher slaves were missing again, which Van Riebeeck described as 'a serious set-back for these people'.[104] In spite of the number of slaves who abandoned the attempt at flight and returned of their own accord, Cape society would continue to be unsettled by regular desertions and the presence of fugitives on the fringes of the colonised territory for as long as the institution of slavery lasted.

When the prospect of obtaining slaves for the Cape was taking on definite form early in 1657, the XVII wrote to Van Riebeeck, as already quoted above, 'they are to be taught all kinds of trades, that in course of time the advantage may be beneficial to yourselves, and a large number of Europeans excused. They are also [especially] to be taught agriculture, as it would be too great an expense to feed such a lot of people from Holland or India.'[105]

Van Goens during his visit that year reduced the number of white employees of the Company to 100,[106] but this was with a view to many of its activities being taken over by freeburghers, and not with reference to the expected arrival of slaves. The intention was that this figure should be even further reduced to 80 when the number of freeburghers permitted.

Van Riebeeck's own plans included the slaves, however. In the winter of 1657, when planning the 'good barn' he intended building near the Company's cornfields at Rondebosch (the present Groote Schuur), he had already envisaged using 'the Company's own labourers and slaves' to cultivate 50 to 60 morgen here 'for feeding the garrison and slaves, etc.', while the freeburghers were to supply the needs of visiting ships.[107]

Early in 1658 the Commissioner who followed Van Goens, Joan (Johan) Cunaeus, raised the maximum number of whites to be stationed at the Cape to 120 'until you have received the slaves expected, when you shall reduce the number to 70 or 80 men. We hope that this will soon be done.'[108] In 1660, however, Commissioner Sterthemius determined 'that for the present the garrison should not consist of less than 120' in order to provide proper protection against the Khoikhoi.[109]

Writing at about the time of Cunaeus's visit, shortly before the arrival of the slaves, Van Riebeeck for his part gave the undertaking that 'as soon as the slaves have been properly trained to their work, we intend to reduce the number of the Company's servants here to 80, especially if everything, excepting the Company's gardens, is left to the freedmen and private individuals'.[110] It may be remarked in passing that this goal was never achieved, and by 1704, during the War of the Spanish Succession, a garrison of no fewer than 800 men was considered necessary for the Cape.[111]

At this same time Van Riebeeck projected an establishment consisting of 82 whites supported by 75 slaves (38 men and 37 women) and 5 convicts or *bandieten*.

According to this scheme the male slaves were intended for service in the Commander's household, in the gardens, and with the millers and grooms, the smiths, the masons and hodmen, the 'cook for the common persons', and the wood wagons. One person was to serve in the forest behind Table Mountain 'for gardening and cooking', and 2 were to be placed at the Company's cornfields at Rondebosch in the Liesbeek valley, one of them 'to act as attendant on the sick and mind the poultry'. Female slaves were to be stationed in the households of the Commander, sick comforter and sergeant, with the millers, masons and cook, and in the gardens. Eight men and eight women were to be used for 'threshing, picking, digging, and gathering of ears, and other work in corn cultivation, &c.', and six men and six women for 'fishing, and for all dirty, useless, and scullery work (*morswerk*)'.[112]

The 7 Angolan slaves who absconded in June 1658 were specified as being 'one from the forest, two from the fort and two pairs from the Company's grain-fields',[113] and a female slave was later mentioned as doing the cooking at the Company's barn near the grain fields.[114]

Van Riebeeck's projected division of labour in April 1658 had provided 12 men and 12 women for work in the Company's garden in the Table Valley,[115] which was gradually being extended along the banks of the mountain streams, covering 15 morgen in that year,[116] and 21 by the time of Van Riebeeck's departure in 1662.[117] This figure could obviously not be attained at first, for when a number of 'garden slaves', 5 men and 7 women, absconded, it was stated that 'the 2 remaining slaves had no time to escape'.[118] Their work would have been particularly heavy when there were ships in the bay, and Van Riebeeck in a letter written in 1659 mentions vegetables being 'collected in baskets within the gardens, and afterwards transferred into bags and thus placed in boats for shipment, (…) they are fetched in the evening in order to be boiled the next day, unless there are only one or two ships in the bay, when they are fetched in the morning early, to be used the same day'. According to him '14 or 15 men had to be employed exclusively in preparing the vegetables for shipment',[119] and they would naturally have been assisted by slaves as available.

Two fugitive slaves were, on being recaptured, scourged and chained, 'and ordered to carry out the slaves' excrement and tubs and to perform other dirty work',[120] though this would presumably have been part of their normal duties as well, and on Robben Island they helped gather shells for the limekilns.[121] There are also glimpses of slaves being used for various other odd jobs as they occurred. When the Fiscal Abraham Gabbema fell seriously ill after having been sent out with the land-surveyor to chart the coast of the Peninsula, 'some men were immediately sent with four slaves and a hammock to carry [him] home'.[122]

In addition to domestic work, the women would probably have been taught laundering. Two years before their arrival Van Riebeeck had requested 'two or three free Mardycker families' from Batavia 'who would be able to earn a living by washing, to the particularly great comfort not only of the people of the Fortress, but also of the passing ships, (…) as the Netherlands' women, however humble their condition may be, when once outside their Fatherland, consider themselves to good (*genereus*) and precious (*waardig*) for such work'.[123] Insofar as they were available, female slaves were probably also used for heavy labour and field work as well as the men, as was already the custom in Batavia.

As far as the slaves of the freeburghers are concerned, they would equally have done whatever work was available and would have been used especially as farm labourers. 'No agriculturist's home, which generally consists of from two to four persons, has less than 50 or 60 sheep and not less than 30 cattle, besides their milch cows,' Van Riebeeck reported towards the end of 1658.[124] Elsewhere he calculated at the same time that the Company owned 1406 sheep, divided between Robben Island and the mainland, and 420 head of cattle, while the freeburghers had 350 and 'almost 200' respectively, the cattle consisting 'mainly of draught oxen, a few milch cows and a number of old cows'.[125]

Slaves have already been recorded as guarding cattle,[126] and during the first winter after their arrival the burghers mentioned how badly they were needed 'on the lands and for wheat farming',[127] while in the winter of 1658, when the time came for planting maize, Van Riebeeck could already remark, 'the slaves know well how to do it'.[128] A slave of Hendrick Boom who had been reported missing was found 'among the grain, where he had been lying hidden out of sheer laziness, which is much in evidence among the slaves'.[129]

Wherever they may have been kept at night, the buildings of that early period were not secure enough to prevent slaves from escaping. After a series of thefts had occurred in the freeburghers' gardens by night, however, all slave owners had to be warned by *plakkaat* in 1661 'to keep their slaves indoors at night, as those who are found out of doors after the bell at the gateway [of the Fort] has been rung will be apprehended by the burgher watch and handed over to the Fiscal in the morning'.[130]

As regards food, rice from Batavia formed the basis of the rations provided for all groups at the Cape, including the slaves,[131] and Van Riebeeck stated that 50 lb. wheat, flour or rice was required per head per month.[132]

After the arrival of the slaves from Angola the freeburghers' boat was dispatched to Dassen Island 'to bring seal meat, salted and dried, for feeding the slaves',[133] and on their return 120 pounds of meat was cooked and served to the slaves, 'who liked it very much'.[134] The following month the *Maria* is mentioned as 'fetching seal meat and birds from the islands for the slaves',[135] probably referring to penguins. At the end of May she was sent to Saldanha Bay 'to salt there so many casks of seal meat and birds and to get such a good supply of fish that the slaves can be fed for a good while, and the barley and rice last longer'—elsewhere in the same document 'gutted harder' is specified.[136] When 2720 pounds of seal meat were sent over to Robben Island as rations for the slaves stationed there, however, the supervisor replied that they preferred penguins.[137] Fish would finally become the basic food used to supplement the rice given to the slaves, and when prices for various foodstuffs were laid down in 1659, is was carefully stipulated that if the Company required fish for this purpose, it was to be supplied 'at the price previously determined'.[138]

Claes Lambertssen who arrived in 1659 as an arquebusier was employed 'as cook for the Company's slaves and as baker of the ration loaves for the men', and had his wages increased from 12 to 18 guilders a month the following year,[139] but the demands made on him cannot have been very high.

With regard to clothing, 'coarse cloth' had been sent out from the Netherlands for the slaves 'to protect them against the cold' when the outfitting of the *Hasselt* and *Maria* was under discussion in 1657, and Van Riebeeck instructed to order further 'clothing' for them from Batavia.[140] Shortly after their arrival he ordered 'negros cloth or Bengal fotas' for this purpose, photas being a cheap, strong cotton often used for loincloths, as well as 'Japanned striped woolly cloth, made and obtained there at a trifling price, especially for clothing the slaves as well in this cold climate'.[141] He had presumably become acquainted with the latter while serving at Nagasaki, for the Council in Batavia replied that it was unknown to them, and sent him instead 'some Wingurla stuffs', textiles from Vengurla on the west coast of India.[142]

'Eastern pilot cloth' was also requested from the Netherlands, with the note: 'Such warm clothing cannot be obtained from India, and is nevertheless indispensable for the slaves here, on account of the cold climate.'[143] In this case, the reference is probably to cloth obtained from the Baltic area ('*Oostzee*'), generally known in the Netherlands as 'the East'. In 1660 there is similar mention of '2 coarse coats, 2 jackets, 2 pieces of St. Thomas negro cloth and one piece of Indian negro cloth' being sent to Robben Island 'as clothing for the slaves there',[144] but the original Dutch ('2 *pijen, 2 baytjens*') could also refer to lengths of coarse woollen textiles ('*pij*' and '*baai*').

Clothing would probably have been elementary in the best of circumstances, with a view to decency rather than the comfort of the wearers, and in the winter of 1663 Van Riebeeck's successor, Zacharias Wagenaer, who was a kind-hearted man, wrote in the Journal of the effect of the 'unceasing cold and harmful south-easterly wind' on all 'not adequately protected against it by warm clothes', 'so that one can hardly send out labourers on public works in the open air or as herdsmen in the fields, much less these poorly clothed [*karig geklede*] slaves'.[145]

An interesting and extremely unusual fragment of information on what may be called the personal hygiene of the slaves is provided in the report of the visiting Commissioner Huybert de Lairesse, who recommended fencing off the watering place of the ships in the immediate vicinity of the Fort 'to prevent as far as possible the freeburghers from washing and bathing there (*wassen ende plassen*), as well as the possibility of the slaves bathing there'.[146]

While a good deal of information about externals such as these may be obtained by sifting through the available documents, however, virtually nothing is known about the individual slaves. The survivors from Angola were mainly children, but among the Guineans there were a number of 'paired' slaves who were regarded by the whites as being man and wife, although it is not known at what stage they were joined in this way. The two slaves belonging to Steven Jansz Botma and his fellow farmer occupied the same bed and the man was called the woman's 'husband',[147] while in September 1658 a couple described as 'a slave and a female slave (his wife)' were sent over to Robben Island with a boat to help load shells,[148] and Van Riebeeck's 23 slaves included one couple from Guinea and 5 from Angola.[149]

These slave unions had no legal status, however, and could not have given the women concerned much protection against the demands made upon them in a community consisting almost exclusively of unattached white males. Although the attestations which provide evidence in this regard date only from 1660, the situation described must have come into being almost immediately after the arrival of the women from Angola and Guinea.

A probably not untypical vignette in this regard is provided by the land surveyor and two soldiers who declared 'that they and the Commander Riebeeck did last night, long after the sentries were posted, arrive at the dwelling of Gunner Willem [Cornelisz], whom they found undressed, lying alongside a female slave of the Commander named Maria',[150] probably a reference to Maria van Bengalen. Similarly, a sailor is said to have stated that Van Riebeeck, paying a visit to his farm Bosheuvel, had asked the superintendent, Barend Waendersz,

'Has any of your men had anything to do with the female slaves and fructified them?', and that Barend answered, 'No, sir.' That Riebeeck replied, 'Barend, did you have anything to do in the matter? Tell it freely, no harm is done, it is for the benefit of the Company.' Barend replied, 'Yes, sir.' Riebeeck answered, 'The go to the Fiscal and settle the matter, no harm is done (it is not of any importance).'[151]

The slave women at Bosheuvel, which lay in an isolated position in the Liesbeek valley, at the very end of the colonised area, must have seemed particularly available, and some soldiers here described how 'whilst walking in the adjoining garden they saw Herman Remajenne of Cologne and Hans Ras of Angel, free agriculturists, going to the female slaves who were in the kitchen'. When reprimanded, Remajenne is alleged to have replied, 'I will visit them, I have visited them before, why should I no longer visit them, you shall not forbid me, &c.'[152]

In a similar statement the freeburgher Steven Jansz Botma, afterwards a prominent member of the community, and his farmhand Willem Willemsz declared that Botma's partner Hendrick Elbertsz,

> living with the latter in one house, had for a long while had illicit intercourse with the female slave belonging to them, named Adouke. Often he had turned her husband from his bed and gone to lie with his wife. The lad said to him, 'Are you not ashamed of yourself?', and he had replied, 'It is nothing to you', &c.[153]

The 'lad' in this translation was obviously the 'boy ('*jongen*') or male slave, Adouke's partner.

In another statement two Company servants declared that the freeburgher Cornelis Claasz 'had confessed to them that the child of the female slave Ysabelle owned by J. Reijniersz was his child, &c.'.[154] Isabella van Angola was to make her appearance in local records again in 1672 when she was sold by Reyniersz to a fellow freeburgher, and her age was then given as 30,[155] which means that she must have been about 19 at the time of her relationship with Claasz.

Contacts of this kind could also be of a more personal nature than is implied in these declarations, as is revealed in a long, rambling statement by the superintendent at the Company's barn, where in a series of complaints about one 'Willem Schalq' (van der Merwe) who was serving under him, he mentions

> a certain female slave by whom he has a child, and whom he had chambered in the kitchen at the time of her lying in. He likewise, every hour of the day, took care of her by preparing her food and fetching water and fuel. Yea! what is more, when she was being confined he knocked me up and begged me to give him his brandy for the reason stated. I gave him two glasses which he brought to her to revive her.[156]

Concubinage, as it was generally termed, does not appear to have been looked upon as criminal in itself or to have been punished unless there were aggravating factors. Hendrick Courts or Coerts was scourged and banished to Robben Island for a year in 1666, for example, after a complaint by a freeburgher's wife that he had twice slept with her female slave,[157] and when the soldier Christoffel Snijman left his guard post the following year for 'the residence of a certain known black woman ["*meijt*"]', he was scourged, deprived of two months' wages, and sent to Robben Island for two years.[158]

Relationships such as these seldom led to marriage, however. Cornelis Claasz who fathered a child by Ysabelle was eventually to marry another slave woman, Catryn van Coromandel, in 1676, but Willem Schalck van der Merwe's daughter, known as 'Marietje Schalk' or 'Marietje Willemsz', ended up in the Company's Slave Lodge, a slave like her mother,[159] while Van der Merwe himself married a European-born wife in 1668 and fathered a white family.

An exceptional case is that of the military man Pieter Everaert, who as Ensign formed one of the small group of senior officials in the Fort, and who on his death in 1664 left 150 guilders to the slave Catharina van Bengalen for the support and upbringing of her unborn child.[160] The child would seem obviously to have been his own.

The birth of children to the slave women can be traced only insofar as they were baptised, which seems in the early years to have been done mainly on the initiative of the owners of the respective mothers. As slaves could contract no legal marriage, these children were inevitably illegitimate and described thus in the church records, and no indication was given of who the father was or whether he was a white man or a fellow slave. Later, when it was realised that this was of importance, the phrase 'the father being an unknown Christian' was added as appropriate.[161]

The first baptism of this nature recorded was that of a boy called Heindrick, the son of an unnamed slave mother, on 17 July 1659, a year after the arrival of the slaves from Angola and Guinea.[162] Over the period 1660–63 the sick comforter Van der Stael recorded 7 more: in 1660 the Revd. François Caron baptised 'a child of my female slave, called Pietertje, and one of the female slave of the Commander, called Reintje; these two are illegitimate children. God grant that these baptised may grow up to His honour.'[163] The fact that the Revd. Caron himself was the son of a senior Dutch official by a Japanese woman who had subsequently been legitimised by his father says a good deal about the multiracial quality of life under the VOC in the East.[164] The following year Van der Stael, besides the baptism of a white child, records that of 'two little boys called Jacob, the fourth a girl called Annetje; these three are illegitimate children'.[165] Once again the mothers are not mentioned.

The most interesting of these baptisms is the last to be noted by Van der Stael before he left the Cape: in 1663 he recorded the baptism of a child 'born of a slave woman and called Louwijs; the sponsors are Gabriel Joosten Cornet and Denijs Otto, both corporals; this child was born illegitimate'.[166]

It may be as well to mention that the children of slave women automatically acquired the status of their mothers, as in Batavia. They were thus born into slavery, irrespective of the status of their fathers or whether the latter were prepared to acknowledge them or not. It was through unions like these that a local 'coloured' or 'halfcaste' population of manumitted slaves or 'free blacks' was eventually to come into being at the Cape towards the end of the century.

As the slaves gradually realised that no return to their homelands was feasible and began to accept their lot, a certain identification with the interests of their white masters took place, even though this was limited, qualified and forced by circumstances.

This holds especially in confrontations with the Khoikhoi, who were the enemies of both slaves and whites, and was clearly seen during the series of cattle raids by the members of local Khoi tribes and armed skirmishes which began in the winter of 1659 and are known as the First Khoi War. When a group of 30 Khoikhoi attacked Van Riebeeck's farm at Bosheuvel, for example, they were repulsed and pursued by farm servants 'with guns and a number of slaves with assegais',[167] and a slave was wounded during an attack on a freeburgher's home at the same time.[168]

In these circumstances a significant decision was taken on 21 May:

> So that the Hottentots may better be overtaken in flight, since they are too nimble for us, it has been decided to release all the slaves from their irons. They are embittered against the Hottentots and would indeed like to wipe them out,[169] so that we may use them against the Hottentots, arming them with half-pikes until such time as they have obtained assegais, which are more effective weapons of offence.[170]

Shortly afterwards Van Riebeeck noted that the necessary weapons were being made for the slaves 'in their own fashion and under their direction, since they are better adepts at wielding them than the Hottentots. An order has been issued that the women of these slaves are to be kept here to prevent the slaves from staying away; it has been found that they are apparently much attached to their womenfolk and do not readily desert them.'[171]

This was possibly over-optimistic, however, if not born of sheer desperation, and it is likely that the slaves were never fully trusted and therefore kept in the background as much as possible during the war. There is no further mention them in the account of the war given by Van Riebeeck in his Journal until August, when the worst was in fact over. 'Not only have the Guinea slaves been stubborn and recalcitrant,' he then noted, but it now appears that they had intended and resolved to escape as a group and join the Hottentots, so all the male slaves have promptly been clapped into chains once more. This has been done so as to prevent such a loss to the Company, for should these sturdy and audacious people link up with our enemies, they would be able to cause more mischief and damage than a hundred times as many Hottentots. Moreover, they would give the Hottentots too much instruction in warfare, since some of them were in Guinea at the time of the European war there.[172]

The reference is to the recent clash between representatives of the Danish and Swedish trading companies in West Africa while their respective countries were at war in Europe.[173]

Nonetheless, the process of adaptation and partial incorporation had already begun, and by October 1658 a Guinean slave belonging to the Junior Merchant Roeloff de Man, who was a bachelor, could express himself in some 'broken Dutch, which he had learnt'.[174] In 1661 there is a reference in the Journal to the sick comforter Van der Stael 'instructing the Company's slaves and the Hottentots in the Dutch language and the Christian doctrine (and with some success)'.[175]

When the Guinean slaves who absconded in the winter of 1659, during the time of the war with the Khoikhoi, were recaptured, Van Riebeeck could also note that all of them 'were again cast in chains, with the exception of the one, who had brought back his companion. He was therefore allowed to remain free and placed in charge of his countrymen, the Company's Guinea slaves, of whom he is one'.[176]

In January 1660 the Journal pays tribute on the death of 'one of the Company's best slaves who had learnt to be as proficient in ploughing, threshing and other agricultural work as the best farmer at the Cape'.[177] In 1661 it was said that the Guinean slaves were 'becoming very handy and they are as good workmen in the gardens as any Dutchman',[178] and towards the end of the year, when their mortality was remarkably high, the Journal noted the death of a slave in the smithy, 'as efficient in his work as any Dutchman', and another who assisted the carpenter, 'who is also as good in his work as any Dutchman'.[179] At the same time the freeburgher Steven Jansz Botma lost a slave 'for whom he had been offered 500 guilders only a short time ago',[180] a very high price indeed.

The relative handful of slaves, important and increasingly essential as they may have been as source of labour, do not seem to have been considered an important segment of the early colonial community, however, and after the difficult early months of arrival and settlement, they are mentioned by Van Riebeeck in his Journal only when one of them had died. In the lengthy Memorial he compiled for his successor in 1662, which runs to 20 closely printed pages in the published version, there are only scattered references to their monthly ration of rice, and the fact that they were learning Dutch and not becoming acquainted with Portuguese.[181]

Furthermore, apart from specific slave transactions, these slaves are seldom identified by name in the contemporary records, unlike whites. A notable exception occured when the surgeon Pieter van Meerhoff, meeting the Chief of the Namaqua during an expedition into the interior, described him as 'a gigantic man, much bigger than Cattibou, our tallest slave who is employed at the Company's granary'.[182]

3. The slave trade: Batavia

The first few years of slavery at the Cape have been described in some detail, as only a relative handful of individuals were concerned and it is possible, by tracing their individual lives, to obtain some idea of the nature of the institution of slavery and the historical framework within which it was established. What follows will be a more general survey of its development under local conditions.

After the unsuccessful second voyage of the *Maria* to Angola in 1658, no further attempts were made to obtain slaves from the West Coast of Africa, as the expense was not considered justified by the results,[1] in spite of Van Riebeeck pointing out 'that a great deal may be done in Congo for ivory and slaves'.[2] An important consideration was that Batavia could at this time still obtain slaves for its own needs cheaply and easily from Bengal and Aracan, although this was soon to change,[3] while the Council of India also reacted unfavourably to the scale on which the early slaves at the Cape absconded and the amount of time and effort demanded from the small white population to pursue, recapture and guard them. 'In our opinion,' they wrote after consideration, 'the colony should be worked and established by Europeans and not by slaves, as our nation is so constituted that as soon as they have the convenience of slaves they become lazy and unwilling to put forth their hands to work (…)'.[4]

For some ten or twelve years the work at the Cape had therefore to be carried on as well as possible with the help of the handful of

Angolan and Guinean slaves who had survived the respective voyages, the Cape winters and an epidemic which killed a further number of them towards the end of 1661.[5] Only erratically and unpredictably were they supplemented by small numbers of slaves from the East and other sources.

The Company continued to use its white employees as common labourers, as it was entitled to do by the terms of its contract with them. It is noteworthy that the building of the Castle which was begun in 1666 to replace Van Riebeeck's ramshackle Fort, 'heavy, hard work' (*'een swaeren bloedigen arbeijt'*) as Commissioner Verburch described it on its completion ten years later, was undertaken with white labour, and Commander Wagenaer complained eloquently about the poor quality of the veterans of various European wars with whom he was obliged to begin it.[6] According to Dr Böeseken: 'Whereas there had been 89 slaves owned by the Free Burghers in 1658, only 39 were left in 1661 and only 23 in 1662. In 1662 the officials had 23 left and the Company 59.'[7]

Van Riebeeck's personal slave holdings have already been mentioned. Over the period 1661–62, when he was preparing to leave for Batavia, he sold several of these slaves, both to fellow officials and to freeburghers,[8] including, on two occasions, the Cape-born child of a Guinean slave couple, which means that these infants cannot have been more than three years old. It is possible that he and his family took only 6 of their slaves with them when they left the Cape in 1662.[9]

When Van Riebeeck's successor, Zacharias Wagenaer, a well-to-do middle-aged man, arrived from Batavia with his wife and widowed stepdaughter they brought with them 'two horses and five slaves', mentioned in that order in contemporary documents.[10] Sales of slaves by both Wagenaer and his stepdaughter to local officials are known to have taken place,[11] and a slave couple were manumitted on Wagenaer's return to Batavia in 1666.[12] The slaves concerned, insofar as they were identified in contemporary documentation, were from Bengal, with one possibly from Japan, where Wagenaer had twice served as Chief of the VOC's trading post at Nagasaki, and one described as 'a Cape slave'. The latter, named Marie, who was sold in 1665, must still have been a child at the time.

According to the muster roll of 1664, which has been published by Kloeke, 'Mistress Wagenaer' at this time owned 10 slaves, which implies a number of unrecorded purchases at the Cape. The young widow of Frederick Verburgh, who had stayed on after his death, owned 4, the wife of the Fiscal, Hendrick Lacus, had a male and a female slave and a child, and the widow of sergeant Van Herwerden, who had meanwhile married the Company's bookkeeper, Jochum Blanck, had 7 slaves. The wife of the Secunde Abraham Gabbema is listed with no fewer than 8 male and female slaves and the same number of slave children.[13] The fact that these slaves are described as the property of the wives of officials seems intended to emphasise the fact that they were privately owned.

Wagenaer is known to have farmed on his own account at the Cape, like Van Riebeeck, if on a smaller scale, which may explain the relatively large size of his slave holdings. This also applies to his successor in 1666, Cornelis van Quaelberg, who bought two male slaves and a female from Wagenaer's stepdaughter on his arrival at the Cape in 1666,[14] but also acquired further slaves during his short stay. In 1668 Van Quaelberg sold to his own successor, Jacob Borghorst, 7 male slaves for a total of 1680 guilders. One was from Bengal and one was described as a 'Malay', but the remaining 5 were all from Coromandel, a reminder of the fact that the VOC was by this time no longer able to obtain slaves from Bengal and Aracan.

In addition Borghorst bought from Lieutenant Abraham Schut, who was on his way to Batavia, a man, woman and child, and from Maria Prignon, the widow of the Revd Wachtendorp, who was also leaving, a Guinean slave, 2 female slaves and 2 children. He thus acquired a total of 15 slaves at a cost of 1832 guilders and 10 *penningen*. These he was willing to transfer to the Company at no profit to himself at the end of 1669 when he himself had been replaced as Commander.[15]

Both Van Quaelberg and Borghorst had arrived at the Cape directly from the Netherlands, and being unable to bring a complement of slaves with them like the Wagenaers, had been obliged to buy them locally.

Up to about 1670, which may be regarded as a turning point in the slave trade at the Cape, transactions took place largely among Company officials, as illustrated by the examples given above. Apart from the slaves brought by Wagenaer and sold here by him, purchases were presumably also made from passengers on ships returning from the East who were accompanied by slaves, and Wagenaer himself, on finally returning to Europe from Batavia in 1668, disposed of his slave Isak van Bengalen to the Company's shopkeeper for 90 rixdollars.[16]

In some cases slaves were also ordered specifically in Batavia and sent out to the Cape. Among Van Riebeeck's slaves was Maria van Bengalen, who had been 'sent hither' in this way,[17] and in 1662 Jacob Does, a prominent freeburgher in Batavia, similarly acquired two slaves who were duly delivered to and paid for by the dispenser, Jochum Blanck.[18] As Blanck was married to the widow Van Herwerden, whose first husband had been Valentijn Does, this may well have been a family transaction.

As far as the Company was concerned, according to the muster roll of 1664 it owned 82 slaves: 30 from Guinea (11 men and 19 women), 17 from Angola (5 men and 12 women), 6 males and females from Madagascar, 2 slaves from Batavia, and a total of 27 unspecified children.[19] As 41 slaves from Guinea and 19 from Angola had been retained at the Cape in 1658, the loss over the past six years had been the greatest in the first named group with its many elderly and sickly slaves.

This nuclear labour force the VOC was unable to supplement in a significant way, although the purchase of the slave woman Gegeima from Guinea from the freeburgher Thomas Christoffel Muller in 1668 is recorded, a transaction from which her daughter Lobbitje, aged about four, was excluded,[20] and there may have been similar purchases. This would explain why the Company was prepared to consider buying Borghorst's slaves in 1669, and also why Isbrand Goske, visiting the Cape as Commissioner in 1671, complained of slaves having been bought from private individuals at 80, 90 and 100 rixdollars each, instead of being hired more economically at 8 to 10 guilders a month, 'apart from their daily food'.[21]

The freeburghers for their part continued to be heavily reliant on hired white *knechten*. The muster roll for 1664 lists 36 male free-burghers with only 27 slaves, 14 of the latter being males and 13 women and children.[22] In contrast they employed no fewer than 46 'Dutch servants' or farmhands, a number of them having as many as 4, while few were without at least one.[23]

The slave transactions between 1658 and 1670 of which records have survived include those of some of the freeburghers, and obvi-ously there were certain individuals who could afford to buy slaves, even at this early stage, when any became available locally. When the Cape was unexpectedly visited at the end of 1664, for example, by an English slave trader on his way from Madagascar to Barbados with a cargo, the two burgher councillors, who at this stage seem to have been Wouter Cornelisz Mostaert and Hendrick van Suerwaer-den,[24] and two unidentified burghers 'living close by the Fort' (in the Table Valley) asked permission to see whether they could buy some slaves.[25]

These individuals were few in number, however, and the names which occur most frequently in the recorded transactions are those Elbert Dircx Diemer, Van Suerwaerden and Mostaert, all of whom were among the relatively prosperous members of the early free white community.

The slaves bought and sold in these transactions continued to be largely from Bengal, with a few from Coromandel and Malabar.[26] The provenance of the '*Indiaan*' ('Indian') Gerrit is not clear,[27] but an '*In-disch slaafjen genaemt Jan*' was probably a child from the present Indo-nesia, while a '*St. Thomese slaeffje*' may refer a little boy from São Tomé off the coast of Guinea, or the place of the same name on the Coromandel coast of India.[28] In 1662 the free fisherman Bartolomeus Borns bought one Jan Vos from Cape Verde on the West Coast of Africa, who was subsequently sold to the surgeon Pieter van Meerhoff.[29]

The year 1670 has arbitrarily been chosen to mark the end of this uncertain period of a limited slave population and small-scale transactions for the reason that the 1670s saw a number of changes at the Cape which were profoundly to affect the fledgling colony.

Firstly, after some fifteen or twenty years the initial difficulties connected with farming in the new country had been overcome, and the early marriages among the white population were beginning to produce a new generation of locally born young people to whom the country was no longer unfamiliar and alien as it had been to their immigrant parents. The first locally born white woman is said to have married in 1675.[30]

Secondly, there were a number of more enterprising freeburghers who had by this time managed to become well established and well-to-do men by local standards,[31] the most notable of whom were probably the three individuals mentioned above.

Diemer began his career as a tailor, but also acted as a grocer and small-scale farmer, and Van Suerwaerden, likewise a tailor by profession, took up pig-farming, while Mostaert was variously employed as a brick- and tilemaker and miller and owned a farm in the Liesbeek valley; more significantly, all three men established themselves as tavern-keepers under the protection of the local authorities. In addition, Diemer was married to a stepdaughter of the late Sergeant Van Herwerden and was a brother-in-law of the Secunde Abraham Gabbema, while Mostaert is also known to have enjoyed the favour of successive Commanders: as early as 1658 Van Riebeeck described him approvingly as 'a good, industrious and sober man, who is now married, evidently to an industrious woman who strives to get on'.[32] All three men held various public offices in the local community, including that of burgher councillor who represented the freeburghers in the local governing body, the Council of Policy. They had thus achieved success, in a manner typical of the time, by a combination of official favour, hard work and diversification, supplemented in all three cases by some connection with the liquor trade. The latter was virtually essential for prosperity in the early economy of the Cape with its population of sailors, soldiers and labourers, where only taprooms and taverns flourished.

A more widely significant development of this period was the fact that in 1672, by means of highly dubious contracts signed by representatives of two small Khoi tribes well-disposed to and dependent on the whites, the VOC had to its own satisfaction obtained possession of the greater part of the territory between the coast and the folded mountains of the interior.[33] In practice this area was still occupied by the Cochoqua, a numerous tribe rich in cattle, but between 1673 and 1677 its power was broken by a series of punitive expeditions which destroyed its cohesion, scattered its members, and deprived them of most of their cattle, which was distributed among the whites.[34]

After this, white farmers were free to move out from the over-populated Liesbeek valley into the valley of the Eerste River, and the south-western Cape or Boland was opened up for settlement. The village of Stellenbosch was founded here in 1679, followed by the colonisation in 1687 of Drakenstein (the present Paarl valley). This was greatly to the benefit of wheat and wine farming at the Cape, while the increased availability of extensive grazing led to the development of cattle farming as a distinctive feature of the colony.

Whereas the economy of the Cape had thus far depended on such credit as the Company was prepared to extend to individuals, it now became possible to obtain money in the form of loans from the *diakonie* or charity board of the local church, followed shortly after by the Orphan Chamber which was established in 1674, as well as from a number of more prosperous freeburghers. In this way the extension of farming activities and the purchase of slaves could be more readily undertaken.

Another significant development during this period was the emergence of an arrangement by which given individuals among the freeburghers could on payment obtain from the authorities the *pacht* or lease for the supply of specified types of liquor for the following year, thus in fact acquiring a monopoly for that period. These *pachters* needed a considerable amount of initial capital, as well as two guarantors prepared to vouch for them, but the holder of the *pacht* was assured of even greater profits, making it well worth the risk. The brandy *pacht* seems to have been especially profitable and fetched high prices, but the wealthiest man during the early decades of the colony, Henning Hüsing, grew rich as a meat *pachter*.

By about 1670, on the threshold of the period which saw all these developments, the more prosperous freeburghers began to expand their slave holdings by the most obvious means at their disposal, namely purchases from passengers on return ships from the East. This may arbitrarily but conveniently be said to have been initiated by W.C. Mostaert, who on 23 February 1671 bought from Jan Jansz de Ruijter, a former freeburgher of Batavia, the 13-year-old slave Jan van Batavia for 40 rixdollars.[35]

As has already been mentioned, the passengers and crews of ships sailing from the East had over the years continued to bring slaves with them as far as the Cape for their own convenience, in spite of official prohibitions. At this time it seems to have become known at Batavia that there was a market for slaves at the Cape, and passengers and crew members not only set out with the intention of disposing of their slaves here, but increasingly bought slaves on speculation for sale both to freeburghers and individual officials.[36] Slaves were even sent out in charge of passengers on return ships to be sold on behalf of their owners.[37]

Simultaneously with the increase in the demand, the supply of slaves available for sale at the Cape would also have improved as a result of the increased numbers of slaves reaching Batavia after the defeat of Macassar in 1668 and 1669. This was followed by what Raben describes as 'the submission of the sultanate of Goa [*Gowa*] and the grafting of the Makassarese slaving network onto the Batavian trade system',[38] while Batavia furthermore established links with the extensive slave trade centred in Bali.[39] It must be noted, however, that the slaves sold at the Cape were at first predominantly from India and Ceylon, though the supply of slaves from Indonesia increased after the turn of the century.[40]

During the 'eighties and 'nineties there were also incidental transactions involving English and Danish ships on their way from their respective trading posts in the East. According to Dr. Böeseken, 'During the last decade of the 17th century the Danes brought more slaves to the Cape than the English.'[41]

The first large-scale sale to private buyers recorded in the 1670s occurred in April 1672 during the visit of the *Sparendam*, when 12 slaves from Bengal, Coromandel, Malabar, Ceylon and the Indonesian island Roti were sold.[42] The buyers were largely Company officials, the local minister, Adrianus de Voogd, buying 3 male slaves and selling a female, but over the following years freeburghers were increasingly well represented in the sales.

Groenewald's calculations of private slave sales, based on the information provided by Hattingh and Boëseken, indicate that over the period 1658–69 no more than 60 slaves were acquired at the Cape in private transactions, 30 of them being from the mainland of Africa (the two big imports from Angola and Guinea), 21 from India and Ceylon, and only 3 from the present Indonesia. Over the following ten years 1670–79, however, 216 slaves were acquired, 100 from India and Ceylon, 18 from Indonesia and 13 from the African mainland.[43]

This increase has also been calculated on a yearly basis: during 1671, for example, no fewer than 16 new slaves were added to those in private ownership, while the corresponding figures are 18 for 1672, and an astonishing 37 for 1676 and 44 for the following year. The annual increase was irregular, depending largely on unpredictable factors, but after the very slow beginning of the slave trade at the Cape, it continued steadily.

As far as the acquisition of slaves by freeburghers is concerned, this not only became much more widespread than it had been, releasing them from their dependence on hired *knechten*, but among the wealthier farmers a number of large-scale slave owners emerged during the final quarter of the century, who by their possession of sufficient labour were enable to increase their land holdings, farming activities and wealth.

The Cape's Asian slaves were of course acquired by means of the trade with return ships from Batavia, and a small numbers of ships which as from 1664 sailed each year from Galle in Ceylon, but a reasonably large complement of Eastern slaves, by local standards, may also have been available from illegal private trade. Shell has, for example, traced at least 30 slave transactions by the skipper Jacob Joppe de Jonge, who was stationed at the Cape, over the period 1690–1704,[44] and there is no reason to believe that his activities were exceptional.

A relatively large number of Eastern slaves also became available after Joan (Johan) Bax had been placed in charge of the Cape in 1676 with the title of Governor, and particulars may readily be found in the available documents. .

Bax was a member of a vaguely aristocratic Dutch family who had been in the East since 1659 and had served as an officer in Malabar and as Commander of Galle in Ceylon during 1672–75; his wife belonged to a branch of a patrician Amsterdam family which had come down somewhat in the world but had also established itself in considerable style under the VOC. They occupied the entire main building of Van Riebeeck's old Fort, which had been standing empty since the Company's administration had been transferred to the new Castle and had become considerably more attractive since the demolition of the surrounding walls. Bax furthermore added a dining room at the back of the building, overlooking a small menagerie containing porcupines, ostriches and wild geese from Saldanha Bay and providing a view of Table Mountain.

Van Riebeeck's son Abraham found the Baxes here when he visited the Cape on his way to Batavia at the end of 1676, and described their Eastern style of living in a household filled with slaves, where the visitors were entertained 'by his black major-domo and another little slave on the harp and the bass lute', the artistry of the former being praised particularly. The party drove out, attended by slaves, for a picnic in the Liesbeek valley, where a tent had been erected for the purpose, and when they left, Bax with his wife and young son, 'together with his domestic slaves and bodyguard', accompanied them to the end of the jetty to drink a parting glass.[45] Gracious living had made its appearance at the Cape in the context of the local slave society.

During his four years at the Cape, Bax and his wife disposed of no fewer than 9 slaves, mainly from Bengal and Malabar,[46] and after his sudden death in 1678 his widow, on returning to Batavia, sold a further 7.[47] As she presumably kept a few women to attend her on board ship, the couple must have been well provided with slaves on their arrival.

Hattingh has made available detailed summaries of slave transactions at the Cape up to the beginning of 1679, while information on the period 1679–1700 is available in the transactions recorded in summary form by Dr Böeseken.[48] During this period private sales of slaves continued and, according to the figures as arranged by Groenewald, showed a spectacular increase towards the end of the century. While 216 transactions took place over the years 1670–79 and 180 over the period 1680–89, the final decade witnessed no fewer than 901.

As far as the total population of the young colony is concerned, according to the census of 1679 there were, not including employees of the Company, 87 free men, with 55 women, 117 children and 30 *knechten*. At the same time there were 133 male slaves, 38 females and 20 slave children.[49] At the end of 1699 there were 458 free white men, 241 women, 519 children and 62 *knechten*; the figures for the slaves were 668 men, 116 women and 54 children.[50] By 1692 the total slave holdings of the freeburgher population had already begun to surpass those of the Company.[51]

There is no point in trying to give full information on the transactions of these thirty years, but some general points may be made and some individual cases touched on.

Young, vigorous slaves with a long working life before them were naturally preferred, and according to Dr Böeseken the slaves sold were mostly young, the largest single group being between 16 and 20 years old, followed by that between 21 and 25.[52] Many were even younger, and Anthoni van Bengalen, who was sold by the junior merchant Willem van Dieden to the Secunde Albert van Breugel, was only 10,[53] while a passing skipper sold to Ensign Hiëronimus Cruse two boys, Michiel van Paliacatte and Jan van Tuticorijn, aged 10 and 12 years respectively.[54]

Small children appear usually to have been sold or otherwise passed on together with their mothers, so that one finds transactions of the type 'Catharina from Madagascar (18/19 [years]) and her son Nagtigaal (8 months) sold by Abraham de Hartog to Gerrit van Wijnegum for Rds. 65';[55] or even 'Paul from Porca (27) and his son Adam (aged two), born in Galen, sold by Bonifacius Ingels to Christina Does, the widow of Elbert Diemer, for Rds.80.'[56] The places referred to are Purakkad on the Malabar coast and Galle in Ceylon.

During the late seventeenth century slaves at the Cape continued to come mainly from the East, and from India and Ceylon more often than from Indonesia.[57] According to Dr Böeseken, Bengal, Malabar (Cochin) and Coromandel (Tranquebar, Tuticorin, Madras) predominated, in that order.[58] The fact that Batavia was by this time obtaining most of its own slaves from the Indonesian archipelago may indicate that the latter were now preferred there to slaves from India and Ceylon. Significantly, the largest single group of Indonesian slaves sold at the Cape during this period was from the sultanate Macassar,[59] which had been defeated and occupied by the VOC shortly before.

Prices for slaves were usually calculated in rixdollars, the rixdollar being equivalent to 3 guilders in the East, and as Dr Böeseken writes, 'Slaves between 15 and 25 were often sold for 80, 90 and even

100 rixdollars. In 1695 the prices paid for slaves reached a peak, when most slaves between the above ages were sold for between 80 and 100 rixdollars and even more.'[60] The prices asked and obtained depended on the gender, age and condition of the person concerned as well as supply and demand and variable economic factors, but Armstrong & Worden give 100 rixdollars as the average for an adult male slave in 1662–4, and 103 rixdollars in 1692–1715.[61]

Sales were sometimes made conditional, depending of the possible return of the former owners,[62] while the buyers could also be obliged to manumit the slaves purchased after a certain time,[63] or it might be stipulated that the slaves concerned were not to be allowed to return to Batavia.[64] The complexity of certain of these transactions is well illustrated by Dr Böeseken's summary of one, which was recorded in 1690:

> Sijtje from Macassar (20/21), given in loan by Franciscus Villerius, skipper of the *Pijlswaard*, to Jan Holsmit who undertook to look after her maintenance until skipper Villerius returns from Holland. A note was added to this document, stating that the brother of the by now deceased Villerius was the only heir and entitled to claim Sijtje of Macassar.[65]

Eight years later Sijtje's position was still uncertain, and a further note states:

> Zijtje from Macassar, who was about 20 in 1690, now given in loan to the Free Black Octavia [*Octavio*] from Macassar, by Jan Holtsmit [*sic*], who was about to return to Patria [*Netherlands*]. Octavia promised to return Zijtje to the heirs of her former master, the late skipper Franciscus Villerius, should they come to the Cape to claim her.[66]

This later period of increased availability furthermore saw the emergence of a class of freeburghers who bought slaves not only for their own use, but also as a business venture, undertaking purchases and sales on a large scale and often making considerable profits in re-sales on the local market. As Worden remarks, with more specific reference to the eighteenth century,

> many Cape Town inhabitants acted as middlemen in the supply of imported slaves to the rural areas. This situation gave a good opportunity to them to engage in slave speculation, and those with sufficient capital could hoard slaves purchased at reasonable prices and wait until demand rose or the potential for selling them inland at profit was presented. Evidence from the more complete records of the seventeenth century shows that this was certainly a common practice then and a number of officials and burghers resold slaves at profit within a short period.[67]

Among the most spectacular of these slave owners and dealers traced by Hattingh over the period before 1700 are Jan Dircx de Beer with 66 purchases and 38 sales between 1687 and his death in 1701, followed by Henning Hüsing with 55 and 10 respectively, Gulliam Eems, with 39 and 2, and Theunis Dircx van Schalkwijk with 32 and 9.[68] As regards De Beer, Hattingh points out

> that his farm Plattekloof was situated on the south-western side of the Tygerberg where he was within sight of Table Bay. He would there have been in a particularly favourable situation to observe the arrival of ships and also to serve as middleman in sending slaves to the interior. Freeburghers far from the Cape could not always be present when new ships from the East appeared in the harbour and they would of necessity have made their purchases from officials or freeburghers near to the Cape.[69]

When De Beer and his wife both died in 1701, he owned, besides Plattekloof, two farms in the Liesbeek valley and a house in the Table Valley which contained, besides the furniture made of ebony and other imported wood, paintings, mirrors and porcelain customary among the very wealthy inhabitants at the Cape by this time, a large Bible with brass clasps, and a chest with cash in various currencies, including 'several bags of silver coin', amounting to more than 23 000 guilders. There were 8 male slaves from Bengal, Malabar, Japara in Java, 'Japauw' and Madagascar in the house, as well as a female slave and a child, and 8 further slaves from Malabar, Bengal, Batavia and Madagscar on the farms, while two French refugees owed money to the estate for slaves purchased.[70]

The Company's servants likewise continued to buy slaves in their private capacity, although none of them could compete with the leading farmers except Commander (later Governor) Simon van der Stel, who in 1685 began farming on a large scale at Constantia (later Groot Constantia). During the period up to 1700 he bought no fewer than 75 slaves and sold 12.[71]

Van der Stel's son and successor as Governor, W.A. van der Stel, farmed on an even larger scale at Vergelegen until recalled to the Netherlands by the Gentlemen XVII in 1707, and according to Hattingh he bought 121 slaves over the period 1699–1707, 87 from passing ships and 34 locally from officials and freeburghers, at average prices of 50,8 and 59 rixdollars respectively.[72] In 1704 he even purchased 80% of the slaves who became available for sale on the local market, and as Hattingh remarks, the scale of his activities in this field must have posed as great a threat to the leading farmers as his actual farming at Vergelegen.[73]

There were, however, a number of other officials who owned a good number of slaves, and Hattingh mentions 13 apart from the Van der Stels who each purchased 10 or more during the seventeenth century, and a further 16 who acquired 3 to 9 slaves each.[74] As early as 1669 the Revd De Voogd obtained special permission to buy one of the Company's slaves, Abram van Angola, for 100 rixdollars, having requested this 'very urgently (…) as a necessity',[75] so that the possession of a slave had clearly by that time become essential to someone of his standing. The scale on which he acquired further slaves when they became generally available five years later has already been seen, and other ministers serving at the Cape followed suit. Pierre Simond, the minister accompanying the French refugees or Huguenots who were settled in Drakenstein in 1688, dealt in slaves on an even larger scale, for he was a well-to-do man who had been given a farm at Banghoek in the Stellenbosch district. Over the period 1690–98 he bought no fewer than 9 slaves and sold 1.[76]

In due course manumitted slaves, the so-called 'free blacks', likewise bought slaves of their own when they were able to do so,[77] and so did Chinese convicts and deportees who settled at the Cape, and the Eastern exiles who were increasingly sent here from Batavia for political and other reasons. The latter could be members of the Eastern aristocracy, such as 'Dain Majampa' from Macassar who in 1690 bought a compatriot, the young Sapatou van Macassar, for 66 rixdollars,[78] and the three-year-old Revan van Madagascar from Simon van der Stel two years later for 60 rixdollars.[79]

A final way in which slaves from the East might have reached the Cape in small numbers was with immigrants. At first this can be observed mainly in the case of officials transferred from Batavia, like Wagenaer in 1662, but towards the end of the century the Cape gradually became more attractive from the point of view of immigration. When Catharina Hoffers, the wife of the free silversmith Christian Mentzing, followed her husband here from Ceylon in 1689, for example, she was accompanied by her children and 3 slaves.[80]

Private sales of slaves, however numerous they may have been, did not solve the labour problems of the Company, which remained dependent on the core group of slaves obtained from Angola and Guinea, with some random additions. When Isbrand Goske, an energetic and enterprising military man, was placed in charge of the Cape with the title of Governor in 1672, he therefore immediately set about trying to obtain additional slaves, specifically for the completion of the Castle.

To Goske's appeals Batavia replied early in 1673 that

to send you slaves for the purpose from here is at present impossible, as we ourselves are but poorly supplied in consequence of their dying off, &c. Much necessary work is therefore to be done with day labourers, but for all that we remain short of hands. Nor do we see a chance of again obtaining an abundance, though slaves are asked for from all places where it is thought they may be obtained.[81]

Goske likewise wrote directly to two of his former colleagues in the East, whose replies were received early in 1674.

From Ceylon, recently captured from the Portuguese, the Governor, Rijckloff van Goens Jr, acknowledged the receipt of 'the garden seeds, the small olive trees and the grape and carnation slips' from the Company's garden, but immediately added that it would be impossible to provide slaves,

as all are urgently required to complete our heavy fortifications, to bring which into a proper state of defence we have this year been obliged to obtain from Wingurla (at heavy expense and trouble to the Company) one thousand *Canarijns*, some of whom we shall be obliged to keep on for a considerable time longer, and hire them instead of the departed and deceased Tutucorijn Coolies. Moreover, our own slaves have been so diminished in numbers by death that we are much in want of others; so that, to our regret, we cannot provide you with any, which we would otherwise have liked to have done.[82]

Van Goens's references are to hired labourers or 'coolies'. Vengurla and Canara were both on the Malabar coast of India, and Tuticorin on the Coromandel coast.

From Malabar, from which the Portuguese had likewise only recently been expelled, the Commander, H.A. van Reede, replied to Goske in a similar vein.

> We regret that we are unable to provide you with any slaves to assist in the building of your new fortifications, partly resulting from a great sickness which has been raging everywhere in this country and carried off a large number of people, and partly because only Paelias [*parias*?][83] would be obtainable here, who are mostly not real slaves, but only under service of their masters. Experience has told us that they have often only been stolen or filched from their masters, as no doubt your Honour experienced too well when you were here. (…) We kindly thank you for the garden seeds. We trust that you will continue to remember us in future in this respect also.[84]

In 1673 a number of slaves from the Indonesian islands of Timor and Roti were sent to the Cape somewhat unwillingly from Batavia for purely practical reasons, presumably of a political nature: 'who, though required here, should be employed by you at the Cape in order to deprive them of the opportunity of deserting to their own country, from which they should necessarily be kept away. They are 39 in number, exclusive of 3 others who are for life to labour in irons (…).' One member of this party died on the voyage, but the remainder were found to be 'strong, healthy fellows'.[85] By the following year, however, the Council of India referred critically to the fact 'that of the 39 slaves and 3 convicts sent to you with the last return fleet only 27 have survived'.[86]

It was not until 1677 that a further group of slaves was sent out from the East, when the return ships from Ceylon brought 93 acquired in Tuticorin, the harbour on the Coromandel coast of India from which small numbers of slaves from the interior were obtained throughout the 1670s.[87] In the meantime the Cape had been able to buy a reasonable number of slaves in Madagascar, so that the local authorities could afford to be generous, and 13 males and 1 female were distributed with 1% profit among 10 of the freeburghers who were considered to be 'the most needy and able farmers'.[88] A year later the purchase price had not yet been paid and the purchasers had to be reminded of the fact.[89]

The private trade in slaves with visiting ships probably continued until the end of the VOC period, and by the turn of the eighteenth century the Company itself seems to have relinquished the control it had ineffectually tried to keep on the export of slaves from Batavia. 'Some freemen returning home have been permitted to take slaves with them,' the Council of India informed the Cape in 1701; 'the latter are to be sold at the Cape or sent back.'[90]

In a passage which deserves to be quoted in full, Fox writes in this regard:

> By the ordinance of 24 August 1700, it became possible by special permission to take 'one or two slaves' to the Netherlands or the Cape of Good Hope, whereas the ordinance of 30 October 1713 seems to imply no limitation on the number of slaves that can be transported to the Cape or to the Netherlands provided their upkeep and the voyage costs to and from Batavia were covered. By a further ordinance of 9 October 1714, however, no slave who made the voyage to the Netherlands and then returned to Batavia could be forced to remain a slave. In effect, a journey to the free Netherlands automatically freed any slave.[91]

4. The slave trade: Madagascar

After the arrival of the slaves from Angola and Guinea in 1658, the Cape's most immediate requirements were satisfied for the time being, but in 1661 the Gentlemen XVII once again took up the subject of its obtaining rice from Madagascar rather than Batavia, in order not to occupy valuable storage space on the return ships.

The earlier voyages to Madagascar from the Cape had been to Antongil Bay in the north-east of the island, with which the Dutch outpost on the nearby island of Mauritius had established successful relations in the 1640s.[1] This was also in accordance with a treaty concluded between the Dutch Republic and Portugal in 1641, by which the east and west coast of Madagascar had been assigned to them as their respective spheres of influence.[2]

After having received extremely promising information about Madagascar, however, the XVII now instructed Van Riebeeck to send an expedition to establish a 'permanent residency' at St Augustine's Bay, conveniently situated on the south-west coast, opposite the mainland of Africa and close to the Cape.[3] It was a well-known port of call for European seafarers, and the English had in 1644 even made an ill-fated attempt to establish a colony there.[4] 'The slaves also,' the XVII added, 'who are obtainable there in great abundance and cheap, though they appear to be of a lazy and dirty disposition, would also [sic] be of great service to us at the Cape.'[5]

The projected expedition, which was dependent on the trade winds, could not be undertaken in 1662, as the final months of this year were devoted to a large-scale and unsuccessful attack on the

Portuguese fortress at Mozambique for which the Cape served as base.[6] In 1663, however, under Zacharias Wagenaer, the dispenser and garrison bookkeeper Jochum Blanck was despatched in the fluteship *Waterhoen*, 'as we may be sufficiently assured of his ability and fitness'.[7]

The *Waterhoen* set off at the end of May with a crew of 24, as well as 11 men intended to establish the desired residency on the island,[8] and returned early in December, having achieved less than expected. Visiting St Augustine's Bay, the company had found the country devastated by local wars, and had with difficulty obtained 'about five lasts of rice, cadjang and round beans or peas, in exchange for copper wire and beads, as well as a vat of salted meat as an experiment, and seven slaves'. The ship's boat with two men on board had been lost in a rough sea, and two soldiers, a carpenter, a sailor and a slave belonging to Blanck had deserted, taking with them five flint-locks, six pistols and some gunpowder.[9] The fact that the fluteship had been unable to round the island and proceed to Antongil Bay at the other end in order to try its luck there was later blamed largely on the bad seamanship of the skipper, about whose failings Wagenaer waxed eloquent.[10]

The slaves obtained were landed at the Cape, however, 'being 4 men and 3 women, among whom 2 small boys and a girl, all of whom seem to be troubled by scurvy, but they were immediately dressed in new clothes and served fresh food'.[11] The 'round white beans' brought by the fluteship were said to have a very good flavour.[12]

In spite of this notable lack of success, Blanck was again sent out with the *Waterhoen* the following year, with a different skipper, as the Cape was running short of rice, and ordered to buy 'as much rice and slaves as he may be able to obtain by trading and send here or bring back himself'.[13] Textiles, tin, copper and beads were sent with him as trading goods. As in the previous year, the ship left in May and returned in December, 'with a modest cargo of not more than 7 or 8 lasts, though of fine white rice from the Bay of Antongil', and a single slave, the local chief or 'king' having this time proved reluctant to do any slave trading. Once again the party had been troubled by desertion, three sailors having decamped with two muskets and two flintlocks. [14]

The lack of success with regard to slaves was all the more frustrating as the Cape had shortly before been visited by the *Eagle*, an English pinnace called the *Arent* by Wagenaer, on its way back from Magelagie in the north-west of the island and St Augustine's Bay where, together with a sister ship, it had obtained a total of 335 slaves for Barbados in the West Indies. Wagenaer, accompanied by the Fiscal, the Ensign, the burgher councillors and two other burghers, had visited the ship in an attempt to obtain some slaves for the Cape. 'Arriving on board, His Honour had seen the slaves sitting on the orlop deck, for the most part younger people, but they were found to be almost completely naked and as thin as skeletons'. The captain, however, had been unwilling to dispose of any of his cargo and had demanded £50 or 500 guilders for a slave, so that no purchases were made. [15]

When reinforcements were sent to the outpost on Mauritius by the fluteship *Hoog Caspel* in 1666, a final attempt was made with regard to Madagascar. She was provided with 'different kinds of textiles, bracelets, beads and other pedlar's wares', and instructed to touch at St Augustine's Bay and try to obtain 'a good number of slaves or at least 20 or 25 lasts of rice (of which we have some need at present)'. [16] On her return to the Cape in December, however, the bookkeeper, Jacob Granaet, reported to Commander Van Quaelberg that 'they were unable to obtain a single grain of rice or a single slave, so much required here, the inhabitants saying that they are in violent warfare with their neighbours like last year, so that they were mutually ruining each other, and destroying everything (…)'. [17]

Quite apart from civil wars in Madagascar, neither St Augustine's Bay nor Antongil Bay where the Dutch had previously traded was, as Armstrong & Worden point out, a major slave port, [18] so that their lack of success is not surprising. The former had a good reputation among slave traders, as the prices there were relatively low, but the supply was erratic and 'fluctuated with the fortunes of local conflicts', as Armstrong phrases it,[19] which explains the success of the *Eagle* and its companion.

In the circumstances Wagenaer could only appeal to the XVII before he left the Cape in 1666 to consider once more the possibility of trading with Angola or Guinea, or else of sending out slaves from Batavia with the return fleet, 'even though only 20 or 25 could be brought at a time'.[20] When Matthias van den Brouck, visiting the Cape as Commissioner in 1670, asked the Council of Policy, 'Whether for the extension of agriculture slaves would not be necessary? And how many would be desirable for this?', the reply, in similar vein, was, 'Yes; and 150 or 200 Angolans would be desirable',[21] which he subsequently incorporated as a recommendation in his official report.[22]

It was possibly in pursuit of this line of thought that the *Marken* was despatched from the Netherlands late in 1671 to the islands of São Tomé and Annabom in the Gulf of Guinea to obtain 'a good number of slaves for this residency', together with some cuttings of the manioc root which was much used for feeding slaves in West Africa. She arrived at the Cape in the winter of the following year to report that the Portuguese at São Tomé

> would not let them trade for slaves or permit them to obtain water or fuel for their money, unless they (…) entered the bay with their vessel and anchored under the guns of the forts; but as this had been expressly forbidden in the Instructions of the Principals [*XVII*], they did not approve of it, as from inquiry among some of the residents and others, the inhabitants and rulers of the said island had no abundance of slaves, whilst those that were there were mostly all Christians, and the rest so highly priced that none could be obtained for less than 80 or 100 reals, who besides might not be sold by the burghers without a previous licence from the 'providoor' or senators.[23]

At Annabom too they 'obtained no slaves, only the cuttings and other fruit trees from the Governor'.

In 1671 a further attempt was made on the East Coast of Africa by sending the fluteship *Zandloper*, 'which is getting too old for these waters', from the Cape to the Mayotte islands (Comoros) off the north-western coast of Madagascar 'for a cargo of slaves', but as it was not anticipated that she would have much success, she was ordered to proceed to Batavia if no slaves could be obtained, as in fact happened.[24]

A somewhat more efficient trading expedition in the area was undertaken shortly after by an old hand, Hubert Hugo, a former employee of the VOC in India and later freebooter in the Red Sea area under a French commission, whom Armstrong describes as 'an ambitious and influential adventurer'.[25]

Having re-entered the service of the Company, Hugo was in 1671 appointed Commander of Mauritius, which he intended to develop into a local centre of trade, including slave trade,[26] and from Table Bay he made his way there by a circuitous route which included Madagascar, the Comoros and the East Coast of Africa. For this purpose he had taken on board at the Cape a slave called Louwijs with his wife to serve as interpreter. This man had been living here for nine years but was a Madagascan by origin, and had probably been one of the party of '4 men and 3 women, among whom 2 small boys and a girl', brought back from the island by the *Waterhoen* in 1663.

The voyage of Hugo's ship, the *Pijl*, was finally to prove disastrous, and among other setbacks a party which was landed for trading purpose at Madagascar, including the interpreter Louwijs, disappeared, presumably killed by the local inhabitants. Hugo returned to Table Bay at the end of 1672 with no more 22 slaves obtained in Madagascar, 17 women and 5 men, who were as usual provided at once with food and clothing.[27]

The following odd batch of slaves which the VOC acquired for its work at the Cape during the years between 1658 and the establishment of successful trading relations with Madagascar in 1676 was that on an English slave ship identified in the Dutch records as the *Johanna Catharina*.[28]

After the Dutch Republic had become involved in war with France and England in 1672, orders were sent to the Cape to capture the island of St Helena from the latter. This was successfully done early the following year, and while the island was not to remain in Dutch hands for long, the expeditionary force also captured a slave ship on its way from Madagascar and Mozambique to Barbados with a cargo of slaves: 'These slaves, obtained so unexpectedly, will come in very handy here,' the Journal noted gratefully.[29]

The ship arrived at the Cape on 12 March, where she was in due course to be renamed the *Helena*,[30] and

> boats were at once sent to her in order to land the slaves. One hundred and eighty-four were accordingly brought on shore, adults and children of both sexes, some of whom appeared lean and *outbacken* [*desiccated*]. Fifteen had died during the voyage. After having been mustered in the square in the presence of the Governor, and inspected by the latter, they were at once provided with some clothing, and for the night were lodged in the second shed of the new Fort [*the Castle*], where they were provided with good refreshments of which those who were almost sick of hunger were so very fond that the cleared off everything as if the cook's kitchen had not smoked for eight days. These refreshments will have to be continued for some days that they may be completely restored to health and strength.[31]

According to Armstrong the ship had originally acquired 270 slaves in Madagascar,[32] and a total of 71 had therefore already died by the time she was captured.

'Heavy South-East wind,' ran the Journal entry for the following day. 'A party of tailors selected among the soldiers and sailors in order to make clothes for the newly-arrived slaves, the stuffs used being unsaleable and moth-eaten, and the lining old sailcloth, so that the whole was contrived in the cheapest and most durable fashion.'[33]

The consignment of slaves had arrived at the Cape on a Sunday. The following Sunday the Journal entry ran, 'Went to church and heard an edifying sermon'; and the next day: 'Excepting the sick, the captured slaves have fairly recovered, and having been provided with clothing, were set to work to fill the second point [*bastion of the Castle*] with earth; it seems as if they will accommodate themselves to labour, and in time render good service to the Company.'[34]

The Cape winter had barely begun, however, when the Journal had to note that 'the Company's slaves, and chiefly those who came from St Helena, are dying very much, a considerable number having been buried within a short time, which is very inconvenient for the Company'.[35]

When a few months later the Cape obtained the 39 slaves sent out from Batavia as a special favour, the Council of India wrote in its covering letter that no more were to be expected from that source. 'Therefore it would be the most convenient thing if you could obtain some from Guinea or Angola, or another place, as very few can be had, as you apprehend, at Madagascar and the Mayotte Islands [*Comoros*], as has been fully experienced from the results of former expeditions despatched for the purpose.'[36]

After the capture of the *Johanna Catharina*, the Cape's most urgent wants were once more satisfied and no further action was taken. The war in Europe likewise impeded any attempt to trade with Madagascar, but early in 1674, as soon as peace with England had been concluded, the XVII wrote urging that it be resumed.[37] By the time these instructions reached the Cape, it was presumably too late in the season to send out a ship, and the following year the Council of Policy claimed to have no suitable vessel, though they attempted to make use of the captured slave ship, the *Helena*, for the purpose.[38] The reason for this lack of enthusiasm was probably that the Castle was by this time almost completed, and as an attack by the English was no longer to be feared, its completion was no longer a matter of urgency.

When Nicolaes Verburch visited the Cape as Commissioner early in 1676, he pointed out in his Instruction, as had many of his predecessors, that more attention must be paid to agriculture. 'So that it is a fixed and immoveable fact,' he wrote in March of that year, 'that the Cape must be provided with more industrious people, and cannot without a large number of slaves be brought to the state in which one would wish to see it, for which the slaves from Madagascar are considered to be the most suitable. For which reason the Company will have to take it upon itself to send expeditions to that island, where they may be obtained cheaply for Spanish reals.'[39] In the Memorial which Isbrand Goske drew up for his successor at the same time, he advised that 'a certain black man, Mockodan Sijmon', be sent out with the ship because of his knowledge of the slave trade in Madagascar.[40]

In May 1676 the *Voorhout*, a yacht which had a few months earlier brought Governor Bax from Ceylon, was equipped with a supply of 'Spanish reals, cloth, glass beads, Japanese copper, iron bars and brandy' and sent out on what Armstrong describes as 'the first successful slaving voyage [to Madagascar] originating at the Cape'.[41]

Though the French had attempted to establish a colony in Madagascar for a good part of the seventeenth century, with little success, they had not taken any noteworthy part in the local slave trade. On the other hand, Arab or Muslim traders, most notably from Muscat and Oman, regularly visited the island to buy slaves and had even established a colony there. Private English traders likewise came here increasingly to obtain slaves for the Caribbean and North American plantations after this had been made impossible in West Africa in 1672 by the monopoly granted to the Royal African Company, and Portuguese from Mozambique visited the island to buy rice. Finally, Madagascar served as a convenient base for English pirates and freebooters who preyed on shipping in the Indian Ocean and the Red Sea area, while Barendse refers to 'slaving along the west coast [of the island], conducted both by [North] American and Portuguese freebooters, (…) mostly wild-slaving, burning down the villages and enslaving their inhabitants'.[42]

One of the few advantages of the voyage undertaken by Hubert Hugo in 1672 had been to establish that the most advantageous slave trading was to be done in the north-west of the island, a fact not previously known to the Dutch. This was likewise where the English slave ship captured at St Helena had obtained its cargo.[43]

The main centre of trade was a town recorded in contemporary sources in various forms such as Nova Mazalagem and Massailly, but known to the Dutch mainly as Magelagie, situated on an island off the coast (the present Nosy Antsoheribory in Boina Bay). By the beginning of the seventeenth century it is said to have had 6000 to 7000 Muslim inhabitants under an Arab sultan, and to have obtained its slaves from all over the island, including Antongil and St Augustine's Bay. It was visited by ships from the Comoros, Muscat and Oman, and more than 3000 slaves were bought and sold there annually. Armstrong calculates a '*low* estimate' of about 40 000 slaves obtained here by Arab traders alone during the seventeenth century.[44]

An equally highly reputed source of slaves at this time was Manigaar or Maringaan (Bombetoka) along the coast somewhat to the north-east.[45] 'The river of Maningaar runs out to sea with 7 mouths,' writes the Revd Valentijn in his compendious work on the trading world of the VOC, 'receiving many rivulets which lose their names in it. It can be sailed upstream by a ship for 16 or 18 [Dutch] miles, and ¾ of the island now falls under an old king who resides 15 or 16 miles from the anchorage and mostly leaves it to his son to govern.'[46] Unlike Magelagie with its foreign trading community, Manigaar was ruled by local chieftains. It was provided, as Van Dam writes in similar terms, 'with an extremely fine big river and a convenient anchorage which may be reached by boats and other small craft sailing upstream as far as the native settlement where the king resides'.[47]

Both these places were in future to be visited regularly by slave ships from the Cape, and by the beginning of the eighteenth century casual reference could be made to 'the usual places at Magelage and Manengaare where the Hon. Company is accustomed to trade'.[48] In this connection Barendse writes evocatively of a coast consisting of 'deep bays with many islands, and impenetrabele tropical swamps, a dangerous, forbidding land for Europeans and Malagasy peasants alike'.[49]

Culturally Madagascar was a strange and alien world, partly linked to Africa across the Mozambique Channel, but to an indeterminable extent also to the wider Malayo-Polynesian world across the Indian Ocean to the east. In the interior it was divided into small territories ruled by individual chiefs, kinglets or kings, and during the late seventeenth century it was increasingly the scene of fierce local wars accompanying the rise to power of the Sakalava tribe.[50] From the point of view of slave traders, this led to a notable increase in the number of slaves available in the form of prisoners of war, and to the demand for firearms as items of trade, and according to Barendse, Sakalava warriors sold captives to the ships of Muslim traders all along the coast in exchange for firearms.[51] In the course of these wars Magelagie was to be burned down and destroyed by Sakalava forces from the mainland in about 1686.

The pattern for the slave-trading voyages to Madagascar from the Cape which were undertaken intermittently over the following century was set by the trade winds, as was usual in an age of sail. Ships leaving the Cape in May would take a month to make the trip, spend three or four months trading, and be back by the end of the year.[52]

The *Voorhout*, arriving in Madagascar in 1676, traded at both Magelagie and Manigaar, and obtained 254 slaves at an average price of over 12 reals, a real or Mexican rixdollar being calculated as approximately equal to the 'Indian' rixdollar of 3 guilders. The ship's officers reported afterwards

[that] that nation is very strict on cash, without which no slave can be obtained there. They only accepted Mexican dollars (*realen*), which they weigh on receipt to see whether the weight agrees with their fancy (*humeur*). If not, they reject it, hence if they (the officers) had been sufficiently provided with the aforesaid heavy standard coin (alloy), they would have been able to buy more slaves.

When they were there, there were also there 4 English ships, also for buying slaves, as well as 3 Arabian vessels. The English intended to take their cargo to Barbadoes and the Arabs theirs to Arabia.[53]

Abraham van Riebeeck, who was present when the ship arrived back in Table Bay at the end of November, noted in his journal: 'Many plump female slaves were to be seen, whom the sailors (as is said) had looked after by day in return for pleasure at night, and who were unable to part with the sailors without weeping and wailing'.[54]

The *Voorhout* is said to have lost 22 of its slaves on the return journey,[55] but when they were counted on disembarking, they were found to amount to 257, 'babes included'.

At once each received a little cloth to cover their bodies, and afterwards all were provisionally lodged in a building at the Company's brick kilns and fed with good, refreshing food, which these poor people were so fond of and ate to the last crumb, so that nothing was left, notwithstanding an abundance had been distributed among them.[56]

A fortnight later, having recovered from their ordeal, 'the sick excepted', the slaves were set to work 'behind the Company's Fortress in the clay pit. They appear to take kindly to the work, and will in time do good service to the Company.'[57] Early the following year a party of 14 were also sent to the Company's outpost at Hottentots-Holland, where the postholder was admonished that they were to be treated well and gently and not to receive commands from anyone other than their own *mandoor* or overseer.[58] There seems to be no obvious reason for this special treatment except the possibility that the Company was already thinking of lightening its own burden by having its farming operations carried out by slaves or ex-slaves, and that these Madagascans seemed to be suitable candidates. The experiment would be carried out in the Stellenbosch district only a few years later.

In May 1677 the *Voorhout* was sent out again, accompanied by a hooker, the *Kwartel* (*Quartel*), and as the Cape was unable to provide sufficient Mexican rixdollars for Magelagie, the crew were instructed to try their luck at St Augustine's Bay and Mozambique as well.[59] At Magelagie they found another VOC ship, the *Hassenburg*, buying slaves at a much higher price in direct competition: 'I must have slaves,' declared the supercargo of this vessel, 'even though I have to pay 20 rixdollars, for I don't intend returning to Batavia without slaves.'[60]

The two ships managed to obtain a cargo in St Augustine's Bay and at Mozambique, but they returned at the end of December with no more than 77 slaves: 'they were so long on the voyage that 43 died'.[61] All of these slaves were said to have been 'under 16 years of age'.[62] A number of them were ill, and the Council of Policy later referred to their 'miserable appearance', 'being in an extremely miserable and sickly condition'.[63]

As it was feared that the new arrivals might spread infection in the Company's slave house, it was decided to make somewhat unusual arrangements to meet the circumstances and hire them out individually to freeburghers and Company servants, 'two Madagascar boys and one girl' per person for a full year at a time, together with a monthly ration of 40 pounds of rice. At the end of the year lots would be drawn for the first choice of the surviving slaves in each case, and one of them would become the property of the temporary owner at a special price of 25 rixdollars, as would also the sole survivor of a group of three, while the Company was to be recompensed with 12½ rixdollars for each slave who had died.[64] The slaves returned to the Company were to be 'well and decently clothed'.[65] By the winter of 1679 the Company was still urging the payment for the Madagascan slaves retained by their temporary owners.[66]

'We have had the last imported [slaves] distributed, for a little at first, among the houses,' reported the acting Commander, Hendrick Crudop, after the death of Joan Bax, 'and their improvement in health is most perceptible; for, however well they are fed and nursed by the Company's servants and slaves, we have found the expence to be greater in the proportion of 3 to 1, and the mortality is that of 6 to 1...',[67] an implicit condemnation of conditions in the Company's slave house.

Apart from the slaves officially brought back for the use of the Company on these two voyages, members of the crews also indulged in slave trading on their own account, probably encouraged by the fact that a market obviously existed at the Cape, and this appears to have happened on a substantial scale. 'It seems likely,' writes Armstrong,

> that roughly ten per cent should be added to the official figures to include slaves obtained in this manner. This private trade was conducted without the knowledge or approval of the Heren XVII or the Council of India. It was not mentioned in official correspondence, nor were the numbers of slaves acquired privately included in the official reports on these voyages. Indeed, it was only after the Company ceased making slaving voyages, near the end of its administration, that the Heren XVII took any official cognisance of this individual trading by its Cape officials. It was defended as a customary

usage, without any specific known authorisation, which compensated the ship's officers and supercargoes for the dangers and discomforts they underwent in the trade, and as an encouragement for them to go on future voyages.[68]

To what extent this happened during the first two expeditions of the *Voorhout* is not clear, but over the first months of 1677 Hattingh's list of slave transactions records three in which crew members sold slaves from Madagascar, and a number of others relating to Madagascan slaves, including a sale by Seuren Seurensz, *mandoor* or overseer of the Company's slaves, who had been recommended by Isbrand Goske for the expedition.[69] After the second expedition, six sales explicitly stated to be by members of the expedition are recorded.[70] In this way the freeburghers were able during the last quarter of the century to obtain Madagascan slaves as well, in addition to the steady supply already reaching them from the East. They soon began to be preferred to slaves from the East for heavy farm work, and Elphick & Shell make the significant point that according to the surviving manumission records for the eighteenth century, 'Not one Madagascan field hand obtained his freedom.'[71]

Groenewald likewise notes 6 private sales of Madagascan slaves in 1676, the earliest sale of slaves from the island recorded here, which had risen to a total of 40 by 1679, while a total of 206 had been sold at the Cape ten years later.[72]

On both its expeditions to Madagascar the *Voorhout* had been accompanied by the 'black man, Mockodan Sijmon', mentioned by Goske in his Memorial. This was the person more generally known as Sijmon de Arabier or 'Sijmon the Arab', who had been found on board the English slave ship captured at St Helena early in 1673 and brought to the Cape.[73] He was apparently a member of one of the Arab or Muslim trading colonies which existed at the time on Madagascar itself, in the Comoros and along the East Coast of Africa, and had been involved in English slave trading in the area, as he spoke English, Arabic and Malagasy. Most likely he was the 'black "Mandador" of the slaves' who is mentioned as providing the Company's officials with information on the captured ship.[74]

A *mandador* was the Portuguese name for a slave overseer, called a *mandoor* or *mandadoor* by the Dutch,[75] while 'mockadon', from the Portuguese *mocadão* and Arabic *muḳaddam*, was used for the overseer of a boat's crew. Sijmon was also referred to by the title of *saiyid*, which is borne by descendants of Mohammed's daughter and indicates a social class among Moslems.

At the Cape Sijmon was regarded as potentially valuable because of his knowledge of the slave trade and languages, and was treated as a prisoner of war with privileged status rather than a captive. He was given a house of his own in the Table Valley and a garden plot,[76] provided with one of the Company's female slaves,[77] by whom he had children, and used as *mandoor* of the Company's slaves, until 1676, when Goske suggested his being sent with the *Voorhout* to Madagascar, but warned against his possibly 'taking his passport under the soles of his feet'.[78] It was he who advised the authorities on the trade goods with which the *Voorhout* should be provided, 'copper and other beads, copper wire, coarse red cloth, &c., as will further appear from the memorial made of them, which according to him are much desired there'.[79] He likewise accompanied the second expedition the following year.

After the second visit of the *Voorhout* to Madagascar, it occurred to the VOC that this successful trading might also be used to the advantage of its operations in the East.

In 1667 the Company had acquired gold mines at Salida or Sillada on the West coast of Sumatra in Indonesia, which it began to exploit three years later. As slave labour from the various areas in the Indonesian archipelago proved unsuitable for the conditions in the mines, the thoughts of the authorities began to turn to the sturdier slaves from Madagascar,[80] and this was one of the reasons why the Cape had been urged to resume trade with the island in 1674.[81]

In 1678 the *Elisabeth* was sent out from the Netherlands specifically to obtain slaves for the mines, and Sijmon de Arabier had by this time proved his worth so well that he joined the ship at the Cape to help with the trading, together with the Company's dispenser and storekeeper Albert Jansz van Breugel, who was to act as supercargo. A cargo worth more than 13 000 guilders was provided, chiefly in the form of Mexican rixdollars, and 114 slaves were acquired at Magelagie, although 51 died before their arrival in Sumatra.[82] Sijmon sailed from Batavia with a return ship which passed the Cape and was thus taken on to the Netherlands.[83]

In 1681 the *Sillida*, a vessel which had been designed expressly for the slave trade, was despatched to Magelagie for the same purpose with a cargo worth more than 21 000 guilders, again chiefly in Mexican rixdollars. Sijmon again acted as interpreter, accompanying her on her voyage out from the Netherlands.[84] On this occasion 168 slaves were bought at Magelagie and 68 at Manigaar, only 144 of whom ultimately reached Sumatra alive, while half of the survivors died within four months of their arrival.[85] The ship's officers later said that on this voyage 'they would have been unable to govern the slaves' without Sijmon's help.[86] It must have been on completion of this trip that he himself died in Batavia.[87]

After the two successful voyages of the *Voorhout*, a further eleven trips to Madagascar were undertaken from the Cape during the years up to the end of the century, those of the *Eemland* (1682), *Hogergeest* (1683–84), *Baren* (1684–85), *Westerwijk* (1685–1686), *Jambi* (1686 and 1687), *Tamboer* (1694), *Standvastigheid* (1694–95), *Soldaat* (1696–97) and *Peter en Paul* (1699).[88] During the eighteenth century a further 21 were to follow.[89]

It is not necessary to dwell on these individual expeditions, though that of the *Eemland* in 1682 deserves more than passing attention because of the fact that a revolt broke out among the slaves on board while the ship was on its way to Sumatra. It was successfully suppressed, but it cost the Company 39 slaves 'of both sexes, who were killed on board or jumped overboard when a slave revolt broke out when the slaves escaped from captivity, to the value of 8395 guilders in all'.[90] The next ship sent out, the *Hogergeest*, was during its long, circuitous journey from Madagascar to Sumatra likewise threatened with a revolt, 'which could be prevented in time'.[91]

In the course of these expeditions, the south-eastern coast of Africa, largely unknown as far as Sofala where the series of Portuguese fortresses and trading posts began, was tentatively explored. The reports, letters and Journal entries of the time include mention of the areas around the Limpopo and Zambesi, and of 'an extremely ignorant people whose king is said to dwell near the gold mines 25 days' travel inland and be called King of Monomotapa, and to have been converted to Christianity by the Portuguese',[92] a reference to the present Zimbabwe.

Firearms continued be in great demand for the trade in Madagascar. In 1697, for example, the Dutch complained 'that (because of their internecine wars) the present King Simanata looks more to good muskets with which to destroy his enemies, than to money or any other merchandise',[93] and two years later the requisition for the Cape included '300 firelocks for the Madagascar slave trade, without which no slaves are obtainable'.[94]

The Company storekeeper Albert Jansz van Breugel accompanied several of these voyages and gave so much satisfaction that he was transferred from Batavia to the Cape in 1680, where he was subsequently promoted from Assistant to Junior Merchant and appointed Fiscal.[95] He died during the first expedition of the *Jambi* in 1686 and was buried in Madagascar.[96] In 1696 the provisional assistant Abraham van den Bogaard was appointed to accompany the *Soldaat* in a similar capacity,[97] and he is subsequently known to have sold a number of Madagascan slaves at the Cape, most notably to Governor W.A. van der Stel in 1700, by which time he was described as 'former merchant in charge of the slave trade with Madagascar'.[98]

For the actual transactions the slave dealers were completely dependent on the services of interpreters, who were often slaves like Louwijs who disappeared during the early trip under Hubert Hugo. In 1699 there is specific mention in a letter from the Cape of 'a Malagasy slave named Inserwole, baptised here with the name of Cornelis', being used in this capacity on a ship bound for Batavia via Madagascar, 'after being already employed as such in the slave trade with that island. As we are badly off for slaves, we beg that he may be sent back as soon as possible.'[99]

In a similar manner the new Commander, Simon van der Stel, writing to the XVII in 1679, remarked that the *Voorhout* had the previous year 'purchased from the natives, at a cheap rate, for some articles of dress, two stout slaves, who were real Kafirs; both are still alive, and as they thrive well in this climate and have been a little instructed, they would be serviceable in making us acquainted with the trade in slaves and other merchandize which has, for the want of such assistance, been hitherto concealed'.[100] Here as elsewhere 'Kafirs' was used in the sense of 'natives of the interior of Africa'.

'Most of these interpreters are known only by their names,' writes Armstrong, 'plus a phrase describing their command of Dutch (and sometimes Portuguese). In the instructions given to the slaving captains on departure, they are mentioned, usually with the admonition that they were to be *rather gently handled*, presumably to ensure their loyalty once on Madagascar. On virtually every voyage recorded, they did as was required of them.'[101]

As far as the slaves themselves are concerned, in most cases it is only in the businesslike records of sales and purchases that these hundreds of people have survived, and some of these random names, ages and prices can be noted here to help rescue them from oblivion: in the case of the private sales from the *Voorhout*, for example, Augustinus Casta Madagascar ('from the coast of Madagascar'), Cornelis, Jan, and Pieter, 'estimated to be 14 to 15 years old', who were sold at the Cape for 40, 87, 87 and 45 rixdollars respectively.[102]

In the lists of the slaves officially purchased for the Company the slaves were recorded by Madagascan names, with their price, gender and age, and the first five names on the list for the *Voorhout*'s first voyage may be cited here arbitrarily: Renecallo, woman, 11 rixdollars; Mangabeen, woman, 10 rixdollars; Manata, boy, 9 rixdollars; Mora, young man, 13,5 rixdollars; and Ingora, young woman, 11 rixdollars. The adult men listed fetched between 10 and 16 rixdollars each. Comparing the prices paid by the VOC in Madagascar with those paid in private transactions at the Cape, it seems clear that the profits made in the latter must have been considerable.

Something more of the strange new world in which these Madagascan slaves suddenly found themselves may be gauged from the detailed instructions for slave traders issued by the VOC at the end of 1685.[103]

Timber was to be provided for a partition near the mainmast on slaving ships in order to separate the quarters of the males and females and for the construction of bunks, and extensive hygienic precautions were prescribed. The bunks were to be washed and scrubbed daily, and the ship was to be sprinkled with vinegar twice a week, and red-hot cannon balls burned in pitch or resin once or twice a fortnight. The slaves were to be allowed on deck for an airing when the weather permitted, their heads shaved and a tub of water provided for ablutions.

Careful instructions were given as to the diet of the slaves, which was to consist chiefly of barley and dried beans, served with diced bacon and pepper, varied occasionally with 'hard bread' or ship's biscuit, and 155 aums of water (about 24 000 litres) were to be taken on board per slave for a three months' voyage. Tamarind was to be available for the scorbutic and the sick, and oranges and limes obtained as long as trading was still going on. Finally, 5000 to 6000 pounds of tobacco and 30 gross (4320) short-stemmed pipes were provided 'in order to issue three to four leaves [of tobacco] to each of them per week'. The clay pipes of the period were disposable.

When above deck the captives were always to be kept occupied, for example by picking oakum, 'in order that idleness does not prompt them to mischief and make them conceive all manner of evil'. They were not, however, to be allowed to get hold of any metalware such as knives, nails or pieces of metal staves, 'with which they are able to do a good deal of mischief', and when the ship was near land, the men were to be kept locked up.

It must be borne in mind, however, that these instructions, prompted by high death rates and the loss of valuable cargo, set an ideal standard which likely as not was seldom if ever approximated in the daily practice of the overcrowded and malodorous slave ships. When slaves were transported directly from Madagascar to Sumatra the death rate among them was particularly high,[104] 'whereas the English took part in this trade so heavily at that time, bringing these people to Barbados, New England and the American regions in large numbers'.[105] This led to the suggestion that slaves bought in Madagascar for the gold mines first be brought to the Cape to be acclimatised and then sent on to the East in batches with outgoing ships.[106] It was pointed out that the WIC similarly took the slaves bought at Popo and elsewhere in Guinea, 'of whom they yearly transport some thousands to Curaçao', to Cape Lopez (near Port Gentil in the present Gabon) 'to refresh them and allow them to rest' before proceeding across the Atlantic.[107]

When the scope of the VOC's trade was enlarged and the *Westerwijk* and the *Jambi* were sent out successively in 1685 and 1686, with room on board for 400 and 600 slaves respectively, it was furthermore thought advisable also to provide the latter with the special instructions quoted above.

Shortly afterwards, however, in 1687, the VOC abandoned the trade in slaves for Salida, 'on grounds of cost, slave mortality, and the danger of piracy in Madagascar waters'.[108]

While the slave traders' preference for 'young, active people' was purely practical, in Madagascar as elsewhere, it is interesting that the Advocate of the VOC in the Netherlands, Pieter van Dam, gives a further reason in his detailed survey of slave trade with the island. This is also, he writes, because older people, seeing themselves being taken away to perpetual servitude outside their own country, immediately begin to grieve and pine away, to which the young people do not seem to be so susceptible and with which they are better able to cope; but this cannot be proved or established, as the kings desire all their people to be accepted, even though old and decrepit, if one is to do any trading or does not wish to be frustrated in it.[109]

This was written in the great compendium of the VOC and its activities which Van Dam began to compile at the end of the century, but it seems to echo the thoughts of Hendrick Crudop, acting Commander of the Cape, in a letter to the XVII in 1679 after the return of the *Voorhout* from its second expedition, in which he remarked on the extreme youth of the slaves she had brought. The age of sixteen, he remarked, was

a time of life which experience and the English have taught us to be the best; for those who are older take to fretting when they but think of their country, and soon die; whereas the young are light-hearted and frolicsome, and thus preserve their health better.[110]

A further characteristic of Madagascan slaves was that they remained remarkably faithful to their own language, and interpreting in Malagasy took place at the Cape from at least 1706 until at least 1766.[111]

To the extent that they managed to adapt to life in their new surroundings and settle in, the good qualities of the Madagascans soon came to be appreciated at the Cape, for as Commissioner-General Van Reede wrote in 1685, they proved to be 'naturally strong, diligent, quick of comprehension and not malicious', and, 'well guided and instructed by our own people, will be able to give good service, yea, better than that of our own nation, as with them it will be possible to do all the farming and field work projected here under the supervision of only a few Netherlanders whose wages burden the profits of the labours'.[112] Batavia likewise had originally been interested in these slaves because they were claimed to be 'of a gentler and more tractable disposition'.[113]

These slaving trips to Madagascar were all carried out by the Company for its own benefit, however, even though private individuals were able to obtain some Madagascan slaves unofficially and incidentally. When Simon van der Stel forwarded a request by local freeburghers to be allowed to trade there themselves after English traders had brought rumours of cheap slaves being available in the vicinity of St Augustine's Bay in 1687, nothing came of it,[114] for the Company was never inclined to encourage potential competition from its underlings.

Of the privately owned English slavers visiting Magelagie and St Augustine's Bay to obtain slaves over the period 1675–1700, no fewer than 40 are known to have touched at the Cape on the return journey to the Americas.[115] These were sometimes willing to dispose of part of their cargo here if the slaves 'were in ill health, or if prices were thought to be relatively low in the Americas (e.g. because of a depression in the plantation economy or because competitors were likely to beat them to the favoured ports)'.[116] For these sales the Company's permission was required, but where it was not given, trade could take place illicitly, so that it is difficult to determine its exact volume.[117]

The most notable and most successful of the English traders was probably William Deeron, captain of the *John and Mary* from London, who, visiting Table Bay early in 1684, 'sold 31 slaves in a couple of days at the Cape for no less than Rds.1633 $^2/_3$'. As Dr Böeseken points out, 'If a slave cost him of an average Rds.10, he made a tidy profit of Rds.1323 $^2/_3$ or f3971.'[118] Deeron paid similarly profitable visits to the Cape in 1686 and 1690,[119] but by 1694 he was dead, and 'Emanuel Fonseca (25), a slave belonging to the late William Deeron, fled from the *Josias*, having stolen several of his late master's possessions: money, a diamond ring, gold and amber worth about f600.'[120]

In 1685 Oliver Cranisborough, captain of an English vessel recorded as *De Margriet* (possibly the *Margaret*), similarly disposed of 11 slaves from Madagascar at prices between 20 and 100 rixdollars each.[121]

A further incidental source from which the Cape is known to have obtained African slaves during this period was the Portuguese ship *Nossa Senhora de los Milagros*, which was wrecked off Cape Agulhas in 1686 when on its way back to Europe, with among its passengers ambassadors sent by the King of Siam (Thailand) to Louis XIV of France. A number of survivors managed to reach the settlement at Table Bay on foot, and as many of them had according to Portuguese custom brought slaves on board with them, certain of whom had likewise survived, 14 individuals were disposed of at the Cape. One of them, Paulus van Mosambique, is described as 'thick-set and small of stature',[122] which distinguishes him as one of the few slaves of whom even a rudimentary description has survived.

The slaves thus sold came from various Portuguese trading posts and colonies, including Mozambique and Mombasa on the East Coast of Africa and Macao on the coast of China. An Augustinian priest, Joseph de la Gracia, sold two slaves from Mombasa and Mozambique, together with '30 ounces of amber, 8 or 10 silver knobs for canes and several spoons', while the Senior Merchant Jan (probably João) da Paiva disposed of ten males from Mozambique belonging to another Senior Merchant, who had survived the wreck but were still at large. 'Governor Simon van der Stel paid de Paiva Rds.25 for the right to sell three of them if he recaptured them. If he caught fewer than three, he would still pay Rds.25.'[123]

According to Armstrong, a total of 1064 slaves were obtained from Madagascar officially for the VOC at the Cape during the period 1652–99, apart from those acquired in private transactions.[124] The latter continued to be considerable, and after the return of the *Jambi* from her first trip, for example, twelve transactions stated explicitly to be by crew members took place between January and April 1687, as well as numerous others involving Madagascan slaves where no information is given about the sellers.[125]

Over the period 1695–1707 Hattingh found 215 slaves from Madagascar among a total of 857 brought to the Cape, more than from any other single region except for Coromandel in India,[126] while Groenewald, covering a longer period, established that by 1700 a total of 344 Madagascans had been sold in private transactions.[127]

It is interesting to note in passing that when the slave trade with Madagascar languished early in 1704, the Council of Policy under W.A. van der Stel decided 'to try again at Angola or the West Indies, with the hopes of better success and less danger'. The XVII responded by pointing out that Angola was within the charter of the WIC, and the Cape duly replied that it would 'refrain from taking any steps in that direction, but renew the expeditions to Madagascar'.[128]

5. The world of the slaves: the Slave Lodge

Insofar as it is possible to generalise about so large and varied a group as the Cape slaves, this can most easily be done with regard to those belonging to the VOC. This considerable body of people, while diverse in origin, was subject to the same authority and discipline, was employed for broadly similar work, received the same food, clothing, schooling and religious instruction, and was largely lodged under one roof.

The small number of slaves privately owned by officials during the early years under Van Riebeeck probably shared their masters' quarters in the Fort, being mostly women, young girls and children, and as likely as not slept on the floor at night, as would be the custom in Cape homes in later years. When the importation of larger numbers of slaves for the benefit of the VOC was being considered, special provision had to be made for them, however, and in 1657, after the visit of Rijckloff van Goens, Van Riebeeck proposed in his Journal,

> the construction inside the fort, along the still unbuilt curtain side, of the projected storehouses approved by the Hon. van Goens. These are very necessary for the purpose of housing slaves below and storing in the granary the grain which, with the help of God, will be won this season and for which we consider our present accommodation insufficient.[1]

Within the earthen walls of the Fort there was a large open square which appears by this time to have been surrounded by buildings

on three sides. The projected new building was probably to be erected against the wall on the western side of the square, on the right
hand side of anyone entering the Fort by the gateway, where an
early plan indicates only a 'projected store'.[2]

Whether the proposed building was in fact built, is not clear.[3]
Evidence with regard to the slaves sleeping somewhere in the Fort
is, however, provided by the Journal entry in 1658 which refers to
two elderly slaves absconding from the building 'when the gates
were opened this morning',[4] and the charge laid in 1660 against
two slaves, Willem and Claes, who had left it without permission
'on Sunday morning at the opening of the gate', concealed themselves in the undergrowth near the dunes (the present Mouille Point)
and killed one of the freeburghers' pigs brought out to scavenge
there.[5]

During the time of the large-scale desertions in the winter and
spring of 1658 there were also references to the chief gardener's
slaves 'breaking out of the building outside the fort in which they
had been locked up',[6] and 14 slaves being confined in 'the gardener's house'.[7] The first garden plots had been laid out immediately
across the mountain streams from the Fort, close to the shore, and
the gardener's house, which in 1655 was described as a wattle-and-
daub structure, must have been in the immediate vicinity. By 1659,
however, Van Riebeeck referred to 'a brick house occupied by the
gardener and slaves and a free family'.[8]

Slaves attached to the new cornfields, gardens and wood-cut-
ting establishment behind Table Mountain in the Liesbeek valley
seem not to have returned to the Fort at night, however, for the first
7 slaves who absconded during the winter of 1658 were specified as
'one from the forest, two from the fort and two pairs from the Company's grain-fields'.[9] During the same period instructions were
given that the slaves working in the cornfields, 'or at the forest, or
elsewhere for the Company, were to be chained to one another at
night; the slaves in this neighbourhood [*Table Valley*] were to be
confined in the Fort at night'.[10]

By the winter of 1662 the gardeners and slaves working 'outside in the Company's orchard under the mountains' were complaining about the fact that their house, '(situated in the same garden, by the side of the highway) had as a result of age become so decayed and leaky that they were unable to live in it during this rainy season and the cold weather'. As the authorities were of the opinion that little could be done to repair the 'old grass house' ('*'t selve oude strooihuijs*'), it was decided to erect a more suitable building in which the Commander might also spend the night when inspecting the Liesbeek valley.[11] This was the origin of Rustenburg, the later country residence of Cape Commanders and Governors.

When Zacharias Wagenaer took over from Van Riebeeck, he immediately began thorough alterations and improvements to the outworks of the Fort. During this time the ramshackle gateway to the garden in the Table Valley and its guardhouse were blown down, and by the end of 1663 Wagenaer noted that it was to be rebuilt on a different site, as the garden had moved 6 roods (20 to 24 metres) higher up the valley after the soil had become exhausted. He envisaged also building 'two long rows of little houses with shed-roofs' on either side of the gateway, each 2 roods deep, resting on walls 1½ feet thick, to be used respectively as a gardener's lodging and a storeroom for garden produce. To this he added the thought that it would be possible to erect similar 'low sheds' in a row next to the gardener's house;

> in which all the Company's slaves (who at present are still living in the Fort, occupying a storeroom very convenient for our wheat) could live, seeing that most of them are employed by day in the said big garden. And if more slaves from Madagascar should be added to their number, it may well become necessary to decide on this, as we would be unable to place them under cover immediately, or otherwise it will be necessary to erect a suitable shed or dwelling for them somewhere on the square [beside the Fort] or along the coast.[12]

His original term for the sheds was '*lage pedackjes*', using a word common in the East at the time which was to survive in Afrikaans in the form *pondok*. In connection with the Company's slave quarters in Batavia a few years earlier, at a time when Wagenaer was officially in charge of them,[13] similar reference was made to the lack of sufficient 'bamboo *petakken*' for new arrivals, who accordingly had to be accommodated 'in the dormitory ["*baijert*"] or common slave house'.[14]

The XVII had suggested moving the slaves to new accommodation in the outworks of the Fort,[15] but according to Wagenaer there was no room for them there, and by April 1665 he could report that the Company's slaves, 'now amounting to more than 80 with women and children', had been lodged

> in the front part of the Company's garden next to the head gardener's [house] and barely a musket shot from the Fort in a row under a good roof (…), where these dirty, slovenly people are always near water and very well situated, so that if anything should occur we may at all times easily take them in and take them under our care [in the Fort].[16]

The reference to water relates to the mountain streams and the ditches and canals led out from them to irrigate the garden.

This was the Company's 'slave house', and given the fact that the Fort was situated on the western end of the present Grand Parade, it must have been somewhere between the present Darling Street and the Groote Kerk. Nothing more is known about it, but it seems very likely that, the question of relative freedom apart, there was at the time no great difference between the living conditions of the Company's slaves and its soldiers in the so-called *corps-du-garde* at the Fort. As Sleigh remarks, a comparative study might reveal 'interesting similarities'.[17]

By the end of 1669, only a few years after it had been built, the 'slave house' was already described as 'very small and much decayed',[18] and early the following year the Journal stated that it had been 'completely rebuilt and repaired, and made comfortable for the slaves and their children'.[19] Comfortable or not, the following winter the slaves were obliged to complain about the inadequate clothing issued to them and the lack of blankets.[20]

Shortly after this the numbers in the slave house began to increase rapidly through the addition of batches of new arrivals from Madagascar and elsewhere. In the course of the 1670s the erection of a new slave house on a further abandoned piece of the garden was several times discussed, but repeatedly put off because priority had to be given to the Castle and fortifications.

By the beginning of 1679 the situation with regard to the slaves had become serious, as the slave house was said to be on the point of collapse and was not judged worth repairing. On 22 February 1679 the Political Council therefore finally decided to begin work on a new building,

> but not according to the old plan which his Honour the late Governor [Bax] had drawn up, but after the example now provided, as the first plan would have demanded too much labour and therefore have been too costly for the Hon. Company, the second, on the contrary, being not only smaller by one third and consequently less expensive, but also equally convenient.[21]

While this new slave house was being erected, additional accommodation for the slaves seems to have been improvised in the recently completed Castle, where they are mentioned early in 1679 as temporarily occupying a building situated against the wall nearest the sea, between the bastions Buren and Catzenellenbogen.[22] A 'slave house' is also shown here on an early plan of the Castle, to the right of the original entrance, which was on the sea side of the building.[23]

The old slave house continued meanwhile to be occupied, for it is recorded that when it burned down suddenly on 19 August 1679 all the inhabitants were able to escape, with the exception of 'a young male slave who had been born at the Cape and had already made good progress in reading and writing'.[24] No plans were made to rebuild it, however, as the adjoining new building was already so far advanced that the slaves were able to move into it immediately. The site where its predecessor had been situated was soon incorporated in the expanding freeburgher settlement in the Table Valley.

The new slave house was situated immediately next to the Company's garden, alongside the canalised stream which was given the ironical name Heerengracht (the present Adderley Street). On the opposite side of the street (on the corner of the present Wale Street) a large new hospital was completed in 1699, and immediately adjoining the slave house the site for a projected church building had been walled in in 1677 and was already used for burials. The church eventually erected here and inaugurated in 1704 was in due course to be replaced by the present Groote Kerk, and its churchyard was only much later separated from the slave quarters by a street (the present Bureau Street).

The new slave house was in its time usually referred to as the *Slaven Logie* or Slave Lodge, and it is as well to retain this familiar name. The word indicates a more or less temporary hut or shed for accommodation or storage,[25] and was later also to be used in both Dutch and Afrikaans in the form *loods* for an aircraft hangar. At a future stage the building, in a much improved form, was to be turned into government offices and subsequently became the Supreme Court and later the Cultural History Museum; it now houses the Iziko Museums. In 1998 what remained of it was given what was apparently assumed to be to the original name of 'Slave House',[26] but however well-intentioned the renaming may have been, it was unfortunate, as it is seriously misleading as far as the present structure is concerned.

The VOC's Slave Lodge, as it was completed for occupation in 1679 and existed until well past the end of the Company's rule at the Cape, was nothing more than a blank enclosing wall, 'a big, rectangular brick building about 28 or 30 feet high,' as Commissioner-General Van Reede described it in 1685,[27] and '77 paces long and 46 deep' according to Valentijn.[28] Originally it was much longer than the present structure indicates, for in 1926 the Adderley Street façade was moved back 44 feet in order not to impede the flow of traffic.[29]

The high surrounding wall was broken only by entrances on the town and mountain sides, and the Lodge, in other words, was nothing more than a compound and prison intended to intern and guard the Company's valuable slaves when they were not at work. It presented a human face to the outside world only on the eastern side, where a new house with a common kitchen had been built for the master and under-gardeners backing onto the slave enclosure.[30] No attempt was made to beautify the structure until it came to serve a new purpose under the British administration and windows, doors, shutters, chimneys and ornamental plasterwork were added.[31]

Much the fullest account of the Slave Lodge by an outsider is that of Peter Kolb, a German with an enquiring mind who lived at the Cape from 1705 to 1713, became closely involved in local affairs, and seems to have acquired a remarkably thorough knowledge of life in the Lodge compared to his contemporaries, though his view of the slaves themselves is inevitably prejudiced and patronising.[32]

Within the wall there was a courtyard enclosed on all four sides by low buildings flat against the surrounding walls, under a sloping roof covered with tiles 'in order to be in less danger of fire'.[33] In the courtyard the slaves presumably spent a good part of whatever free time they had when the weather was fine, and presumably the children would have played here as well. According to Kolb they cooked here and also kept pigs,[34] and here too were the privies, 'vats or tubs, which are used more or less shamelessly in public, and cause no little stench and filth, if not unhealthy air as well', and which had to be emptied daily.[35] 'I have been inside this building only once to deliver a waggon of salt for the slaves,' wrote the German O.F. Mentzel, who was at the Cape from 1733 to 1741, 'but I can give no description of the quarters inside, for the stench made me beat a speedy retreat.'[36]

Finally there was a small lock-up in a corner of the courtyard for the temporary accommodation of offenders, and a whipping post where punishment was publicly administered. Kolb describes the scourging as being so severe 'that the blood not only flows down the back, but entire pieces of flesh are torn from it, (…) and all the others must be present, who are then exhorted to take example by this'.[37]

Insofar as the curiously elongated plan of the Lodge given with that of the Company's garden in Valentijn's book is dependable,[38] the buildings surrounding the courtyard housed storerooms, a common kitchen and separate schoolrooms for the slave boys and girls: this would reflect the situation as Valentijn himself became superficially acquainted with it during his brief sojourns at the Cape over the period 1685–1714, and was most likely compiled by or for him in the latter year. Like everything else sketched in this chapter as though it were fixed and unalterable, it would inevitably have undergone changes in the course of time.[39]

The greater part of the buildings served for the accommodation of the slaves, who are also described as sleeping in the attics under the sloping roof: this is what Kolb refers to when he writes about a building 'only two storeys high, in the first of which a man can barely stand upright, while the second is immediately under the roof'. Elsewhere he mentions the building being so low 'that it is almost possible to touch the roof'.[40] He also specifies that these two storeys were not subdivided internally, but formed two large dormitories or *baaierds* with wooden shelving along the walls which served as beds,[41] and refers to 'double bed shelves' ('*dubbelde bed planken*'),[42] presumably implying two rows, one above the other.

Commissioner Van Reede, visiting the Lodge after working hours one day in the winter of 1685 to investigate conditions for himself, found there many small children, white as well as black, all speaking the Dutch language, running about quite wild. The bunks in which they slept were very dirty, as was the floor, as a result of the leaking roof and the strong winds blowing in the rain. The sick lay there with no greater comfort, like animals. Small white children too big to be carried by their mothers and too small to follow the troop in cold and wet weather sat about on the bunks like chickens in a coop. The married and unmarried, small and older girls and those of marriageable age, as well as boys, young men and unmarried men, lay about on the beds without any distinction among them, and lived herded together like animals.[43]

When individuals or families required privacy, it was obtained, according to Kolb, by hanging 'a piece of cotton or any other linen cloth around their planks'.[44] 'The greatest hardship of the slave family,' comments Heese, 'and especially of those belonging to the Company, was probably the lack of privacy.'[45]

By 1799 Lady Anne Barnard writes of the enlarged Lodge building that 'the slaves of [whom] there are between 200 & 300 sleep in rows in the large rooms each has his or her bed & rags of curtains hung round them, they burn candles & lamps all night without restriction & a spark of fire would in five minutes consume the whole'.[46] This was presumably based on hearsay, but when the French-born architect and engineer L.M. Thibault reported on the state of the building for the British administration five years later, he referred with some horror to a space 'divided and subdivided in a multitude of little lodgings made of coarse rags which obstruct the air and prevent it from circulating'.[47] He recommended breaking through 18 windows in the exterior walls, which signalled the beginning of the process of improvement the building was to undergo under the new administration.[48]

Mentzel further mentions that 'a number of hammocks, given by sailors to the female slaves, are hung around a small court and are occupied by various couples',[49] while Kolb states that in the heat of summer the slaves preferred sleeping on the earth, presumably in the courtyard as well, whereas in the winter they made themselves ill by using their wet clothes as bedding,[50] probably for the lack of an alternative.

In these conditions it is hardly surprising that there was a high rate of mortality among the Company slaves. 'Death visited the Lodge in the coldest, rainiest months,' writes Shell, 'and dropped to a very low rate in the summer',[51] and not untypical in this respect is a Journal entry for the winter of 1673, referring to the old slave house, which reads that 'the Company's slaves (…) are dying very much, a considerable number having been buried within a short time, which is very inconvenient for the Company'.[52]

'For example,' write Armstrong & Worden with reference to the slaves imported from Madagascar,

> of the 221 Malagasy slaves of the *Joanna Catherina*, 129 died within fourteen months of their arrival in 1673. Of the *Voorhout*'s 257 slaves (mostly children) landed in 1676, 92 were dead in three and a half months. Of the *Soldaat*'s 119 slaves, the largest part were dead within a year of their arrival in 1697.[53]

In the Lodge there was likewise little resistance to epidemics, and Heese mentions an epidemic in 1701 which claimed 220 victims,[54] while the great outbreak of smallpox which devastated the entire local community in 1713 caused the death of nearly 200 of the Company's approximately 570 slaves.[55]

'A comparison of the birth and death statistics,' observe Armstrong & Worden, 'shows that deaths far exceeded births, and confirms the observation made above that the Company's slave force was not self-reproducing, but relied for its survival on replenishments from imports.'[56]

Under the Company, the upkeep of the building was neglected

from the beginning, although Kolb writes feelingly about the expense caused by the maintenance of the slaves' lodgings.[57] Commissioner Van Hoorn found in 1710 that 'from the outside it makes a certain impression because of the wall, but inside it looks very slovenly and mean', and described it as 'extremely dilapidated'.[58] K.J. Slotsboo, 'upper *mandoor* of the Hon. Comp.'s slaves and convicts', submitted a brief two-page report on the Lodge on Van Hoorn's orders,[59] but nothing was said in it about the condition of or conditions in the building. Under Van Hoorn's chairmanship the Council of Policy paid some attention to improvements to the hospital building across the street,[60] but nothing seems to have been done about the Lodge.

In 1717 the tiled roof of the Lodge was described as being so 'leaky everywhere' that the slaves were unable to keep dry in their beds, while the door and window jambs had decayed beyond repair, and the Council was advised to demolish and improve the structure,[61] advice which was confirmed in a detailed report the following year.[62] At this stage the building was described as being 'approximately 180 feet in length and 85 feet in width',[63] and was stated to be 'much too small for so large a number of slaves'.[64] In the same year reference was made to the discomfort caused to 'both the hospital and the slave lodge, yes, and the church as well', by the canal alongside the Heerengracht,[65] so that the Lodge must also have been damp.

It was not until 1732 that the 'renovation and enlargement' of the Slave Lodge authorised by the XVII shortly before came to be discussed by the Council of Policy,[66] and as a result a second storey was added to the structure around the courtyard,[67] basically giving the building its present shape. According to Dr Mary Cook, writing in about 1950,

the side walls of the Old Supreme Court and the rooms lining them may claim to be the second oldest building in Cape Town, and the lower part of the walls and the lower row of

137

rooms are probably of greater antiquity than any building now standing, excepting only the foundations and lower parts of the Castle.[68]

Given these conditions it is hardly surprising that the Slave Lodge had an unsavoury reputation. 'Who can blame the prudence of the burghers in forbidding their slaves to visit these contaminated and rapidly dying slaves or have contact with them?' demanded Kolb rhetorically. 'Who can criticise the fact that the barber-surgeons who in the absence of physicians have to act as doctors have not assisted them?'[69]

The food provided for the slaves continued to be whatever happened to be cheap and readily available, and for the time being this was still mainly fish: in 1672 they received 20 pounds of salted fish per head per month, and the following year the total consumption was 10 000 pounds. According to Sleigh, this consisted mostly of salted and dried harders and steenbras, while the freeburghers fishing at Saldanha Bay also supplied the Lodge with salted seal and penguin meat and penguin eggs for the same purpose.[70]

By 1678 the consumption of fish had decreased to 5500 pounds, although Simon van der Stel is said to have done pioneer work in encouraging fishing for this purpose in False Bay, where Simon's Bay was named after him.[71]

Rice imported from Batavia likewise continued to play an important part in the slaves' rations, and in 1669 'most of the Company's female slaves and their children came to complain to Commander Borghorst that they were not able to come out on their rice rations. This his Honour heard with surprise,' according to the Journal, 'as that ravenous folk receive daily ¾ lb. per head', and on due investigation it was decided 'that the complaint was groundless, and that these people received enough'.[72] When they complained about being issued with rice eaten by weevils the following year, it was decided to compensate by supplying them with 50 pounds a month instead of 40.[73]

In 1672 the slaves likewise complained to Commissioner Aernout van Overbeke about the 'vile and scanty food received by them, notwithstanding their heavy daily labour'.[74] They were receiving at the time a ration of 40 pounds of rice and 20 pounds of salt fish a month, but stated that it had formerly been the custom to give them fresh fish or meat once a week, a privilege which was now restored to them 'as circumstances might permit'.[75]

It may be noted that this was in the same period during which the slaves complained twice about the clothing and blankets issued to them, the years 1668–71, during the brief terms of office of the sickly Commanders Borghorst and Hackius, when the Company's affairs at the Cape were in a state of general neglect.

Meat was rationed as much as possible, and when '16 casks of fine salted breams, harders and other fish' were brought from Saldanha Bay in 1672, this was welcomed for reasons of economy: 'Thus a large quantity of [salted] pork and meat will be saved.'[76]

In the early years game was still plentiful in the vicinity of the Liesbeek valley, however, and when in 1666 an employee of the Company arrived at the Fort with 'a wild dead buffalo on a wagon' which had been shot behind Bosheuvel and it proved unsaleable on the market, Wagenaer had it 'cut into pieces and salted for our slaves'.[77] Before the colonists moved into the Berg River valley in the 1670s, game was likewise readily obtainable here, and in 1673 three soldiers are mentioned in the Journal 'who have for a considerable time been busy obtaining wild meat by the shooting of elands, rhinoceroses and harts for the sustenance of the slaves'.[78] A few years later Lieutenant Cruse was sent to shoot hippopotamuses in the same area, 'their flesh being much wanted for the Company's servants and slaves'.[79]

The consumption of fish decreased as cheap butcher's meat gradually became available towards the turn of the century, and by 1687 the Council of Policy decided to supplement the rations of the Company's slaves with 'the heads, feet, intestines and further offal of the Company's cattle slaughtered locally'.[80] While the Company reduced its farming operations and stopped farming with sheep altogether as from 1701, a number of indigenous or fat-tailed sheep were traded from the Khoikhoi 'to feed the slaves with occasionally, for their health and well-being, as they were as cheap as fish'.[81] Among the statistics supplied to Commissioner Van Hoorn in 1710, one finds 'Hottentot sheep got by barter as food for the slaves, 123'.[82] When a contagious disease broke out among the slaves in 1709 and about 70 were said to be indisposed, 'some already dead', the meat ration was increased, and it was ordered that they were to be supplied 'daily with 300 lbs. of fresh mutton to be boiled in rice'.[83]

When regulations were issued concerning the official meat contract in 1705, it was furthermore stipulated that 'the bad meat shall be condemned and forfeited for the slaves'.[84]

Though this is well beyond the period under discussion, Mentzel noted in the 1730s that 'the slaves and Hottentots have to eat the meat of animals that die, which, however, they enjoy just as much as that of slaughtered animals'.[85] And elsewhere, 'Mutton costs two, and fat three stuivers a lb. The head and pluck are sold to the slaves very cheaply, while the rest is given to the dogs.'[86]

References to large quantities of fish for the slaves nonetheless still occur regularly in the early eighteenth century.[87] W.A. van der Stel in the course of his dispute with the freeburghers stated that a boat manned by Company servants was kept at Vishoek (the modern Gordon's Bay) in False Bay, 'that the fish caught there have always been, and still are, being salted and dried there by the persons mentioned'; and, 'That the same salted and dried fish have always been, and still are conveyed thence during the whole year by persons in the pay of the Company, and in wagons of the Company, and brought to the Cape as food for the slaves of the Company—about 600 in number.'[88] There is also a reference to some vats of salted herring 'which were already going bad' being brought to the Cape from Van der Stel's estate Vergelegen 'for the Company's slaves'.[89]

In 1710 reference was made to the slaves' official fish ration being increased to a half aum per 50 head per week,[90] and by 1717 the Company required 56 half aums of salted fish and 94 bundles of dried fish per week, the latter, also known as 'slaves' fish', being mainly dried stumpnose, with a bundle weighing a little over 5 kg.[91]

As regards the issuing of rice to the slaves, Commissioner Abbema in 1680 noted with satisfaction that the Cape was able to satisfy its own needs with regard to wheat, but that rice would still have to be provided for the greater part of the slaves.[92] At the end of 1681 it was officially decided to begin issuing bread to the garrison in the new year,[93] but Rijckloff van Goens Jr in 1682 likewise stated that 'although the prospects here are very good for harvesting more wheat than the colonists with their slaves and those of the Hon. Company require, experience nonetheless teaches that the slaves cannot thrive here without rice, and the Hon. Company will therefore remain obliged to continue the troublesome importation of [80 to 100 lasts of] rice'.[94] The Council of Policy remarked in this regard that 'apart from the fact that they have all been brought up on rice, there is here also no inexpensive foodstuff ["*toespijs*"] to serve with dry bread, while they are able to get the rice down with water and salted fish, &c.'.[95]

By 1685, however, Van Reede noted that the slaves were already growing used to bread, 'which supplies better nourishment and strength',[96] and in 1687 the XVII learned with pleasure that 'the slaves begin to grow accustomed to bread and thrive on it as well as on rice'.[97] By 1688 their rations were said to consist of 'fresh bread, meat and fish, together with good accompaniments ["*toespijs*"] and cooked food ["*potagie*"]',[98] and in 1699 it was mentioned that 'bread mixed with rice has been found to be very healthy for the [slaves]'.[99] After an abundant rye harvest in 1707, it could even be decided 'to feed the slaves entirely on rye bread, that the rye may be used up and not remain on our hands'.[100]

'They receive one loaf a week (the same as the garrison), with some old rice, some vinegar, pepper', Van Hoorn was told in 1710,[101] while Slotsboo gives the rations of *mandoors* or overseers, slaves and convicts as a loaf of bread and 10 to 12 salted fish each per week, with 40 jugs of vinegar and 20 pounds of pepper for the entire slave community per month, and makes no mention of rice in his report.[102] The purpose of the pepper was medicinal, as it was considered to be good for the health, and as early as 1680 it had been decided to supply the slaves with a quarter pound per head per month, as was customary in the East.[103] In 1706 the Cape also demanded 300 pounds of turmeric from Mauritius for the slaves, possibly for the same motives.[104]

The Council of Policy, on examining the matter during Van Hoorn's presence at the Cape, decided that the existing rations were 'too frugal and scant', and increased the monthly quantities to a half aum of salted fish per 50 slaves and 40 lbs of rice per person, 'and when they receive bread instead, half a pound of fresh meat will be issued to each per day'.[105]

In 1677 the authorities noted with concern the illness and deaths among the Company's slaves, which they attributed to the slaves 'through their own laziness' eating their rice uncooked, and it was decided to divide them into eight groups, as was customary on board ship, and appoint a quartermaster for each group, who would not only prepare their food but be allowed vegetables from the Company's garden twice a week.[106] This arrangement must have lapsed over the years, as Kolb mentions the Company providing salt fish, rice, bread, pepper and other provisions, which the slaves ate uncooked, as according to him they were 'too sluggish, too lazy and too negligent' to cook their food, 'unless compelled by blows'.[107] They may also well have been too tired after a day's hard work.

While extensive use was made both of arrack (Eastern rice-brandy) and brandy from Europe in the cattle trade with the Khoikhoi, the Company's slaves do not appear to have been given strong drink officially, and Sleigh notes that none was given to those working on the outposts.[108] According to Kolb they drank only water, 'unless they happen to obtain some money here or there in order to buy wine. And when they have wine, they do not drink it moderately, but pour it into their stomachs in such quantities that they are too drunk to know who or where they are.'[109]

This was illustrated in 1669, after a slave died as a result of a heavy drinking bout, and a *plakkaat* was issued noting the fact that colonists not only sold 'strong drink such as brandy and arrack' to the slaves, 'but provided them with room in their own houses for drinking, thus giving the said slaves such encouragement to this debauch that the latter, apart from the loss of their time, when they have finally become intoxicated, could rise up against their superiors, as has already occurred and been complained of to us'. Supplying them with drink was therefore forbidden under penalty of a fine of 150 rixdollars and the refusal of any further liquor licence.[110]

The illegal sale of strong drink continued to occur nonetheless, and Mentzel at a later stage mentions cheap wine, 'the worst of all the wines that can be sold to the dealers', as being sold mostly to 'soldiers, sailors and slaves'.[111]

In these circumstances tobacco, also used extensively in trading with the Khoikhoi, was the only solace left to the slaves in their bleak lives, and this was used as a special reward. On New Year's Day 1674, for example, 'to encourage [the Company's] slaves, each was presented with a small present of money and clothing, as well as a piece of almost spoilt (*bedurven*) tobacco, which generosity made these poor menials very cheerful and happy'.[112] Similar gifts are recorded in later years,[113] and when in 1686 the tobacco received from Mauritius was said to be so bad that it could not be disposed of to the colonists, 'and still less to the Hottentots', with the result that it was daily 'deteriorating and growing worse', it was decided to 'distribute it thriftily to the Hon. Company's slaves', rather than throw it away.[114]

As regards the clothing it issued to its slaves, the Company continued to import light cotton textiles from the East and heavier stuffs for winter wear from Europe: on one occasion 'duffle jackets and pilot cloth trousers' were mentioned,[115] and pilot cloth was described 'as the only comfort to protect the common agriculturists and slaves against the winter season'.[116]

As far as the Eastern textiles are concerned, literally hundreds of different types of cloth were produced in India at the time and the VOC dealt in dozens, of which only the names are still known: the explanations given by modern writers often differ, while those of contemporaries are mostly vague and confusing. The varieties of Eastern cloth most often referred to with regard to slaves at the Cape were bafta, bouling, chintz, geras, nequanias and photas, which were naturally cheap, strong materials, often striped or checked in bright colours such as red or blue. Valentijn refers to clothing distributed twice yearly, 'of sailcloth and blue linen'.[117]

As in the case of weevilly rice and spoiled meat and tobacco, so too spoiled cloth and clothing were often given to the slaves. When the Company in 1673 disposed by public auction of clothing, hats and shoes in its stores 'which had been unsaleable for a long while, and been much injured by moths and rats', it was noted that 'what was left on hand will not be unwelcome to the slaves'.[118] In 1695 it was similarly decided that some lengths of worsted and serge which were so moth-eaten as to be unsaleable would be distributed among to 'the Hon. Company's slaves in the lodge for clothing'.[119]

Likewise the Company in 1667 distributed to the slaves and convicts on Robben Island 48 blankets used when official French visitors were lodged in the Fort shortly before and scorched by the visitors smoking in bed. As the visitors had slept on the floor and the blankets piled 'mostly two upon each other', they were presumably palempores or quilts from India which were in common use at the Cape.[120]

The fullest indication of the materials the slaves were given for their clothing is provided by Slotsboo's report in 1710. According to this the slave officials in the Lodge received 12 ells of pilot cloth, a piece of bafta, 2 pieces of sailcloth or bouling, a quarter pound of thread and 6 dozen buttons each, as well as jackets of pilot cloth and sailcloth respectively, and two pairs of trousers. Female officials were given a length of photas for four dresses or skirts ('*kleties*', '*kleedjes*'), pieces of geras and bafta and 2 pieces of sailcloth (presumably for linings), and thread. The other slave women each received a piece of photas sufficient for four dresses or skirts, a length of nequanias, a piece of sailcloth or chintz for a *kabaai*, 4 ells of white linen for head cloths, and a supply of thread.[121]

There are also interesting lists of the winter and summer clothing issued to the slaves under Governor De Chavonnes some years later,[122] stipulating the same materials mentioned above. According to these the male slaves receiving double quantities of clothing were also given 3 dozen brass buttons each.

While all this may sound well enough on paper, especially as regards the brightly coloured Eastern cottons and the brass buttons, the reality was often much drabber and grimmer, quite apart from the quantities of clothes supplied frequently being alleged to have been inadequate.

In the winter 1670 the Journal notes complaints by the Company's slaves

that for a long time now, excepting their scanty clothing annually supplied to them, they have received no other change of garments or anything that they might use to cover themselves with as a protection against the cold during the night. The result has been that much sickness has broken out among their young children and old people, and therefore the Council decided, in order to prevent these discomforts, to provide them with some common Coast blankets, as they required them.[123]

Here too blankets referred to were probably the palempores or quilted cotton blankets from the Coast of Coromandel which were in common use at the Cape during the VOC period.

In 1672 again the slaves complained to Van Overbeke about receiving only a plain pilot cloth ('*pije*') jacket and trousers, besides some coarse Dutch ('*vaderlantsche*') shirts, a year, and they were promised new clothing twice a year in future.[124] The supply of clothes seems to have varied very much from time to time and to have depended on how conscientious the local officials were in this regard. Simon van der Stel discovered during his first winter at the Cape that the slaves were again receiving new clothes only once a year and were unable to change their wet clothing in winter, which caused much sickness. Once more it was therefore decided to issue two sets of clothes a year,[125] but only five years later Van Reede was nonetheless greatly troubled by the inadequate supply of clothing.[126]

It was Van Reede who, concerned mainly about the lot of the half-caste children, painted a vivid picture of the Company's slave force in the winter of 1685, describing

how the slaves suffered great discomfort, especially when they were wet as a result of the rain or other causes; that the women draped themselves in all manner of old rags and tatters against the cold, that many of them, especially the younger ones, were dressed in the jackets of soldiers and sailors, that there were girls and boys among them as white as Europeans, that many mothers had small infants bound and wrapped on their backs while at work who seemed more like the children of European mothers than of black women, and that the whole troop seemed to suffer from a considerable and miserable lack of clothing (…).[127]

The men's clothing was made up by the Company's tailors, and there were complaints about their dilatory work.[128] The women were given lengths of cloth and thread, as mentioned above, and made their own clothes, a division of work customary in Europe, where women's and children's clothing and 'linen and wool' were normally made up at home.

As to the actual appearance of the slaves there is little information, but gathering together the visual evidence from both the Cape and the East over the entire VOC period and making no allowance for changes in style, taste or availability of materials, male slaves would appear to have worn long trousers or else breeches ending shortly below the knee and short or long jackets (a *hemdrok* or *rok* respectively): illustrations may be found in Johannes Rach's well known view of the market square in the Table Valley in 1762.[129] Mentzel in the 1730s refers to 'a coarse close-fitting woollen doublet and trousers',[130] but elsewhere elaborates on this costume as it had evolved by his time: 'each male slave wears a doublet and trousers made of a coarse white woollen cloth with black streaks and lined with a cotton cloth called "sailcloth". The doublet is adorned with 12 brass buttons. The outfits are made up by the garrison tailors.'[131]

As regards the women, there is slightly more reliable visual evidence in a drawing by Caspar Schmalkalden, a German who was in the East in 1642–52, of a slave woman, wearing a long skirt and a short, loose blouse, the typical Eastern combination of *sarong* and *kabaja* or *kabaai*.[132] It may be assumed that this is approximately the way in which the earliest Eastern slaves at the Cape were dressed and that it served as model for the clothing provided for the slave women from Angola and Guinea, forming an acceptable compromise with Western clothing. The young Khoi woman Krotoa (Eva) is likewise said to have adopted 'the Indian way of dressing' while living with the Van Riebeecks in the Fort.[133]

Evidence which seems more relevant and may also be more reliable is provided by one of the so-called 'Khoi sketches', a series of drawings of traditional Khoikhoi made by an unidentified artist in about 1700. In the background of one of them appears the figure of an Eastern woman who may safely be taken to be a slave, and who is dressed in a style similar to Schmalkalden's female slave, though with a scarf wrapped around her head and knotted under her chin.[134] Mentzel refers to the female slaves in his time being given a 'veil or head-cloth'.[135]

Tentatively interpreting the vague and imprecise Dutch names used by Van Reede in his journal entry, his account of the slaves' clothing in his time reads,

> that no more than two lengths of cloth are given to the women in a whole year for skirts ('*rocken*') and two jackets ('*baatjes*' or '*kabaaien*') or half-shirts, and to the men an unlined pilot cloth jacket ('*rock*') or *casjack*,[136] besides a pair of sailcloth breeches and nothing more, with which it was quite impossible to make do for a full year, or to protect them against the cold one experiences here.
>
> I therefore ordered the Commander to have the women supplied in winter with two skirts and two jackets and an unlined coat ('*rock*') of pilot cloth, and in the good season with two skirts and two jackets, as well as a coarse, thick blanket per person according to the season. For the men in winter each a coat ('*rock*') of pilot cloth lined with sailcloth and two pairs of sailcloth breeches, and in the summer a coat of cheap gingang or some other material with a pair of breeches, with which they will be well equipped.[137]

According to Mentzel, writing some fifty years later, 'The female slaves wear smocks imported from Batavia. It [*sic*] is made up of six yards of coarse cotton cloth.'[138]

While it is necessary within the limitations of this book to summarise information covering half a century or more, this may give the erroneous impression that the world of the Cape slaves was monolithic and that their lives were static. However, even when it remained largely unaltered in broad outline throughout the VOC period, it changed constantly in its details, and information such as that given by Mentzel for the 1730s, for example, cannot necessarily be made applicable to part or all of the period under discussion here. At most it can serve as indication of a form that developments had assumed by his time, in this particular instance with regard to clothing.

One point worth making specifically is that the servants of the Company, in spite of its many faults and failings, were always free to make known their grievances, and that this privilege included the slaves. However strict discipline may have been, they are still to be found complaining to Commissioner Van Overbeke about their food and clothing in 1672,[139] while the *mandoors* likewise complained about their rations to Commissioner Van Hoorn in 1710.[140]

In sickness the slaves, being valuable property as far as the Company was concerned, were cared for, as mentioned by Kolb above, by the Company's barber-surgeons, who were not necessarily highly qualified men, but were very often the only medical personnel available. Slave women appear to have been assisted during their confinements by whatever midwives were available locally, and Van Reede specifically commended Sara van Rosendael, the wife of the Company's master carpenter Adriaan van Brakel, in this regard.[141] Kolb in passing provides the information that pregnant women were excused from work for six weeks before giving birth and six weeks after.[142]

When necessary, sick slaves were also admitted to the Company's hospital, apparently on an equal footing with the whites, and at any rate received the same food, namely a pound of meat with vegetables: this was decreased to half a pound in 1677, as it was believed that this lavish diet encouraged malingering.[143] Slaves arriving from Madagascar in a poor condition after the long voyage were likewise sent here 'in order to be refreshed and nursed'.[144]

The corpses of slaves were buried in the unwalled general cemetery described by Kolb as being 'between the town and the Fort in the direction of Table Mountain', where Christians and heathen lay together.[145] Around the turn of the century it was moved some distance to the west of the settlement (the present Somerset Road area), where a 'common cemetery for soldiers, sailors and slaves' was mentioned in 1710 when the decision was taken to have it walled in.[146]

Presumably the dead were simply wrapped in their blankets, for at the same time it was decided that Europeans would, 'in accordance with Christian charity and the general practice in India [*the East Indies*]', in future be provided with coffins, 'insofar as planks can be spared for this purpose'[147]—' in order to maintain the status of the Europeans as far as possible with regard to the indigenous races,' as the Council of Policy phrased it at a later stage.[148] The was so far outside the settlement, however, that the burgher watchmen and the *caffers* assisting the Fiscal had to be instructed to patrol the area regularly to prevent the theft of the planks used for coffins.[149]

It was not until 1720 that the 'great stench' of the earlier cemetery in the Table Valley led to it finally being filled up and closed.[150]

The VOC not only provided its slaves with shelter, food, clothing and medical attention, however, but also took some care of their presumed spiritual needs, according to the teachings of the Reformed Church (*Gereformeerde*, later *Hervormde Kerk*), the so-called 'public church' of the Dutch Republic, which was the only church permitted in areas governed by the Company. Ministers and rudimentally instructed sick comforters attended to its white servants, but from time to time also paid attention to the slaves in a somewhat erratic way. What was done depended largely on the interest taken by the individuals concerned, or the current Commander or Governor, in the spiritual well-being of the slaves, and their ministrations suffered from the fact that most of these officials succeeded one other quite rapidly and there was no continuity in the work.

The Synod of Dordrecht, which in 1618 had formally established the doctrine of the Reformed Church, had laid down that the children of non-Christian parents might only be baptised as adults, but the VOC was a law unto itself, and in the territories it governed the offspring of Company slaves were automatically baptised, the Company itself guaranteeing that they would receive Christian instruction.[151] It was presumably on these conditions that the illegitimate children of slave women were baptised during the early years under Van Riebeeck, although there appears to have been some doubt in this regard, which was only removed by a formal reassurance from the Council of India received at the Cape early in 1664 in response to a query.[152]

In 1665 the Revd Joan van Arckel became the first ordained minister at the Cape and founded a local congregation, and according to Dr Böeseken he 'tried to record the names of the children who had been baptised before his arrival by visiting ministers. As for the slaves, the first entries were Cornelia and Lijsbeth Arabus ['*the Arab*']', this referring to the two 'Arab' girls presented to Van Riebeeck's wife. 'Then followed Heindrick, Pietertjie, Reintje, two Jacobs, an Annetje, Cathalisa, Mary and Louwijs (…). Another Mary and Jan Bruijn are registered as children of mixed marriages.'[153]

Van Arckel himself likewise administered baptism on the existing terms,[154] and after the Sunday afternoon service a month later, 8 children of slaves were presented at the font, together with the son of the Secunde Abraham Gabbema.[155]

On 31 March 1666, however, Van Arckel having died suddenly in the interim, the Revd Philippus Baldaeus, on his way back to the Netherlands after a term of office in Ceylon, caused some consternation by baptising the child of 'Christian Dutch parents' but turning away that of the slave woman Susanna.[156] The Council of Policy reacted with great indignation to his presuming to oppose local custom in this way, and Van Arckel's successor was ordered to baptise the child the following Sunday,[157] which was duly done: he received the name Andries.

The following May the Cape church council conformed with the decision of the authorities and decided, 'Firstly, that the children procreated by freemen with slave women are to be baptised on the word of their masters or mistresses, publicly given before the congregation. Secondly, that the children of slave women of the Hon. Company are similarly to be admitted, on the word of the Council or one of its members, simply by giving some sign or other.'[158] On 20 September of the same year the first recorded baptism took place at which 'a member of the Hon. Council' was given as sponsor, and this now became the custom, as in a similar case a year later: 'The child of a female slave of the Hon. Company, was named Catharijn; the mother's name is Fransike. The sponsor on behalf of the Hon. Council was *dominee* Victor [*the sick comforter*].'[159]

At this early stage there were relatively few slaves in private hands, but a number of baptisms were also noted among this group: Elisabeth the daughter of Susanna, and Dominga the daughter of Helena, both belonging to 'L. Wagenaar', who was probably the Commander, Zacharias Wagenaer; Johannes, child of a slave of the Secunde Hendrick Lacus, whose wife, a minister's daughter, acted as sponsor; and Dirk, the son of Sabba who belonged to the prominent freeburgher W.C. Mostaert.[160]

By the time of Van Reede's visit in 1685 uncertainty and confusion had once more arisen due to the belief that baptised slaves had of necessity to be manumitted afterwards. Finding that baptisms of Company slaves had ceased accordingly, Van Reede ordered them to be resumed as regards the children of slave women by Dutch and therefore presumably Christian fathers, under sponsorship of the Company.[161] He likewise made arrangements for the manumission of Company slaves on certain conditions which included profession of the Christian faith.[162]

The first baptism of a halfbreed child was administered during Van Reede's presence at the Cape to a child of four, he himself acting as sponsor,[163] but at some stage the general baptism of slave children seems to have been resumed, irrespective of their origins. The Revd E.F. le Boucq, who arrived from Batavia in 1707 and caused a great deal of unrest during his brief stay, objected specifically to the fact that Captain Oloff Bergh of the Council of Policy had not been present in church to stand as sponsor to a slave child on behalf of the Company, so that the child had to be sent away unbaptised, but also criticised the way in which baptisms of this nature were handled, and queried the fact that 'all the Company's slave children are baptised without distinction', which reopened the old controversy, with much the same result.[164]

152

Kolb in the same period left a brief sketch of a slave woman presenting her child for baptism,

carrying the child on her arm, or as usually happens, having it carried by another slave woman, on which the minister enquires concerning the origin of the child's mother and what it is to be called. If it is black or yellow, according to the nature of the reputed parents, no further investigation is necessary, as the apple never falls far from the tree; if the child should be more white than yellow, and the mother pitch black, this is a sure sign that it must have had a European father; concerning his identity the minister can establish no more than that the mother or the slave woman carrying the child replies: I don't know, father gone long ago, father gone to Holland long ago. Whether this reply is always to be believed and the father is not in many cases available, cannot well be guessed. It is at any rate readily conceivable that the women often do not know themselves who the true father was.

But however this may be, the child is not left unbaptised for this reason, and an official from the Council always acts as sponsor, who when the minister reads the baptismal formula after the sermon and asks whether N.N. wishes to be baptised, invariably replies: Yes, in the name of the Honourable Company; with which the said sponsor wishes to convey that he is acting in the place of the said Company and on its orders, replying not in his own name, but that of the illustrious Company.[165]

In 1666 the church council requested that evening prayers be conducted 'in the Company's garden 'for the male and female slaves', which refers to the slave house of the time.[166] During his visit to the Cape as Commissioner in 1671, Isbrand Goske likewise urged that the slaves, young and old, be obliged to attend 'Christian prayers' every evening and twice on Sundays, 'and that they should also try to repeat the reader's words aloud, these being in the Dutch language, as is done in the case of their children, in order to retain that which they have heard better in their memories, in the hope that more of them will in this way be animated and arrive at the desired felicity, to which may God give them His blessing and grace'.[167] In 1677 'a suitable black person' was employed for this purpose, and reference was made to both morning and evening prayers.[168]

In 1671 Goske also expressed concern about the fornication between white men and slave women, and considered means to prevent this. He also pointed out the drawbacks to allowing unions between slaves: 'to join the male and female slaves together as man and wife, and to keep them in this state without permitting them to marry formally, however, before they have been baptised and instructed to such an extent that they thoroughly comprehend the institution of marriage and understand to what extent man and wife are by these means bound to one another (…)'.[169]

Van Reede, in an attempt to combat promiscuity, immorality and the birth of further half-caste children, ordered that the names of all the slaves in the Lodge 'married voluntarily after their fashion' be noted and these couples be warned again immorality and promised official protection.[170] He likewise ordered that separate quarters in the Lodge be assigned respectively to these couples and to the children and single people of either sex.[171]

In his Instruction for Commander Van der Stel, Van Reede wrote movingly and at length about the Company's obligations to its slaves, more specifically as regards evangelisation.

The slaves in the Company's service provide considerable profit by their labour and promise no less for the future, but it will be necessary to look upon these poor people with different eyes, because they are the Company's own, not hirelings, who are unable to leave the service of their master when they tire of it, not only for their whole lives, but also for those of their children and descendants. The more we improve them, the better they will be able to give service, to love their lords and masters and be faithful to our nation. They are heathen, alienated from and ignorant of the true God, and we are Christians: their bodies are in our power, yea, almost their very lives; if we take care to look after dumb cattle, it would be a cause of shame to let people grow savage and leave them in a condition worse than in their own country. Our Lords and Masters [*the XVII*] are also the foster fathers of the Church of Christ, and we close its doors if we neglect to make use the means on hand and do not do all in our power to bring these people to knowledge of the sanctifying faith; for what do we know of that which God in His grace has decided concerning these people, and what will they and all foreign nations say to our disgrace if we leave them to live in fornication and wantonness, without doing anything about it, as with our own people.[172]

It was in this context that Van Reede introduced far-reaching improvements in the Slave Lodge and in the lives of its inmates, although it must be admitted that they were intended mainly for the benefit of the halfbreeds present among the slaves and with a view to preventing as far as possible the birth of further halfbreed children.

In spite of the racial mixing and miscegenation in the overseas colonies of European nations such as the Portuguese and Dutch, the latter remained conscious of the so-called purity of their blood or stock, and utilised a variety of terms to define and describe it. The Portuguese term *mestiço* (mestizo) was much used in various forms for a halfcaste,[173] the Dutch being *mesties*, and the future Governor of the Cape, Simon van der Stel, with his coloured grandmother, was officially described as a *mesties* when he left Batavia for Europe in 1660.[174] Much use was also made in Dutch of the terms *heelslag* and *halfslag* to indicate people of 'pure' indigenous stock and those with an admixture of European blood (halfcaste) respectively. For the sake of convenience these terms will be translated here as 'full-breed' and 'halfbreed' when referring to a contemporary situation. There was also a category of *kwartslag* or 'quarterbreed' which is irrelevant in the Cape context.

The morality of keeping the halfbreed children of Christian fathers in a state of slavery and the question of their baptism, education and possible manumission was one which was much discussed in the VOC and particularly engaged Van Reede when he visited the Cape. His sentiments were, however, highly unusual for the time, both among slave owners and the officials of the VOC, and Van Reede himself spent no more than twelve weeks at the Cape before continuing his tour of inspection, so that he was unable to see to the implementation of the detailed instructions he left behind. As the basic situation remained unchanged, however, no amount of improvement in details could possibly be effective. Casual relations between white and black continued, the Slave Lodge continued to be used for purposes of prostitution, and halfbreed children continued to be born.

In the brutal world of slavery a woman was helpless, and the reason so many of the early Angolan and Guinean slaves were described as 'paired' is probably that the women had at an early stage sought and found male protectors among their fellows. These would not have been able to protect them against the attentions of whites, however, whether on board ship or on land, and protectors may also not have been readily available. As far as the Slave Lodge is concerned, Shell points out that 'from 1652 through 1714 the Lodge housed the largest number of women in male-dominated Cape Town', many if not most of them single and unprotected.[175] In some cases the attentions of white men may even have been sought because of the more effective protection they were able to provide and the favours they could grant. The relationship established between the slave women arriving from Madagascar on the *Voorhout* and members of the crew, as observed by Abraham van Riebeeck in 1676, has already been described.

The lot of a slave woman sent out from Ceylon in about 1706 was sketched in a revealing statement by the Revd Kalden after he had, in the course of the violent and often unedifying dispute between a section of the freeburghers and Governor W.A. van der Stel, been accused of fathering a child by her. In this he declared,

> That this woman ['*meyd*'] was sent to me from Colombo, thence conveyed by ship to Galle, where the Revd. Shwem [*Swem*], worthy minister of that place, understanding that she was my property, wished her to come to his house as long as the ship lay there, but this was not permitted, on which this gentleman wrote to me, You can imagine what conditions will be like on the ship. In about six months [after arrival] she was duly confined, and the child publicly baptised in the church, as will be confirmed by the church register.[176]

According to De Wet, 60% of the male freeburghers over the period 1657–1707 remained single for lack of suitable partners, amounting to 970 men out of a total of 1613,[177] in addition to the large and steadily increasing number of soldiers, sailors and artisans in the Company's service at the Cape in normal circumstances. Even when Commissioner Verburch reduced the size of the garrison early in 1676, it was still considerable: '200 soldiers, apart from military officers, clerks, sailors, artisans, etc., who together probably amount to 150, under three chief officers, namely a captain, a lieutenant and an ensign who are in command, as well as 4 sergeants and 16 corporals'.[178]

Frequently, however, circumstances were not normal. The successive wars of the Dutch Republic with the English in 1665–67 and 1672–74 and the French in 1672–77 required the Cape to be heavily garrisoned with a view to possible attack by sea, and the Castle, which was begun at the end of 1665, was built with the help of drafted white labour. As from 1665, large numbers of soldiers and sailors were 'lifted', as it was known, or commandeered from passing ships, for example, and 400 men were at one stage stationed here, causing severe problems with regard to accommodation.[179] In 1670 again, a letter from the XVII gave permission for 300 extra men to be drafted, together with ammunition and other requirements.[180]

To this must be added the daunting number of visitors the Cape received each year as passengers on passing ships. During the decade 1680–90, for example, the first decade after the completion of the Slave Lodge, a total of 345 VOC ships sailed in both directions between the Netherlands and Batavia, carrying a total of well over 50 000 people, by far the greater part of them men, and most of these ships called at the Cape. Over the succeeding decades, the corresponding figures increased steadily.[181]

In spite of the vast numbers of seamen and others visiting the Cape each year, however, it appears to have been mainly local white men who fathered the steadily increasing halfbreed population of the Slave Lodge which caused so much concern to Van Reede and others, and with reference to the relevant statistics Shell points out that 'the mulatto conception cycle does not tally with the fleet arrivals. In fact, conceptions were the lowest in the months of the heaviest fleet movement at the Cape. The mulatto conception rates in the Lodge were based in the equinoxes, as in most other populations, and the Lodge women chose local European partners'.[182]

This was made clear after the sudden death of Governor Bax in 1678, when the Secunde Hendrick Crudop served as acting Commander during more than a year.[183] A fit of morality seems to have taken hold of the Council of Policy during this time, and it devoted a good deal of attention to the fact that

a number of imprudent servants of the Company and certain of its officials stationed here and in the country have not hesitated or been ashamed not only to keep and to use slave women of the Company and of private people as their mistresses and concubines, but even to hold vile converse with them ('*alle vuijle conversatie daarmede te plegen*') like shameless people on the public roads and other public places, as though this were a permitted matter and neither culpable nor evil.[184]

The 'vile converse' singled out for disapprobation probably meant no more than that the men concerned appeared openly in public places with their slave mistresses, but the Council, under the chairmanship of Crudop, objected to relationships of this nature between Christians and heathen, which according to them invited 'God's just anger and retribution'. Moreover, they led to the birth of half-breed children to the Company's slaves which the Company, because of their Christian fathers, felt obliged to manumit after a given time. This combination of fervent morality and questions of profit is quite characteristic of the VOC.

The result of these deliberations was that a *plakkaat* was issued at the end of 1678 in much the same words, but referring even more explicitly to 'the shameful crime of fornication or whoredom', the involvement of freeburgher men, the presence of mixed couples 'in taverns and at other gatherings', and the fact that the slave houses of the Company and of private persons, filled with 'illegitimately procreated children', provided sufficient evidence of such relationships, 'to the shame of the Dutch and other Christian nations'. White men were therefore strictly forbidden to keep mistresses or concubines and threatened with unspecified punishments.[185]

This seems to have had little effect, and in 1681, under the commandership of Simon van Stel, the Journal expressed its concern about a situation described in much the same terms as under Crudop.[186] At the same time the minutes of the Council of Policy complained more specifically about the 'scandalous and disgraceful households of two families, the one being a Timorese family and the other a certain manumitted slave named Catarijn, where the slave women of both the Company and private persons gather at certain fixed times and deliver their bodies to all manner of vile fleshly lust and allow themselves to be used by Europeans'.[187]

This new fit of concern led to the issuing of a further *plakkaat*, only three years, almost to the day, after its predecessor, couched in largely the same terms. An interesting addition, however, was the statement that the gatherings objected to took place on Sundays, which was normally the day on which the slaves were free from work, and in 'the Company's Slave Lodge, and further places suspected of serving this purpose', the Lodge having in the meantime replaced the ramshackle old slave house and obviously being regarded as a convenient meeting place.

In this case the injunctions and punishments were, however, much more explicit and much stricter.

> (…) we hereby forbid both Company servants and others to attend gatherings of this nature where slave women are present, wherever these may be held, and with this in view to refrain especially from making their appearance in the Company's Slave Lodge under whatever pretext this may be, on penalty of whosoever being found there, whether by day or by night, being thoroughly whipped in the case of the Europeans, without distinction, while the slave women, whether those of the Company or those of private persons not living there, are without the least exception to be bound to a post and severely whipped and thus sent back to their masters. And in order better to apprehend the contraveners of our orders, the masters and supervisors of the Company's Slave Lodge are earnestly instructed to pay close attention to all such persons entering the Lodge, who should in the first place report themselves, those found negligent in this regard being punished as though guilty, and finally each of these free colonists is strictly forbidden to permit such gatherings in their homes.[188]

In the given circumstances at the Cape there was, however, little that mere legislation and threats of punishment could do, and Van Reede in 1685 was distressed to discover that 'concubinage among the slave women with our own people was so openly and generally known that it was discussed as something tolerated', while poverty and the lack of clothing in the cold 'drove many of the women to let themselves be misused for an old jacket or blanket'.[189]

Apart from making very practical arrangements to have both the supply of clothing to the slaves and living conditions in the Lodge improved, Van Reede appears also to have suggested even severer punishments for relationships with the slave women of the Company, and in his private journal he mentions that servants of the Company should be deprived of a year's wages and freeburghers sentenced to the public works for six months with slaves' rations, while the fathers of children by slave women should pay 150 guilders a year for each child.[190] These seem to have been only suggestions, however, and they probably encountered opposition locally. In his journal Van Reede refers to a *plakkaat* 'against debauchery, seduction and concubinage with the Company's slave women' being 'publicly proclaimed and posted up everywhere',[191] but no other record of this has been found, and it possibly means no more than that the legislation of 1681 was promulgated anew.

The Slave Lodge thus continued to be used as a brothel and to be generally known as such. In the course of his wide-ranging controversy with the freeburghers, for example, the Revd Kalden, who left the Cape in 1708, in referring to the 'excesses' to which people in 'Indian lands' were inclined, added that they had special opportunities to 'satisfy their lecherous lust' at the Cape, 'both by means of the military stationed there and the visiting ships, which is also the reason why such a shameful number of white children are to be seen walking about the Hon. Company's slave house'.[192]

This was similarly acknowledged by the Cape authorities, not only tacitly but also explicitly. Among the *plakkaten* formally renewed in 1716 under Governor De Chavonnes was one which stated, 'Any person found by day or night in the slave quarters will without distinction be thoroughly scourged ["*dapper gelaerst*"]',[193] but this obviously continued to have little effect.

When concern was expressed at irregularities in the Slave Lodge in the same year, these included the fact that the inmates, 'receiving servants of the Company, chiefly the sailors and soldiers, in the Lodge, allowed them to camp out there all night, by which means unclean diseases break out to such an extent that are not to be eradicated or overcome'.[194] The regulations which were issued for the Lodge a week later merely regulated these visits, however, stating that if the provost marshal were to find any Europeans in the building on inspecting it in the evening, he was to send them away and to arrest those who were unwilling to leave.[195] This was in other words a mere safety precaution, aimed not so much at preventing the birth of halfbreeds or even the spreading of venereal diseases, in which it would have been of little effect, as the prevention of fire in the Lodge. The authorities no longer kept up any pretence of concern about the morality of its slaves.

'They herd together like animals,' Mentzel wrote disparagingly of the Company slaves some twenty years later, 'and have no higher moral sense. Female slaves are always ready to offer their bodies for a trifle; and towards evening one can see a string of soldiers and sailors entering the Lodge, where they misspend their times until the clock strikes 9.'[196]

The fertility of slave women is said to have been low compared to that of the whites, although the lack of exact statistics makes this difficult to judge,[197] but given the situation in the Slave Lodge, and the fact that there was no form of birth control whatsoever, there was a comparatively high birth rate in the Lodge, a fact which the Company was not inclined to discourage as it increased their own slave holdings. H.F. Heese mentions the Company slave Fatima van Madagascar who had 14 children baptised over the period 1690–1720,[198] although she was not necessarily typical.

The muster roll for 1693 lists surviving infants born during the three previous years in three distinct groups numbering 13, 14 and

11 children respectively, and a total of 61 schoolchildren, 29 of these being halfbreed and 32 fullbreed. The three lists of clothing for 1720–21 refer to lengths of photas, a sturdy cotton cloth commonly used for loincloths, distributed to the mothers of infants in three age groups, whose numbers are here given as 17, 20 and 32 respectively.[199] These figures are perhaps not high when seen in terms of the total number of slave women owned by the Company,[200] but the army of children probably seemed formidable in the extremely confined space of the Lodge. According to Kolb it was 'crawling' with young children, 'who, whether black by nature or born from the union with a European and yellow or brownish, are not yet able for work'.[201]

The rule of thumb in compiling statistics for the Lodge was probably that the infants were not yet old enough for school, and the schoolchildren not yet old enough to be set to work, which seems to have meant in practice that they were under twelve. During this time some rudimentary attention was given to their education.

As early as 1663 Wagenaer reported that the sick comforter Ernestus Back was 'diligently' teaching reading and the catechism to a number of children in the community, his school at the time consisting of 11 young white children, 4 baptised, halfbreed slave children whose names are given as 'Armasie, Crisme, Zou and Basol' (in a variant reading, Crisin, Zon and Basoe), and a 'little Hottentoos'.[202] Back was deported to Batavia two years later, however, with his wife and daughter, because of his 'drunkenness',[203] after which the existing arrangement seems to have lapsed.

In 1666 the newly formed church council requested the authorities that 'the children of the slave women from the garden', in other words in the slave house, might be allowed to attend school,[204] after which there are irregular references to a school, usually conducted by the sick comforter. In 1671 Commissioner Goske mentioned 12 slave children as being at school, 9 of whom had white fathers, and regarded their education as a 'pious work', 'so that these children may above all not be alienated and remain in slavery all their lives, no, but may in due course acquire the freedom to which they have been born on their fathers' side'.[205] The following year Alexander Carpius, an educated man from Meurs (Mörs) in the indeterminate frontier area between the Netherlands and the German-speaking regions, arriving at the Cape as a freeburgher, was immediately employed by the authorities as a sick comforter, and was reported to have shown 'great industry' in teaching the slave children.[206]

The situation as regards schools and schooling at the Cape remained unsatisfactory, however, and Commissioner Verburch remarked in 1676 'that thus far no fixed schools have been established here to teach the young people reading and writing and to educate them in Christian virtues, which in a commonwealth are generally termed the nurseries of the State.'[207] The schoolmaster he appointed was to instruct the children of the 'poor and destitute' as well as those of the wealthier freeburghers and officials, but though his services seem to have been intended for the whites only, by the following year the 'cleverest black children' were allowed to attend the 'Dutch school' until a schoolmaster could be found for them.[208]

Van Reede during his visit in 1685, referring to the slaves, made special mention of 'the great desire for learning among these people, yea, so that one among them who had learnt something earlier, of his own volition would instruct the others'.[209] It was he who first seems to have given more than divided attention to the education of the slave children, largely because of his concern for those who had white fathers, and as a result a school was established in the Slave Lodge, teachers appointed and all children under twelve obliged to attend. Older children were to spend two half days a week here to be instructed in the Christian faith and taught reading,[210] but no other slaves and no white children were to be admitted.

Van Reede also drew up a set of rules for the schoolmaster and children, with the characteristic heading, 'The Lord God and the wellbeing of the Honourable Gentlemen Directors of the East India Company is the highest law.' There were to be two sessions a day, starting at 8 in the morning and 4 in the afternoon respectively, and the master was to teach the children 'to sing psalms and to write, and let them recite their ordinary prayers every day'. He was furthermore to instruct them in the Heidelberg Catechism twice a week and teach them 'good Christian principles and manners', not tolerating any 'vile talk'. The children in turn were 'to show respect to their teacher, as well as to the Commander and other officials whom they might encounter in the street or other places'.[211]

During Van Reede's stay, the slave children, 'boys and girls, with their master and mistress', on his orders attended the Sunday church service in the hall of the Castle,[212] and he left instructions that they were to receive catechetical instruction in public after the service.[213] The local minister at the time was Johannes Overney, described by Van Reede as 'a pious minister who demonstrated great inclination to convert these people from the blind ignorant state in which they had been left to knowledge of the true God, to the honour of God's Church'.[214] He had arrived at the Cape in 1678, but died in 1687, so that he too was unable to achieve much for the slaves, however good his intentions may have been, and this seems to have been typical of the work undertaken sporadically for their evangelisation and education.

The school founded by Van Reede appears to have continued, however, and in 1688 there were said, by the Council of Policy, to be 79 children being instructed 'in all Christian honour, doctrine and virtue, in reading, sewing and other arts, while we take equal pains with the education of the infants to the number of 19'.[215] The catechetical instruction also seems to have been kept up, and in 1710 white and slave children attended the Sunday afternoon catechism service together, where members of both groups might be asked to answer questions.[216] It was also decided to examine them all on Christmas Day each year in 'reading, writing, ciphering and the Articles of the Faith', although a distinction was made as regards the prizes. The freeborn would receive pens or money and each would be given a 'sweet cake', while the slave children would receive the cakes only.[217]

Subsequently the Council of Policy gave orders that the girls were to be taught 'all forms of handiwork common in the fatherland, particularly the sewing of linen and woollen clothing' and were to work for members of the Council free of charge, but might keep whatever money they earned in this way elsewhere, 'on condition that they use it wisely for their own clothing and necessities'.[218]

Inside the Lodge any number of languages may have been in use at any given moment, as slaves from the same region would naturally have communicated in their own tongue. Those from the Indonesian archipelago may have known Malay, the modern *Bahasa Indonesia*, though according to Franken the first example of interpreting from Malay in the Cape courts took place in 1713.[219] It is known that some use was also made of Portuguese during the early years, and the Khoi interpreter Krotoa (Eva) was able to pick it up, for example, probably from slaves from the East, where a form of it was widely spoken.

By 1696, where three convicts from the Indonesian archipelago were attached to the *Zwaag* as interpreters, all three were said to speak Malay, Portuguese and Dutch, as well as various local languages'.[220] The description of their linguistic abilities gives a fascinating insight into the way in which the multifaceted world of the East was represented at the Cape:

Aje of Clompong speaks Malay, Lampoender, Bima, Sambauwe, Tambora, Taey, Sanger, Macassar, Javanese, Portuguese and Dutch; Moegadua of Macassar speaks Macassar, Boni, Malay and Javanese, Goenouw[,] Ambonese, Portuguese and Dutch;[221] and Jongman of Bali speaks Javanese, Malay, Balinese, Portuguese and Dutch.[222]

These individuals cannot have been completely unique, though none of these local languages was able to maintain itself at the Cape.

According to Kolb, who spoke from experience, it was always possible to make oneself understood at the Cape in Dutch, and Europeans might best learn Portuguese or Malay in addition, 'which languages are spoken not only here, but almost in the whole East Indies'.[223]

As far as Portuguese is concerned, however, the VOC was anxious not to introduce the language of its main commercial rival into the settlement, and even before the arrival of the first large shipments of slaves Rijckloff van Goens warned Van Riebeeck to 'take care that the Portuguese language is not introduced here, and prevent this in every possible way'.[224] It was only after a significant number of slaves from India and Indonesia had been established at the Cape at a later stage that Malay and a form of Portuguese gained the importance as a common means of communication which they are both known to have enjoyed during the eighteenth century.[225]

There is evidence that a number of whites at the Cape also knew either Portuguese or Malay, at any rate sufficiently to be able to follow the arguments in court cases in later years and act as interpreters.[226] Officials and interpreters able to speak Malagasy became essential as slaves from Madagascar started arriving in large numbers in the 1670s, and according to Franken it was first used in a court case in 1706.[227]

The official language of the VOC, however, was Dutch, which it also used in its dealings with its slaves, and in his Memorandum for his successor in 1662 Van Riebeeck emphasised, 'The slaves here learn nothing but Dutch and so too the Hottentoos, so that no other language is spoken here'.[228] Prayer services held in the Lodge were conducted in Dutch, and the children were taught it at school and learned their catechism in it: Van Reede refers to the latter in 1685 as 'speaking the Dutch language without exception'.[229]

This was probably the main factor in the propagation of this language among the slaves, and while the Company obtained its slaves largely from Madagascar, and this group was sizeable enough to be able to preserve its own language in the Lodge, the increasing group of halfbreeds used Dutch among themselves.[230] They would have grown up possibly understanding but not speaking the languages of their respective parents, which would thus have died out within a generation or two, leaving only scattered fragments behind.

By the age of twelve slave children normally joined the adult slaves who made up the labour force of the Company. Working hours were from early in the morning, presumably from daylight in the winter months, with a break between 11 and 1 o'clock, until 6, when they were allowed to fetch water 'and other necessities for themselves' before being locked up in the Lodge.[231]

For the greater part the slaves would, during this early period, have been common labourers or assistants to the Company's white artisans, as has already been indicated with reference to the Angolan and Guinean slaves. The Castle, begun in 1665, was largely built with white labour; but by 1674 so many of the Company's slaves were occupied with the final stages of the work that Khoikhoi had to be hired 'for a trifling wage' to carry manure from the cattle kraal to the Company's garden.[232] In this regard it is also significant that Rijckloff van Goens Jr in his capacity as visiting Commissioner, discussing further building to be done within the walls, the digging out of the moat and the levelling of the surrounding terrain, remarked in 1681 that this would give the slaves enough to do.[233]

By the time the building of a church and a residence for the Landdrost at Stellenbosch was begun in 1687, the team sent there consisted of 2 brick makers in the service of the Company, 5 Dutch *knechten* and 14 slaves, all under the supervision of the master carpenter.[234] The muster roll of 1693 lists no fewer than 103 Company slaves, 36 men and 67 women, apart from convicts, as employed on the public works, which would include building operations of this nature.

Slaves were also used to load and unload the Company's ships and carry ballast,[235] and in 1700 a list of articles to be written off includes '½ chest Surat soap stolen by the Company's slaves while being dragged from the jetty to the Castle'.[236] They are likewise known to have carried from the shore to the hospital the seamen who arrived seriously ill, usually from scurvy caused by malnutrition during the long outward voyage. Kolb gives a graphic description of male and female slaves transporting these men, 'partly on their backs and partly on light planks',[237] although hammocks were also used.[238] After the hospital was transferred from the vicinity of the shore to the new building at the top of the Heerengracht, opposite the Slave Lodge, Kolb adds, 'that especially when there are many sick, a strong guard is posted along the route to see to it that the sick are not robbed; which otherwise could happen very easily, and the distance from the shore to the hospital is very great and each sick man lying on a bed is carried by four men or women'.[239]

At any given moment a large group of slaves was also employed in the Company's garden, where in 1657 20 white men had been at work, although Van Goens thought at the time that 13 would be sufficient.[240] In 1693 there were no fewer than 42 slaves here, and by 1708 Commissioner Simons remarked in his report, 'It is incomprehensible why 72 male and female slaves are employed in the garden, since the vegetables delivered from it do not cover one-tenth of what their labour is worth.'[241] As late as 1789, according to official statistics, 34 men and 14 women were still posted in the garden.[242] The 1693 census also lists slaves working in the stables, the smithy, the apothecary's shop and the kitchen of the hospital.

Female slaves appear to have been used mostly for domestic, garden and field work, the former including laundry work, and when the return fleet visited the Cape early in 1713, it was they who were first stricken with smallpox by means of infected laundry sent ashore. The beginning of the epidemic which ravaged the Cape in that year was recorded in the Journal on 9 April, the day before the departure of the fleet.[243] Women could equally serve as labourers, however, as appears from the examples quoted above. In Batavia 31 women were employed in 1685–86 'on the ships, in carrying sand, lime, bricks and the like', while 224 were working 'with the masons, diggers and other labourers'.[244]

An idea of the range of activities entrusted to slaves is given by the fact that when the possible replacement of slave labour by whites was being considered in 1717, it was stated that the approximately 250 white workmen required to replace them would have to have knowledge of 'gardening, digging and weeding'; 'carrying of bricks, mixing of lime, etc.'; 'quarrying; brick-making'; 'discharging and shipping cargo, working in storehouses, at jetties and sailors' work'; and 'working with rakes, wheel-barrows, shovels, spades and scythes'. [245]

While the majority of the Company slaves were used as common labourers, there were also a number, however, with more special-ised tasks and duties. In 1710 the cook in the hospital was stated to have two slaves as assistants, and the following year the presence of 16 slaves was approved 'for the comfort and convenience of the sick housed or arriving there, as well as keeping the said hospital clean and so forth'. [246] Kolb mentions eight or ten slaves as being on duty in the hospital day and night by his time, [247] and by 1717 there were varying references to 11 men 'accustomed to attend to the sick or to help in the hospitals', [248] and 13 slaves 'who are used both to tend to and watch by the sick as for other necessary work'. [249]

A privileged position among the Company slaves was probably occupied by those who were assigned to the households of the senior officials, as was customary since Van Goens's visit in 1657, the exact numbers being determined by the status of the officials con-cerned and by the availability of slaves.

When Simon van der Stel started reducing his household in the Castle in 1686 after his sons had grown up and left home and he himself had begun farming at Constantia, three halfbreed women who had been in his service since his arrival at the Cape were due to return to the Lodge. [250] The slaves Jan Figoredo and Pintura van Ceylon, who had served as his butler and cook respectively, were at the same time manumitted on account of their good service, 'but on the condition that during the presence of the [Governor-]General or members of the Council of India, or on occasion of any public banquets, they shall remain available to be used in the service of the Hon. Company'.[251] In 1693 Van der Stel, who by this time was living mainly on Constantia, officially had only 2 halfbreed men and 2 female *bandieten* or convicts in his service,

Among the perquisites of the Governor early in the following century, Valentijn listed a monthly allowance of rice, flour, mutton, olive oil, vinegar, brandy, wine, beer, butter, wax and tallow candles, salt meat or bacon, 20 pounds of spices and 31 loads of firewood, to which he added, 'The male and female slaves needed for his house with their food and clothing, gratis'.[252] W.A. van der Stel who, unlike his father in his later years, had a young family, stated rather vaguely, 'That is his quality as Governor of the Cape he had in his service, like all other commanders in all the Company's possessions, about 20 male and female slaves, who were the property of the Company, and certainly necessary for all kinds of work and house service in such a large dominion as that of the Company.'[253] In 1710, under Governor Van Assenburgh, who was unmarried, there were 8 slaves in the Governor's house.[254]

According to the census of 1693 no fewer than 11 senior Company officials each had the use of one or two slaves, including the Landdrost of Stellenbosch, who occupied an official residence in the small village, and Pierre Simond, minister of the Drakenstein congregation, who farmed at Banghoek in the district. By 1710 all Slotsboo mentioned in his report to Van Hoorn was, in dramatic contrast, 2 slaves each placed with the 'chief administrator', the dispenser and the Landdrost of Stellenbosch,[255] although in the circumstances this may have been a question of deliberate under-reporting.

In addition there were also slaves stationed on several of the outposts which had over the years been established by the Company outside the Table Valley. The latter served mainly for agricultural purposes and as cattle posts, to supply the constant demand for cattle, sheep, garden produce and wheat for the Company's own wants and more especially those of visiting ships.[256] As virtually nothing is known about Company slaves outside the Lodge in the Table Valley, some information on these outposts may conveniently be given here.

In 1656 Van Riebeeck first had wheat sown in a sheltered spot at Rondebosch in the Liesbeek valley, at some distance from the Fort, and the Company's operations here and at the adjoining Newlands increased over the following years. Vegetable gardens, orchards and vineyards were laid out, and in 1657 a barn (the subsequent Groote Schuur) was erected where wheat could be threshed, cleaned, placed in sacks and loaded on wagons under cover. By 1666, 25 white men and 'a large number of male and female slaves' were said to be stationed at De Schuur, and the Company's wagons and draught oxen were kept here as well in order to be close to the wheat fields and the forests where the woodcutters worked.[257] The post provided 500 wagonloads of manure annually to the garden in the Table Valley.[258]

This was followed by the erection at Rondebosch of the house later to be called Rustenburg, which soon developed into the official country residence of the Commanders and Governors. Slaves are described as working in the vineyards and irrigating the vegetable garden and the orchard at Rustenburg,[259] and female slaves as weeding the cornfields.[260] In the census of 1693, 5 men and 6 women were listed here, which by 1727 had increased to 25 and 8 respectively. Some idea of the latter's daily lives and their back-breaking work is given by the equipment listed at the same time: spades, shovels, hoes, pick-axes, bushel baskets, vine cutter's knives, axes, crowbars, pitchforks, wheelbarrows, buckets, watering cans and mole traps.[261] At Newlands in the same year there were 25 men and 15 women.[262]

Meanwhile, from about 1679 the role of De Schuur changed and it was used entirely as transport centre, where 23 wagon drivers and 7 cattle herdsmen were listed by 1705,[263] although the presence of slaves is mentioned incidentally at a later stage.[264] By 1719 more definite figures are available, giving 28 whites, 4 slaves, 414 draught oxen and 19 wagons.[265] It was mostly responsible for supplying the

Cape with wood, timber and firewood from the mountain forests, and brushwood and stumps from the Cape Flats. For want of an alternative the latter were much used at the Cape, and Mentzel describes the bushes found on the Flats as 'excellent fire-wood'. 'Freshly dug out roots burn like turf or charcoal, while those that are dry burn with a flame and give out much heat.'[266]

The census of 1693 lists 2 slaves and 2 *bandieten* 'in the forest' and a single slave woman 'at Paradise', the latter referring to Het Paradijs or 'The Paradise' at the back of Table Mountain. Here Simon van der Stel in 1688 planted 40 000 oak trees on land immediately adjoining the existing indigenous forest in the mountain ravines from which the Cape had obtained its wood since the early years.[267] In 1693 he planted a further 24 000 young oaks on the mountain slopes above the house at Rustenburg,[268] and it is for his tree-planting that he is largely remembered still. However, while this is the way in which events are normally recorded and recalled, it would be more correct to say that Van der Stel took the initiative, made the decisions, gave the orders and deserves much of the credit. Here as in all similar cases it must be borne in mind that the work of actually clearing and preparing the ground and transporting and planting the trees was done by labourers, who by this stage of the colony's development would for a good if not the greater part have been slaves.

The workmen at Het Paradijs seem to have led an isolated, semi-independent life with a communal kitchen,[269] which explains the presence there of a single slave woman. There were also scattered camps of woodcutters in the forests around Hout Bay over the years, where 6 slaves from Malabar absconded with their axes in 1677,[270] and at the post where the master woodcutter lived with three men there is likewise mention of a single female slave,[271] who would similarly have been needed to cook for them.

The Company outpost at Hottentots-Holland was situated on a fertile plain to the east of the Cape Peninsula, near the shores of False Bay and at the foot of the Hottentots-Holland mountains. It had been acquired for the VOC in 1672 by means of its highly dubious treaties with local Khoikhoi. It was used as a convenient resting place for cattle-bartering expeditions sent to the Khoi tribes of the Overberg beyond the mountains, and slaves stationed here were usually called upon to help carry the baggage of these expeditions up the steep mountainside. The cattle kept here were often attacked by wild animals, while Van Reede mentions seeing large troops of buck in the vicinity. Wheat was also sown and wagonloads of hay regularly dispatched to the Cape.

It was decided early in 1677 to send a number of slaves recently acquired from Madagascar to work at Hottentots-Holland, this being more economical than the use of the Company's soldiers who had been employed on agriculture up to now, and the decision may well be seen as signalling the official change-over from white to slave labour. Orders were also given to erect accommodation for them.[272] When the land was subsequently let to freeburghers for a short period, the Company undertook to hire out 12 male and 12 female slaves to them and allow them to employ as much additional white labour for the harvest as required.[273] In 1688 there were 9 male and 6 female slaves at the post,[274] and five years later they had remained much the same, 8 and 6 respectively.

Van Reede during his tour of inspection found the post house at Hottentots-Holland a 'miserable building consisting of two rooms under a thatched roof', and mentioned in addition 'four or five slave huts ["slaevenkotten"]', a large barn and a number of cattle enclosures, 'suitable enough, but rude and rough'. 'A garden with a vineyard and some cabbages and vegetables was all that was to be found here apart from the wheat fields.'[275]

The outpost Klapmuts, further in the interior, between Stellenbosch and Drakenstein, was established in 1683 as a cattle post and wheat farm, where Van der Stel subsequently also had trees planted on a large scale.[276] Van Reede found 120 of the 400 to 500 morgen under cultivation two years later, an 'extremely long barn' which also served as a dwelling for the postholder, and a cattle enclosure. Besides the postholder and 8 white knechten, there were no fewer than 46 slaves and convicts busy clearing the ground for plough-ing.[277] In 1693 the slaves at Klapmuts numbered 11 men and 14 women, with 5 convicts. Large concentrations of slaves such as these inevit-ably encouraged large-scale attempts to escape, such as that which was planned at Klapmuts in 1687 by the harvesters, who had already collected and buried an assortment of flintlocks, pistols, swords, lead and gunpowder by the time their plot was discovered.[278]

The post at De Kuilen (Kuils River), about 25 kilometres inland from the Table Valley, was established in 1680 as a halting place for travellers to Hottentots-Holland and Stellenbosch across the Cape Flats, and at the time of Van Reede's visit it supplied most of the reeds used for thatching 'houses, barns and stables' in the vicinity of the Cape. He found a supervisor and 7 herdsmen stationed there, besides 'six male and female slaves who tend a vegetable and cabbage gar-den',[279] while in 1693 its slave complement consisted of 3 men. The cattle in the fold were often attacked at night by lions and leopards, and troops of as many as 200 wild dogs attacked and killed the sheep.[280]

The number of whites stationed at these three posts is known for 1695, the full tally at Hottentots-Holland in that year being 9 whites 'as agriculturists, cattle herdsmen and shepherds', with 11 male slaves and 10 women and children; at Klapmuts 5 whites, with 13 male slaves and 14 women and children; and at De Kuilen 9 whites and 2 male slaves. In this year a single male slave was furthermore listed at each of the posts Bommelshoek, Vissershok and Rietvallei, while there were four further posts at which no slaves were mentioned.[281]

The VOC's most outlying outpost in the seventeenth century was in the bleak and barren area around Saldanha Bay to the north of Table Bay, where the Company several times established a station with a view to fishing, seal hunting, trading cattle with the local Khoikhoi and frustrating the French in their attempts to establish a refreshment station of their own on the African coast. The number of men stationed here always seems to have been small, and slaves do not appear to have formed part of the regular establishment, although 9 slaves are mentioned as having been sent here in 1686 expressly to gather salt from the salt pan, extra rice being provided to feed them.[282] A plan for considerable improvements and extensions drawn up in 1738 but never executed made provision for a number of slaves to work in a projected hospital and gardens, man the rowing boats and catch fish.[283]

By 1789, at the end of the VOC period, when many new outposts had meanwhile been established, but a great number closed down and disposed of as well, a total of 183 male and 39 female slaves were still distributed among them.[284]

The assignment of a slave to a given task or place of work was apparently reasonably stable,[285] but could of course be altered at very short notice as needed for specific tasks. Slaves from elsewhere were for example sent to Hottentots-Holland and Klapmuts temporarily to help with ploughing and harvesting,[286] though by 1690 so many Khoikhoi offered their services in exchange for arrack and tobacco that the help of slaves could be dispensed with at the latter post.[287] In 1686 when bricks had to be made for building at Hottentots-Holland, 20 slaves were requested to chop firewood for the ovens,[288] and in the same year 8 were transferred from Klapmuts to help with the building of the drostdy at Stellenbosch.[289] The result is that statistics such as those quoted above are dependable only up to a point, and must be regarded as a general indication of how the Company disposed of its labour force rather than an exact account.

It would appear that by the turn of the century at the latest, Company slaves were on occasion also hired out to private individuals, as was customary with private slaves, and that this is what Commissioner Simons referred to in 1708 with 'the calling-in of Company's slaves used by private persons', adding, 'And Y[our] E[xcellencies] should also see to it that the[se] artisans be not exchanged for any strangers'.[290] When the Company was short of slaves, on the other hand, labourers might be hired from freeburghers: in 1718 a fee of 24 stivers (a little more than a guilder) per day was mentioned in this regard, with the corollary, 'an even then they are hardly be obtained because of their scarcity'.[291]

Initially the slaves served merely as mechanical labourers and factotums to the whites, but they would have been given such instruction as they required in order to perform their various tasks, and in individual cases would probably also have received some degree of informal in-service training. In practice certain of them may thus have become as proficient as their masters and supervisors. Van Reede, however, urged in 1685 that halfbreed slaves formally be taught trades with a view to their future manumission and the fact that they could replace the more expensive white labour in various ways, mentioning as examples 'tailors, shoemakers, smiths, carpenters, wheelmakers, herdsmen, builders, woodsmen, gardeners and whatever else might be to the general advantage here'.[292]

Whether this was done in any purposeful manner may perhaps be doubted, but as they became more proficient, individual slaves were given relatively more responsible work. When four white servants of the Company were sent to the Overberg by W.A. van der Stel to construct a palisade on one of his cattle posts, they were accompanied by 'one of the Hon. Company's slaves, named Ley (as wagon driver)',[293] and in 1710 Andries Barendse, who had been born in the Lodge of a slave mother, was on his manumission immediately employed by the Company as a mason.[294] Nevertheless C.J. Simons, visiting the Cape as Commissioner about the same time, could make the general observation,

a point which was so strongly ordered in the Instruction of H.E. the Lord van Meydrecht [*Van Reede*] has not yet been put into force, namely to use the slaves as waggon-drivers for the Company, first accompanied by Europeans and later in pairs without them, which [I believe] would have been done long since, had it not been neglected for private ends, since if the Freemen can let thrice as heavy loads of firewood be brought by their slaves, why not the Company also?'[295]

While the work of the Company's slaves was hard, monotonous and mechanical, men with knowledge of other languages could be placed arbitrarily on passing ships to serve as interpreters, as has already been mentioned in the case of the slave trade with Madagascar. When the *Zwaag* was dispatched from Amsterdam in 1696 to investigate the mysterious 'South Land' (Australia), instructions were likewise given that 'should there be any slaves at the Cape born in the South land or the neighbourhood, resembling in colour or form the natives of that country, and acquainted with the Portuguese or any other language, to send them with the ship as interpreters, with the promise of emancipation and reward'.[296] Three convicts were duly attached to the ship, and on reaching Batavia on the *Zwaag* at the end of the voyage were set free. However, the Cape informed the Council of India that Jongman van Bali 'has entreated us to ask you to let him return to the Cape, as he has a wife and children here, and when liberated will be able to support himself'.[297]

Female slaves could similarly be assigned to passengers on the return ships who had not brought slaves of their own with them and required the assistance of a slave in some unforeseen emergency, in spite of the ban placed on this by the authorities.

A former Governor-General like Joan van Hoorn was naturally a law unto himself, and when he returned to the Netherlands in 1710 with his wife and stepdaughter, they took with them 3 male and 2 female slaves, as well as a Chinese physician, though their cook, 'the *jongen* Juni', was sent back to Batavia from the Cape with '2 gunny bags of rice, 1 small basket of onions, 12 salted fish, for him to eat on the voyage as he is used to eating rice'.[298] When in 1689 vice-admiral Wouter Zeeman of the return fleet paid the local authorities 'for his male and female slaves whom he was permitted to take with him to the fatherland' this likewise seems to refer to his own slaves from Batavia, but at the same time the bookkeeper Jan Gaspar Lagenbergh was able to obtain the services of the female slave Calamatacke from the authorities at the Cape on depositing her fare with them and 'on condition that he places a slave in the Company's Lodge in return'.[299] What was eventually to happen to Calamtacke is not clear.

Similarly the Journal noted in 1707: 'The widow of the late artillery major, Christoffel Wild, being in poor circumstances and lame, is allowed to take a female slave with her free of expense': '(As she is a helpless widow)' is probably an explanatory note added by Leibbrandt in his English translation of the text.[300] Here too the reference appears to be to a slave brought from Batavia and being allowed to continue her journey with her mistress as a favour. As against this, when the wife of the skipper Steeven Scheideruijt was, in 1711, 'on account of her indisposition, inclined to take the girl ("*meijt*") Marie (…) to the Fatherland with her, in order to receive assistance from her during the voyage', the reference was to a local woman, the Company slave Marie or Maria Stuart van de Caab. The expenses involved would be paid, and a 'boy ("*jonge*") called Tandewa', probably a slave brought by the Scheijderuijts from Batavia, left to serve in her place.[301] This was 'gladly' accepted by the Council, 'as there is at present a serious shortage of male slaves ("*jongens*"), in addition to which it so happens that he has always done gardening'. After three years Tandewa was to be returned to Batavia 'in full freedom', while Maria Stuart would presumably be sent back from the Netherlands.[302]

When a senior Cape official returned to Europe with his family after the expiry of his term of office, the same arrangements were most likely made, and so too when freeburghers repatriated, although this occurred less often and they were frequently not able to afford the expense involved. A notable exception in this regard would have been the widow of the wealthy Henning Hüsing, who repatriated with some female relatives in 1718, but her arrangements are unknown.

When Johanna Wessels, widow of Frans van der Stel, who had been recalled to the Netherlands together with his brother, the former Governor, left the Cape herself in 1717, she received permission to take with her two chests 5 feet long by 2 feet wide and high, 'as also a female slave, on condition that she pay transport and board money for the outward and return journey'.[303] When Johanna Constantia Elsevier, wife of the Revd Beck of Stellenbosch and daughter of a former Secunde, left her husband to return to the Netherlands four years later, she was allowed to take female slave, Catharina van Macassar, on the same conditions, together with one similar chest, 'one clothing chest ["*plunje kist*"] and one cellaret with 12 bottles'.[304]

Apart from the 'debauchery' of the slave women decried by the authorities from time to time, little is known of the existence of the slaves outside working hours. They sometimes received small amounts of money as a gift or reward, and could occasionally earn modest sums, as in the case of girls from the Lodge with their needlework. In 1675 Governor Goske informed his successor that a piece of ground in the Table Valley set aside to be planted with fruit trees 'had meanwhile been granted to the Company's slaves, to level and cultivate outside working hours and sow for their own benefit until circumstances permit the Company to take possession of it again':[305] the produce was possibly sold. In 1709 again, the Journal refers to Company slaves 'who on Sundays or at other times, by labour or fishing, know how to earn a penny and so provide themselves properly with clothes',[306] with the implication, presumably, that the Company itself had failed to do so.

Slaves also had various other ways of acquiring small sums of money, and with reference to the rules governing the Company's garden in the Table Valley, which was open to the public, Valentijn writes, for example, that 'there are many slave-spies everywhere who well know how to keep watch. However, one very seldom hears of any (…) [infringement], and if by bad luck anyone ever happens [to be detected], such an imprudent person will prefer to give a bribe to the slaves rather than expose himself to the wrath of the Gardener, or of the Governor.'[307]

Apart from this, the slaves had to satisfy their wants as well as they were able by bartering the little they had for what they wanted or needed even more. Their wants probably included alcohol, tobacco and food most prominently, and as early as 1677 many of the

Company's soldiers, who in this period received no uniforms, and others were said to be wearing the pilot cloth jackets issued to the slaves, obtained from them for 'a little tobacco or a handful of rice'. As this caused illness and death among the inadequately clad slaves, a *plakkaat* was issued to forbid such barter, and repeated in 1700 and 1709.[308] Often too this barter took the form of trading in stolen goods, but this was general in the world of the slaves and by no means restricted to those in the Lodge.[309]

Except for the valuable but random details supplied by Kolb, information on life inside the walls of the Slave Lodge during the early decades of its existence must be extrapolated from Slotsboo's report of 1710, and the regulations drawn up in 1716, which most likely consolidated the situation as it had developed up to then.

The Fiscal or public prosecutor had overall responsibility for the Lodge, and Shell mentions a 'commissioner of the Company slaves' under him at a later stage, which probably refers to the office of what was also called *oppermandoor*.[310] According to Kolb a house for the superintendent of the slaves formed part of the Lodge complex, and it was situated at the eastern end, behind the kitchen and the square courtyard of the building occupied two gardeners, but he seems not to have lived here.[311] He was assisted by 'two upper foremen' or *mandoors* who were Europeans.[312]

In 1685 Van Reede appointed as supervisors of the slaves the administrator Andries de Man, Captain Hiëronimus Cruse and the Revd Johannes Overney,[313] but how they fitted into the existing hierarchy, what their duties and powers were, and how long they constituted a distinct body, is not clear.

Lieutenant Kaje Jesse Slotsboo, a Dane, was appointed *oppermandoor* of the Company's slaves in 1707, a post of which he was relieved three years later when he had become too heavily burdened with other duties.[314] In 1677 and 1678 respectively Seuren Seurensz (Sören Sörens), likewise a Dane, and Jacob Stevensz are mentioned as 'supervisors of the Company's slaves', presumably in the sense of *mandoors*,[315] and Seurensz was also referred to by Governor Goske in his Memorandum for his successor, in which he was described as 'a fine honest man who can speak the Madagascan language quite fluently'.[316] Two Dutchmen, Lambert Jansz and Jan Albertsz Brons, are listed as *mandoors* in the muster roll for 1705,[317] and in 1708 the former sent a power of attorney to the Netherlands for drawing his salary or other money there.[318] He seems to have died in 1710, on which occasion his surname was given as Broens, and to have been a well-to-do man in possession of a considerable quantity of gold and silver, two houses and a slave woman and her child, though the estate was heavily in debt.[319]

External and internal matrons or 'mothers' ('*buijten en binnen moeders*') for the Lodge are mentioned as early as 1687.[320] As in the case of the hospital, the former were probably the wives of officials or other white women with a supervisory function, and the latter privileged slaves actually living in the Lodge,[321] although the office of *buitenmoeder* seems to have lapsed. Other white personnel appear to have been added in the course of time, and in 1716, for example, the German Burchard Heinrich Brand, who had arrived at the Cape as a soldier a few years before, is mentioned as 'clerk in the slave lodge'.[322]

Under the white *mandoors* there were a number of coloured officials, male and female, who were slaves themselves and lived in the Lodge, and these *officiers* and *officierses*, as they were called, occupied a privileged position in the slave hierarchy. So it was decided in 1710, for example, to issue the 'black *mandoors*' with double rations, 'except for rice and bread',[323] while the lists of clothing dated 1720–21 likewise provide extra rations for *officiers* and *officierses*, the latter being distinguished from the *werkmeiden* and *schoolmeiden*, 'working females' and 'schoolgirls'.[324] In most if not all cases they appear to have been halfbreeds.[325]

Immediately under the two whites were the coloured *mandoors*, the most notable example being Sijmon de Arabier, who served the Company in the 1670s, although he enjoyed special status at the

Cape and did not live in the Lodge. By the time of Slotsboo's report in 1710 they seem to have been nine in number,[326] and to have been responsible for internal discipline in the Lodge.[327]

A good deal of random information is available on Johannes Kemp, 'the former convict and mestiço [*halfbreed*] burgher from Batavia', who was sent to the Cape in 1688 from Ceylon but appointed *mandoor* by Simon van der Stel in 1693 after his term of banishment had ended.[328] In 1699 and again in 1703 he transmitted money to the Netherlands, on which occasion he was variously described as 'headman over the slaves' and '*mandoor*',[329] and in 1710 he was allowed at his own request to return to Batavia, 'on condition that he will work on board for his keep'.[330]

Especially prominent among the officials in the Lodge besides the *mandoors* were the schoolmaster and -mistress.

After the institution of a school for the slave children by Van Reede in 1685, Jan Pasquaal and Margriet van de Caab were appointed as the first teachers.[331] 'That same year,' Upham reports, 'Margaretha married a prominent free burgher and relocated to the new colony at Stellenbosch',[332] while Pasquaal by 1687 had been accused of succumbing to 'vile unchastity and fleshly lusts' with various of the schoolgirls.[333] In the context of the charges against him, he was described as a 'black *bandiet* [*convict*] who was scourged and branded in Batavia and publicly exhibited below the gallows with the halter around his neck, and banished from there for ever',[334] and he was now sentenced to be banished to Mauritius in turn.[335]

Pasquaal was replaced by Claas Cornelisz van de Caab, a halfbreed slave who was described as 'a person of good comportment and the required competence', and who was to receive 3 reals a month in addition to food and clothing.[336] By 1691 he had in turn been succeeded by Daniel Rodrigo, who would appear also to have been a convict from Batavia like his predecessor Pasquaal,[337] and who was still in office as late as 1707.[338]

Klein Armozijn van de Caab (Armozijn Claasz), the sister of Claas Cornelisz, was listed as a schoolmistress by 1693, and after her manumission early in the following century she was succeeded by her daughter Manda Gratia van de Caab.[339] This was the office of *matres*, a title commonly used for a schoolmistress at the time,[340] but in practice the female teacher also seems to have acquired the status of a matron. The plans for an enlarged building drawn up in 1717 provide accommodation not only for 'commissioners or supervisors', 'Dutch *mandoors*', and 'native *mandoors* and schoolmasters', but also for a '[school] mistress and matron of the sick', who appears to have been a single individual.[341]

According to Slotsboo, the schoolmaster and -mistress by 1710 each received 2 reals a month as ration money in addition to the customary slave rations,[342] while Kolb seems to imply that they were allowed to live in their respective schoolrooms,[343] which given the conditions in the Lodge would have been a great privilege.

By 1717 a midwife is mentioned for the Lodge as well,[344] while in the census of 1693 one Sevelin, a fullbreed male, was listed as 'cook in the slaves' quarters'.

As far as the routine of the Lodge is concerned, some information is available from the point of view of white officials viewing it from outside the gates. According to Slotsboo, when the gateway of the Castle was opened in the morning, the under-gardener fetched the keys of the Lodge from the Fiscal and the Lodge was unlocked 'at 6 o'clock precisely', after which the slaves were counted 'outside the Lodge at the usual mustering place', and the *mandoors* sent out with their working parties. After work they returned to the Lodge, and at 8 'the bell in the Lodge is rung and the rattle sounded, and after evening prayers the roll called by the *mandoors* and the gate locked, and the keys are returned by the under-gardener to His Honour the Independent Fiscal with a report on absentees'.[345]

This obviously proved insufficient, and in 1716, under a new Governor, Maurits Pasques de Chavonnes, concern was expressed at the lack of discipline in the Lodge, and the fact that soldiers and sailors were allowed to stay there and lights and fires lit overnight. Regulations for the Lodge ('*een reglementje nopende de huijshoudinge door s. Comps. slaven in de logie'*) were therefore promulgated on 17 November, consisting of five articles.[346] The most important change was that the assistant of the Fiscal, the provost-marshal (*geweldiger provoost*), was now required to call the roll at eight o'clock each evening, to inspect the building to ensure that no lights or fires were burning except in the kitchen, and to lock it, handing the key to the under-gardener for delivery to the Fiscal in the Castle. The slave *mandoors*, who remained in the Lodge overnight with the other slaves, were enjoined to maintain discipline there and to report any irregularities in the morning.

Implicit statements as to the quality of life inside the Lodge after the locking of the gates are rare, and violent incidents have not been preserved in the records of the Council of Justice as is the case with regard to slaves in private ownership. As Shell remarks, 'The implication is that the Lodge inmates dealt with such matters themselves.'[347]

The inevitably violent nature of life in the Lodge is probably illustrated well enough by a single incident which has been recorded because it was brought to the attention of the Council of Policy and preserved in its minutes for May 1686. According to a statement made in this connection, the recent miscarriage suffered by a slave woman in the Lodge was to be attributed to 'the severe beating (…) which one of the Hon. Company's slaves had given her, plucking her from her sleeping place and mistreating her by beating and hitting her until her husband had come to the aid of his pregnant wife'.[348] This may explain why the Council during the same time decided to manumit three baptised halfbreed female slaves whose services were no longer required in the Commander's house, 'as these unfortunate people could not without the utmost danger be returned to the Company's slave house and among these uncouth and heathen peoples.[349] As the Commander, Simon van der Stel, was himself particularly interested in these manumissions, it may also explain why the incident was brought to the Council's attention in the first place.

The incident may likewise help to explain two further decisions made by the Council early the following year:

Whereas Paul van de Caab, aged one and a half years, son of Hector, slave of the Hon. Captain Hieronijmus Cruse, and of Maria van Madagascar, a slave of the Hon. Company, has since his birth been kept and brought up in the house of the said Hon. Captain and by his father up to the present; it is therefore understood, considering what he would cost the Hon. Company before he would be in a condition to serve it, also as regards the education of the child, who will succeed better in the care of his father than that of his mother, to grant him his full freedom.

It is also been understood to grant to François of Macao, manumitted slave, at his iterated request, that his son Bartholomeus, aged three years, procreated by the Company slave Cingala van Madagascar, be allowed to follow him from the Company's slave house in a state of freedom.[350]

Nothing is known about the possible contacts of François van Macao, but Hiëronimus Cruse was a member of the Council which took the decision on little Paul van de Caab, and it is obvious that he influenced it just as much as Van der Stel did that concerning the three slave women some eight months earlier.

On the whole the Company's slaves did not have a good reputation, and W.A. van der Stel early in the eighteenth century stated heatedly,

That he was often very badly served in his house by these same slaves of the Company, and would have been much better served, more honestly and cleanlily, by the best of his own slaves. That in consequence he took for housework [in the Governor's residence] on some occasions some of his own best slaves, who during the night were not taken to the Slave

Lodge, in order not to be spoiled by [that] crowd of dirty and stinking creatures.[351]

'The slaves belonging to the Company are undoubtedly the most rascally of all,' declared Mentzel in similar terms some thirty years later, although he added in all fairness:

They also receive the worst treatment. Their food is scanty and coarse; their weekly dole of tobacco is often kept back. It would be dangerous to give them the slightest latitude; a tight hold must always be kept on the reins; the taskmaster's lash is the main stimulus for getting any work out of them. Those slaves who are privately owned are, with few exceptions, much better treated and more amendable to good treatment.[352]

It was in these circumstances that halfbreed slaves were able to attract favourable attention and to enjoy such limited advantages as they possessed, being locally born, partly Europeanised and Dutch-speaking, in contrast to the imported slaves, whether from Angola, Guinea, Bengal or Madagascar. Shell, basing his research on the Company's slave holdings in 1693, finds halfbreeds occupying all supervisory positions, while 'in the clerical category, full-breeds outnumbered mulattos by two to one, but in all the other "soft" occupation categories the mulattos are present in a greater proportion than one would expect from a random distribution of descent and occupation.'[353]

According to Mentzel, by whose time several generations of mixed-breed slaves had already been born in the Lodge, 'these slave children are found useful at a very tender age and cost little to bring up. They are likewise better-mannered and better educated than imported slaves. Some of them are taught certain trades and become skilled artisans.'[354]

While the slave officials in the Lodge possessed only limited authority over their fellow slaves and those specifically in their charge, there was a further category of Company slaves who likewise possessed a certain status in local society in general. They were the assistants to the Fiscal or public prosecutor who were known as *caffers* and served in practice as a local police force.

In Batavia the department of the advocate-fiscal included 8 male slaves, later increased to 14, who acted as *caffers* or assistants to the sheriff, and who by the end of the century were paid 3 rixdollars a month. They are described as 'muscular negroes from Angola or Mozambique', and were thus literally men from the interior of Africa, as their name suggests, and foreigners within the Eastern society in which they operated. There were many complaints about their behaviour, especially by white inhabitants, which led to an attempt at restriction in 1670.[355] Reference is made to the 'half-gallows and whipping posts' opposite the *caffers*' quarters where they were able to execute summary justice, and similar posts in public places elsewhere in the town.[356]

At the Cape the earliest reference to these slave officers occurs in the Journal entry in 1667 which describes how a Khoi 'convicted of housebreaking, theft and other crimes, was sentenced to be whipped by the "Caffers", and transported to Robben Island to gather shells there'.[357] Early next year the same source records the execution of a number of white mutineers on a visiting ship: 'Five were hanged, and seven were scourged and branded. As we had no executioner, the work was done pretty well by our Provost and Caffers.'[358]

The *caffers* were responsible in general for arresting delinquents, administering summary chastisement to slaves, and helping to execute official punishments.[359] 'A high proportion of the sentences handed down by the Court of Justice,' writes Shell, 'ended with the words "to be handed over to the executioner and to be beaten by the Caffers".'[360] They also had various other official and semi-official duties, and in legislation issued in 1686, for example, the Fiscal 'assisted by his Caffers', together with the *klapperman* ('rattle watch') or night watchman, was instructed to supervise the extinguishing of fires in the Table Valley.[361]

The office of *caffers* was filled by Company slaves, and the muster roll of 1693 lists 6 *Caffers van de Justitie*, who are all described as fullbreeds, and judging by their names were all Guinean slaves, therefore likewise '*caffers*' in the literal sense of the term as it was used at the time, namely non-Muslim natives of Africa. In 1709 there is a reference to 'Jan Roscam, Company slave, "kaffir" at Stellenbosch. Helps slaves escape from prison. Whipped, branded on right cheek, chained for 20 years.'[362] It may be worth mentioning that while the slave's ostensible Dutch nickname is derived from *roskammen*, meaning to curry a horse, the word can also have the extended meaning of beating or belabouring;[363] although it was equally a Dutch surname not unknown at the Cape.[364] In 1728 the *caffer* here was called Janever, which seems equally to have been a surname or nickname (*jenever*—'juniper' or 'gin').[365]

While nothing can be deduced about these individuals' origins from their names and nicknames, from at least 1713, if not earlier, *caffers* with Dutch or Eastern names were used in Cape courts to interpret Portuguese and Malay.[366] Where toponyms are given, these are invariably of Eastern origin, such as Ibrahim van Batavia,[367] Boetjoe van Boegies,[368] and Meij van Boegies,[369] the name of Benjamin van Malacca recurring frequently over the period 1763–71.[370] Elsewhere the names of Sacodien van Java and Said van Java are mentioned in the same period, and even that of a Chinese, Oensien van Tantjoeng,[371] but the old name *caffers* with its African associations was retained, although it no longer indicated race but solely office.

In this context it is interesting to note that a list of '*Justitie kaffers*' issued in 1804, under the short-lived regime of the Batavian Republic, gives 16 names, in addition to those of two warders and the hangman and his assistant, but while no toponyms are provided, as far as can be distinguished all of them are likewise of Eastern origin.[372]

The *caffers* were the only non-whites at the Cape, and above all the only slaves, who had any authority whatsoever with regard to whites. Moreover, they alone of all slaves and *bandieten* were armed, and Adam Tas early in the eighteenth century writes disparagingly about a sword he received from his uncle Henning Hüsing, 'it resembles a hangman's sword', the original Dutch referring more explicitly to '*een kaffers zijdgeweer*'.[373] Mentzel refers in this connection to 'a sword with an iron hilt' and 'a "palang" or heavy club'.[374] The *caffers* in Batavia are said to have been dressed in red,[375] and by Mentzel's time those at the Cape likewise wore a rudimentary uniform, which he describes.

Isbrand Goske, visiting the Cape as Commissioner in 1671, shortly before becoming Governor, stipulated that the Company's slaves should be recorded in the bookkeeping system individually with their names, places of origin and children, not as mere totals, and entered monthly, with the number of children updated every six months.[376] Commissioner Abbema, however, visiting the Cape nine years later, found no adequate record, 'not only of the slaves, but also the horses, asses and other articles of trade', and feared that this would enable the supervisors and administrators of the slaves to enrich themselves, 'selling the latter to passing ships'.[377]

In 1685 Van Reede once more left instructions that the Company's slave holdings be recorded as part of the elaborate bookkeeping system of the VOC, and a record kept of marriages, births and deaths. On the same occasion he stipulated that they were not to be 'exchanged, sold or decreased in number, nor to be transported from here by anyone, regardless of his rank', the latter with reference to the custom of senior officials taking slaves on board ship with them for their own convenience during the voyage.[378]

This finally led to results as far as local records were concerned, and in December 1686 all the Company's slaves, who had been brought to the Table Valley from their various places of work by their supervisors, were listed by the Commander after the Sunday service together with the places of work to which they were assigned. The undertaking seems to have occupied three days in all, at the end of which 'the Hon. Lord Commander had the malefactors punished for their misdeeds as an example to others, urging them all most earnestly to fulfil their duties and presenting each with a piece of Mauritius tobacco'.[379] To the slaves themselves the spring excursion must have been a pleasant break in the monotonous routine of their lives.

The actual recording of the Company's gains and losses with regard to its slaves seems to have remained careless, however, and in 1708 Commissioner Simons once again issued a reprimand, reminding the authorities that the slaves should be recorded 'by name in the Company's books, in which should be added their age, and on what ship they had arrived, and in what year, which should be done [at the next survey], and in the presence of the Independent Fiscal (…)'.[380] According to H.C.V. Leibbrandt, who published an edited and translated version of the official Journal, the deaths of Company slaves were recorded in this source as from January 1720.[381] By 1724 the Council of Policy referred to the fact 'that none of the Company's slaves may by order be written off in the books unless it has previously been established by means of a proper declaration how and in what way such a slave has come to die'.[382]

The practical and businesslike spirit in which these records were kept may be illustrated from an entry in the minutes of the Council for 1717.

Furthermore [the chief administrator Abraham Cranendonk] produced a memorandum concerning some worsted and half-hourglasses found to be short, also of some slaves who had died between the first of September and the last of December, as well as some cattle which had died during the same time, all of it autheticated with declarations by deputies, with the request to be allowed to write off these goods, viz. 25 ells of blue worsted short in a piece of 84 ells, 2 half-hourglasses broken in a crate, 4 male slaves died in 3 months, 18 head of cattle died or injured by wild animals, 14 horses ditto, and 1 ass.[383]

Figures of this nature, while informative, are of limited value only, however, as the total slave holdings of the Company were liable to fluctuations which could on occasion be sudden and dramatic, taking the form of large-scale desertions, accessions of new arrivals from Madagascar or elsewhere, or epidemic diseases. As far as the Slave Lodge is concerned, however many inhabitants it may have had at any given moment and however overcrowded it may have been, the full complement of the Company's slave holdings was never lodged here at any one time, and statements with regard to the population of the Lodge are often misleading. According to Shell, 'About 85 percent of Company slaves lived in the Lodge.'[384]

Large as the Company's slave holdings may seem, they were also comparatively modest by the standards of the time and in comparison with the East, remaining 'well below 1,000 during the whole of the VOC period,' as Armstrong & Worden remark.

> The very circumscribed nature of the Company's slave population was due to the Company's realistic calculation of its labour needs. Moreover, its economic needs were fairly constant, being linked mainly to activity in the port (which expanded only slowly) and to occasional construction projects in Cape Town. The Company played only the slightest role in enterprises in the interior.[385]

According to Van Reede there were 335 Company slaves by 1685, 137 men, 106 women and 92 children under twelve, and of the latter 25 boys and 19 girls were said to be the children of 'Dutch fathers',[386] figures he subsequently raised to 32 and 26 respectively.[387]

The 'general survey and muster roll' drawn up on New Year's Day 1693 lists the names of 322 slaves and 47 convicts, grouped by their places of work, subdivided by gender and subdivided again into full- and halfbreeds.[388]

In 1710 there were 560 Company slaves according to one account,[389] and 440 according to another,[390] which may well be explained by the difference between the total slave force and the slaves housed in the Lodge.

Kolb, giving the total as 600 at about the same time, writes with much sympathy about the expense caused to the Company by its slaves: 'according to the simplest calculation, and reckoning only 50 guilders a year for each slave, although food and drink, clothing and medicines amount to a good deal more, the abovementioned 600 slaves cost 30 000 guilders per year in all'.[391] Officially, however, the 'expenses of the Company's slaves' were stated to amount to no more that 18 000 guilders, as against more than 53 000 guilders spent on 'garrison pay', almost 10 000 guilders for the hospital, and just over 1000 guilders for 'Governor's table'.[392] The official figures quoted in 1710 for the amounts spent on winter and summer clothing for the slaves run to just over 3500 and 2700 guilders respectively, making a total of almost 6300 guilders.[393]

When in 1717 the possible advantages of white labour were assessed by the Council of Policy, the Governor, Maurits Pasques de Chavonnes, declared, 'Wages would have to cover all the work to be done, not only in the fields, but also the daily work usually performed by slaves,—work, too, which could not be demanded of a European in this climate. The Company would therefore find it more useful and cheaper to keep slaves.'[394] The Secunde, Abraham Cranendonk, an experienced official of the VOC, went into greater detail on the subject, writing to the Gentlemen XVII, 'I find on examining the books for the expenses of the last five years, that every slave—adults, boys and girls—costs the Company about 40 gulden a year, including expense of clothing.' A soldier, in contrast, 'cost the Company ƒ14 odd per month and ƒ175 per year. For this sum at least four slaves could be employed, and moreover, each slave would have to serve his whole life long for the same wage whereas a European's wage would have to be raised from time to time and thus cost our Masters [the XVII] more and more.'[395]

Only Captain Dominique Pasques de Chavonnes, the Governor's nephew, strongly opposed the system of slave labour during this discussion was, and complained about the cost of 500 to 600 slaves, pointing out especially the incidental expenses of the system.

> The old slaves, the pregnant and nursing slaves, and also the children, can do practically no work, and yet, year after year, they cost the Company 23,000–27,000 guldens, exclusive of the expense occasioned by death, runaway slaves, the long sea-voyage necessary to obtain slaves, the interest on the capital, the clerk of the slaves, the overseer, the school-master, school-mistress and the midwife, for all of these involve additional expense.[396]

No essential change was ever brought about in the system, however, and by the final years of the VOC's regime it owned a total of 946 slaves, of whom 510 were housed in the Lodge, which had meanwhile been enlarged, while 291 worked elsewhere but were also housed and fed there, and 145 were stationed at various outposts.[397]

Under the British administration, write Armstrong & Worden,

> Those remaining were, in March 1811, removed from the lodge, and settled in other rented premises. In 1820 they were transferred to a new lodge in the Cape Town garden. Two years later, they numbered 'about 200 of various ages'. By 1826 their numbers had fallen to 171, and their emancipation came in 1827, several years before that of the colonists' slaves.[398]

6. The world of the slaves: the slaves of private owners

Concerning the slaves belonging to the VOC, a certain amount of generalisation is possible, as has been said; but as far as the slaves belonging to freeburghers and to Company officials in their private capacity are concerned, it is impossible to generalise. While they all inhabited the same colony and were ultimately subject to the same authority and the same laws, the condition of private slaves depended in daily practice on a multiplicity of variable factors such as the professions, social and economic status and personalities of their respective owners and the size, constitution and geographical location of the domestic communities of which they formed part.

In this regard, even more than in that of the Company's slaves, it is well to remember the admonition of Howard Temperley, writing about slavery in North America: 'One thing that is immediately apparent is that there was no such thing as "the slave experience". Slaves had many different experiences.'[1] These words must be borne in mind in reading the present book, and more particularly the chapter which follows.

As has already been shown, private slave ownership started to become general only during the 1670s, but by 1692 the total slave holdings of the freeburghers already surpassed those of the Company,[2] while from about 1710 the slaves outnumbered the freeburgher population.[3] By 31 January 1711 there were 545 white men, 337 women, 874 children and 114 white *knechten* in the colony; as against 1232 male slaves, 290 females and 249 children.[4] By 1735, to present the available figures in a slightly different way, African and Asian slaves made up 58,9% of the entire Cape population, and free white settlers 35,9%.[5] Or as Guelke & Shell summarise the implications of this development: 'By 1705 the economy of the south-western Cape was partly dependent on slave labour and in 1731 it was largely dependent on slave labour. The slave population (excluding Company slaves) grew from 1,057 in 1705 to 4,030 in 1731, an increase of 307%.'[6]

By 1717, when the Gentlemen XVII belatedly set about enquiring into the use of slave labour at the Cape, it appeared that the system was already entrenched. To the question 'Whether European farm hands and agriculturists would be less expensive than slaves', the eight members of the Council of Policy, in a series of individual replies, with a single exception replied with a decided negative,[7] the main arguments being the relative expense of white labour and the demeaning nature of the work for Europeans.[8] 'Each labourer's wage was reckoned at the rate of a soldier's pay—ƒ9 per month,' wrote the Fiscal Cornelis van Beaumont,

> for he would hardly accept less even for work done by slaves, add to this the cost of his board and further emoluments, and a great difference will be found, as a slave costs annually (everything included) about ƒ40. Set against this the fact that the emoluments of a soldier vary from 8 to 10 gulden, let alone the wages which the Company would have to pay. Further, one will not find Europeans of nearly as much use as slaves, especially in the daily menial tasks; besides it is more fitting that slaves rather than Europeans should be used.[9]

In similar terms the Junior Merchant Jan de la Fontaine remarked that 'the wages paid to a farm-labourer for a year and a half would often pay for a slave, as the usual wage of such a labourer is 15–20 guldens a months, exclusive of food, which would be considerably more for a European than for a slave'.[10]

In addition, K.J. Slotsboo, a Dane who had come to the Cape with W.A. van der Stel in 1699 and by this time had acquired the rank of 'Captain-Lieutenant', remarked, 'No matter how poor a person is, he will not accustom himself to perform the work of slaves, as he thinks in this way to distinguish himself from a slave. Moreover, the fact that they have left their country makes them think that they should lead an easier life than at home (…).'[11]

The Senior Merchant Jacobus Cruse, who had been born at the Cape and had no other standards of measurement, even declared himself unable to believe 'that farm-labourers or other Europeans will be found more useful, industrious, convenient or cheaper than slaves, as one can accomplish everything with slaves (who only require food and a little clothing) even better than with Europeans. This opinion will, I am sure, be confirmed by the farmers and others who have been here for many years and who can speak from experience.'[12]

Finally, the secretary of the Council, Hugo van der Meer Pietersoon, pointed out that 'the farm servants here usually earn from 10 to 16 and even 18 guldens and more, in addition to good food and drink, besides 1 to 2 lbs. of tobacco per month', while 'the slave of a private person is usually estimated at f60, reckoning 1 rixdollar per month for food, a length (span) of tobacco per week, 2 pairs of trousers and one coat per year. It is quite true that they sometimes run away, but it is no less true that many more, in fact, quite three times as many, are born.'[13]

It was likewise Van der Meer who pointed out a further practical advantage of the slave system. 'But supposing many of these [white labourers] live together on a farm,' he asked rhetorically,

farms being sometimes hours distant from one another, would there not be reason to fear that these labourers would always be the master, would one servant if ordered to do so by his master, dare to bind and punish the other if the latter had displeased his master? I do not think so; the slaves do this, however, when ordered to do so, always remembering who

197

they are, in the hope that by means of good service they may one day earn their freedom.[14]

Only Captain Dominique Pasques de Chavonnes, the nephew of the Governor, queried these arguments or the advantages of slave labour, and dissented from his colleagues in some detail.

The ordinary purchase-amount of a slave is 80–150 rixdollars for a labourer, 150–300 rixdollars and more for a herdsman, mason, wagon-driver or workman's apprentice. Clothes, tobacco and food, whether in service or not, the never-ending sicknesses, accidents, maimings, deaths and burials, whatever is stolen or neglected by this class or person, and the fact that 3 slaves are required to do the work of 2 Europeans,—all add to the expense, and it will therefore be acknowledged that I am right in saying that a farm-labourer, earning 8, 9, or 10 guldens a month and his food, will be more useful to the country and a better investment to the farmer than a slave.[15]

Captain De Chavonnes had been stationed at the Cape in 1686–89, and again since the appointment of his uncle as Governor in 1713,[16] so that he was not without knowledge of local conditions, but this was not the general opinion of the Council, and the Gentlemen XVII were swayed by the majority. The Cape was to remain a slave society until the emancipation of the slaves was proclaimed at the end of 1834, under British rule.

In the early years particularly, only a relative handful of richer individuals were able to acquire enough slaves to serve as basis for the extension of their activities, thus accumulating greater wealth in order to buy more slaves and continue the cycle of economic progress. The great majority of the freeburghers during this period owned one or two slaves at the most, and in many cases none at all.

By 1688 a reasonable degree of stability and prosperity had been attained in the Cape district, the older and more settled area in the vicinity of Table Bay and the Liesbeek valley, and the freeburghers here owned a total 166 male and 37 female slaves, while in the Stellenbosch district, which had been opened for settlement only nine years before, pioneering conditions still obtained and the corresponding figures were 64 and 7.[17] The average farmer in the Cape district owned 10,6 slaves,[18] while the hypothetical 'average' household in the Stellenbosch district is estimated to have consisted of one or two white men (depending on the presence of a *knecht*), a white woman, 5 children and one or two slaves.[19]

These figures would of course have varied from one specific case to another, in some cases dramatically, but the averages increased gradually over the years. 'In 1706,' writes Shell,' only 34 percent of the free population owned slaves; by 1731, a generation later, at least 56 percent did.'[20]

Even when slave owning became general in the course of the eighteenth century, however, slave holdings were never spread evenly over the entire white population. 'Although by 1682 the free population numbered only 102 census households (…),' remark Guelke & Shell with reference to the period immediately after the opening up of the Stellenbosch district for colonisation, 'there were already marked differences in the size and wealth of individual undertakings. Twelve census households employed or held over 50% of the farm servants, slaves and livestock, and between them produced most of the Colony's wheat, barley and rye.'[21]

In the case of the largest slave owners it must, however, be borne in mind that they were in most cases also in possession of more than one farm or cattle post, and as Shell points out, 'in cases where the slave owner owned more than one property, the number of slaves on each property was always much smaller than the census entry. The ostensibly large Cape slave distributions, when disaggregated from the census, universally reveal themselves to be small slave holdings spread over several properties.'[22]

As a specific example Shell refers to Hendrik Sneewind, who according to the census returns for 1701 owned 14 adult male and 3 adult female slaves, but when he died later the same year was shown to be in possession of three farms:

> a market garden along the Liesbeeck River (this was the main farm, identified in the inventory as the *hofstede*), a subsidiary freehold farm in the Tijgerberg region, and also a loan farm in the frontier reaches of Tijgerberg. Each of these farms required slave labour. One of his daughters, who had married his neighbour Abraham Diemer in 1697, was already running the Tijgerberg farm, and those slaves, included in the January census, were not included in the November inventory of the *hofstede*. His widow, Abigail Vroom, inherited the main farm, for which she reported only 6 slaves. If one relied solely on the rough census entry that reported that Schneuwindt owned 17 slaves, inferences about owner-slave relationships would be entirely different from the reality of only 6 slaves on the *hofstede*.[23]

Bearing this in mind, there were nonetheless a number of comparatively spectacular estates at the Cape by this time. The pioneer freeburgher Steven Jansz Botma, who had come out under Van Riebeeck and had been the leader of one of the first groups of freeburghers in the Liesbeek valley, owned 250 head of cattle, 1800 sheep, 4 horses, 11 male slaves and a single female when he died in 1700, and left an estate worth more than 20 000 guilders.[24] Henning Hüsing, who started his career as a freeburgher in 1678, owned a single male slave by 1682, which had increased to 16 men by 1692, and to 59 by 1700, by which time he was probably the wealthiest freeburgher at the Cape.[25] Governor W.A. van der Stel, in addition to the large number of Company slaves he is alleged to have employed for his own work, is known to have purchased a total of 121 for his personal use over the period 1699–1707.[26] These required their own administrative system, and Corporal Jan Jacobsz de Caron is said to have served as '*mandoor* of the female slaves' on the estate.[27]

As regards the urban area in the Table Valley, the hypothetical 'average' white household here owned 1,3 slaves in 1700, but while many families possessed more than one, others would equally have had none.[28] The legal records, in which so much valuable incidental detail about everyday life at the Cape has been preserved, provide a glimpse, for example, of the German Detlef Biebow, former corporal under the VOC and later free barber-surgeon, going to fetch two buckets of water 'at the fountain near his house' in the Table Valley one summer evening in 1689 while his wife waited for him at home,[29] so that the couple, who had been married for only a month or two, obviously owned no slaves. In 1692 and again in 1693 Biebow bought a young female slave,[30] but when he died in 1695, leaving a widow and three small children, the couple owned only a woman called Lijsbeth, together with a horse, some shabby kitchenware and crockery, an old table and an old chest, and lived in what was described as a small and equally shabby mud walled house.[31] There must have been many other families like theirs.

In spite of the increasing economic stability, the welfare of a section of the freeburgher community and the emergence of a small number of wealthy men among the large wheat and wine farmers and the *pachters*, life at the Cape by the turn of the eighteenth century was still relatively simple. In the Table Valley a few more imposing public buildings had been erected and some larger private houses were being built, but in the remainder of the colony the white inhabitants still lived in rectangular thatched cottages, mostly with earthen floors and unglazed windows, the window openings being covered with Guinea linen or wooden shutters.

Threshing floors and simple cattle folds, often constructed of branches, would not have been listed in probate inventories, but as farming conditions improved, the latter began to record the appearance of outbuildings, the earliest mentioned in the Stellenbosch district being wine cellars, which indicates the growing importance of wine farming. On large farms belonging to obviously affluent men further buildings such as barns, dairies, distilleries, smithies and even wagon-builder's shops are mentioned from time to time by the turn of the century, all indicative of the growing scale of farming operations, but also of the largely self-supporting nature of life on the isolated farms in the colony, and the widely varying demands which might be made on the slaves working there. These farm complexes were, however, little more than an untidy huddle of buildings situated in a bleak landscape, for it was only during the 'eighties and 'nineties that the planting of oak trees was gradually begun with the active encouragement of Simon van der Stel.

Roads were primitive tracks and often impassable in winter, and not everyone owned horses, so that travelling was often done on foot, the French refugees who were settled in Drakenstein in 1688 even walking in to the Table Valley on occasion. When the Berg River came down in flood, farmers on the far side were cut off for months from the church and mill at Drakenstein and the Landdrost in Stellenbosch.

Scattered Khoikhoi still roamed about the area, and there were incidental clashes with the farmers now moving into what had until recently been their pastures, although they increasingly entered the service of the whites as herders or harvesters, usually on a temporary basis.

Wild animals were also to be found all around the areas of white settlement, and in 1688 Van der Stel still had to explain to the XVII that slaves could not be used as herdsmen, as the latter had to be armed. 'To allow them such arms,' he explained, 'was nothing less than putting a knife in their hands with which they could unexpectedly "cut our throats"'.[32]

As money gradually became available, farmers tended to invest it in the purchase of stock, farming equipment and a few slaves, and one reads of estates comprising '242 sheep, big and small' and 'a female slave with her child',[33] or '14 head of draught cattle, 1 slave, 1 horse, 1 old wagon', the total value of the estate in the latter case being 1000 guilders.[34] Even where relatively large numbers of cattle and sheep and some horses and slaves are mentioned, the household furniture in the surviving inventories is often surprisingly scanty: for example, 'one piece of land with a little house ["*huijsken*"] on it', 3 horses, 'some pieces of household furniture ["*weijnig huismeubeltje*"]' valued at 30 guilders, and a slave for whom 50 rixdollars were still owing;[35] 40 head of cattle valued at 600 guilders, 60 sheep at 120 guilders, and 4 slaves at 1200 guilders, with 'a few pieces of furniture' at 50 guilders;[36] or 600 sheep, 50 head of cattle, 'a few household effects' at 100 guilders, 'some men's clothes' at 75 guilders, but 1 woman with a child, and no fewer than 7 male slaves.[37]

Caroline Woodward has estimated on the basis of probate inventories for this period that for 300 guilders 'a house could be furnished with a modicum of comfort and for 1 000 guilders with comfort and some of life's luxuries. Where property is concerned, a farm or house worth 4 000 guilders apparently represented prosperity.'[38]

Seen in these terms, insofar as the word 'typical' has any meaning, a 'typical' prosperous Cape farmer of the late seventeenth century may well be Christoffel Esterhuijs who in 1689 was in possession of a farm of 50 morgen which had been cultivated for eight years, so that he must have been one of the early settlers in the Stellenbosch district, as well as the following: '16 oxen, 12 cows, 4 calves, 3 horses, 5 leaguers of wine, 100 sheep, a wagon, plough and harrow, [and] 1 slave'. No valuation is given.[39]

In most cases when money began to be spent on the house, as opposed to the farm, it seems initially to have been used in a practical way for equipping the kitchen, which was often surprisingly well stocked. The lists of iron pots, copper kettles, trivets, hearth chains, gridirons, meat forks and skimmers provide the outline of the world in which slave women spent a good part of their lives, cooking over an open fire on a floor-level hearth, and often bringing in their bedding to sleep on the kitchen floor at night.

It was only towards the end of the century that more prosperous households began to acquire such goods as porcelain, feather beds, large quantities of table and bed linen, and silver objects such as buttons and spoons which were regarded as a form of investment as much as land or slaves. Their models would no doubt have been senior officials of the VOC such as Lieutenant Adriaan van Reede and his wife Christina Does, who had formerly been married to the pioneer freeburgher Elbert Dircx Diemer. On her death in 1703 they occupied a large house in the Table Valley filled with furniture, porcelain, silver, mirrors, lacquerware, jewellery and clothing, and owned 25 slaves 'large and small', of whom 7 were said to be the property of the deceased woman's son-in-law, the Fiscal Joan Blesius, who had owned a farm in partnership with her.[40]

Shell graphically illustrates the process of social and economic progress during this period by citing the case of Matthijs Greeff, who was a prominent inhabitant of the Stellenbosch district in his day, serving repeatedly as Heemraad or member of the local court of justice over the period 1684–1701.

Matthijs Greef appeared on the 1692 census in the Stellenbosch district with no adult children and no slaves and as cultivating a few vines and running a few sheep: this was a farm in the making. He had a Company knecht, and hired two free knechts, Pieter Andriesz and Pieter Meijer. Nine years later the family reported 8 of their own children, 13 male slaves, 2 female slaves, 1 male slave child and 2 female slave children. The husband and wife were now presiding over an established and extremely productive farm: with the eldest son now 14 years old, and with a number of slaves, Greef could dispense with his Company and free knechts. By 1706, his eldest son, 19, was listed in a separate household, and Greef senior once again hired a Company knecht, this time keeping him on for a year before letting him go.[41]

When Greeff's wife died in 1709, two farms in the Stellenbosch district, an unspecified number of cattle outposts deeper in the interior, a house in the Table Valley, 19 male slaves and 2 females appeared in the probate inventory,[42] and on his own death three years later the number of male slaves had increased to 22, while three farms and three outposts were specified. His home was also very well furnished, with porcelain, paintings, feather beds, an ebony four-poster and a chest with brass clasps.[43]

The Secunde, Abraham Cranendonk, declared officially in 1717 that, 'broadly speaking, there are not 30 families which can be regarded as wealthy. As for the rest of the inhabitants, there is not one who has sufficient to support himself, or who has not mortgaged his property, either to the Orphan Chamber, or to the Poor Fund, or to a fellow-citizen. None of these men have any hope of being able to clear their property or of becoming wealthy.'[44] Such statements must be qualified, however, like the judgements in the report sent to the Netherlands by Governor De la Fontaine thirteen years later.[45] In this case Cranendonk had arrived from the East only two years before with standards very different from those obtaining at the Cape, and as likely as not did not realise the extent to which an extensive system of credit and debt underpinned life in the colony and was accepted as normal.[46]

This then was the world in which the early Cape slaves found themselves, and in which they lived, worked and died. What must be emphasised is that the 'world of the slaves' at the Cape was essentially domestic by nature,[47] and apart from the work force of the VOC, it was inhabited by relatively small groups of slaves working in private homes or on moderately sized wheat or wine farms. It cannot be compared, in scale or nature, to the plantation farming of the Caribbean or North America, and attempts to understand or explain the local system by reference to the latter are largely meaningless.

Individual slaves in private ownership are on the whole not as fully documented as those belonging to the Company, who were official property of whom a record of some sort had to be kept. While there is a reasonable amount of information available on the activities of slaves in the eighteenth century, especially in the urban settlement, it is not clear, however, to what extent such information may already be applied to the period under discussion in this book. Where evidence from sources later than 1720 is used in the chapter which follows, this will be made clear either in the text or in the notes.

In this context some use will inevitably also be made of the writings of the German O.F. Mentzel, an intelligent and observant man with an enquiring mind who spent the years 1733–41 at the Cape, for some eighteen months of which he moreover served as private tutor to the children of a well-to-do farmer in the Stellenbosch district.[48] Information will even be used, when apposite, from an observer with an even livelier eye, Lady Anne Barnard, who spent some years at the Cape during the very last years of the eighteenth century, but whose observations are often revealing of the local situation.

Information on slaves is scarce and random, however, and must be gathered from over a very wide field.

Normally at least the name of any slave recorded in contemporary documentation is given, but this is a dubious source of information on the individual concerned. The VOC for the sake of consistency in its records retained the given names of the slaves it acquired, with the result that many African, Asiatic and Madagascan names are to be found among them, albeit in garbled or mangled form.[49] For the rest, slave dealers and owners were free to impose whatever names they chose on the slaves under their authority.[50] Hattingh found 550 different slave names in the records of slave transactions at the Cape, of which by far the most common among the men were Jan and Anthony (in various spellings), followed by Titus, Claas, Pieter or Piet, Jacob, Coridon and Aron, in that order. Among the women the most common names were Maria (with variants), Susanna and Sara. Common Dutch names seem to have been preferred, although Portuguese names such as Domingo serve as a reminder of widespread Portuguese influence in the East. Biblical names such as Abraham, Gideon and Rebecca, names from ancient history and classical mythology such as Caesar, Cassandra, Cupido and Hannibal, and the names of months (January, February, Maart) also occur regularly.[51] The range was relatively small, and it is often difficult to distinguish given individuals, even with the help of toponyms.

Certain names such as Bygeval, Clapperdop or Domingo Apekint, or those of the trio Weggesonken, Behouden and Dikbeen van Kaap Verde who were bought by Simon van der Stel in a single transaction in 1698,[52] look like nicknames or appear to have been derogatory or disparaging by nature, but it is also possible that they were in some cases simply corruptions of indigenous names by Dutch speakers.

Slave dealers and owners could also change the names of slaves at will. Mousa from Guinea, who was sold to Elbert Dircx Diemer in 1684, was renamed Gideon,[53] while Coridon van Madagascar, bought by the free black Maria Evertsz, was 'according to the wishes of the buyer called Cupido'.[54]

This may seem a minor point in the context of the violence and injustice to which slaves, given the nature of slavery, were habitually subjected. As Armstrong points out, however, in discussing the lists of the Company's Madagascan slave purchases, 'A *slave* is but a slave, an abstraction, but a slave with a name becomes a man, a woman, a child. Hence lists of slave names have an essential and peculiar interest, an actualizing power, that derives from their symbolic intersection with individual existence and social anonymity.'[55] The deprivation of something as personal as a given name, the name by which an individual has thus far been identified and known to family and friends, is equally an act of violence and injustice.

In cases where a slave's given name is accompanied by a toponym the latter may appear to provide some biographical information on the individual concerned, but this is not necessarily the case. The slave called Ary van Bengalen himself stated that he came from the area 'between Suratte and Persia',[56] although he had presumably been sold in Bengal, on the other side of India from his birthplace. Christina van Canarie (Canara on the Malabar coast of India) was on one occasion listed as Christina van Coromandel,[57] while Diana van Coilang (spelled in various ways, but referring to Quilon, likewise on the Malabar coast) also appears in contemporary documents as coming from Bima, and was on occasion recorded as Lena van Ceylon.[58] Sara van Solor (in the Indonesian archipelago) arrived at the Cape according to Hattingh's transcription as Sara van Ceylon.[59]

Few slaves were ever given the opportunity to record anything about their former lives, like Ary van Bengalen who in 1706 told the freeburgher Jacobus van der Heiden 'that during his childhood years (…) when he was playing on the beach, he was carried off by the Dutch and was eventually sold as a slave'.[60] A similar vague, uncomprehending reminiscence emerged when 'a certain Malabar, to all appearances rescued from the Ceylon return ship *Bennebroek* and brought here some days ago', was interrogated by interpreters at the Cape in 1714 and declared,

> That his name is Mieje, and that when his brother and other Malabar slaves were brought from Galle [in Ceylon] on board four of the Company's ships last year, he was brought in a boat and subsequently put on board a fifth ship, without however knowing the name of the ship or that of the skipper, but that he left with the fleet of the Lord Fiscal of Ceylon.[61]

Similarly one reads in the judicial interrogation of Titus van Ternate in 1727: 'In what year he came here and with whom?—Says he does not know, but that it is about six years ago that he came to this place with a master ["*seur*"] whose name is unknown to him.'[62]

Most of the slaves transported to the Cape like these men probably found the experience no less incomprehensible and bewildering and underwent it with much the same passivity. Caesar van Madagascar, '26 to 28 years old', was said in 1707 'to have been at the Cape 13 years, and to have been very young when he arrived, and furthermore not to know his age'.[63]

While the slaves of the VOC were possibly manumitted at some late stage, they were, with certain rare exceptions, never sold.[64] They would thus have had no other owner than the Company, and to this extent experienced a degree of relative stability unknown to private slaves. In the case of privately owned slaves, a change in the financial or other circumstances of his or her owner or even a sudden whim could transform their situation overnight in a way over which they themselves did not have the slightest control, and which contributed notably to the inherent insecurity and instability of a slave's life.

Margaret Cairns gives the example of the slave Piet Snap van Bengalen, aged twenty, who was sold by skipper Hendrick Janse Bontekraai to the freeburgher Tobias Marquart on 21 May 1683 for 48 rixdollars. On 2 June 1684, Marquart sold him to his fellow free-burgher Gerrit van der Bijl, together with a slave called Andries, for 170 rixdollars, and on 5 April 1696 Van der Bijl sold him to Willem Jansz ter Wereld for an undisclosed amount.[65]

For a slightly later period Mrs Cairns provides similar information on the slave Moses, likewise twenty years old, sold by skipper Jan de Heij to the new Secunde Abraham Cranendonk in 1716 for 100 rixdollars, by Cranendonk's widow to Noach Bakker in 1722, by Bakker to Catharina Elizabeth Meyer for 160 rixdollars in 1725, and by one Catharina Lambrechts, who may or may not have been the same person, to the widow Meijboom for the same amount in 1727.[66] Moses therefore had at least five owners over a period of eleven years.

Initially all slave transactions were handled by the secretary of the Council of Policy and formally recorded in the presence of two witnesses, but as from 1698 an increasing number of slave sales were dealt with by the Council of Justice.[67] As both the number of sales and the number of manumissions increased, however, the freeburghers were correspondingly inclined to enter into informal or *onder-handse* transactions, to such an extent that these had to be forbidden by the Council of Policy in 1722, apparently with little effect.[68] Transactions during the period covered by this book were reasonably well recorded.

The interesting collection of accounts, receipts and other ephemera forming the Joubert Papers in the Cape Town Archives Repository includes a number of documents relating to the sale or purchase of slaves, the earliest referring to a visiting English ship.

December the 26th 1714
Recd. of Peter Joubert by the hands of Monsr. Sollier, one hundred & fifty rix dollars for two Madagascar negro ladds, the one named Indien, the other Lombo, imported in the ship *Delicia*, Woodes Rogers commander, witness my hand, [*signed:*] J.W. Ker.[69]

The second document, which is in Dutch, refers to a similar transaction:

I the undersigned acknowledge to have received from Madam Jubert [*sic*] for two slaves one hundred and twenty rix-dollars. *Actum* Cape of Good Hope the 29th November a[*nn*]o. 1715. [*Signed:*] [*illegible*] Cnollendam.

No more is known about this transaction, but it may be worth noting that the *Leidsman* had returned from Madagascar on 21 November, 'having been very successful in trading for slaves, and buying about 200 of good quality'.[70] This may well have been a private sale by a member of the crew.

As distinct from these two informal receipts, the Joubert Papers also include nine formal documents relating to further slave transactions between 1729 and 1738, Jan Smiesing, former schoolmaster in the Slave Lodge, acting as witness in one case.[71]

A similar transaction is recorded incidentally among the outstanding debts in the probate inventory of Jan Dircx de Beer, who has already been identified as a leading figure in the local slave trade: '[Owing] by Isaac Bisseux 200 guilders and 25 guilders for a slave, makes 225 guilders, and for a load of wheat 100 guilders, [total:] 325 guilders.'[72]

A unique record of bookkeeping by a slave owner in the early eighteenth century is provided by the account book of the Revd Henricus Beck of Stellenbosch, where two facing pages, both headed 'Praise God' according to his custom, provide details of his transactions. The 'Credit' page begins in 1710, but entries are not further dated, while entries on the 'Debit' page are dated over the period 1710–16. All prices are given in rixdollars.

Credit

For the slave Diana 46 rds, ditto the slave Aaron, 90, both my
　　wife's
For Marise, 70 rds
Sara died
Maaij Jubse died
Corilon sold to Pfeil for 130 rds
Antonij sold to ditto for 100 rds
Jan van Baly, Caatje, female slave: these two have been chosen
　　by my wife for herself

Debit

For a slave bought called Titus at 65 rds
For a female slave Marise at 60 rds
For a slave of Uncle Vander Duijn, Sara at 50 rds
For the female slave Jubse of Papa's [*his father-in-law*] at 38 rds
For the slave Corilon at 65 rds
For Jan Baly at 82 rds

For Prins van Bengale, rds 55

For Honsaar at 130 rds

For Elias at 70 rds

For Siphron at 110 rds

For Caatje at 110 rds

For Adam van de Cust [75 rds][73]

According to these notes, covering a period of some seven years, Beck bought 12 slaves, of whom 2 appear to have died, and sold 3, while his wife owned 4 slaves, of whom 2 were sold in the period under discussion. This seems a not inconsiderable number, given the fact that Beck was childless, occupied the parsonage at Stellenbosch where he would presumably also have had the services of a Company slave, and was by this time no longer farming. It can possibly be explained partly by what was considered necessary for the prestige of a minister, and partly by the needs of his wife, who was a daughter of the former Secunde Elsevier and had grown up in the East, where slaves were plentiful.

The acquisition of slaves, while normally in the form of a purchase, could also take the form of an exchange, as the following in 1695: 'Manuel (20) and Domingo (21), both from Malabar, exchanged by Theunis Dircksz van Schalkwijk for the slave Arent from Madagascar, belonging to Jan Maarschalk. Domingo was permitted to keep any money he had in his possession.'[74] More usually, however, the exchange involved goods. The freeburgher Jan Pietersz Broertje in 1671 acquired the slave Isaacq, 'about 16–18 years old', for 4 draught oxen and 'an almost worn out wagon',[75] while Adam van Madagascar was 'exchanged by Willem Jansz for 38 ewes belonging to Gerrit Cloete' in 1686,[76] and Arent van Madagascar was sold by Henning Hüsing to Frederick Russouw de Wit 'for one hundred wagonloads of wood' three years later.[77] When Gerrit Elbertsz died in 1713, a note was made in the probate inventory 'that the deceased had sold a *jonge* to Albert Meijburgh for 100 sheep on the condition of selecting the said sheep from among 700'.[78]

Slaves were property, could be bequeathed and inherited, and were listed in probate inventories along with the household furniture, farm equipment and stock: in the town house of Hans Rutgertroost in 1715, for example, 'In the kitchen: 1 female slave named Suzanna; 2 iron pots; 2 skillets; a copper kettle'; and so on.[79] They were likewise disposed of with other property at the auctions which at an early stage became part of the economic and social life at the Cape: this happened in the case of legal separations between husband and wife, as also that of certain insolvent or intestate persons.[80] After the recall of W.A. van der Stel there was an auction lasting five days at which his agents disposed of 'some of his moveable goods, such as male and female slaves, oxen, wagons, ploughs, a great quantity of prepared buckskins, paintings, chairs, beds and other household equipment'.[81] Similarly, when the farm of the widow Trijntje Theunisz Gansevanger, a very successful farmer, was sold by auction in 1715, 7 male slaves were listed casually as having been sold between the household items 'table and bench' and '1 bedstead', fetching prices from 60 to 225 rixdollars each.[82]

One reads similarly in contemporary records of 'Catharina from Madagascar (13) sold by Cornelis Pieter Linnes at the public auction of the possessions of the late Barbara Geens to Diederick Potter for ƒ150 [*guilders*], Cape valuation';[83] of 'Anthonij from Mozambique (18) sold by public auction by Andries de Man and Cornelis Linnes ex the estate of Hans Erentraut to Nicolaas Loupscher for ƒ26',[84] or 'Half of the slaves belonging to Hendrick Ulm (Oulm), together with cattle, wagons, a plough and farm implements sold by the owner to Guilliam Eems for ƒ2675'.[85]

One wonders what the slaves felt with regard to transactions in which they themselves were so directly and personally involved without being able to influence the events in any way. One wonders, for example, what lay behind Anthoni van Goa's seemingly impassive statement, 'That Oberholster, as his former *baas* [*master*], had sold him on his auction to the aforementioned Beatrix [Verweij], without knowing the correct date',[86] especially when it appears that he was by this sale forcibly parted from the woman he regarded as his wife.

De Kock quotes an early public notice of a slave sale.

> On Saturday morning the 1st August [1699] within this Castle at 10 o'clock it is intended to sell for cash by public auction on behalf of the Honourable Court of Justice a certain slave named Alexander of Bengal, aged 16 years....
>
> The buyer must undertake to keep the slave in chains for six successive years in accordance with his punishment; only on this express condition can he be alienated or transferred to another.
>
> Those interested should come on the day and hour specified and thereby make a profit.[87]

This probably refers to the boy who two years earlier, when he was said to be 15, had been sold by the first mate of a passing ship to the burgher Johannes Pithius for 50 rixdollars.[88] Pithius was a well-to-do man and future *pachter*, who at the time of his wife's death in 1699 owned 2 adult slaves, a boy and 2 children,[89] but he seems to have sold Alexander to a fellow freeburgher Jacob Vogel, living in the Table Valley, with whom he had business dealings.[90] Alexander absconded from Vogel early in 1699, taking refuge with Sergeant Christoffel Heuning who lived at the foot of Table Mountain and who sheltered him, even though this was against the law. While staying there, Alexander three times entered the house of the free tapster and innkeeper Joris Pietersz at night and stole money, as well as a blanket, a bucket and a dish, showing considerable cold-bloodedness, daring or effrontery in the process. He was caught, however, and sentenced to be scourged, branded, riveted in chains 'to both his legs' for six years, and returned to his master, Jacob Vogel.[91]

Vogel was a well-to-do man who was repeatedly in possession of a *pacht*, but was seemingly in financial difficulties at the time, for the following year he requested to be relieved of his obligations as *pachter*. He also appears to have been unable to pay the legal costs arising from Alexander's trial, with the result that he transferred the slave to the Council of Justice, a common procedure at the time.[92]

What is known of individual slaves is largely a name and a price, and at most one can hope for an additional fragment or two. In the case of young Alexander van Bengalen one has a number of fragments relating to sale, escape, trial and re-sale which together amount to a sizeable piece of biographical information, even though nothing further is unfortunately known of him.

The few readily available descriptions of slave auctions at the Cape date from the end of the eighteenth century, when Lady Anne Barnard was informed by her husband 'that it was a place I could [not] find myself in with comfort to myself, that I should not merely see the slaves put up on a table & bid for, that I should see each almost naked, but examined in a very protracted and indelicate manner to ascertain that he or she had no disorder'.[93] Auctions would hardly have been conducted with greater delicacy a hundred years earlier.[94]

Slaves could furthermore be transferred from one owner to another as gifts.[95] In 1686 Jan Pietersz Broertje made over to his son-in-law Willem Jansz 'a small slave girl of seven years of age, named Marie van de Caab, born in his own house, which slave he gives as dowry to his legal daughter, Anna Pieters Broer, on the condition that she ultimately frees the slave'.[96] In 1688 Herman Gresnich, who seems to have been disposing of a number of slaves at the time, gave Diana van de Caab, who was six, to Hendrik Sneewind 'in friendship', 'on condition that Snewint does not sell her and, when he dies, she be set free'.[97] Cornelia, the eldest daughter of W.A. van der Stel, received the little slave girl Catharina van de Caab, aged three, as a gift in 1706, in circumstances which are not quite clear,[98] and when the wealthy farmer Henning Hüsing was temporarily reconciled with her father, the event was sealed by Hüsing presenting the latter with 3000 sheep and 2 slaves.[99]

Slaves could also be bequeathed and distributed like other property, and when the wealthy Jan Dircx de Beer and his wife both died in 1701, the probate inventory noted that 3 of the 9 slaves listed in their town house 'are to be sold', while the remaining 6, suitably allotted to new owners, 'are not to be sold with the estate but remain among the said children as divided'.[100] In 1728 the ex-slave Armozijn Claasz or Armozijn van de Caab could herself leave the slave Sabina van Malabar to her freeborn granddaughter.[101]

Like other property, finally, slaves could serve as surety, and in 1672 the freeburgher Henrick Barents gave his 'house and grounds, all his other goods, moveable and immoveable, slaves, animals and his own person' as surety for the sum of 1000 guilders he owed the Sergeant, Hiëronimus Cruse.[102] They were likewise included with other property in deeds of sale.[103]

As has been said, the life of a private slave could differ widely from one household to the next, and insofar as incidental information does not happen to have been preserved in the available documentation, one can only make general deductions from what is known concerning the better documented slaves of the VOC.

Here too the basic items in the diet would have been rice and bread, and after the abundant rye harvest of 1708, for example, the Company decided not to buy any further supplies from the freeburghers, who were told that it might be 'used as food for their families and slaves'.[104] This would have been supplemented with fish, where readily available, and W.A. van der Stel had the workmen and slaves on his estate fed with fish caught and salted for him by Company servants operating from Vishoek (Gordon's Bay) in False Bay.[105]

Elsewhere meat such as offal from slaughtered animals, the flesh of animals which had died from natural causes or game would have been provided. Much of this is necessarily guesswork, but W.A. van der Stel is stated to have had game shot, 'such as hippopotamuses, elands, hartebeest, bontebok, &c.' to feed the many workers on his estate in Hottentots-Holland.[106] In the country vegetables would also have been readily available, and in 1681, when the authorities began cutting down on the importation of rice, Simon van der Stel advised the farmers to supply 'nutritious supplementary food' cheaply for their slaves by cultivating 'maize ("*milie*"), cadjang, pumpkin, sugar cane, &c.'.[107]

Wine was probably more readily available to private than to Company slaves, especially on the wine farms of the Boland. 'On occasions such as the end of the sowing season, during the harvest, after the vintage, or for work on Sundays and other special days,' writes Mentzel, 'well-meaning masters would give their slaves some wine, which has an immediate refreshing effect on them.'[108] He also mentions that slaves received 'a glass of brandy and a small slice of bread' before going out to their work in the morning.[109]

According to the same source, 'The quantity of tobacco consumed here is enormous, for it is the custom to give each slave—male or female—a span of tobacco weekly.'[110] And elsewhere, 'Every slave or Hottentot must be given a weekly dole or a span of tobacco to get any work out of him. This forms their most cherished comfort.'[111]

Clothing would have depended on the benevolence of the owners. In some cases it could have been specially made, or the women would have been given the cloth to make their own clothes. In others, slaves would have worn the cast-off clothing of members of the family, while Mentzel lists 'second-hand clothing for his slaves' among the basic purchases which the farmer is obliged to make in town.[112] When Christina de Beer, wife of Willem Helot, secretary to the Council of Policy, died in 1710, leaving a considerable amount of clothing, a dress of coarse striped woollen cloth, obviously a less elegant garment, was for example annotated in the probate inventory, together with a blanket, as 'given to the slave woman'.[113] In this way, both Eastern and Western models could therefore have been in use among the slave population.

Most likely it was mainly the light, brightly coloured Eastern cottons imported by the VOC in such large quantities that were worn here by the slaves, although there are also references to heavier European textiles. The freeburgher Johannes Phijffer placed an order in the Netherlands in 1700 for '20 ells of the cheapest worsted ("*dat alderslegtste laeken*") for my slaves',[114] and during the 1730s the Company official J.N. von Dessin is known to have ordered both 'coarse blue cloth for slave clothing' from the Netherlands and 'fine and common slave cloths' from the East. But full information on the clothes made for and worn Von Dessin's large slave household is not available until the 1750s, too late to be relevant here.[115]

Styles most likely varied, and very probably slave clothing, beginning by following the examples set by Batavia, became progressively more Westernised during the course of the VOC period.

By the turn of the eighteenth century, if not earlier, there appears to have been a recognisable category of clothing known as 'slave clothes', which were presumably characterised by their simple, practical cut and the coarse, strong and cheap materials from which they were made. There are also stray references to 'slave frocks' (possibly camisoles, short workman's jackets),[116] and 'slave trousers',[117] and one is reminded of the '2 pairs of trousers and one coat per year' described as a standard outfit for a male slave in 1717.[118]

In the probate inventory of the wealthy Matthijs Greeff in 1712, 6 'slave jackets' and a pair of 'slave breeches' (*rokjes* and *broekje* respectively), all made of pilot cloth, are recorded in the lean-to in the house which served as storeroom and also contained a small medicine chest, garden seed, empty bottles and 8 sickles.[119] When the widow of the extremely wealthy Pieter van der Bijl died in the Stellenbosch district 1744, there were likewise '1 slave jacket and 4 pairs of breeches' in a chest in the attic of the farmhouse, and '4 blue slave shirts' among the linen on another farm at Riebeek-Kasteel,[120] which links up well enough with earlier data, even though some time after the period under discussion.

The male slaves on W.A. van der Stel's estate are said to have been supplied yearly with trousers and jackets made from the prepared skins of game shot for him,[121] and leather trousers were commonly worn by labourers at the time.[122]

The wearing of hats by slaves was expressly forbidden by the Statutes of Batavia 'unless they can clearly speak and understand Dutch' and had received official permission.[123] Phijffer's order for clothing mentioned above also included a dozen 'English caps' ('*Engelse mutsen*') for his male slaves,[124] but head cloths or scarves seem to have been the general form of headgear at the Cape, and were sufficiently common and characteristic by the end of the eighteenth century to be commented on by visitors.[125]

There is no express prohibition in Cape legislation on the wearing of shoes, but bare feet seem in practice to have been regarded as a badge of slavery, and Mentzel states, 'The bare foot is the mark of the slave. Hence at the Cape, unlike in ancient Rome, the shoe, not the cap, is the mark of freedom'.[126] An English traveller who visited the Cape in 1744 observed in similar fashion: 'no slave is permitted to wear shoes, no man-slave a hat, nor woman-slave a cap.'[127] In reporting on existing legislation regarding the clothing of slaves in 1813, however, the Fiscal remarked that 'nothing else is observed than the prohibition of slaves wearing shoes and stockings, and even this prohibition is now but little attended to, as experience of a few successive years has taught us.'[128] The oblique criticism probably refers to the deleterious effect of British administration.

There are references in contemporary documents to slaves' blankets,[129] and to a coarse woollen cloth which is described as 'the only material used here for coverings by the ordinary farmers and slaves during the winter'.[130] These were presumably imported Dutch or 'fatherland' blankets, as opposed to the more expensive palempores or cotton quilts from the East which were in general use.[131]

Apart from what they could manage to obtain in the form of gifts, cast-offs or theft, slaves could have acquired personal possessions by means of purchases with their incidental earnings. In legal documents of the eighteenth century casual mention is made of knives, pipes, tinderboxes, combs, cooking utensils and chests,[132] and the women would often have had trinkets or items of adornment. The possessions of favoured female slaves might, on occasion, be considerable. When arrangements were made in 1696 for Maria van Bengalen to be manumitted on the death of Jan Coenraad Visser, it was stipulated that she 'was to be allowed to take her possessions, kist and clothes out of the estate',[133] and in the probate inventory of Bartholomeus Franse or Bartholomeus Vos, whose slave Flora van Bengalen was likewise to be manumitted, 'a chest belonging to the *meijt*' and '1 bundle of bedding for the *meijd*' were similarly listed in 1719.[134]

Slaves were often given a piece of ground to cultivate and allowed to keep the proceeds,[135] while servants in town were sometimes permitted to work for their own profit, against payment. Domestic servants in the Table Valley were tipped by visitors boarding in the house where they worked,[136] and there are regular references to gambling by slaves. Gambling by Europeans 'with a male or female slave or other mean ["*vil*"] persons' was forbidden by a *plakkaat* as early as 1658.[137] Among the *plakkaten* formally renewed in 1715 was one strictly forbidding 'anyone', by which whites were by implication meant, gambling with 'a male or female slave, *bandiet* of any similar vile ["*veragt*"] person',[138] and in 1728 Jacob van Bocum van Ceylon stole a signet ring and other goods from the house he was supposed to be guarding during his master's absence, and lost them in gambling with other slaves and Chinese.[139]

As regards accommodation it is equally difficult to generalise. The orphan Adriana van Jaarsveld, living in the house of Johannes Mulder, former Landdrost of Stellenbosch, declared in 1694 that a male and female slave slept on the floor before her bed, and this was quite likely common practice.[140] According to a declaration made in 1713, Tryntje van Madagascar, a slave of the well-to-do Elizabeth Lingelbach, who lived alone in a house in the Table Valley, slept 'in the same room and before the bed of her mistress', but moved successively to a 'lean-to in the yard', and the attic, which was accessible from the house by means of a ladder. Tryntje's companion Flora slept in 'the little house in the kitchen', by which a pantry is presumably meant,[141] all of which indicates the variety of sleeping places available to a house slave in the early eighteenth century.

Lady Anne Barnard, who in 1797 stayed in a double-storey house in Cape Town, wrote of a staircase leading up to the bedrooms, 'which all go off one Square apartment, where the female Slaves sleep in the best manner they can contrive, for there is *little nicety observed*'.[142]

It was not until the smallpox epidemic of 1755 threatened the white community that official attention was paid to the matter of accommodation, however, thus making some contemporary information available. In a *plakkaat* issued at this time, it was observed

that in most houses no apartments are to be found for housing slaves, the people [*white inhabitants*] are therefore obliged to let the said slaves stay in the rooms of the actual houses, while in those houses which are provided with some special rooms for slaves, these are invariably so cramped that healthy slaves can only just find sufficient room there.[143]

By the 1730s Mentzel, writing about the accommodation provided for the staff at the Company's stables, adds, 'the slaves squat in a few outrooms',[144] and in connection with archaeological investigations carried out in Stellenbosch but not specifically dated, Hennie Vos writes similarly and evocatively that the 'the backyard position' of a given building, 'its economical construction materials, the nature of the remains and the untidy, communal living space suggest that the dwelling may have been occupied by servants or slaves'.[145]

Elsewhere Vos remarks of an archaeological site: 'On the basis of the amount of charcoal, fish scales, bones, artefacts and organic materials that was trampled into the clay floors, the kitchen and back rooms were apparently not kept tidy. It is postulated that such rooms were also the abode of slaves.'[146] This is borne out by Mentzel, who remarks, referring to his own observations in the 1730s, that 'it is usual at the Cape for a couple of slave girls to bring their beds into the kitchen towards night-time, sleep there, and clear out again early in the morning'.[147]

Yvonne Brink, in observations of a general nature based on archaeological and other research, remarks that it was possibly 'considered quite in order for slaves to crowd together. To phrase it even more positively, indications are that they were probably *made* to huddle. They appear to have occupied the same types of spaces in which goods (furniture, implements, crops, and so on) were stored. These include lofts, cellars and outbuildings in which other articles were stored.'[148] Where the contents of the wagonmaker's shop of Adam Leendertsz van Nieuwenbroek in the Table Valley are listed baldly as wagonmaker's tools and woods, 2 male slaves, 1 female, and 2 incomplete new wagons, it seems likely that the slaves slept in their workplace as well.[149]

It would seem that only the very wealthy had special accommodation for their slaves, at any rate of a nature to make it worth including in probate inventories, such as Cornelis Stevensz Botma, for whose house in the Table Valley a skillet, an old barrel, 4 harnesses with their bridles and 4 tin chamber pots are listed 'in the back of the little slave house' in 1716.[150] This is the earliest reference found to such an arrangement in the town, but Botma was a very rich man. The equally wealthy widow Engela Breda had a slave house on her garden plot in 1719, which contained 3 iron pots, but this was outside the town and seems in fact to have been a small farm where a sheep shed, a wine cellar, 11 slaves and 181 sheep are likewise listed.[151]

These examples have been taken from the Table Valley and Stellenbosch, but on farms the arrangements appear to have been similar, although there would have been more space available and possibly more choice. On the farm of the wealthy widow Ten Damme (Helena Gulix), who herself lived in the Table Valley, the *knecht*, who obviously acted as farm manager, in 1726 had a room opening off the kitchen, but three slaves slept in the house as well, one of them in a lean-to room,[152] while in 1715 Adriaen van Jaarsveld's slaves slept in the barn ('*corenhuijs*').[153] Here as elsewhere arrangements would have differed from one farm to the next, and these random examples are meant as illustrations only: 'they slept in kitchens, attics, and barns or out of doors in the summer,' write Armstrong & Worden. 'Slave shepherds and herders often slept with their flocks in sheep and cattle-pens.'[154]

It would seem that housing intended specifically for slaves, the so-called *slavenhuis* or 'slave house', was by no means common even on farms during the period under discussion, and was in fact only beginning to make its appearance on the farms of the wealthier slave owners who had reasonably large numbers of slaves. The earliest mention found in the course of research for this book was on Onrust, the Tygerberg farm of Johanna Victor, widow of the well-to-do freeburgher Johannes Pretorius, who died in 1694, and subsequently married to Johannes Starrenburg, who later became Landdrost of Stellenbosch. A '*slaven huijsje*' or 'little slave house' was listed in the probate inventory of her estate when she herself died in 1709, together with a stable, cowshed and wagonhouse 'all under one roof', a barn, a wine cellar and 6 male slaves, although it is not known at what stage it was built or by whom.[155]

Even where references to 'slave houses' occur in probate inventories during the early decades of the century, these tend to have been sparsely furnished if at all.

When Matthijs Greeff died in 1712, the slave house on his farm in the Stellenbosch district contained '5 old spades, 3 old manure shovels, 3 manure forks, 1 manure hook, 1 pickaxe, 1 old club-hammer'. Greeff owned no fewer than 24 slaves, as already mentioned, though all of them were listed as being on his three outlying farms at the time.[156] On the death of Abraham Diemer, a son of the pioneer freeburgher Elbert Dircx Diemer, the following year, he was in possession of 21 slaves, who seem all to have been males, while his slave house contained '5 vats, one with salt, 1 lot of rope, 1 lot of wood'.[157]

Cornelis Stevensz Botma, with 14 males slaves and a female on his farm at Rondebosch in 1716, had two iron pots in his slave house apart from gardening tools.[158] In 1717 the slave house of Theunis Dircksz van Schalkwijk seems also to have served as a wagon-house, for its contents were listed as '8 teak planks, 1 stretcher, 1 baking trough, 2 harrows, one with wooden and one with iron teeth, 2 ploughs, 1 'ceijs' [chaise?], 2 ox wagons, 1 horse wagon, 1 cart, 2 old vats'. Van Schalkwijk owned 15 slaves.[159] Finally, in 1732 the 'slavenhuijsje' of the former Landdrost of Stellenbosch, Johannes Mulder, who owned 21 slaves, contained no more than 'a set of rafters and pumpkins'.[160]

While some of the slaves' working implements seem to have been kept in the slave houses, the simple bunks or cots and blankets, the night soil tub and the personal belongings of the slaves themselves, if any, were obviously not thought worth recording.

The ultimate example of a Cape slave house in the period under discussion was of course that on Vergelegen, the estate of W.A. van der Stel in Hottentots-Holland, a structure 40 metres long and 12 metres wide which formed part of the symmetrical group of buildings around the manor house. Its remains have been investigated archaeologically, and evidence has been found for the existence of a partition dividing the building into two unequal sections with further subdivisions, two hearths with wooden smoke hoods, which possibly served as cooking fires, and floors of crushed brick mixed with clay.[161]

It is interesting that in two of the cases cited above the inventories listing slave houses also refer to the presence on the farm of a slaven combuijs or 'slave kitchen'. That on the farm of Abraham Diemer contained a wide variety of farming implements, saddles, harnesses, rye and barley, but cooking was also done there, as is indicated by the presence of a small square table and the following equipment: '1 bread chest, 2 vats with salt, 1 handmill, 4 iron pots, 1 copper skimmer, 1 water half-aum, 1 frying pan, 1 iron lamp, 1 iron hearth-chain'.[162] A slave kitchen is likewise mentioned on the farm of Sofia van der Merwe, widow of Roelof Pasman, in the same year.[163]

The widow of Jan Stevensz Botma, son of another Cape pioneer, Steven Jansz Botma, left an even better equipped slave kitchen on her death in 1724, although it also housed tools which were obviously used by the slaves, such as carpenter's equipment, axes, pickaxes and a tar-bucket. The widow had owned 9 slaves, and her own house appears to have been comfortably furnished, but the inventory makes no mention of a slave house on the farm.[164]

In most cases, however, even where quite large numbers of slaves are enumerated in an inventory, there is no mention of a slave house, or at any rate there was none judged worth mentioning. A separate kitchen for the slaves must have been even rarer, and confined to those households with an inconveniently large work force, or where the woman of the house preferred them to prepare their own food. In all these cases, however, the owners of the farms concerned were also among the wealthiest farmers of their day.

During the VOC period it was only the settlement in the Table Valley that could by any stretch of the imagination be called a town, though for most of this time it was little more than a straggling village. Its total population in 1710 was given as 'fully five hundred', and there were 155 households which paid *ratelwachtsgeld* or 'watch-money',[165] that is, contributed to the upkeep of the watchmen who patrolled the streets at night armed with wooden rattles.

The Table Valley was the nucleus of the VOC's administrative system, however, for within the walls of the Castle were concentrated the residences of the Governor and other officials, the council chamber, the administrative offices, the barracks and the Company's storerooms. The most imposing buildings in the freeburgher settlement a little distance from it, the thatched, cruciform church, the hospital and the Tuynhuys or official summer house in the gardens, were likewise Company property.

Apart from this the *Vlek* or 'hamlet', as it was sometimes called, consisted of little more than a few badly kept streets between the

Company's garden and Table Bay, a market square (the present Greenmarket Square) and a scattering of thatched houses, some of which served as taverns or taprooms, while in others the inhabitants conducted an informal retail trade in their living rooms for want of shops. By the turn of the century, however, a number of larger and more imposing houses, some of them with two storeys, were being built for the wealthier members of the community, often as the town houses of farmers such as Henning Hüsing.

The Company's gardens had by this time developed from a functional vegetable garden into a botanical garden much admired by visitors. Further gardens surrounded the settlement, stretching up the slopes of Table Mountain, while at some distance to the west, in the area later to be known successively as Hottentot Square, Boerenplein ('farmers' square'), Riebeeck Square and Heritage Square, were the huts of detribalised Khoikhoi who had become dependent on the whites and were often employed by them.

The male slaves in the Table Valley worked mostly as house or stable boys and gardeners. A house slave, Carel van Bengalen, for example, mentioned 'fetching wood or water for his mistress', and specified going to the 'pump' or the 'jetty' for water on one occasion with two buckets.[166] This probably refers to the fountains of running water on the Heerengracht end of the present Parade, at that time near the coast and the jetty, although there was also a fountain on the market square.[167] Carrying water was regarded so specifically as the task of slaves that a *plakkaat* could be issued in 1708 to regulate their activities and threaten their owners with a fine in case of damage.[168]

Fuel gathering was also an important task in the barren valley, and as Ross points it, this was no luxury, 'but had to do with one of the major necessities of life, and with one which was otherwise difficult to acquire in Cape Town'.[169] As time went on and the size and the demands of the settlement itself as well as the needs of visiting ships increased, the wood-gatherers had to travel greater distances each day, and they became a steadily more important part of the local community. Their work is described in some detail in various books relating to the Cape in the eighteenth century.[170]

Commander Wagenaer referred in 1666 to the market master selling produce 'for the benefit of those who have no slaves and who cannot vend it themselves', which indicates that slaves were already used for this where available.[171] In later years slaves earned so-called *koeliegeld* or 'coolie money' for their masters by selling garden produce in the market place or hawking goods about the streets of the town, mostly foodstuff such as vegetables or fruit,[172] and Mentzel describes the owners of the gardens on the slopes of Table Mountain 'sending their slaves into town with baskets and supplying regular customers or casual buyers'.[173]

The sale of fruit, vegetables and firewood by slaves is mentioned as early as 1676,[174] and in 1706 a number of local bakers protested at the fact that certain of their colleagues sent out three or four slaves at a time to hawk their bread, which they regarded as unfair competition.[175]

Hawkers also went out on the small boats to meet the ships entering Table Bay, and according to the C.P. Thunberg, who arrived here in 1772, 'We had hardly come to anchor before a crowd of black slaves and Chinese came in their small boats to sell and barter for clothes and other goods, fresh meats, vegetables and fruit.'[176] By this time the supply and demand had probably become more sophisticated, and according to Georg Naporra, who had visited the Cape twenty years earlier, these boats sold hot buttered white bread, roast sheeps' heads and fowls, boiled crayfish, fried fish, salted harders and steenbras, apples, pears and grapes.[177]

'Owner of carts and horses make money as coachmen, goods carriers or wood-sellers', writes Mentzel with reference to the situation by the 1730s. 'This work, too, is usually done by slaves.'[178] He likewise refers to slaves offering their services for hire as 'coolies'—the common term for a labourer or porter.[179]

Furthermore, the small number of white artisans and craftsmen in the settlement in due course acquired slave assistants, and when repairs were carried out to the church building in 1715, for example, payments were made to 'Harmen the thatcher with slave', 'Jan Pretorius with 2 slaves', 'Anthonij the thatcher with 1 slave' and 'Jacob Paessen for his slave'.[180]

Slave owners could likewise make a profit by 'the letting out of slaves for hire', as Mentzel calls it, which seems to apply in the case of Jacob Paessen's slave mentioned above. 'The usual terms are that the hirer should pay to the owner of the slave 4 Rds. [*rixdollars*] per month and provide the slave with food and tobacco but not with clothes.'[181] It was in this way that slaves participated in the fishing industry. 'At least early in the eighteenth century,' writes Ross,

> the fishing community working Table Bay was made up of small men owning ships, which were manned very largely by other people's slaves. Thus, for instance, in 1728, four *schuyten* [*fishing boats*] were arrested for fishing in an illegal stretch of water. The crews were all slaves, but only four of the sixteen were slaves of the owner of the boat on which they worked.[182]

When the building of the new church in Stellenbosch was begun in 1719, slaves were also hired from private owners as labourers at one guilder a day. 'This is the hire per day which at that time was regularly paid out to the owners of such slaves (...),' comments A.M. Hugo. 'For many people, especially widows, it was a welcome source of income.'[183] In the same connection the historian Theal refers to slaves being hired out to farmers for the harvest.[184]

Mentzel further mentions that slaves in his time were sometimes permitted to earn their own livelihood 'on the payment of 6 stuivers a day; such slaves must find their food, but can save up money for their own use according to their earnings',[185] and writes of others paying their masters a skelling a day for being allowed to gather firewood independently, for their own benefit, whether on the mountain slopes or the Cape Flats.[186] Where the debts of Ferdinand Appel, who died in 1717, include more than 50 guilders owing to

'Jacobus, free slave of the widow Phijffer', this probably refers to some such arrangement,[187] and so also two interesting scraps of paper preserved among the Joubert Papers.

> Acknowledge having received from Madam Juber [*sic*] a sum of eight rixd. for the account of Apsalon van Malgasker [*sic*], for the service which he had to render here at the Cape, [*signed:*] [*illegible*] Hendricksz, Cape of Good Hope, the 6th January 1735.

> [I], Apselon van Mallegassij, a slave bought[?] from Stockvliet, acknowledge having received a year's wages from Leijsebet [*Elisabeth*], widow of Pieter Jobert [*sic*] with a receipt for thirty-six rixdollars. Thus I have signed this with my own hand. This is the X of Apselon van Mallegassij. On the Breede River, the 19 March *anno* 1735.[188]

Similarly slaves were said by Mentzel to frequent 'the cheapest type of wine shop', 'not so much to drink as to gamble. They have their master's permission, for which they pay 6 stuivers daily, and are free to pocket their winnings.'[189]

These various systems of making money by means of slave labour led in the eighteenth century to what Ross describes as 'the rise of a rentier class in Cape Town, living not off land but off the so-called "koeli geld" brought in by their slaves'.[190] Once again, it is not clear whether any of these arrangements had already come into being by the beginning of the eighteenth century, or to what extent, but this is the way the more sophisticated form of slavery was developing in the relatively urbanised Table Valley.

The slaves employed by artisans and craftsmen inevitably acquired some knowledge and skill, even if they received no formal instruction from their masters, and it is probably by these means that a class of slave craftsmen came into being. 'If the market gardeners on the mountain slopes are excepted,' Ross writes with reference to the eighteenth century, 'almost all the productive slaves worked either as craftsmen or fishermen',[191] although Kolb, describing local weddings, refers to 'music which the slaves have learned to make very beautifully on all manner of instruments',[192] an aspect of the slave society of the Cape which is not often remembered.

A further source of possible income for slaves, whether on their own initiative or on behalf of their owners, was beachcombing, especially after a ship had been wrecked in the Table Bay area. In 1722 a *plakkaat* issued in this connection referred disapprovingly to 'many of the local residents as well as Company servants and also slaves' being 'more inclined to undertake expeditions along the beaches and elsewhere to carry off jetsam' than to help with salvage operations.[193]

Finally, slaves could obtain money or goods by the sale or exchange of stolen goods, and Ross refers to 'the world of "domestic theft and receiving" of Cape Town', in which

> the slaves were able to finance their pleasure—above all wine and gambling, but also opium-smoking—by stealing from their masters and passing the goods (above all cloth) on to the Chinese community that for the first half of the eighteenth century had the receiving business in its own hands. The Chinese had been recruited for the work, it would appear, most of them having been sent to the Cape as punishment for similar crimes in Batavia.[194]

Probably this network was only just beginning to take shape during the period under discussion, and is not yet reflected fully in the available records. As Ross remarks: 'Especially in the 1730s and to a degree early in the 1760s, the regular life of the Cape Town slaves becomes clearer for us because what was tacitly accepted in normal times was now persecuted.'[195] By 1700, however, thefts by slaves had already become such a serious problem that a *plakkaat* was issued forbidding trade with them in 'clothing, household goods, (…) weapons, gold, silver, cattle, corn or any goods whatsoever'.[196]

According to the sentences listed by Heese, two Chinese ex-*ban-dieten* were hanged in 1705 for theft,[197] but the earliest case of a Chinese acting as a receiver of stolen goods occurs in 1725, when two female slaves, Caatje van de Caab and Pater van Batavia, were tried together with Tio Tjanko who had incited them to steal from their mistress, Gesina Meijboom. Four other Chinese and a free black, Jacobus Hendricksz van de Cust, were also mentioned in connection with the case.[198] In 1733 Cornelis van de Caab stole porcelain- and silverware which he sold to two Chinese who were sentenced together with him to five years hard labour in chains.[199]

In 1813 the Fiscal, summarising the existing body of laws on slaves and slavery as these had come into existence under the VOC, gave a remarkably vivid little sketch of this Cape underworld which is probably, all things considered, equally applicable insofar as it already existed a hundred years earlier: 'No slave may sing, whistle or make any other noise at night in the streets, by which they are accustomed to induce one another out of the houses, thereby affording an opportunity of committing irregularities or of concealing stolen goods, on pain, if detected therein, of being severely flogged.'[200]

Female slaves were employed as domestic workers, cooks and washerwomen, and there is an early reference in 1668 to Dorothea, a slave of the Secunde Hendrick Lacus, 'standing by the river washing'.[201] Lacus and his family lived in the Fort, and the 'river' was one of the mountain streams in the immediate vicinity, which was the customary laundering place at the time. Washing was usually done in any convenient river or stream, and throughout the eighteenth century there would be horrified accounts by Europeans of the way in which fine linen was manhandled by Cape laundresses.[202] As early as 1717 reference is made to cotton clothing, 'which is washed by being beaten on a stone or plank in cold water. Linen could never be handled in this rough way.'[203] 'Dutch linen after it has been washed twice here, falls to pieces because it is beaten [on the stones]. It is impossible to teach the slaves to wash on their hands— this way of washing would take too long and be more expensive.'[204]

Female slaves also acted as personal attendants to the women of the house, nursemaids, wet nurses and seamstresses, while Mentzel mentions that slave women from Surat and Bengal in India 'and other similar places' were able to embroider 'most beautifully', 'so long as the designs are provided for them'.[205]

On the farms slaves were of course employed for all kinds of garden and field work. The opponents of W.A. van der Stel later alleged that he had used '40, 50, 60 and more of the Hon. Company's slaves, both men and women', for 'clearing the 400 morgen of thickets, shrubs and heath' in laying out Vergelegen, a task which would have been necessary wherever white farmers settled during the early years of colonisation,[206] as well as for subsequent work on the estate, 'mostly digging ditches, digging in the vineyard and weeding the orchard and other lands'.[207]

Adam Tas came out to the Cape from the Netherlands under the patronage of his uncle by marriage, Henning Hüsing, the richest man in the freeburgher community, and within a few years married a wealthy widow and became the owner of the farm Libertas in the Stellenbosch district. Probably no man achieved success at the Cape during the VOC period more effortlessly than he, and his surviving diary for the years 1705–06, a unique personal record of the time, reflects a leisurely, carefree existence consisting mainly of driving about, visiting or entertaining neighbours, gossiping, drinking wine, smoking and playing cards. His work on the farm seems to have consisted mainly of strolling about to see what was being done.

While Tas cannot be considered a typical farmer, even for this class, his diary at any rate illustrates a way of life which was by this time becoming common among the bigger farmers and slave owners of the Boland. 'Sowed this day: Sicilian corn, 2 muids; wheat 1¾ muids', he recorded in a marginal note that winter, and in another: 'Sowed this day: ½ muid barley, ½ bushel peas.' One muid or *mud* equalled 120 litres. Throughout the diary, however, slave labour, casually referred to, was constantly going on in the background.

This day three of our slaves began pruning the vineyard; the others busy repairing the wall or bank in several places…. Pruning of the vineyard was resumed and straw carted into the pens…. Progress was made with the pruning of the vine-yard. The rest of the slaves have been cutting wood at the river…. When the rain stopped in the afternoon, the slaves resumed digging…. There had evidently been some rain over-night, and it still looked like rain, accordingly all our slaves were busy digging in the vineyard near the house…. This day our labourers ['*volk*', *slaves*] were again weeding among the corn…. This day our labourers were busy cutting rye and Sicilian wheat…. In the afternoon our slaves were busy cut-ting the ripest corn…. This day our rye was carted home, being 2,500 sheaves…. In the afternoon our labourers were busy stooking corn…. A start was made this morning with carting corn to the house…. This day our labourers have been busy threshing…. Our labourers were busy cleaning corn. The rest of the rye was weighed and stored in the loft. The total rye crop amounted to 34½ muids….[208]

Other activities were also mentioned casually: 'Shortly after mid-day I despatched 3 leaguers of wine to the Cape with one of our own wagons and two wagons hired from Barend Lubbe,' for example; 'This morning a load of corn was brought to the mill, and having been turned into meal, the load was brought back at evening'; or 'This day 51 of our draught oxen sent to Groene Clooff.' One leaguer or *legger* was approximately 600 litres, and the oxen were sent away to Groenkloof in the present Darling area for grazing.

'Farm work was highly seasonal,' write Armstrong & Worden in a particularly evocative passage,

but farms producing both grain and wheat provided work steadily throughout the year. On grain farms the major tasks were sowing and ploughing between May and July and harvesting between December and February. In the vineyards, cutting and pruning took place in July and August, weeding in October and November and grape-picking in late February and March. (…)

There was no mechanisation on the farms, and some tasks were back-breaking, such as the harvesting of grain with sickles, the picking of low-hanging grapes or winnowing with sieves. In the Cape Town hinterland harvesting had to be performed swiftly, between the ripening of grain and its flattening by the onset of strong southeasterly winds. (…) Work began at dawn and continued until midday when the heat caused the grain to fall out of the husks as it was reaped. It was resumed in mid-afternoon and lasted until dusk at about 8 p.m. After dark the labourers took sheaves to the threshing floors and laid them out ready for trampling by horses and winnowing the next day. (…)

At other times of the year, slaves performed a variety of tasks. Field labour included the seasonal occupations of sowing and ploughing, pruning vine stocks and weeding, as well as herding livestock. (…) Other regular chores included the collection of wood, 'an arduous and daily task' as forests became denuded in the arable regions. (…) Older farm slaves often worked as shepherds or as ox-drivers in the ploughing season.[209]

'Industrious farmers,' reports Mentzel, 'let no hour pass unused.'

Even in the season between sowing and harvesting, when the countryman could sometimes have an easy time, they keep themselves and their servants busy; and when the weather is so inclement that nothing can be done outside; the slaves under cover of a roof, in the barn or in their dwellings, will at least make ropes and cords out of old anchor cables, for tying oxen and knee-haltering horses (…).[210]

Occasionally one finds some detail of the world of the slaves sketched incidentally in contemporary documents, such as the declaration by a cooper in Company service who described how he had made four large winepresses for W.A. van der Stel, 'in each of which four boys [*slaves*] could press out the grapes simultaneously'.[211] There are also references to slaves acting as wagon drivers, fetching firewood for their masters,[212] or taking wheat to the mill at Stellenbosch or Drakenstein.[213] and in a probate inventory compiled in 1713 there is a chance listing of 'one white man's shirt given to the slave woman ["*meijt*"] to wash'.[214]

Slave children on farms were not exempt from work as were Company slaves under the age of twelve. 'Slave children,' writes Mentzel, 'are found useful for work from the ages of ten or twelve, especially during harvest time. At such time slave children have the task of following the reapers and gathering the wheat into piles, ready for tying into sheaves.'[215] They also 'scared birds and animals from the crops, weeded and did other field tasks during the peak seasons'.[216]

As the large farms grew progressively larger, some degree of specialisation would probably have been called for among the more able of the slaves, as was foreshadowed by the fact that the Company cooper, Hans Pietersz, was asked to give instruction in barrel-making to a slave of W.A. van der Stel, 'who advanced so far that he could make all kinds of barrels and halfaums from staves'.[217] By 1717 Captain Dominique Pasques de Chavonnes, as a member of the Council of Policy, could point out that a 'herdsman, mason, wagon-driver or workman's apprentice' cost twice as much as an untrained slave,[218] and where the slaves belonging to Theunis Dircksz van Schalkwijk were listed in his probate inventory in the same year, one Titus was distinguished from the others as a 'cattle herder'.[219] Such slaves could also be hired out profitably to others in the neighbourhood in a way which was to become general in the town.[220]

In the Liesbeek valley and in the immediate vicinity of Stellenbosch, farms were possibly within walking distance of each other, and according to his diary the wealthy Adam Tas in the early years of the eighteenth century regularly walked to neighbouring farms and to the village.[221] Where homesteads were more widely scattered, situated in mountain glens or separated by rivers, slaves probably had contact with the outside world only when they were sent to other farms with messages or to help with the work, or had occasion to travel to the local smith or mill.[222]

Sunday was traditionally a free day for slaves, though this was often ignored when there was work to be done,[223] and as early as 1670 the Council of Policy expressed concern about the fact that 'a portion of the residents do not hesitate to let their slaves and servants work on Sabbath and sermon days, not only before, but during the sermons'.[224] Only two years later, however, the Journal itself could note: 'This second Christmas Day celebrated in the usual manner by going to church, the Company's slaves only being kept at work.'[225]

Adam Tas let 'our slaves and the Hottentots' continue harvesting or digging in the vineyard on a Sunday,[226] and a visiting missionary was surprised to find this work continuing while Tas himself went to church.[227] 'Fortunate are those slaves whose masters still have so much religious feeling as not to grudge them their Sunday's rest,' wrote Mentzel by the 1730s.[228]

Writing from his own observations in the 1730s, by which time there were probably more locally born than imported slaves in the community, and a relative degree of stability may have been achieved, Mentzel observed rather wilfully that

it may be said that even the slaves are quite happy in their bondage. This may be clearly perceived in fine weather and on moonlit evenings. For although the slave has worked fairly hard and suffered from heat during the day, yet he is happy and sings, and plays on his *raveking* (*ramkie*)[229] and even dances. But on winter evenings they sit round the fire with a pipe of tobacco and tell each other stories of their fatherland in Portuguese (*lingua franca*).[230]

In a rural context he refers to farmers sometimes having 'a slave or mixed-breed Hottentot who can strum a bit on the fiddle'. 'Among the slaves and Hottentots there are generally womenfolk who can pluck the strings of a *raveking* (…), and to whose highly unmelodious sound another slave or Hottentot adds a few discords on the *gom-gom* [*ghomma*, *drum*] to the dancing of the slaves.'[231] By the end of the century Lady Anne Barnard, describing a 'Sunday Slave Ball' in Cape Town, 'by the side of a long & high wall', refers similarly to 'a Hottentot instrument—a gourd at the end of a bit of wood with a few strips of catgut, it makes an uncouth and wild sound'.[232]

Kolb mentions the inclination of slaves to use any extra money they might obtain to make 'Sunday clothes' for themselves; 'for although these people appear to be the most forlorn and miserable creatures who depended on the whims of others, most of them are marked by incredible pride; so that when they are a little spruced up they hardly know themselves, and cannot bear be laughed at or made fun of for this reason'.[233] For festive occasions, Mentzel observes likewise, 'they buy ornaments and fine coloured kerchiefs to bind round their heads, puffs, i.e. small pieces of taffeta to sew to the edge of their trouser-legs, and articles of like nature',[234] in which one may possibly see the burgeoning of a tradition which was to lead, in due course and under many divergent influences, to the development of the 'Coon Carnival' of the Cape.

In the country the possibilities of obtaining some money were considerably fewer for slaves than in the town. Those who were given ground to cultivate by their masters were allowed to keep the money if they sold the proceeds, although this would, of course, imply a local market,[235] and sometimes they would be rewarded for capturing or killing buck and other wild animals which could harm the crops and gardens.[236] Opportunities for making money by gambling probably occurred only in and around Stellenbosch, or when slaves congregated in larger numbers at the mill at Stellenbosch or Drakenstein or accompanied their owners to church at these two places, even though Kolb refers loosely to their indulgence in 'gaming, boozing and whoring'.[237]

In 1686 a *plakkaat* referred to freeburgher slaves 'gathering and meeting both in public and private beside paths and streets, in corners and recesses, as well as in the countryside, not only to gamble and play, but also become intoxicated and commit other vile excesses'.[238] At the time of the general unrest surrounding the conflict between W.A. van der Stel and a section of the freeburghers in 1706, the Landdrost of Stellenbosch, Johannes Starrenburg, referred heatedly and in very similar terms to the fact that

> great sauciness and unbridled license are being observed among the slaves in the country, who are beginning to despise and neglect their duties, so much so that many absent themselves from their masters during the night and congregate in the back slums of certain freemen's houses to gamble, get drunk, and commit other irregularities. That their impudence and daring have become so great that on Sundays when they do not work, they cause great commotion in Stellenbosch and neighbourhood by fighting, beating and throwing one another, making the highways unsafe and not even hesitating to molest and frighten the minister there, &c.[239]

The meetings objected to were probably no more than the boisterous gatherings of people briefly released from bondage, but there was always a good deal of underlying tension in the community at the Cape, and it was necessary for the authorities to be watchful. In 1686 the Council of Policy, noting with disapproval the gatherings of slaves mentioned above, expressed the opinion that these served 'more particularly (as daily experience teaches) to consult with one another, either to desert and thus deprive their masters, or to commit robberies, yea, manslaughter and murder'. 'Gatherings, whether in the town or the country, of three, four or more boys [*male slaves*] belonging to different owners' were accordingly forbidden and the slaves concerned were to be delivered to the Fiscal 'to be corrected and punished, in order that the slaves may thus be taught greater respect and better held to duty and obedience towards their masters'.[240]

When a *plakkaat* was issued the same year to guard against fire, slaves were, together with soldiers and sailors, forbidden to be out of doors 'after nine o'clock at night or after the ringing of the bell',[241] referring to the curfew bell at the Castle. A year later it was ordained more fully that no freeburgher slaves were to be allowed in the streets or outside their masters' grounds or lands after ten o'clock, unless sent out by their owners and supplied with a pass, in which case they had to carry 'a lighted lantern, flare or torch'. The punishment for transgressors was to be brought before the Fiscal or Landdrost 'to be bound to a stake or tree, as may be convenient, and well scourged and beaten with rods, a stick or a cane'.[242]

In 1709 it was further laid down that slaves sent from home by their masters on an errand had to be provided with a lead token with the name of the slave and the Company's monogram, to be obtained at the Castle at a skelling each.[243] Franken, writing in 1931, described this as 'the basis of the pass system at the Cape and later in the [Boer] Republics'.[244]

In 1686 it was likewise forbidden to allow slaves to handle or carry their masters' guns or side arms, 'even in tending the cattle',[245] as had apparently been permitted in newly settled areas where wild animals still constituted a threat, and in 1688 slave owners were warned against their slaves managing to appropriate their firearms 'and collect and hide them with evil intentions, by which means this colony might easily suffer a great and irreparable disaster'. Reference was made specifically to 'flintlocks, blunderbusses, carbines or pistols hanging on the walls or on racks'.[246]

Typically enough, the freeburgher Balster Christaensz Wever of the Stellenbosch district was in 1701 unwilling to leave home to help search for a fugitive slave as he was ordered to do 'as his boys [*slaves*] were behaving in such a way that he had not dared go to bed for seven or eight nights, but constantly kept watch in order that they might not run away also'.[247] No less typical is Pieter van der Bijl, a prominent inhabitant of the same district, who promised in the same year to manumit his slave Hannibal van Tuticorijn after ten more years of faithful service, on condition that the man would not steal from him or try to abscond, and would warn him if any of his other slaves tried to do anything to his disadvantage.[248]

The outbreak of violence which slave owners were always expecting and dreading seldom took a personal form, however, such as occurred in the case of Claes van Malabar, 'aged about fifty years', a slave of the veteran freeburgher Jan Coenraed Visser, who was broken on the wheel in 1692 for killing his master's wife.

Claes himself stated, as recorded officially in the phraseology of a Company official,

that when, towards evening, he was busy chopping some firewood about eight or ten paces from his master's ['*patroons*'] house, he was so negligent about it that his mistress ['*patronesse*'] (…), coming home from her daughter's house, reprimanded him for his negligence, asking him at the same time what had kept him busy for so long, and further saying that he knew well that she had to bake the next day and afterwards go in to the Fort [*Castle*] as well. To which he replied with the excuse that he had been to look for the cattle on the mountain, and his mistress in turn that the cattle were nearby and did not need to be looked for.

That he, at these words, setting aside all due respect, was driven to the outrageous extravagance of daring to say to his mistress, eighty-two years old: You old dog, then you can go and fetch them yourself!

That his mistress, justifiably angered at this offensive abuse and improper reply, picked up a little branch from the ground, threatening to hit him with it. That he, through his evil nature, was driven by this to such inconceivable and inhuman cruelty that he did not hesitate to lift up the axe and with it give his mistress a blow in her face on the left side of the temple of the head to the cheek, in such a way that she immediately fell to the ground.[249]

In attempting to interpret all this, much depends of course on the relationship of the Vissers with their slaves, which must remain unknown, although it is recorded that Visser as a widower in 1696 manumitted the young slave Maria van Bengalen with her three small children. 'The deed was to take effect on Visser's death and Maria was to be allowed to take her possessions, kist [*chest*] and clothes out of the estate',[250] a rare mark of thoughtfulness in the early annals of Cape slavery. A further twist is added to these developments by the fact that one of these children, who was to marry a white man, later called herself Susanna Visser,[251] though this by itself need not necessarily prove that Visser was her father.

In this particular case much depends too on the relationship between Claas and his mistress as built up over a longer period, the exact wording and tone of the murdered woman's reprimand and threat, and the size of the '*kleijn tackje*' she picked up from the ground.

In attempting to interpret the inadequate and one-sided evidence on this particular incident, it must be born in mind as well that Claes appears to have been of a somewhat truculent disposition, which cannot have made his position easy in a context of slavery, servility and subservience. Finally, he was a Malabar from the west coast of India, and the Malabars had an unfortunate reputation at the Cape among both black and white, their name duly becoming a general term of abuse.[252] The Journal notes, for example, that Claes remained cold-blooded when interrogated after the murder, and that when God was mentioned to him, he declared 'that he knew neither God nor Devil, that he was a Malabar by descent, that he was satisfied if he received enough to eat and drink and was content to die'. He was duly broken on the wheel, on a day of a raging south-east wind, and was found to be dead by one o'clock that afternoon.[253]

The murder of Margaretha Gerritsz or 'Grietje Grof' as she was known remains enigmatic in many of its details, but it is a clear illustration of the suppressed resentment and constant threat of violence which existed in the slave society at the Cape, and which might erupt at any moment, often with seemingly little obvious or immediate provocation.

The 'average' slave household of the late seventeenth century in the Stellenbosch district has already been described as consisting of one or two white men, a white woman, 5 children and one or two slaves, and this may well have been typical as well. The origins of these people would in most cases have been varied, the men being of Dutch, North German or Scandinavian origin, the women and children typically Cape-born, and the slaves of different origins, as is illustrated by a casual reference to three slaves of Johannes Holsmit being sent out with a wagon in 1692 to chop wood: Claas van Malabar, David van Coromandel and Jommat van Batavia. Their places of origin were the west and east coasts of India and the Indonesian archipelago respectively.[254] Of the 7 slaves on the farm of Trijntje Theunisz Gansevanger in the Tygerberg in 1715, the origins of 6 are given, and they represent an equally wide area in the East: Alexander van Ternaten, Abram van Macassar, Arent van Ceylon, September van Bengalen and Joseph van Batavia, in addition to Jan Caffer van Madagascar.[255] A Khoi or two might also have formed part of these establishments, possibly as casual labourers, and in 1705, for example, the wealthy Adam Tas recorded in his diary his *knecht* Jacob (who is identified only by his first name), 6 slaves and 2 'Hottentots' had been driven out to the coast 'to conduct seine-fishing'.[256]

An extreme example of this diversity is given by the slave holdings of Arnoldus Willemsz Basson, who died a wealthy man in

1724. On his farm in Drakenstein there were 13 male slaves, of whom 2 each came from Cochin in Malabar, Angola and Madagascar, and the others variously from Coromandel, Bengal and Tuticorin in India, Macassar, Bouton Bali and 'Mandarij' (Mandar in Celebes), all in Indonesia, besides 2 female slaves from Madagascar and one from Bengal. On Basson's two further farms at Piketberg and Four-and-Twenty Rivers deeper in the interior, where he kept most of his cattle and sheep, there were a further 10 male slaves, 3 from Bengal and one each from Malabar, Tutucorin and Surat in India, Ceylon, and Batavia, Nias and Maccassar in Indonesia.[257]

This example illustrates even more of the diversity of early slave society at the Cape if one bears in mind that Basson himself was a grandson of the free black woman Angela van Bengalen,[258] while his wife, Maria Vosloo, appears to have had a coloured mother.[259]

Living in close intimacy on an isolated farm, many of them in the same house, working together indoors or out and sharing the common challenges and threats of existence in a pioneering country, farming communities such as these came to form a close-knit little world in which there was of necessity a good deal of interdependence and at least some measure of mutual trust. Their relationships could thus, for all the tensions innate in the situation, also be characterised by a remarkable degree of solidarity.

As far as the slave owners are concerned, it would have been in their own interest to take good care of their slaves, and most of them probably did so according to their own lights. Many of them, for example, paid not inconsiderable sums to such medical practitioners as were available at the early Cape for the treatment of their slaves,[260] but education was not required in a slave, and as likely as not only Company slaves received any schooling.

It appears too that slaves in private ownership were not often baptised,[261] though there was a custom among many of the well-to-do slave owners to have child of one of their slaves baptised on the same day as a child of their own, probably as a social convention or status symbol rather than a matter of conviction.[262] Here Simon van der Stel and the members of his family formed a notable exception among Cape slave owners.[263] It was not until the very last years of the eighteenth century that some of the latter, influenced by the pietistic and evangelistic movements in Europe and the missionaries from Europe who had begun to work locally, grew concerned about the spiritual welfare of their slaves and began informal evangelisation among them.[264]

Kolb likewise mentions that slaves who were Christians were left free, 'and not compelled to attend church if they have no wish to do so themselves. As most of them live at a distance from the church, it happens barely once a year that they are to be seen there, the more so as they spend Sunday cultivating and planting their own piece of ground'.[265]

If there is little information available on the lives of the private slaves, this is of course even more applicable as regards their deaths. Some slave owners promptly sold elderly slaves who were no longer of use, or set them free, while others kept them on in old age and cared for them until they died. There is a casual reference to a slave of the widow Robbertsz at Riebeek-Kasteel on the fringes of the colony, probably at a cattle post, being buried about 300 paces from the house, 'in a blanket with a mat sewn around it',[266] a normal arrangement at the Cape given the shortage of timber for coffins. By 1728 there was a slave cemetery on the estate Constantia, which then belonged to Bastiaan Colijn, the son of the free black Maria Evertsz by a Dutch father, but he probably owned a large number of slaves.[267] In the Table Valley the official grave digger complained of slave owners preferring to bury their slaves themselves and having the graves made so shallow that the corpses were soon exposed,[268] while the village of Stellenbosch had a *slavenkerkhoff* or 'slave cemetery' by 1723, where the sexton charged a rixdollar for 'burying the corpse of a slave', the same amount as for a European.[269]

While the world of slavery was essentially harsh and violent, the relations between whites and slaves in specific cases, on the other hand, were not infrequently characterised by a surprising degree of loyalty and affection. When the slave Samel in 1709 tried to persuade three fellow slaves belonging to different owners to run away with him, they replied, by their own evidence, 'that they (…) did not want to do that since they have good *basen* [*masters*] and are not in want of anything', and 'I have a good *baas* [*master*] and mistress, why should I run away then?'[270] There must have been others who felt like them.

Often too this relationship could be surprisingly informal and even intimate. One reads in the contemporary records, for example, of the wife of Pieter Jansz van Marsseveen, who in 1692 not only felt free to shelter three male slaves overnight in the house where she was apparently alone with her sister, but let them sit on a bench by the fire in the same room where the two women were lying in bed,[271] and in 1714 of the wife of the surgeon Dirk Snith letting a slave who was too weak to walk a great distance ride behind her.[272] During the following decade, Joost Hendriksz, a freeburgher living in the Stellenbosch district, made his slave Carel van Bengalen his universal heir,[273] but was banished in 1728 after the two of them had assaulted the *caffer* of Stellenbosch, while Carel was sentenced to be scourged in public and chained for five years.[274]

The explanation for relationships such as these may well be that slavery was a new and unfamiliar phenomenon both to the immigrant whites and the imported blacks, and that there were no precedents at the Cape for behaviour in a slave society, except insofar as these could be provided by the handful of officials and slaves from the East. A modus vivendi had therefore to be established experimentally.

However, one must be careful too in interpreting records such as these, for the information provided is mostly cursory, the events recorded occurred several centuries ago, and the world in which they took place has become largely incomprehensible and liable to misinterpretation by a modern reader. It is not possible to understand the past fully, or to be certain of interpreting it accurately.

Whatever intimacy or affection there may have been in individual cases, there was, however, always an innate distance between masters and bondsmen, which was essential to the institution of slavery as a whole, and not only respect was insisted upon, but even servility. All white men came to be addressed as *seur*, *sieur* or *sinjeur*, terms derived from the Portuguese *senhor* or 'sir' or the French *seigneur*, which were common under the VOC and appear in the records of Mauritius as early as 1677.[275] An increasingly common form of address at the Cape, however, was *baas* or 'master', which was originally used for the foreman of a group of workmen or *knechten* such as, for example, the VOC's *baastuinier* or 'master gardener'.[276] This would remain the general form of address of white by non-white until the end of the apartheid era, on the threshold of the 21st century.

White women were addressed as *nonje*, from the Portuguese *dona* or 'lady' via the Malay, a common synonym for 'woman' or 'girl', which would develop in Afrikaans into *nonna* or *nonnie*, as well as the more modern *nooi* or *nôi*.[277] *Juffrouw* or 'madam', originally used at the Cape for women of standing, in the early years more especially the Commander's wife, also came to be used in this connection.[278]

The degree of servility expected in a slave is illustrated tellingly in a letter written in 1719 on behalf of Jonas van Manado, from the Indonesian archipelago, to his mistress, the widow Hermina Gillis, to request his freedom. While it was obviously drawn up by an educated person acquainted with legal documents, it seems equally clear that he largely made use of Jonas's own phrasing.

To the virtuous *juffrouw* Aarmintie ['*Hermientje*'] Gilles,

Your honourable *juffrouw*'s obedient slave gives notice, with all humility and sadness of heart, with the presentation to your honourable *juffrouw* of how he, the suppliant, had served your honourable *juffrouw*, since fully ten years ago now, with faithful service, without complaining to anybody, consequently he, the suppliant, is finally seeking your honourable *juffrouw*'s aid with hands clasped and knees bent, praying humbly that it would please your honourable *juffrouw* to look upon him, the suppliant, in keeping with her innate mercifulness, with the eyes of compassion, and to please permit him, the suppliant, a letter of freedom. He, the suppliant, promises to serve your honourable *juffrouw* with faithful service.

Which I do, &c.[279]

The request was refused, as a result of which Jonas attempted to kill his mistress with a knife. He was sentenced to have his right hand chopped off and to be hanged.

Male slaves were referred to as *jongen* (*jong* in Afrikaans) or 'boy' and *meid* (in varying spellings during the period under discussion) or 'girl', common terms applied to white servants in Dutch which at the Cape came to be used exclusively for slaves and other non-whites, irrespective of age.[280] On the other hand, for elderly non-white people the respectful though perhaps slightly patronising terms *paai* and *maai* were in use, from the Portuguese for 'father' and 'mother', which had also reached the Cape via the East.[281] An entire colonial world with its variety of language, its hierarchies, gradations and general obsequiousness is illustrated in a few forms of address.

As far as the wider world is concerned, Dutch was of course the official language of the VOC, the language of the courts, of proclamations and *plakkaten* emanating from the authorities, the church and such schools or informal instruction by private teachers as existed. While the French refugees at first persisted in using their own language in dealings with the authorities, their church council was instructed to use Dutch in 1709, and after the 1720s church services were no longer held in French. Members of the smaller domestic world would likewise have used some form of Dutch in their official communications with the authorities in Stellenbosch or the Castle, especially in writing.

In a purely local or domestic context, Dutch-born men and those from the Southern Netherlands (Belgium) would have represented a variety of Dutch dialects, while the others probably spoke the language in various broken forms. Freeburghers who through earlier service in the East under the VOC had some knowledge of Eastern languages or Portuguese would naturally have used these, insofar as appropriate, in their dealings with slaves during the early years. Much the same applies here as has already been said with regard to the Company slaves in the Lodge, especially during the early eighteenth century, when not only the number of slaves in private hands increased, but more specifically those from India and Ceylon, where a form of Portuguese served as *lingua franca*, and Indonesia, where Malay served the same purpose.

Franken draws attention to 'the evidence for the widespread use of Portuguese as general everyday language among the slaves and to a certain extent acquaintance with it among the whites *during the first half of the eighteenth century*'.[282] Some colonists seem to have acquired a working knowledge of one or both of these languages at the Cape,[283] and there is even reference to a locally born white woman on a farm in the Roggeveld, deep in the interior, who in about 1760 communicated 'as best she was able to bring forth in an imperfect manner in Malay and Portuguese' with a new and inexperienced slave who was described as 'unable to speak a word of Portuguese but only Malay'.[284]

With all due allowance for the ignorance of new arrivals, however, the main means of attempted communication would in the case of most whites ultimately have been some variety of dialectical or broken Dutch, which the slaves would in turn acquire from them or from each other or from Khoi servants on the same farm. It is in these circumstances that one finds what Groenewald describes as 'the earliest forms of the restructuring of Dutch at the Cape which eventually resulted in the formation of Afrikaans'.[285] Raidt has written specifically about the role played by Cape-born women, 'and this includes manumitted slave women', in this process of linguistic change, in a limited domestic context of children, household slaves and Khoi servants.[286]

A further significant element in this domestic microcosm was the white farmhand or *knecht*, about whom there had been so many complaints during the early years of settlement.[287] Rather than disappearing from the local scene with the general acquisition of slave labour, the *knecht* was increasingly promoted from white farm labourer to overseer of black labour, especially on larger farms or cattle posts.

In 1670 an attempt had already been made to regulate the hiring of *knechten*.[288] By 1692, when the number of slaves in the colony was beginning to increase considerably, they were still so much part of Cape society and still gave so much cause for complaint that it was made compulsory to have a formal contract drawn up between master and *knecht*.[289]

These *knechten* often entered into a contract for no more than a year at a time, but sometimes also served longer, and in 1701 Simon van der Stel described his own *knecht* Pieter Marreveld as 'a man of good comportment who had previously worked for four years for Hendrik Sneewind, eight months for Matthijs Greeff and two years for Jan Vosloo'.[290]

As was explained to the XVII in 1717, many farmers would have liked to free themselves of the expense of keeping white servants, 'were it not that the great distance of the farms from each other compel[s] some [to keep European servants] to look after their slaves, cattle and other property'.[291] As Henning Hüsing's slave holdings increased steadily, for example, so too did the number of *knechten* he employed, from one in 1682, to 10 in 1692, and 24 in 1700.[292] Over roughly the same period the number of free *knechten* in the colony increased from 30 in 1679 to 62 in 1699, and 114 in 1711.[293] This number, however, did not include the Company's servants (*leenknechten* or loan *knechten*) hired out to the colonists, who in 1708 numbered 120.[294] De Wet has traced the names of no fewer than 424 individual free *knechten* over the period 1657–1707, the first half-century of free-burghership, and notes that a quarter of them subsequently began their own undertakings 'with varying degrees of success'.[295]

The *knecht* is of importance in the story of slavery because where he was present on a farm or outpost he was in immediate contact with the slaves, often acting for the master himself in the latter's absence, but his social position was ambivalent, and this caused uncertainly between the two groups. Although freeburghership had been instituted on a basis of social equality, social divisions very soon began to emerge among the whites, determined by origin, authority, ability and relative wealth.

'Between the highest social group and most of the people in the middling group there was a strict division,' writes De Wet with reference to an incident which occurred as early as 1692. 'The farmer and burgher councillor Cornelis [Stevensz] Botma for example called Arij Gerritsz Prinsloo, an illiterate freeman of unknown origin, by his name, while the latter addressed him as "Monsieur Botma".'[296] He also quotes a similar episode which took place in 1707: 'That some of the freemen on the higher social rungs expected marks of respect from the lower officials appears from the incident in which the blacksmith Hans Jacob Conterman struck the veldwagter [*local legal official*] Hartwig Jacob Alsleben with his fist for not having taken off his hat to him.'[297]

'The labourers,' continues De Wet with specific regard to the *knechten*, 'were the lowest social class among the freemen and especially between them and the highest class there was virtually no intercourse. (…) Between the *knechten* and their masters there were likewise social divisions. They addressed the masters as *baas* and did not live in the house but usually in an outside building.'[298] Their standing in local society was strikingly illustrated when the shrewish wife of the freeburgher Jan Cornelisz, known as 'Jan Bombam', burst out at him in 1699 with the words. 'You're lower than a *knecht*, yes, lower than a Hottentot, yes, lower than a dog', and declared 'that she thought less of him than of a slave or a dog'.[299]

It is a further interesting indication of the *knecht*'s status that it was apparently possible for his employer to loan him out for payment. According to Biewenga, the abovementioned Conterman in 1704 demanded 33 guilders from Jan Sanders 'because Conterman's *knecht* had worked for him'.[300]

On the other hand the *knecht*, while not part of his master's family, was his employer's representative with regard to the slaves and shared in his authority, while at the same time he was white, a Christian and a free man, which clearly set him apart from and above them. This inevitably led to tensions and clashes, and there are many instances of *knechten* using violence to assert or maintain their authority and mistreating slaves.[301]

Mentzel, referring to slaves in private hands, albeit for a somewhat later period, writes: 'if the *knecht* does not give the servants enough to eat, the slaves would on occasion complain about it and the proprietor would have to consider such complaints; for in such a case every slave assumes the right to say: *Kammene kumi, kammene kuli*, which means: If I have nothing to eat, I cannot work.'[302] He probably reveals more about the relationship between *knechten* and slaves, however, when he adds:

> No master will listen with patience to complaints about ill-treatment or blows, but would rebuke the slaves, and even command the knecht, in their hearing, to give them a good thrashing if they refuse to obey them; but at the same time he would in private reprimand the knecht for such brutality, and point out to him that the slaves were human beings and that he had to pay a high price for them.[303]

This raises the question of how far the 'domestic correction' permitted by the Statutes of Batavia to the slave owner or his representative might be carried before becoming excessive or degenerating into outright sadism. A slave owner or *knecht* was sometimes put on trial when a slave died after particularly severe punishment, and sentenced, but the question itself was never clearly answered, and men and women in charge of slaves obviously felt free to set their own limits. The slave Valentijn, for example, was made to remove his shirt and then tied to a ladder, after which he was beaten by Pieter Schalk van der Merwe 'till the middle of the night',[304] and when the slave Andries and the Khoi Caffer were beaten by the Frenchman Jean de Thuillet, he 'tied them, pulled them up by the hands to a beam and thrashed them wretchedly with a halter and continued so long with this until he grew tired'.[305]

A single striking case of serious cruelty to a slave during the period under discussion may be described in greater detail as an example.

In 1697 Godfried Meijhuisen, a wealthy man and former owner of the brandy *pacht*, was found guilty of the ill-treatment of Bastiaan van Canarie or Canarij (Canara on the west coast of India), who was accused or suspected of having stolen a copper kettle, as well as a variety of other goods found in a bundle which had been hidden in a haystack: 'two stones of soap, about a pound of thread, a pair of underdrawers, a shirt, and some long neck-ties, both with and without lace'.[306]

Having been tied to a ladder, Bastiaan was subjected to a protracted beating with a thick cane and lengths of thatching cord, in which Meijhuisen's wife, young children, *knechten* and slaves all seem to have taken part in succession, 'excepting Claas van Paliacatte, who meanwhile held the ladder'. This was followed by further collective beatings which lasted for several hours and included Bastiaan being strung in a so-called *Poolse bok*,[307] 'although they sometimes paused, drinking a jug of wine and smoking a pipe of tobacco'. The result was that he eventually died, 'notwithstanding the slave Maria van Madagascar sprinkling his face with water, but in vain, and some time being spent in this'.

Meijhuisen was sentenced to have a sword swung over his head while kneeling blindfold before a heap of sand, a symbolic punishment customary at the time, which was commuted by Simon van der Stel because of the 'public scandal', to be followed by hard labour for life on Robben Island, where he died in 1704, and his possessions were confiscated. The latter included a town house in the Table Valley, and a new house with several rooms on his farm, a considerable amount of clothing, '7 paintings representing the

7 Sybils', some porcelain and pieces of silverware, a fashionable octagonal table, a large Bible with brass clasps, and 7 male and 2 female slaves, while 400 guilders were still owing by the estate for 'the purchase of a female slave in two payments'.[308]

This was an extreme case, but it was by no means unique, and in 1731 a *plakkaat* had to be issued forbidding slave owners to bury slaves without the bodies having first been examined officially, with specific reference to 'cruel chastisement and other barbarous treatment' suffered by slaves from owners 'forgetting their Christian duty'.[309] Such cases might well be dismissed as the work of pathologically disturbed individuals, were it not that they occur with such monotonous regularity among the relatively small group of Cape slave owners during the entire period in which slavery existed here. Meijhuisen himself, who had directly caused the death of Bastiaan van Canarie, was clearly a successful businessman by local standards and a prominent member of the small white community, with a relatively elegant style of life. Lord Acton's famous dictum about absolute power corrupting absolutely applies equally to the absolute power over other human beings conferred by slavery.

All that can be said in defence of the system is that though the limits to what was permissible under 'domestic correction' were very vague, they nonetheless existed. When a slave owner went too far, there were members of the white community who would express concern and disapproval and bring the matter to the attention of the authorities, and the authorities when informed would duly take it up as in the case of Meijhuisen. When Isak van Ceylon in 1686 complained of mistreatment by his master, Tobias Marquart, and claimed that a fellow slave had recently died after a heavy beating, he was likewise heard, and sold by order of the Political Council 'in order to liberate him from his master's vengeance and wrath and threatened harsh treatment', the purchase money being made over to Marquart.[310]

Complaints by the slaves themselves could also be dangerous, however, when not believed, and Heese mentions the case of Antony van Malabar, the slave of Hendrik Moes, who was scourged, branded and returned to his owner in 1718 after having falsely accused the latter of killing the slave January van Malabar.[311]

When the movement of cattle farmers on to the inland plains beyond the Cape mountains began in the early decades of the eighteenth century, there was no control over what happened on the widely scattered farms and cattle posts of the interior, and the Bokkeveld and Roggeveld regions are said to have become 'especially notorious' in later years for the mistreatment of slaves which took place there.[312]

This leaves the question of the sexual lives of the slaves.

Among the Company's slaves there were usually many more women than men, for the ships it sent out to Madagascar and other slave markets were mostly obliged to take what was given to them, in spite of their objections. The freeburghers in their individual transactions were free to choose, however, and preferred men who could serve as labourers on the farms, and Shell points out that their slave holdings were predominantly male, although there was 'a relatively higher proportion of female slaves in the town than in the rural areas'.[313]

Given the facts that men were by far in the majority, no form of marriage or other legal union was possible and there was no guarantee of stability in the casual relationships which were the norm, there was naturally a great deal of competition, jealousy and sexual tension in the slave community. Regular glimpses of this are to be caught in contemporary court records and legislation and in casual references by white observers.

According to Dr Böeseken, 'When it was discovered that Paul, a slave from the Coast of Malabar, who belonged to the Free Black Anthony from Bengal, had hidden Calafora, a slave woman belonging to the Company, for three days and nights in his room, he was flogged and branded. The woman, who was pregnant, was to be punished after the birth of her child.'[314] This incident, which took place in 1679, presumably indicated a personal relationship between the two people concerned.

Kolb mentions an early case of a crime of passion with which he was involved while serving as secretary to the Landdrost and Heemraden of Stellenbosch in 1710–13, when 'a slave of Mr. Pieter van der Beyl [*Bijl*] cut the throat of a female slave who was his concubine and likewise belonged to the said Mr. van der Beyl, in the garden, under the impression that she also had connections with another man, on whom I together with two other persons and a surgeon had to perform an inquest and order her to be buried'. The slave concerned cut his own throat a few days later while in custody with a razor he had concealed under his clothing.[315]

This is as far as information is available for the period under discussion in this book, but in Heese's lists of sentences pronounced in the eighteenth century one finds, during the early period, the names of Adolph van Madagascar, found guilty of arson 'in rage at the infidelity of his "wife"' and sentenced to death in 1720,[316] and Antony van Goa (possibly Gowa in Macassar), who in 1721 was scourged, branded and sent back to his widowed owner in chains for assaulting a slave woman 'who had been unfaithful to him'.[317]

The documents relating to the latter case have been transcribed and published and help to make what seems to be an arbitrary act of violence explicable and even excusable. Antony, 'about thirty years old at a guess', who had been sold to a new owner at a public auction, returned without permission to the home of his previous master, and the assault took place when he found that the female slave Jannetie, 'who was the prisoner's concubine (as he asserts) when he too was living there as a slave, and who had promised him she would not take another man for as long as he was alive, (…) was lying with another *jongen*'.[318]

Or in his own words as recorded during his interrogation, 'she was my own wife while I lived there (…). This *meijd* had sworn, I will never take another man for as long as you live, yet when [I] saw that she was lying with another man, then my heart ached, I then pushed away the *jongen* and I stabbed her with a knife in the abdomen'.[319] As the editor of this document remarks: 'It is a rare example of a slave's direct testimony, albeit mediated through the scribe of the court.'[320]

While slavery in the seventeenth century in many respects remains an area of darkness, or at any rate a twilight zone, as far as the eighteenth is concerned it is remarkable how many of the cases selected for publication by Worden & Groenewald in *Trials of slavery* and those listed by Heese in *Reg en onreg* concern crimes of passion or jealousy or others having similar sexual motives.[321] The forcible parting of partners or the infidelity of one of them could mean that a whole little world of personal affection and security painfully constructed in the unfavourable context of slavery was disrupted and destroyed, with results which could on occasion be dramatic.

This was realised and acknowledged by the slave owners and attention was paid to the fact, if only with a view to greater stability among their labour force. While slaves could not contract a legal marriage, Kolb observes that farmers in possession of a 'faithful and willing' slave took care to provide him with a wife and help them support their children, 'and thus he lives with her in an unmarried state, but not before his master has consented'. A further advantage of such a union to the master, also pointed out by Kolb, was that the children were automatically born into slavery and became his property,[322] and Botha observes, 'Slaves had no "potestas" over their children, even while minors, such children being the property of their masters.'[323]

Though this form of union was sanctioned by the slave owner who had the required authority to do so, neither in the union itself, nor in the family, was there accordingly any real stability or security, and the individuals concerned remained wholly dependent on the goodwill of their master and his heirs or successors.

It was on the children born of slave women, whether from approved unions such as these or casual liaisons with white or black, that slavery at the Cape depended for its continuation as much as on the erratic importation of slaves from the East and elsewhere, which meant that casual sexual relations on the part of slave women and the resulting pregnancies were not necessarily discouraged by their owners either. Relations between white men and slave women were as common outside the Slave Lodge as within, although they attracted considerably less attention, and the fathers of halfbreed children were not infrequently known and identified as such.

The German Detlef Biebow already referred to, to mention an interesting and probably not untypical example, had a child by Diana van de Caab, the slave of a freeburgher, who was baptised in 1687. Not only was he openly acknowledged on this occasion as the father, but after he married a white woman contact was apparently kept between the members of his respective families, illegitimate and legitimate, coloured and white. His daughters both married German immigrants, and when Susanna Biebow, the coloured daughter, had a child baptised in 1711, her white half-sister and brother-in-law acted as witnesses.[324]

It would seem too that the situation of these two young women in local society did not differ very much either. When they died within a few months of each other in 1713–14, most likely in child-birth, Willem Odendaal, the husband of the elder, illegitimate daughter, owned some blacksmith's tools and a slave and his estate was valued at 672 guilders, while Philip Morkel, who married the younger, legitimate child, was in possession of 10 empty wine leaguers, which seems to indicate farming activities, 4 male slaves, a female and two 'little girls', and his estate was worth 1030 guilders.[325]

Hans Rutgertroost in 1688 referred openly in his will to 'my two children Karel and Hendrik Rutgertroost, procreated illegitimately by my former slave, now freely manumitted, Maria van Bengala [sic]', appointing them as his universal heirs.[326] Likewise Dirk Pretorius, stable master in the service of the Company, 'had three illegitimate children with a non-white woman Maria van de Caab and appointed them as his heirs';[327] this was in 1707, and the mother of his children was Maria Hansdochter, one of the early free black residents in the Table Valley.

There were also a number of relatively stable unions between white men and women of slave origin. Cornelis Claasz, an early member of the Cape community under Van Riebeeck, had three children by Catryn van Bengalen, a 'baptised black', who were baptised themselves over the years, and he married their mother in 1676.[328] He is possibly the same man who was in charge of the outpost De Schuur until 1671, when he became a freeburgher, and subsequently leased the ground from the Company in 1678–79.[329]

When the Khoikhoi began to settle on white farms as labourers it happened increasingly that a male slave had a child by a Khoi woman, in which case the child, usually known as a 'Bastaart-Hottentot', was free,[330] and likewise contributed to the establishment of a free coloured population at the Cape. In 1721 a number of white farmers petitioned the Council of Policy, pointing out that these children, being brought up on their farms, had obligations towards them and requesting that they be obliged to serve their white 'foster masters' for a given period.[331]

The inability of slaves to contract a legal marriage or be assured of a reasonably stable union, and the fact that they had no power or control over their own children, is a reminder of the inexorable fact that whatever palliatives there may have been in given cases, the slaves' lot was essentially unbearable. This applies not only to their unfree state as such, but equally to its implications, which affected their daily lives in every possible way, reminding them continually of their legal helplessness and social inferiority.

According to the summary of the legal position of the slaves given by C. Graham Botha,

Slaves were not competent to make or take under a will, and in general they could acquire no property except for their masters, nor could they enter into binding contracts, either on their own account or on behalf of their masters. It frequently happened that a well-disposed master would allow his slave to have the free administration of whatever he might acquire for himself either by his own labour or otherwise. (…) A slave could not be injured verbally, but a corporal offence against him was punished according to the circumstances. Killing a slave was technically murder, though the fact that death was due to excessive punishment on the part of the master appears to have been regarded as an extenuating circumstance. (…) The law that slaves were not competent to give evidence in Courts of Justice, though observed during the Dutch period, was repealed, in so far as Christian slaves were concerned, in 1823.[332]

The situation of the slave population under the VOC may be further deduced from the proclamation referred to here, which was issued under the British administration by Lord Charles Somerset on 18 March 1823,[333] with the declared object of 'the removing of any existing evils' in the system of slavery, and the propagation of Christianity among the slaves.

According to this, slaves who had been baptised might henceforth legally marry with the consent of their respective owners, and a married couple might not subsequently be sold separately, nor could children under their ninth year be separated from their mothers. Children above three and under ten years of age were to be sent to school for at least three days a week where this was feasible, 'and those whose residence will not permit them to afford this consoling advantage to their slave children are anxiously invited to avail themselves of any means which may offer for giving them instruction'. Slaves were allowed to possess property, 'whether acquired by work in extra hours (with the permission of the proprietor), by donation, legacy, inheritance or by any other honest means)', and the evidence of baptised slaves was to be accepted in court.

Slaves were 'daily to be supplied with sufficient and wholesome food' and 'good and sufficient clothing'. The working day in gardens or fields was not to exceed ten hours in each 24 in the winter and twelve hours in the summer months, and no slave was to be compelled 'to perform field labour on the Sabbath-day, or any other work but such as is ordinarily considered work of necessity'.

As regards misdemeanours, slave owners and their representatives were 'not at liberty to inflict any punishment on a slave beyond what may be considered a mild domestic correction'. This seems already to have been limited to a maximum of 39 lashes under British administration in 1813,[334] but it was now for the first time defined: 'this correction is only to be given with rods or other implements of domestic punishment, it is not to exceed twenty-five stripes, and is in no case to be repeated within twenty-four hours, nor until the delinquent shall have recovered from the effects of any former correction'. This was further reduced to a maximum of fifteen stripes in 1831, while the flogging of female slaves was forbidden in 1830.[335]

Finally provision was made for the lodging of complaints by slaves with the local magistrates who had under the British replaced the Landdrosts of the Dutch era.

Modest as its stipulations were, this proclamation may well be regarded as the bill of rights of Cape slaves, 170 years after the stowaway Abraham from Batavia made his appearance in Table Bay.

There were, however, also other issues deeply influencing the lives of the slaves, and this, surprisingly enough, was recognised by the members of the Council of Justice in 1795 when justifying to the new British authorities the 'degree of severity' with which capital punishment was inflicted at the Cape. While pointing out that this severity should deter slaves 'from the commission of crimes', they also mention that 'the source of these very crimes, as well as the origin of that enmity which slaves bear towards free persons, is to be found in circumstances totally unconnected with the punishment of death'.

We think, under correction, that these causes originate from the consciousness which a slave has of his condition—from the great improbability of his being able to ameliorate his condition—from the difficulties that prevent him from even using means to effect that end—from the abuse which masters often make of their authority—from the want of those principles which might direct and comfort them in their unhappy situation. (...)

The measures we recommend are the following, viz. that masters should zealously endeavour to conduct themselves as fathers rather than as judges in their families, and act according to the strictest rules of virtue and humanity, not only in punishing, but also in rewarding. (...) Upon these principles we would flatter ourselves with the hopes that it is not impossible to inspire slaves with affection for their masters, for it is indisputably true that affection is a reciprocal sentiment, and always increases in proportion to the good actions of him towards whom such sentiments are exerted.[336]

This suggestion, self-seeking though it was, was made after the existence of slavery had exerted its blunting influence on the sensibilities of the population for almost a century and a half, but the thought expressed is probably not much less applicable to the beginning of the period than to the end.

The evidence concerning the effect of all this on the slaves is indirect, although it may be deduced from the repeated occurrence of desertion and arson in the records. However, the voices of the slaves have sometimes been captured in these records as well, and they themelves have on occasion been allowed to formulate some of their grievances. Tellingly enough, these often relate to relatively minor details within the wider framework of slavery. Though it is not a factor often taken into account when writing about slaves, simple loneliness or lack of companionship was, for example, of considerable importance in their daily lives.

In a wider sense the slaves from various parts of the extensive Indonesian archipelago may have had some general sense of cultural or linguistic unity,[337] but this would not have been the case with slaves coming from Malabar, Coromandel, Bengal and Ceylon respectively, while slaves from Madagascar would have been completely alien to the others. As the average slave community on a given farm was relatively small and its members differed in origin, and as farms were mostly widely scattered, few slaves would have had regular contact with anyone from their own region or speaking their own particular language or dialect.[338] Pieter van Batavia, a slave of Jan Stevensz Botma, declared in 1683 that he had absconded 'because at night he was not allowed to sit near the fire, and had no companions with whom he might converse (*"vermits hy des avents niet by 't vier kon komen en geen mackers en had daar hy mede konde praete"*)'.[339]

There was also, however, the question of physical loneliness, which worsened as the colonists began to turn from labour-intensive wheat and wine farming to cattle farming. Towards the end of the century white farmers increasingly established cattle posts further in the interior to the north of the colonised area. While this was opposed by Simon van der Stel, it received the official approval of his son and successor, who in 1699 also opened up for colonisation the remote area beyond Roodezand pass in the folded mountains known as the Land van Waveren (Tulbagh valley). Here one or two servants or slaves often manned an isolated hut while they herded their master's cattle, and they must have had little human contact. So for example when the wealthy widow Anna Hoeks, who owned six farms in Jan de Jonkershoek, in the vicinity of Stellenbosch, died in 1723, she left a total of 15 slaves, some of whom were claimed by her heirs; Aron van Tutucorijn, however, was listed as being 'over the mountain', a reference to a further farm on the 'Swarte Rivier' or 'Black River', where there were at the time 98 head of cattle and 340 sheep.[340]

One finds a brief reference to this in the diary of Adam Tas in 1706: 'A slave of my uncle Hüsings, whom he had lent to Hendrik Mulder, arrived here. The same had made his way over the mountains from Rode Sant, and he declared he could not live there as it was too far from home. I had the fellow brought to Meerlust, and myself rode there.'[341] Meerlust was Hüsing's farm in the more settled and relatively well-populated Stellenbosch district. Just a few years later there was a similar case, referred to by Ross, of Simon van Malabar, who 'took exception to being sent away from the farm on which he lived to live on a lonely cattle post.[342]

With reference to the desertions and outbreak of violence which took place in 1688, Ross writes of similar dissatisfaction on the part of the ringleader Francis van Batavia.

> At least one of the slaves involved himself lived in Stellenbosch. He had been sold some four years earlier by an official of the Company to a farmer there. Evidently he resented the change. The heavy work on the farm, the deprivation of the company provided in the town, the closer supervision of his master, these all led him to feelings of insupportable exploitation, to decisions to take action against the masters.[343]

More often mistreatment, harshness or misunderstandings were a cause of complaint, and the fugitive Jacob van Siam, a slave of Jan Stevensz Botma stated after his capture in 1693 'that he was a greenhorn and ignorant concerning his master's work ("*een baar of een onweetende was omtrent syne meester's arbeyt*"), and had therefore received many beatings'.[344] Worden again mentions the case of Augustus van Batavia, 'a slave in his mid-twenties, [who] was sentenced by the Council of Justice in December 1728, because he had repeatedly tried to escape and, "being of a godless and malicious nature ran away three or four times on the abominable pretext that he was getting no food but a great amount of work from his master"'.[345]

The slave Cinna, who did not know his own age, '(but has grey hair)', ran away in 1705 from his master Arij van Wijk in the Stellenbosch district, 'Because of getting no clothes, nor tobacco, and continually being abused as an old dog by the wife and children, and being further tormented', and went 'to the Cape to his sister to get breeches ('een broekje') and some tobacco',[346] a rare example of family feeling among the slaves. Ary van Bengalen absconded from his master Jan Lourensz 'with the intention never to return again because he was tired of life',[347] and Aaron van Bengalen, '40 years old at a guess', stated that he had tried to set fire to his master's wine cellar and kill himself because of bad treatment by his master's stepson: 'because of the continual harshness and bad treatment of Gerrit Mos, but that he cannot complain about his baas, Pieter van der Westhuijsen'.[348]

Sometimes frustration, depression or despair could lead to a slave taking his own life, and cases of suicide in four successive years can serve as an example, although the motives must remain unknown. In 1702, a slave of the Revd Henricus Beck, hanged himself 'in the shed, with a whipcord, from a beam'.[349] In 1703 the slave Alexander Kaffer hanged himself from an apple tree in the orchard of Henning Hüsing. 'The inspectors saw "above his head various flowers, [and] his tobacco pouch with comb and flint". The ladder with which he had climbed up into the tree still stood below.'[350] In 1704 'a slave of the ex-burgher councillor Cornelis [Stevensz] Botma cut his own throat. He was dragged over the high road towards the gallows and there hung by the legs.'[351]

While suicide in general caused great horror at the time, the suicide of a slave was in addition an act of defiance to his owner and the authorities which was punished accordingly, as shown by the treatment of Botma's unnamed slave. After the suicide of Ventura van Malabar in 1705, it was likewise decreed that the body, 'as unworthy of the earth, and for the deterrence of other servile people, be dragged through the streets from his owner's house or the gaol house to the gallows field and there hung by the legs from the gallows to be devoured by the birds of the air'.[352] In his history of the Dutch Reformed Church of Stellenbosch, A.M. Hugo refers, with some details, to a particularly high incidence of slave suicides over the period 1725–35, and quotes a letter written by the Landdrost in 1729 in which he suggested erecting a gallows behind the church for the public display of the corpses.[353]

Further difficulties which might be found in a slave's life were caused by the tensions which had from the beginning existed between slaves and Khoikhoi, which would of course have led to daily friction as detribalised Khoikhoi were incorporated into the economic system of the whites and employed as farm labourers or herders. Equally there were tensions among various groups within the slave community, for example Africans and Asiatics, as was illustrated by the breaking up and scattering of a large group of fugitive slaves in 1709.[354] In a farming community which was often of extremely mixed origins, this could be a source of serious discord.

7. Resistance and control

On the whole the VOC, like the civil and ecclesiastical authorities in Europe, tended to punish insubordination severely, whether that of its employees towards itself or slaves towards their masters.[1]

This had occurred already in the case of the Angolan and Guinean slaves who absconded in Van Riebeeck's time, and while there seems to have been a lapse of authority under the sickly and ineffectual Commanders Borghorst and Hackius in 1668–71, discipline was restored when the former military man and visiting Commissioner Isbrand Goske became Governor in 1672. The fact that the Dutch Republic was at war with both England and France at the time, and that the Second Khoi War was launched the year after, would have increased the need for discipline and control in the small white community, and this was shown by the authorities in their dealings with Company servants, freeburghers, slaves and Khoikhoi alike.

While the 1670s may still be considered as part of the pioneering years, there is a strong tendency to see the term of office of the two Van der Stels, father and son, the thirty years around the turn of the eighteenth century, as a period in which colonial culture flourished at the Cape, characterised as far as the white community was concerned by what is generally called 'gracious living'. This is erroneous, to say the least. Since the first freeburghers had begun farming, conditions on the whole had certainly improved, and the existence of a number of very wealthy officials and farmers in the small community has already been illustrated. It must always be borne in mind, however, that these developments took place in terms of a slave society, in an atmosphere of constant tension and fear, where arson and desertion were possible at any moment. The white population could maintain its control only by unrelieved vigilance, severe discipline and draconian punishments, alternating with sporadic outbursts of senseless violence and cruelty.

In contrast to the Company slaves, where a good deal of information is available on their acquisition and their living conditions, as far as the 'private' slaves are concerned it was mostly only when they were accused of some crime or misdemeanour that greater attention was paid to them, further information about them taken down, their own statements recorded or incidental detail about their lives preserved. With few exceptions it is only in legal documents that the voices of the slaves may still be heard, albeit in muffled and distorted form.[2]

While this limits the nature of the information available on the private slaves, it does not make it invalid, nor does it mean that the information concerns only a criminal and therefore deviant section of the slave community. Given the nature of slavery, the control which the authorities and slave owners tried at all times to maintain, and the frustrations among the slaves themselves, it was only too easy for slaves to commit offences which were judged to be crimes by the standards of white society, without themselves being or becoming 'criminals' in any significant sense of the word. While such a diverse group of people inevitably included deviants, misfits and asocial or unbalanced individuals, and the nature of slavery probably aggravated any existing weaknesses, whether moral or psychological, it is likely that the slaves whose lives are recorded in the legal records were on the whole a representative group.

What follows on crime and punishment among the slaves is applicable to the entire slave population of the colony, irrespective of whether they belonged to the Company, officials or freeburghers, there being no distinction between them is this respect, so that all the available information may be grouped together for convenience.

Ross stresses the point 'that resistance, not acquiescence, is the heart of the history of human slavery'.[3] According to Heese the most common crimes among slaves in the eighteenth century were desertion or absconding (*drossen, aufugie*), theft, murder, rape and arson, in descending order,[4] and more than two of every three sentences passed on slaves arose from desertion.[5] The situation is likely to have been similar during the previous forty years.

The prevalence of desertion among slaves is hardly surprising, given the fact that they were kept in bondage against their will and wishes, something which not even the kindest and most considerate of masters could alter; added to which by no means all masters were kind or considerate, but many were thoughtless, many selfish, and not a few deliberately harsh or cruel.

Desertion may be seen as an act of protest on the part of the slave concerned, an act of sabotage, which was said often to occur at the time of the harvest or vintage or of ploughing and sowing when slave labour was particularly needed, or as an attempt to harm the slave owner concerned by depriving him of a valuable piece of property. Sometimes flight was planned long beforehand and weapons and provisions were collected, but it was often unpremeditated, arising as the spontaneous reaction to some specific slight, injury or act of injustice.[6]

It was moreover noted at the time that there were certain slaves who seemed to have made a habit of absconding—'*die hun werk van 't weglopen schijnen te maken*'[7]—and who might be called habitual or compulsive absconders. In some individuals the desire to abscond in spite of repeated capture and punishment may well have been inspired to some extent by an uncontrollable spirit of recklessness or adventure.

It was inevitable that absconding slaves in the course of their flight committed acts of violence or other crimes such as theft, arson and murder, and it was for these as much as for the act of desertion itself that they were subsequently tried and punished. Nonetheless, the mere fact of one or more slaves, possibly armed, having escaped from supervision and control and being at loose was enough to cause panic in the small white community.

The slave Anthony from Madagascar is known to have decamped from the Fort in 1655, while desertion on a large scale took place shortly after the arrival of the slaves from Angola and Guinea in 1658.[8] It presumably continued to be a feature of life at the Cape, but it received attention only when Isbrand Goske arrived here in 1672 with the rank of Governor and proceeded to set the affairs of the colony to rights after the neglect it had suffered under his immediate predecessors over the previous six years.

One of the results was severe legislation with regard to aiding and abetting 'the Company's servants, freeburghers, *knechten* and male and female slaves who abscond and flee', who are here described as 'fugitives, vagabonds, cattle thieves and brigands'. As far as they were not actively assisted by members of the white community, these fugitives naturally preyed upon them, and they formed a very real danger to a population which in the year this *plakkaat* was issued consisted of no more than 64 adult white males spread out in the Table and Liesbeek valleys with their families.[9] Permission was therefore also given to the freeburghers 'that they may freely defend themselves with buckshot should any vagrants and brigands at any time of the day or night attack their houses, barns and stables violently and break into them, without being held responsible or answerable'.[10]

At this time the Liesbeek valley still formed the frontier of the colony, under constant threat from wild animals and potentially hostile Khoikhoi of the Cochoqua tribe in the interior, and runaway slaves with their feelings of resentment towards the whites formed a particular threat. The panic they caused is conveyed graphically by the history of a large-scale attempt at desertion early in Goske's administration and immediately after the first punitive expedition against the Cochoqua, as described in successive entries in the Journal.

August 25th, [1673]. A few days ago eight slaves ran away, four of the Company and four of the freemen. One of them returned and acknowledged that the others were hiding in the neighbourhood. Accordingly the ensign and some soldiers were sent out to capture them.

August 26th. Two of the slaves of the freemen captured, professing that they had returned yesterday with their comrade. They had wandered away from the others, and were found near their masters' homesteads. Their intention had been to proceed to Angola, to the Portuguese there, in order to live a better life there and never more to return to the Cape. Alas! too idle a conception, which will cause the remaining five much misery and finally their destruction.

September 2nd. The runaway slaves of the freemen, not wishing to confess in what manner they had effected their escape, were brought to a successful confession by castigation with rods. From it it appeared that these gallows birds had seduced the Company's slaves to accompany them.

September 22nd. The runaway freemen's slaves, who had induced 4 of the Company's slaves to run away with them, were sentenced to have their ears cut off and be scourged and branded. The two principal instigators to serve for life as convicts in the Company's service.

For the rest we had pleasant weather (…).[11]

Only a year later there was an even more dramatic attempt at escape involving 27 slaves in all, 15 of whom belonged to the Company, and the length at which it is described in the Journal clearly shows the fear and horror it caused in the white community. The account is quoted here in full both for its narrative interest and the vivid and illuminating information it provides.

[*15 November, 1674*]. An ensign was quickly mounted and sent inland with as many horsemen as he could collect at the Fort, whilst all the burghers residing in the country were ordered, on pain of a fine of Rds 25, and without the least delay, to

270

come together at the Ruyter Wacht [*Ruiterwacht, cavalry stables in the Liesbeek valley*], and according to the orders of the said ensign, whether together or divided, to block the thoroughfares to the interior, follow the fugitives on their heels, and endeavour to capture them.

15th. One of the fellow conspirators of the fugitive Indians from the new Fort [*Castle*], who appears not to have been able to follow the others, was early this morning discovered at one of the lime kilns, whilst a second, belonging to one of the burghers, was recaptured below Table Mountain, who on examination confessed that the 27 had induced each other and agreed to run away to Mosambique, but that they (the two), having very soon regretted it, had left the troop. This we shall have to believe until further evidence is obtained. In the mean time the two are imprisoned.

This afternoon two more of the fugitives were sent in by the ensign, in charge of a horseman, with the information that a little before daylight they had unexpectedly found themselves in the midst of the fugitives, who becoming aware of their presence, and favoured by darkness, succeeded in escaping, so that only the two now sent in had been captured. A Javanese convict who defended himself against the ensign, and had previously with his knife ripped open the stomach of a Hottentoo so that the latter's entrails fell to the ground, as he thought that the Hottentoo intended to seize him, was shot dead.

They are said to be provided with muskets and other arms for their defence. Where this wretched lot got them, must in time be investigated. In the meanwhile the ensign was provided with 12 more men and some pork and bread, and ordered in every way to watch the fugitives.

16th. The ensign sends in seven more of the fugitives in charge of some burghers on horseback, and as he wished to be informed from here how he was further to act in search-

271

ing for the rest, he was told that he was to continue the search as long as practicable, for that purpose retaining all his men with him, and that to-morrow some biscuit will be sent him on a pack ox for his people.

November 17th. Two men and two pack oxen with biscuit despatched to the ensign, with orders to the latter that he was to search all the hiding places in the neighbourhood with his men and the Hottentoos with him, and to send a party of Africans [*Khoikhoi*] with some Dutchmen towards Saldanha Bay, provided with sufficient victuals, in order to intercept the fugitives in that direction. For that purpose, and in order to encourage the Hottentoos the more, 8 lbs. of tobacco are also sent to him to be distributed among them, with authority that all who may show fight and do not voluntarily surrender may be freely shot down. It will however be more pleasant to us if they can be captured alive.

18th, Sunday. Last night one of the fugitive slaves belonging to a private person returned of his own accord, and this morning another, loitering between the Wijnberg and Coornschuur [*Groote Schuur*] among various houses of the burghers, was caught by the Schuur people and brought in. He stated that he had wandered from the rest. It was accordingly decided to let our people know of this, and to let the aforesaid slaves, in charge of a corporal and three soldiers, go out with the latter in order to point out where they had parted from their comrades, with further orders to the ensign, as he is at present sufficiently provided with Dutchmen and Hottentoos, to let the freemen whom he still had with him go home, and allow the aforesaid slaves and their masters also to return.

November 20th. As no more of the fugitives have been found, and the absence of our men in the country has very much retarded the necessary works, we ordered our ensign that in case he had captured no more fugitives to return, unless for reasons he might decide otherwise, when more provisions will be sent to him.

21st. The ensign returns bringing two more fugitives, who had been captured behind the Tijgerberg. Before he left he had persuaded a large number of Sonqua Hottentoos [*hunters, 'Bushmen'*] with large promises to search the country in every direction, and who had undertaken to do so faithfully, so that it is believed that more will be caught, as these Hottentoos, in consequence of the desperate act of the Javanese convict who had been shot, committed against one of their own nation, are so bitter against the slaves that they would not entertain the request of the ensign unless he promised them that they might be permitted to resent the injustice done them in similar coin. This the ensign agreed to, subject to our ratification, as we would rather see that the fugitives were hacked to pieces than be left alive to make the roads unsafe and create other street [*public*] offences, besides affording them an opportunity of getting more recruits.

The Sonquas had also promised that they would show certain proofs (*lidtteijkenen*) that they had killed those whom they had been unable to capture alive.

November 23rd. The Court of Justice meets and sentences the captured fugitives in various ways, in proportion to the magnitude of their crimes. Some were merely thoroughly scourged, of others the ears were cut off, and others again were branded on both cheeks, excepting a certain Javanese convict who had most stubbornly resisted our men and endeavoured to hurt them in every possible manner. Having been reprieved from death, he had to undergo all the above mentioned punishments, after which both his thumbs were to be cut off and his tongue cut out.

The sentences were at once carried out, after which all the condemned were heavily chained in pairs, so that any attempt to run away again may be safely abandoned.

To date we have recovered 15, viz. 10 of the Company and 5 of the burghers. Eleven are still missing, viz. 11 of the Company and 1 of a freeman [*sic*].[12]

In spite of the example made of the captured slaves, attempts at desertion continued regularly, and in 1686 Simon van der Stel expressed his concern at the 'daily and incessant escaping and absconding of both the Company's and freeburghers' slaves, who run off armed and in groups and support themselves in the wilderness'. With a view to deterrence it was decided that all captured fugitives would summarily be bound to a stake and severely thrashed by *caffers*, have an ear cut off and be sent back to their place of work in chains.[13]

In 1688 a group of 10 or 12 freeburgher slaves escaped under the leadership of Sante and Michel, two slaves from 'Sant Jago' (São Tiago in the Cape Verde islands), to which Van der Stel reacted violently and emotionally in the Council of Policy, pointing out the possibility of the gang launching attacks on the colonists by night, 'reducing one house after another to ashes and robbing the owners of all they have and hold'. The two leaders were outlawed and rewards of 25 and 15 rixdollars offered for each, living or dead respectively, while the other fugitives were to be shot if they resisted capture.[14] 'All the passes were occupied by the Company's servants and freemen,' Van der Stel reported in his account to the Gentlemen XVII;

the conspirators were surrounded on all sides, and in a river thickly covered with rush and trees they fought four hours desperately against six of the freemen, and were only overpowered after having killed one of the latter. Three of the ringleaders were killed fighting to the last. Four others and a female were conveyed to the Castle, where they will be rewarded according to their deserts.[15]

In the same account he described no less emotionally 'what terrible anxiety, painful days and sleepless nights we pass through, for often we are hard pushed and threatened by conspiracies of slaves and convicts, fortunately always discovered in time by God's grace'.

Reference has already been made to the inherent dichotomy in the system of slavery, with practising Christians, including ministers of the Gospel, owning and dealing in slaves on a large scale, and expeditions sent to Madagascar to buy slaves being instructed that 'above all, God's Holy name shall always and at fixed times be invoked for His blessing…. If this is done, we need not doubt the good success of the slave-buying expedition.'[16] A further dichotomy may often be detected among the slaves themselves, for many of them seem implicitly to have accepted the system and to have co-operated with it to their own advantage, even if this was to the disadvantage of their fellows.

When a further mass escape of slaves took place in 1690, it was, for example, a slave belonging to a freeburgher who first helped the pursuers discover the hiding place of the 'conspirators', as the deserters were called,[17] while the last of the fugitives was found 'by two convicts, described as slaves in chains, on the slopes of Table Mountain. He fought for his freedom, but was overpowered after a fight which lasted about an hour (…).'[18] Of this man, a freeburgher slave called Francis van Batavia, Dr Böeseken reports: 'He had been baptised, and spoke excellent Dutch. He knew the 12 Articles of the Catechism as well as the Lord's Prayer.'[19] His sentence was to be broken on the wheel, and he was attended during his last moments by a minister of religion.

After this, slave owners were obliged by *plakkaat* to give notice of missing slaves within 24 hours to the Fiscal at the Castle or the Landdrost at Stellenbosch, after which a blue flag would be hoisted as a warning signal to the freeburghers both at the Castle and 'on the road between De Kuijlen and Stellenbosch'.[20]

In addition to the steady desertion of individuals and small groups, mass desertions such as those described above continued to occur regularly over the years, and to pose a considerable threat to the colony. In 1709, for example, a group of 39 armed slaves made off in the direction of the Breede River and wandered about for a considerable time until they were weakened and divided by internal dissensions and captured. Their leader, Jacob van Ceylon, also known as 'de Smid' or 'the smith', was sentenced 'to be bound to a pole on the place of public execution, well whipt on his bare back, branded on both cheeks, to have his ears and nose cut off, to have the ears nailed to the gallows, to be rivetted in chains for life, to work as a convict for two years, and after that to be sent home to his master'.[21]

By no means all fugitive slaves were recaptured, killed or otherwise accounted for, and at any given moment there must have been a number of them at large at the Cape. While the freeburgher slaves among them would presumably have been omitted in the next census returns, one finds 6 slaves listed in the probate inventory compiled after the Heemraad Jan Oberholster lost his wife in 1714, with the note, 'another slave who has already been missing 4 months, named Alexander, 100 guilders'.[22] Similarly when the Heemraad Pierre Rousseau died in 1719, his slave holdings 'on the lower farm' were recorded as comprising 17 'jongens', 'including one who has deserted'.[23]

As far as Company slaves are concerned, however, Armstrong & Worden point out that such losses were not reflected in the statistics, 'for no regular bookkeeping procedures existed for writing off successful escapes. For example, in 1753 there were no fewer than fifty such escaped slaves among the roughly six hundred slaves the Company then "held".'[24]

A surprising number of absconding slaves remained in the area where they had up to then been living, which was familiar to them, where they had friends and contacts, and where they could manage to exist by theft from the colonists' stock, gardens and houses. Many deserters, for example, took refuge in the thickly wooden ravines on the eastern slopes of Table Mountain, and according to Sleigh, the postholder and workmen of the woodcutters' post at Het Paradijs were often called upon to hunt for them.[25]

There was less possibility of evading capture among the farms of Stellenbosch and Drakenstein, but here too fugitive slaves often lingered. This is illustrated vividly by the information provided in the Journal on Daniel van Coromandel, who in 1704 escaped from the messenger of the court, Christoffel Hasewinkel. When he was sentenced, it was stated,

> That he had deserted from his master and returned a week later; that he was then charged with having killed a sheep of his master in the field; that thereupon, through fear, he ran away again and went from one place to another; that in the night of 12th March last he had stolen grapes in the Rev. Bek's [*Beck*] garden; that he then went to the Clapmuts mountain to hide himself and die there of hunger; that after lying down half an hour a slave of Rev. Bek met him, named David, who said that he intended to run away also. That the following night they stole some quinces in the garden of Cryn [*Trijn*] Ras. That when prisoner wished to return to Clapmuts, David prevented him and wished him to show where the sheep were of Mr. Elsevier. That he refused to do so; that thereupon David quarrelled with him and finally beat him; that thereupon he drew his knife and wounded David in the throat. That David thereupon fell down and finally died; that prisoner then went to the land of Monsieur Mulder, where he slept; that thereupon he went to meet those sent out to capture him, and so was taken prisoner by the burgher Jurgen Smacky.
>
> The court sentences him to be hanged, and further decrees that his body shall be left hanging and exposed to the birds of the air.[26]

All this took place over a relatively small area in the immediate vicinity of Stellenbosch.[27]

Three months later Jacob van Bengalen, another slave belonging to Hasewinkel, deserted, together with Matthys Caffer of 'Nova

Guinee',[28] a slave of the Revd Van Loon of Stellenbosch. In this case it was stated,

> That Jacob had deserted from his master and remained a long time in the fields, living on pumpkins &c. stolen by him in the gardens of Drakenstein. That four months ago Matthys, who had also absconded, joined him, that together they went to Drakenstein to the house of Pieter Malmer, whose boy [*slave*] gave them food, and also a file to Jacob with which he filed off the chain in which he had been riveted for crimes committed. That thereupon they went to French Hoek to hide themselves. That there they had stolen a horse belonging to Jacob van Driel out of the garden of the Heemraad Pieter Rossouw [*sic*], that they brought it to their hiding place, killed and ate it; that a month later they stole a horse of Abraham de Villiers which they ate likewise. That after that they stole and ate an ox belonging to Pieter Hubert [*Imbert*], a horse of Jacob de Villiers near his farm at the French Hoek, and another horse of the before-mentioned Pieter Rousseau, all of which they ate, and that whilst cutting up the last animal they were apprehended by some farmers, &c.
>
> The Court sentences them to stand under the gallows with the rope around their necks, to be severely whipped with rods, after that to be branded and sent for life heavily ironed to their masters.[29]

Hasewinkel seems to have been particularly unfortunate as regards his slaves, for in 1710 a further three of them, Cupido van Macassar, Hannibal van Macassar and Matthijs van Bengalen, were found guilty of having stolen and sold some pigs. That these were the property of Captain Oloff Bergh, a member of the Council of Policy, may have been an aggravating factor, but their sentence was remarkably savage compared to that imposed on Jacob van Bengalen and Matthys Caffer for killing and stealing 4 horses and an ox only a few years before: each of them was to be scourged and branded on the right cheek and a piece of his nose was to be cut off, and they were condemned to hard labour in chains for two months.[30] The general impression is that disproportionately harsh sentences, often involving mutilation, again became common during the term of office of Governor Louis van Assenburgh (1708–11).

Patrols searching for fugitive slaves traversed the Boland regularly, and Sleigh gives a graphic description of the panic caused by four armed fugitives in 1690, when Commander Van der Stel 'had a net of patrolling horsemen placed around the entire colony and plains, wood, mountains and ravines searched'; the postholder at Klapmuts took part in the search with six soldiers and five or six Khoikhoi 'who know how to handle firearms'.[31] Within less than forty years the Khoikhoi had become dependent on the whites to such an extent that they could be regarded as allies against the threat posed by the slaves, and even armed.

At a time of great unrest during the agitation against W.A. van der Stel in 1706, there is a stray reference in the Journal to the fact that a corporal sent out by the Landdrost of Stellenbosch with some armed men had alleged that this was done because

> a troop of fugitive black men were wandering about the country, and as they had arms, that everyone should be careful and on his guard; and that they were out to capture them. Although he told this in an off-hand manner, it is nevertheless true that near the Paarel [sic] a troop of six or seven boys [male slaves] are wandering about, and have stolen and killed cattle of Bouman and others, and on Brommert's farm have stolen some things from the house.[32]

In 1702 the Journal contained the note: 'The postholders of the Groenkloof [Malmesbury district], the land of Waveren [Tulbagh valley] and the Vogelvalley ordered always to send out armed patrols in search of fugitive slaves and clear the country of these malefactors. Those armed with guns and showing resistance to be shot if they cannot be caught. The Governor, however, would like them only to be wounded sufficiently in order to be easily apprehended. This latter course to be adopted only when all others are impossible.'[33] In the instruction sent to the corporal of the military post at Riebeek-Kasteel, established shortly before to protect colonists in the Berg River valley against Bushman attacks, he and the superintendents of these three outlying posts were instructed 'every day to send one of your men, properly armed, through the country from station to station in order to overtake the fugitives.'[34]

Valentijn states that in the same period, under W.A. van der Stel,

> Corporal Samuel Paske made an inland journey of 80 [Dutch] miles with 8 or 10 soldiers and 50 Hottentots, to the Zwarte River, chiefly to search for runaway slaves, of whom he caught 4. They were away for 6 weeks, finding everywhere a Company's Post, a Company's House, a Company's Salt Pan, and the necessary utensils for cooking their food. They passed the most beautiful fields of flowers imaginable, at last reaching a deep marsh which extended to the Zwarte River, a pretty large stream. Here they could go no further. They met with no wild animals on their journey, except for three large lions, which got out of their way, nor made any discovery of importance.[35]

Nothing further is known of Paske, the 'Zwarte River' or this expedition, which seems to have been to the northward;[36] but the passage is quoted for its vivid and evocative quality.

There were other fugitives, however, who made for the fringes of the area in which the colonists had settled, especially the mountains immediately adjoining Stellenbosch and Drakenstein, where white deserters and renegades likewise gathered. In 1708 Commissioner Simons could refer to colonists 'being molested by stowaways, vagabond Freemen or farm-hands run off from their employ',[37] adding that no fewer than 120 of the Company's servants were at that time hired out to the freeburghers as farmhands, 'many of whom run off from their employers, going out as vagabonds and doing much harm'.[38]

In 1696, during the Nine Years' War in Europe, when there was a very real danger of the Cape being attacked by the French, the Council of Policy expressed serious concern at the number of white deserters and condemned criminals at large both in the countryside and in the surrounding mountains. Mention was made explicitly of 'fugitive black boys [*slaves*]' among them, and a *plakkaat* issued in this regard shortly afterwards referred to the group as including 'various slaves, both armed and unarmed'. It was alleged that these men were supplied with arms, gunpowder, lead and tobacco by colonists in order to undertake illegal cattle-trading expeditions to Khoikhoi in the interior and that they were also responsible for raiding expeditions. They were outlawed and rewards offered for their capture, and it was permitted to shoot them in the legs with buckshot or otherwise injure them should they attempt to escape.[39]

When legislation in this regard was once more issued in 1722, it referred to escaped white criminals and convicts and deserters from Dutch and foreign ships, adding that they were not only guilty of 'cattle theft, murder, housebreaking and robbery on the public highway', but 'often did not even hesitate to gather together absconded slaves and other vagrants and vagabonds and set themselves up as leaders of these people in order to execute their evil misdeeds and thieving with greater security'. It was also alleged that they established contact with the colonists through *knechten* and slaves herding cattle in the open.[40] Ross mentions colonies consisting specifically of runaway slaves, most notably, from about 1725, at Hangklip on False Bay, in the mountainous area at the furthest extremity from the colonised area,[41] but he emphasises that 'they were spread along the length of the mountain chain and the largest consisted of at most sixty men and women'.[42]

Many fugitives attempted to flee the settled area, however, and at first they mostly took the route northwards along the coast. Some details are known of the path followed by three slaves of Jan Stevensz

Botma who escaped in 1683, Pompstok van Madagascar and his companions Pieter van Batavia and Jacob van Siam—a further small illustration of the varied composition of the Cape slave community. 'They made their way along the strand of Table Bay,' writes Mossop,

> and journeyed northwards for a month; they passed Saldan-ha Bay and crossed the broad mouth of the Berg and Verloren Vlei Rivers, and so amongst the white sand dunes which fringe the scrub covered red ones of the South Sandveld by Leipoldtsville and Lamberts Bay. They kept themselves alive with shell fish, tortoises, and ostrich eggs, and such else as they might find.[43]

In the early years slaves at the Cape had on occasion hoped to reach Angola or Guinea by following this route along the shore,[44] but Madagascan slaves, with a confused sense of both direction and geography, seem to have believed that they could reach their homes as well. Heese mentions a group of fugitives under Coridon van Madagascar who in 1706 travelled northwards in the direction of Piketberg, stole sheep from the Khoikhoi and tried to force a Khoi to show them the route to Madagascar.[45]

In later years the goal of these fugitives was often the Khoi tribes beyond the Olifants River, among whom they hoped to find refuge, as in 1707, when five fugitive slaves 'decided to proceed to the Hottentot nation the—Namaquas'.[46] If they survived the perils of the journey through a semi-desert area, they were more often than not killed by the Khoikhoi, or else captured and returned by Khoi tribes on good terms with the Dutch authorities or anxious to be so,[47] or by freeburghers and presumably also free blacks from the Cape fishing along the West Coast.[48] In 1680, early in his administration, Simon van der Stel could state that 'neither hunger nor thirst, neither the murderous hands of the Hottentots living far into the interior, nor the impossibility of escaping death deters them from running away'.[49] In the same year the Council of Policy decided to reward

Khoikhoi returning one of the Company's fugitive slaves 'with as much tobacco, beads &c. as the Hon. Company is accustomed to pay for a head of cattle', and a European with 3 rixdollars.[50]

The Company's outpost at Saldanha Bay, being situated the furthest to the north, on the outskirts of the colonised territory, soon became the centre to which these fugitives were returned. As early as 1673 there is a reference to a fugitive slave being brought here 'on a Hottentoo's pack ox, a distance of 3 (Dutch) miles from our lodge',[51] and to the Company's sloop *Bruidegom* bringing back four fugitives who had been kept there for some time,[52] while reference is also made to the free fisherman Willem van Dieden buying back fugitives from Khoikhoi.[53] Slaves who seemed dangerous were not kept at the post itself but on one of the islands in the bay.[54]

Two of Botma's three fugitive slaves were apprehended by the Grigriqua, a Khoi tribe inhabiting the Sandveld between Piketberg and the modern Graafwater,[55] who forcibly detained them for five months and finally took them to the Olifants River to be handed over to the expedition of Ensign Oloff Bergh on its way back from Namaqualand. 'Marched onwards again in the afternoon,' Bergh noted in his journal the following day. 'We took the two slave boys with us, placing them before the wagons to lead the oxen.'[56] Back at the Cape Pieter van Batavia was scourged three times, had his right ear cut off for attempting to escape from custody, and was chained for life, while his companion Jacob van Siam had to witness his punishment and was likewise chained.

In 1706 a group of five armed fugitives roamed about the area for some time, attacking and fighting with the small Khoi tribes living there, three of them finally being killed by the Khoikhoi, one fatally wounded and the fifth captured and executed.[57] The following year the Journal notes, 'The corporal stationed at Saldanha Bay brought in five male and three female slaves belonging to some freemen who had deserted from their masters some weeks ago.'[58]

Not all Khoi tribes killed or returned the fugitives, however, and in 1696 Ensign Isaq Schrijver, having been despatched on a bartering expedition to the north, reported 'that he had heard that the Grigriquas, a nation living beyond the Olifants River and having no intercourse with the Company, harboured many deserted slaves of the freemen and kept them in their service, without [the owners] ever being able to find out where these deserters were hiding.' 'This being considered by us conduct at variance with the laudable custom among the surrounding Hottentots,' declared the Council of Policy,

> who, being of a more civil nature, and in order to show their fidelity to the Company, are accustomed to deliver a runaway slave to the Company so that his owner recovers him; and further, it being probable that such deserters, growing in numbers, might either conspire with the Grigriquas or, having overcome the latter, make raids upon our people, who live scattered far and wide from each other, it was decided in Council on the 13th December (…) to send the ensign, a sergeant, nine men and some burghers of Stellenbosch to the far side of Olifants River in order to visit the Grigriquas, and either by barter or in any other convenient manner recover the fugitives, or otherwise to carry off to the Castle as hostages some of the tribe—a captain or some of the women or children—until the slaves have been given up.[59]

This plan did not succeed, but from captured Grigriqua it was subsequently learned 'that besides 15 or 16 [slaves] whom they had killed, they still had a few among them'.[60]

This route to the north continued to be followed in spite of its drawbacks, and in 1707 a group of deserters set out northwards under Augustyn van Batavia, having equipped themselves with a bayonet, knives, plates, a cheese, a bottle of brandy and clothing, while in 1709 a group under Jacob van Ceylon set themselves the same goal. Both groups committed murders during the course of their travels, and were apprehended and their leaders punished.[61]

The tendency of absconding slaves to flee northwards changed after a large party of whites early in 1702 travelled 'across the high mountains' on an illegal cattle-raiding expedition to 'certain Cabucquas, called the Great Caffres, more than 120 Dutch miles distant from this Castle'.[62] In this way the existence of Xhosa tribes deeper in the interior to the north-east was established, and by 1709 Jacob of Ceylon was to be found inciting a large group of deserters to proceed to 'Kaffirland' along Olifantspas in the mountains above Franschhoek, attempting to cross the Breede River on rafts: 'Ary [van Bengalen] would show them the way, he having roamed about a long while as a shepherd in the country beyond the mountains',[63] i.e., the Overberg. In 1712 a group of deserters were likewise described as making their way over the Hottentots-Holland mountains,[64] and by the 'thirties Mentzel could state, 'should a fugitive slave succeed in reaching the Kaffirs [*Xhosa*], he would be protected against all danger, for they never give the slaves up, because they become their best fighters, more courageous than the Kaffirs themselves'.[65]

Apparently slaves also managed to escape to Europe on ships of the return fleet, which was possible with the connivance of members of the crew, the more so as their were sometimes coloured seamen on the ships of the VOC, although French and Danish vessels seem to have been preferred. When nine men, 'both slaves of the Company and Indian convicts', were found to be missing in 1685 they were immediately suspected of having taken refuge on a French ship then at anchor in the bay.[66]

This may have occurred quite frequently without being detected, for in 1705 the Council of Policy addressed a note to the XVII on the subject, which Leibbrandt summarises as follows.

> Slaves often missed. Supposed that they escape in the return fleet. Two again gone. Fugitives write to the slaves here about the vast difference between liberty and slavery, and about the Fatherland, making them also anxious to escape. This should be stopped; and we therefore beg you to have all the

ships examined before the men leave them, and also to see whether the two runaways are on board and to send them back in irons to be punished, to deter others. This is a matter seriously affecting the Company and the people.[67]

On which they elaborated some two months later with the statement that 'the light colored slaves are getting into the habit of escaping with the return fleet'.[68]

Between 1724 and 1747,' writes Ross of a slightly later period,

some forty-four slaves completely disappeared from the Company's slave lodge in Cape Town. Of these no fewer than thirty went in the first three months of each year, This improbably high proportion is significant because these were the months during which the fleets were in town. The Indian ocean monsoons combined to congregate both outward and homeward bound ships at the Cape at that time of the year, although there were a few sailing at other seasons. The obvious explanation for the concentration of escapes in January, February and March, then, is that the slaves took advantage of the crowded harbour to find a passage to freedom as stowaways.[69]

Among the documents published by the freeburghers in the course of their dispute with Governor Van der Stel there also is an unexpected and detailed account of the way in which a slave who originated in Batavia managed to make his way back there. In a subsequent declaration in 1711, the Cape brewer Willem Menssink described how a certain slave bought for himself or his mother from Adam Tas for the sum of 60 rixdollars came to abscond;

who according to the report received, having spent some time in the wild veld ['*in 't woeste veld*'], finally sailed to Batavia on an English ship, where on arrival a boomkeeper,[70] having been his former master, is alleged to have asked him how he had got there, to which he had replied that he was free, but when asked about his letter of freedom and previous master at Cabo [*the Cape*], he said that a letter of freedom had been judged unnecessary and he did not have it with him, but that the brewer and burgher lieutenant at Cabo Willem Menssink had been his master, on which the said boomkeeper became suspicious, as the said slave had been sent from Batavia only a short while before to be sold at the said Cabo, and forthwith had him fettered ['*heeft doen vleugelen*'] and sent onto a return ship then lying there with the request to the skipper of that vessel that he would return the said slave to his said master at the Cape.[71]

While arson was much less common at the Cape than desertion, it was greatly dreaded in a community in which all the buildings except the Castle and the Slave Lodge had thatched roofs, and quite often committed for this reason by slaves seeking revenge.[72] Fire was also a constant danger when the corn was ripe in the cornfields.

The fugitive slave Ary van Bengalen in 1706 gave a vivid description of falling in with a gang of arsonists in the vicinity of Paarl Mountain, stating,

That Anthonij then said to him, Ari: 'The weather is right now and the wind strong for setting fire to houses' and immediately added to this: 'Come, let us set this house alight', whereupon Ari said: 'I have no fire', and received as answer fron Anthonij: 'We have sufficient fire'. That together with Anthonij he left the other two *jongens* ['*boys*'] there and went to the house, and that when Anthonij struck fire, he handed Ari half the burning tinder and told him, because he was dawdling with it: 'Hurry up, or else the fire will go out'. That hereupon Ari threw the burning tinder onto the thatched roof, while Anthonij shoved what remained of the burning tinder into it [*the thatch*], upon which the house instantly caught flame.[73]

One night in 1715, when a strong south-east wind was blowing, 'a bundle of inflammable material' was similarly thrown onto the roof of a house in the Table Valley, 'in which a piece of lead was also found, presumably placed there in order to be able to throw it onto the roof of the said house more easily and thus set it alight'. The result was that the regulations concerning the nine o'clock curfew were repeated explicitly for 'all Company servants, artisans, soldiers and sailors, as well as the convicts and the slaves of both Company servants and freeburghers', and severe penalties threatened for transgressions.[74]

While property was often damaged or attacked, it would appear from the available data that slave owners were seldom killed by slaves, though the possibility was naturally very real at all times and contributed to the general insecurity. Basing his calculations on the information concerning just over a hundred slaves tried and condemned for murder during the eighteenth century, Heese states that in little more than 30% of the cases the victims were whites;[75] and these were as often as not probably individuals killed in the course of flight, where colour and status were not the most important issues.

The main principles of slave ownership at the Cape in the early eighteenth century, as distilled from some fifty years of practical experience, are probably formulated well enough by Kolb where, after eight years spent among slave owners, he writes as follows.

> Above all it is essential to make a careful distinction (...), and keep a tight rein on those who are recalcitrant ['*steeg*'], unless one wishes to run the risk of losing one's life; for there are

already all too many examples of such miscreants having killed their own master and murdered him in the most appalling manner; but those who willingly do what they are ordered must be treated gently and not be made unwilling, as this has evil results and bring about great disasters.

Especially one must take care that they have no lack of food; for whoever should wish to reward their heavy labour with hunger and not give them as much as they can eat, may be assured that they will repay this form of restriction with desertion at a time when they are most needed and their labour is the most essential; from which the master may expect nothing but expense, and even a total loss, for if they return of their own accord, he is lucky, which however does not happen once in a hundred cases. If they are captured by someone else and returned to him, he must give the finder 3 rixdollars for his pains; should he wish to have such fugitives openly or secretly punished by the officers of justice, this will cost him as much again; if he intends laying a charge against them and have an iron horn made for their heads or fetters for their legs, this too will cost him a handful of money, so that he will have nothing but expense as a result.

If they remain away altogether and do not return, so that they have either been devoured by wild animals or killed by the Hottentots, who cannot get on with the slaves at all (…), the disadvantage is considerably greater, because the master then loses the entire capital he had spent in acquiring them, apart from the fact that he has again to buy others (…).[76]

Broadly similar opinions were expressed by the members of the Council of Justice in 1795, immediately after the first British occupation of the Cape, at a time when the numbers of slaves in the colony had grown much greater: they were responding to a letter from the new Commandant, Major-General Craig, on the 'relative degrees of severity with which capital punishments have usually been inflicted here'.[77] In their extensive reply, available in print only in an incomplete and imperfect translation from the Dutch, they point out bluntly that many of the slaves

> are descended from wild and rude nations, who hardly consider the privation of life as a punishment unless accompanied by such cruel circumstances as greatly aggravate bodily sufferings.
>
> It may also be observed that in every family (with a very few exceptions) the number of slaves is so great, that the safety of the family depends on them. This requires the greatest precautions that they may not make use of their superior force, because such an event would bring the whole colony to the brink of ruin.
>
> In order to render the precautions essential, they should comprehend sufficient motives to prevent the slaves from disturbing the tranquillity of the family, and at the same time leave in the hands of the master such power as is necessary for him to exercise in the direction of his family. Experience has taught that gentle means are inadequate, even amongst free persons, to maintain good order (…); consequently, altho' strongly actuated by motives of humanity, and viewing the slaves in the most favorable light, it becomes necessary to adopt severe measures to deter them from revolting against their masters & taking advantage of their superior strength.[78]

In the final analysis, strict control of slaves and the discouragement of insubordination and rebellion were essential both for the protection of their masters and for the preservation of slavery as an institution. The first absconding slaves in 1658 were publicly scourged 'to make a proper example of all of them',[79] and in 1660, when two Company slaves were found guilty of killing one of the freeburghers' pigs grazing in the Table Valley, they were likewise sentenced to be scourged and branded, not only to prevent similar damage to property in the future, but also 'to keep the black nation in greater awe'.[80]

Punishment, here as elsewhere in the seventeenth century, was meant to act largely as a warning and deterrent to others, and in the community at the Cape the punishment of slaves tended to be particularly severe, as has already been made clear by the examples given above. The nature of the punishments imposed here for various common crimes and trespasses can best be conveyed by a chronological list of bald statements, compiled from the Journal and similar sources.[81]

1674: 'A freeman's slave who had dared to set himself against a certain Netherlander by inflicting two wounds on him was ordered to be scourged, branded, riveted in chains and to serve as a convict for two years, the owner retaining his ownership.'[82]

1676: 'Two slaves, one of the Company, who had stolen some cabbages from the garden of a freeman, were condemned to be scourged and branded and have both their ears cut off. Moreover, they were to be riveted in irons, and thus sent home to their owners.'[83]

1680: 'Emanuel of Bengal, Company's slave: theft of cabbages. To be flogged, with a cabbage hung round his neck. (…) Two slaves: desertion and theft of various articles of food. Sentenced to be flogged and branded, to work in chains, 1st prisoner 10 years, the 2nd 5 years.'[84]

1681: 'Pasqual of the Coast [of Coromandel], slave: desertion. (It is stated in aggravation that the prisoner stole some ears of corn from the garden of the freeburgher Louis of Bengal, and that a fire which he made to roast the corn had spread and done some mischief.) Sentenced to be flogged and branded and work in chains for one year.'[85]

1681: 'Anthony of the Coromandel coast, slave of the free burgher Louis of Bengal: desertion and wounding in the hand with a knife Lieutenant Baptista [*Jan Baptiste Dubertin*] who tried to apprehend him. Sentenced to be pilloried, with a halter round his neck, to be severely flogged, marked on the back with a hot iron, to have the middle finger cut out of each hand, to be rivetted in chains *ad vitam* [*for life*], and thus sent back to his master, with costs. (…) In the minutes it is added, "the nose to be cut off".'[86]

1702: 'Leander of Batavia, slave of Jacobus Cruse, [aged] c.16. Deserts, steals firearms, kills the shepherd Joseph who refuses to give him a shirt. Hanged.'[87]

1703: 'The Court of Justice sentences Titus of Macassar, slave of the widow Lingenbach [*Elizabeth Lingelbach*], for deserting with two female slaves (after having been punished several times for theft), and for various thefts committed at various places. (…) To stand exposed under the gallows with the rope round his neck, after that to be bound to a pole, severely whipped, branded on both sides of his back, and for life to wear a chain on one leg; also to pay the costs.'[88]

1704: 'The provisional Landdrost [*of Stellenbosch*], Pieter Robberts, authorised to thrash some runaway slaves and put them in chains to prevent them from again escaping.'[89]

1707: 'Augustus of Batavia, slave of the Company, [aged] c.22. Deserts, cattle theft, murder of a slave and white man. Pinched with red-hot pincers, broken on the wheel.'[90]

1708: 'Coridon of Macassar. Slave of Ariaantje Jansz, wife of Pieter Malmer who was missing. Assault on mistress. Right hand chopped off, broken on the wheel, hand exhibited above body.'[91]

These examples have been taken more or less at random from a variety of printed sources, but it must be emphasised that crimes and punishments such as these were by no means uncommon or atypical of the period, and by no means infrequent in the slave society of the Cape.

The mildest punishment available, which in the case of slaves seems to have been applied mostly to accomplices whose guilt was regarded as minimal, was *pronken* or 'displaying', by which the offender was publicly exhibited, often with a noose around the neck,[92] or with some symbolic object relating to the offence committed, such as a sheepskin in cases of sheep theft. It was similar in purpose to being placed in the pillory in England, and was regarded by whites as disgraceful and demeaning. The term 'public exhibition' will be used here.

The most common form of punishment for white and black, free-born and slaves, was of course scourging or whipping, which in the form of 'domestic correction' was also permitted to slave owners by the Statutes of Batavia. The latter had already become notorious at the Cape by 1658, when Van Riebeeck had to warn the freeburghers against mistreating their slaves. It soon became firmly entrenched as a method of trying to maintain control of the slave population, and by the early eighteenth century, if no earlier, it had become custom-ary to measure the duration of a flogging in terms of the time it took to smoke a pipe of tobacco—'*een pijp tabacq rookens lang*'.[93]

One of the many grievances, often of a very petty and personal nature, expressed by the freeburghers in their petition against Gov-ernor Van der Stel in 1706 was tellingly enough that he allegedly harboured fugitive slaves at Vergelegen,

> which is a matter with grievous results and greatly to the detriment of the freeburghers, as the slaves take advantage of this, and when they have received the least castigation from their masters, they run to the Governor, apart from the fact that some of them are incited to do so, consequently they are in this way completely spoiled, which is a hard matter for the freeburghers, for should this continue, they cannot re-tain control of their slaves.[94]

'Sensible slaves want nothing but food, clothing and tobacco,' declared Mentzel dogmatically some thirty years later; 'sensible mas-ters do not deprive them of any of these, but take into consideration the heavy yoke of slavery and do not treat them reasonably nor have them flogged unduly.'[95] The word 'unduly' is worth noting.

When in 1813 the Fiscal, Daniël Denijssen, submitted to the Brit-ish authorities a 'Statement on the laws regarding slavery', as they had come into being under the administration of the VOC and existed at that time, 'domestic offences' liable to correction by the slave owners themselves were summarised as follows:

Neglect and negligence in performing the proper duties required from slaves by their master.

The occasioning of loss to the master by the neglect or carelessness of the slave.

Wilful disobedience of the legal order of their masters, but by no means of such commands as are contrary to morality or the laws, and which a slave is not obliged to, and may not, obey.

Drunkenness.

Impudence, not amounting to force, or to assaulting the master or openly resisting his commands.

Desertion or running away.

The committing of domestic thefts (…).

All other transgressions against the master or those in whose service the slaves are, in case they should not be classed under the head of *crime*.[96]

Under the VOC no definition of 'domestic correction' was ever given, and the maximum number of stripes was not even laid down, although the Fiscal stated in the above document, at a time when the old laws and customs were still in operation, that 'it is recommended to every person not to punish any slave in his private house on the naked body, or otherwise than on the back or buttocks, nor to make use of any other instrument for that purpose than samboks, leather thongs, their rattans [*canes*] or the like, by which there is not any danger of occasioning contusions or open wounds'.[97]

A flogging could also be administered to a slave by the authorities at the request of his owner. During his visit in 1685 Commissioner Van Reede, who had spent some twenty years in the East and was acquainted with the phenomenon of slavery there, was nonetheless shocked at the ease with which slave owners at the Cape

could summon the *caffers* of the Fiscal to their homes to chastise
their slaves without any form of authorisation, 'bound and severely
scourged with canes,' as he himself described it,[98] or 'bound to a
post and scourged'.[99] He therefore ordered that the permission of
the Commander be obtained in future.

The Fiscal, with whom Van Reede took up the matter, made a
point concerning the slave owners of the Cape which has already
been made in connection with the early slaves from Angola and
Guinea:

> that many of these people, having been of extremely low con-
> dition and grown up in a servile situation in the fatherland
> or Europe, did not possess sufficient knowledge or reason,
> and did not know how to govern the people who had fallen
> into their hands as slaves, so that they abuse the advantages
> and the rights of ownership and act badly in their ignorance,
> with the result that the slaves are not only driven to despair,
> but filled with revulsion and hatred with regard to our na-
> tion, from which no good may be expected in a newly estab-
> lished colony.[100]

The privilege of having one's slaves chastised at will by the *caffers* continued, however. The freeburgher Christoffel Groenewald
is even recorded as having taken three of his male slaves and a
female to the Landdrost in Stellenbosch for punishment in 1707 and
being so dissatisfied 'because the woman had not been punished
sufficiently in his opinion' that he took them back with him.[101]

According to Mentzel, writing about a period half a century
after Van Reede's visit, the victims of these informal floggings 'are
tied naked to the stocks, and two "*kaffirs*" armed with rods (consisting of a bundle of split bamboo-canes) scourge them unmercifully
until the blood runs down their backs'.[102] Earlier in the century
Kolb was apparently an eyewitness to a particularly severe castigation by an alternative method, administered by *caffers*, presumably

in Stellenbosch where he was at one stage employed, to 'an obstinate slave who could not be governed by good and gentle means'. The man to be punished

> was undressed by them outside the gaol and strung in a *Poolse bok*; after they had uncovered his posterior and passed a stick though his hands and legs, which had been tied together, so that he had to remain lying on one side as long as it pleased them. They took their bundles of split Spanish canes and whipped him until the blood flowed and the flesh began to swell and turned as black as coal.[103]

After this the victim was turned over and beaten in a similar way on the other side, and was unable to work for three or four weeks. Salt water, or water to which pepper and salt had been added, was rubbed into the wounds in such cases to prevent mortification, and there are also examples of urine being used for this purpose.

The *Poolse bok* or 'Polish rack' apparently referred originally to some kind of frame or similar apparatus used for the purpose of chastisement in Poland, although the method was by this time used equally for the punishment of slaves in the West Indies, where it was known as a *Spaanse bok* or 'Spanish rack'.[104]

Scourging as part of a court sentence was often complemented by a sentence of hard labour on Robben Island or 'at the public works', sometimes in chains, or alternatively slaves were sent back chained to their owners, who were thus not deprived of their services. 'They may be chained by one leg to a log,' writes Mentzel, 'which they have to drag after them or carry in their arms to enable them to walk. Another punishment is to rivet heavy iron rings on each leg. Such chains and rings have to be paid for by the slaveowner at a fixed tariff.'[105] After a number of local slaves had absconded in 1704 the Landdrost of Stellenbosch, Pieter Robbertsz, likewise asked permission 'at their masters' request', 'that they might be scourged, branded or "horned" (*gehoornd*)',[106] a reminder of Kolb's slave with an 'iron horn on his head',[107] and at the same time the Council of Policy gave instructions for the punishment of fugitive slaves on the island outpost of Mauritius, which presumably also reflected local practice at the time.

> It was resolved, in order to terrify the slaves, to empower the Mauritius Commandant and council to punish a slave with a slight corporal punishment if he or she has been absent from his or her owner for more than three days without permission, and if longer than six weeks, to whip them severely at a stake, with rods, and clinch them in one or two irons, or put an iron band with horns round their necks for a time, as may be deemed necessary.[108]

In 1728, Galant van Banda is said to have chopped off the iron collar his fellow deserter Jan van Cochin was wearing,[109] and legislation on the treatment of slaves passed in 1731, in referring to the use of 'too heavy chains', gave instructions that slaves were only to be chained, freed from their chains or 'provided with so-called horns' with official permission and by blacksmiths appointed and approved for this purpose.[110]

Ary van Bengalen was sentenced to hard labour on Robben Island in 1706, after absconding and committing arson, for refusing to name his accomplices, 'with a heavy chain and block on both legs connected to an iron collar around the neck',[111] and on his death two years later he was buried in his chains. 'The death of the slave Ary of Bengal has relieved us of a useless eater,' wrote the Cape authorities to the island, 'but you might have taken his irons off before burying him, they could have been used again'; in reply to which the superintendent referred to 'the strict orders of Governor W.A. van der Stel that the convict was never to be released from his bonds, and that he still has the written order'.[112]

More severe punishments were branding on the back or face, as well as mutilation in the form of the loss of ears, nose or fingers, although this may also have been intended to identify and set apart convicted criminals or deserters. Hamstringing or severing the Achilles tendon of the right leg was possibly a precaution against further attempts to abscond. This form of punishment seems to have been applied quite regularly, according to Heese for the last time in 1766,[113] though he lists a further sentence of this type pronounced on a Khoi who took part in an armed rising in the Roggeveld in 1772.[114]

In 1711 the Council of Policy decided unanimously, as scourging had no deterrent effect on the Company's fugitive slaves, 'to scourge and brand them for the first offence; for the second, another brand on the cheek; and for the third to have their ears and nose cut off, if during their flight they have committed no murder'.[115] By 1715 the Independent Fiscal had to admit that this was ineffective, as there were 'divers slaves who appear to have made a habit of deserting', and was given permission to have captured deserters chained together in pairs as well to prevent further escapes.[116] In 1727 these drastic measures were repealed, however, 'taking into account how appalling such punishments are for other people, especially pregnant women, encountering such mutilated slaves, and the mishaps which could occur in this way'. In future, slaves would be marked with one or more brands on their backs according to the number of times they had absconded;[117] with which the Council seems itself to have acknowledged the futility of trying to prevent desertion.

Torture was used, or at least threatened, as a matter of routine, both at the Cape and in Europe, when a confession was not made voluntarily,[118] and most commonly consisted of scourging—'castigation with rods' as it was termed when it was used at an early stage at the Cape to make recaptured fugitives confess how they had escaped.[119] Thumbscrews were also in use,[120] and Mentzel, in mentioning them, adds, 'I have never known of any case where a slave was firm enough to defy the thumbscrew and the rack.'[121] The third form of compulsion, the 'rack' to which he referred, involved drawing up the victim by his bound arms with weights attached to his feet. When a white man accused of having killed a Khoi was being interrogated in 1707, 'a 50 pound weight was suspended from each of his great toes, but though he confessed a little, he confessed nothing of what was required'.[122]

As far as capital punishment is concerned, hanging was common, while Mentzel describes the 'process of slow strangulation, while a "kaffir" holds a bundle of burning reeds close to the face'.[123] Strangling was frequently used for women condemned to death.

In 1713 a young slave woman, Tryntje van Madagascar, who had killed her small child, was condemned 'to be tied to a stake and subsequently strangled with a cord in such a manner that death follows; furthermore her dead body is to be taken to the external gallows field and there fastened in a fork until such time as it has been consumed by the air and the birds of heaven'.[124] The following year a white woman of about the same age, Maria Mouton, was executed in the same way for the murder of her husband.[125]

Infinitely more spectacular, and more painful, was breaking on the wheel, joint by joint, with an iron bar:[126] there is a reference in this regard to breaking the joints 'with eight strokes'.[127] The *coup de grâce* could then be administered in the form of a final stroke over the chest, or the victim might be allowed to linger on the wheel until he died of natural causes. After the murder of a white man by slaves in 1706, for example, 'the hand of the slave who had committed the murder was to be cut off, and after that both were to be broken from below upwards, and so left until they died. Their bodies were afterwards to be exposed on a wheel at the outside place of execution until destroyed by the birds and wind.'[128]

The sufferings of a person condemned to death could be further intensified by tearing out pieces of his flesh with red-hot pincers, which was apparently done according to a fixed pattern, four, eight and ten applications being specified in various sentences.[129] This was the fate of Antony van Mosambique, sentenced in 1713 for the rape of a young white girl, after which he was broken on the wheel,[130] and Heese lists this additional form of punishment eight times in all for the eighteenth century, the next occurrence not being until in 1745; though his is not intended to be a complete record of punishments. While not unknown in Europe, this form of punishment seems to have been applied only to slaves at the Cape.

Arson was punished by death at the stake. Ary van Madagascar was put to death in this way in 1698,[131] and Kolb describes witnessing the death of Moses van Bengalen for the same crime in 1712 after he had attempted several times to set fire to the house of his master, the former Secunde Samuel Elsevier, in revenge, according to Kolb, for having been sold. He was condemned 'to be fastened to a stake by a chain around his body, and wood piled up about him, and to be burned or roasted alive'.

> I had never thought that a human being could live so long with a living flame playing constantly on his eyes and face as this man did; for he not only walked about around the stake and kept off the flames from him, but moved his arms and legs for a long time, crying out aloud, *O Deos mio pay*! O God my father! and kept alive in the fire in this fashion for a quarter of an hour.[132]

Heese records two more executions of this type during the eighteenth century, and in 1796 the combined members of the Council of Justice could still state in a matter-of-fact way to the new British administrator, 'An incendiary is punished by fire, &c., &c.'[133]

These were all common punishments in Europe at the time, but one which was confined to the East and imported to the Cape from Batavia was impalement, known in the East as *caluete*.[134] For this an incision appears to have been made at the lower end of the spine, and a thin iron rod with a sharp point inserted and driven along the spine under the skin until it emerged at the back of the neck. The rod was then set up on a tall pole with the weight of the victim resting on a ledge, and he remained in this position until death intervened.[135] Mentzel refers to it as 'a form of crucifixion whereby death may not take place until two or three days have elapsed'.[136] It does not appear that the rod was inserted in the anus, as is commonly supposed, which would immediately have been fatal to the victim.

It is not known when impalement was first practised at the Cape, but the slave Titus van Bengalen was impaled in 1714 for the murder of his owner after having become the lover of the latter's wife, Maria Mouton,[137] while Tromp van Madagascar, who was sentenced to impalement in the same year for absconding and killing a Khoi, strangled himself before he could be executed.[138] For the eighteenth century, Heese lists three further occurrences during the years 1741–42,[139] and this punishment also seems to have been reserved for slaves.

Punishments were normally administered by the Fiscal and the *laksman* (hangman) and *caffers* serving under him, and other officials involved in the process appear to have been lost sight of. In 1707 the secretary of the Council of Justice, Abraham Poulle, and the messenger of the court, Marinus Keestok, accordingly submitted to the Council of Policy a memorial

> showing that they had never yet drawn any fees for slaves condemned to death for crime and executed, notwithstanding all such verdicts have been given with the costs and expenses of justice. The Council consider this reasonable, and as the funds of the Court were in a reasonable condition, it was decided that henceforth the Court shall pay them the expenses earned by them in the execution of the slaves of the inhabitants, for whom it would be hard to pay the costs, besides losing the value of their slaves; but no payment shall be made for slaves of the Company, and only when it is found that there is enough on hand in the Court's chest.[140]

As stated above, these various punishments were equally common in the slave society of Batavia,[141] and as likely or not it was merely the Batavian models that were followed at the Cape. They were no less common elsewhere in the world of colonial slavery, as may be seen by the 60 articles of the *Code Noir* or 'Black Code', intended for regularising the treatment of slaves in the West Indian colonies of the French in the Antilles, and issued from Versailles in 1685 by Louis XIV himself.[142]

In many ways this in a unique document for its day, but though it set certain standards and introduced certain safeguards, it was essentially no more concerned with improving the lot of the slaves than the relevant sections of the Statutes of Batavia. What is of interest here, however, is the punishments prescribed or permitted: slaves striking their master of mistress or the latter's children so as to leave a mark or draw blood were to be executed, while the theft of sheep, pigs, chickens or vegetables was to be punished by scourging with rods and branding with an emblematic fleur-de-lis. A fugitive slave who had been at large for more than a month was to lose his ears and to be branded on one shoulder, and for a second offence he was to be hamstrung and branded on the other shoulder, while a third was punished with death. Slave owners who believed that their slaves deserved punishment, were allowed to chastise them with rods or cords.[143]

This was the universal attitude of the period towards slaves and punishment, and as Mentzel remarks, 'if the natives were not deterred from ill-doing by the infliction of severe punishments such as hanging, breaking on the wheel and impaling, no one's life would be safe. A European, on the other hand,' he could add by the 1730s, 'must have committed a very serious crime before he is punished by death. In the eight years that I was at the Cape only six Europeans were put to death, and they had thoroughly deserved it.'[144] And elsewhere: 'Torture seems to be reserved for slaves only, as in my time no European was ever put to the torture.'[145]

This illustrates a telling point. During the course of the eighteenth century the use of torture and the harsher forms of punishment such as mutilation or breaking on the wheel were gradually abandoned in Europe and in many countries officially abolished. At the Cape, however, they remained in use for controlling the slave population, or at any rate for attempting to do so.

In 1796 the members of the Council of Justice pointed out that one of the factors governing 'the degree of severity with which punishments are inflicted' was: 'The person who commits the crime, and also the person upon whom it is committed; as when a subject murders his sovereign or a slave his master', and again: 'with regard to slaves, the equality of punishment ceases when they commit offences against Europeans or free persons, particularly their masters'.[146]

Or as the Fiscal reported to the same authorities more specifically in 1813:

> The care requisite for the maintenance of a good police [sic] has also occasioned that the transgressions of slaves by which the peace and tranquillity of the inhabitants and the safety of their persons and properties could be disturbed, especially in the public streets and roads, are by the laws of the Colony subject to punishments free people are not liable to.[147]

And in the following paragraph of his report:

> Such is the law enacting that a constable seeing a slave wilfully jostle or push against a European, even of the lowest class (that is actually European or descended from one) or otherwise insult him, is obliged, in the absence of the master, immediately to apprehend such a slave and have him punished with flogging by order of the magistrate.[148]

In discussing the administration of justice under the VOC, Heese writes,

> that justice was administered with regard to non-Europeans (slaves) which differed from that in the Netherlands where

slavery was forbidden by law. In addition, colour discrimination, which had been virtually absent during the seventeenth century, also came into being during the eighteenth. 'Coloured' people, whether free of enslaved, received heavier punishments than 'whites' who had committed the same crime. This tendency was, however, not unique to the Cape; it was the rule rather than the exception in all colonial territories.[149]

The last time that a Cape burgher was condemned to death for killing a slave, according to Groenewald, was in 1707,[150] when the French refugee Jean de Thuillet was sentenced *in absentia* after a slave named Andries and a Khoi worker called Caffer had died as a result of severe whippings administered on his orders.[151]

8. Uncertain freedom:
the first free blacks

As long as the VOC was in charge of the Cape, the institution of slavery remained in force, unmitigated and unchanged, and by 1793 there were 592 inmates in the Company's Lodge, which had meanwhile been enlarged, 74 of whom were convicts: 'Thirty-six of these slaves were incapable of doing any hard work owing to old age or physical disability; they were responsible for cleaning the Lodge and nursing the small children'.[1] In 1795, the year in which the first British occupation announced the end of the VOC regime, the total slave population in the colony according to Shell's calculations amounted to 22 442.[2]

By this time a considerable body of legislation on slavery had accumulated, which served mainly to safeguard the slave owners and their rights. Cumulative *plakkaten* in this regard, consisting of 29 articles in each case, were issued in 1754 and 1794.[3]

It was only after the British occupation that the influence which philanthropic and emancipationist bodies had already acquired in British society began to affect the situation here too, at first in a general way only by the abolition of torture and punishments that were by then regarded as barbaric. In 1807, however, an act was passed forbidding the importation of slaves as from 1 March 1808, although a further 500 reached the Cape during the year before it came into effect.[4] After this date the Cape acquired some 2100 so-called 'prize negroes', mostly from Madagascar or Mozambique, these being slaves found on the slave ships brought to the Cape as booty or prizes by British vessels and apprenticed here for fourteen years before being set free.[5]

On 18 March 1823 extensive legislation was issued setting forth conditions for the treatment of slaves and assuring them of certain basic rights,[6] and on 1 December 1834 all Cape slaves were formally emancipated, although they had first to serve three years' apprenticeship with their former masters.[7] By this time the slave population had swollen to 36 169,[8] and these people were now, with little training or preparation, turned out into free society to make their way there as best they could, without much help from anyone except the churches and missionary societies.

As far as the slaves at the Cape were concerned, for the entire period of Dutch domination, 143 years in all, the slaves' only hope for any improvement in their situation lay in individual manumissions, infrequent though these may have been.[9]

Provision had been made in the Statutes of Batavia for manumitting or freeing slaves which stated baldly, 'Whoever wishes to free any slave shall do so before a secretary and two witnesses', before proceeding to enumerate at length, in a number of further clauses, the obligations manumitted slaves continued to have towards their former masters. For manumission 'reasonable knowledge' of the Dutch language was required, although slaves whose masters were by reason of illness no longer able to support them might likewise be freed, and so too any slave who could make known his master's murderer.[10]

The first slave known to have been freed at the Cape was Catharina Anthonisz van Bengalen who was manumitted by Jasper van den Boogaerde after the return fleet arrived at the Cape from Batavia in 1656, and married the assistant Jan Woutersz. In 1658 the former soldier Jan Sacharias bought Maria van Bengalen from the sick comforter Pieter van der Stael in order to manumit and marry her, and she was as far as is known the first Cape slave to be freed.[11] Both these women were eventually relegated to Robben Island when their husbands were appointed there, and Catharina van Bengalen died on the island, while Maria followed her husband to Batavia.

On 13 April 1666 the former Secunde Abraham Gabbema on his departure for Batavia set free Angela van Bengalen and her three children, on condition that she first undergo six months of training from the freeburgher Thomas Christoffel Muller.[12] Five months later, on 25 September, the Commander, Zacharias Wagenaer, on his own return to Batavia, granted freedom to Anthonij van Japan,[13] his wife Annica van Bengalen, and their children Elisabet and Abraham, apparently against payment of 60 rixdollars.[14] A few days later he granted to 'my former slave, called Anthonij', a piece of ground in the Table Valley; and during the course of this year the Cape free black community numbering at least eight people may be said to have suddenly sprung into being.

According to Dr Böeseken, the term *vrijzwart* or 'free black' occurs only twice in the official annual missives of the Governor-General and Council of India to the Gentlemen XVII in the Netherlands, both times clearly intended as synonym for the Mardijkers, a group of free coloured Christians of foreign origin living in Batavia. At the Cape, however, it was used specifically for manumitted slaves, and its earliest recorded appearance is said to have been in 1671.[15] Other members of the free coloured community which soon came into being at the Cape were described as *vrijgeboren* or 'freeborn', so that a more accurate and distinctive name for the manumitted slaves might rather be '*freed* blacks'.

The Cape church in its baptismal registers kept the distinction between the two groups,[16] but the civil authorities were not so precise. The distinct body of non-white civilians formed in the Table Valley in 1722 for service during fires and in other emergencies, for example, was to consist of 'free blacks and free Chinese', though obviously all the coloured residents were meant.[17] Likewise Heese points out that in the census for 1725, manumitted slaves and free-born blacks were lumped together as 'free blacks'.[18] Modern writers have also tended to use the term 'free blacks' loosely when discussing the non-white or coloured community in its widest sense, including Elphick & Shell,[19] who add, 'The vast majority of the free blacks were ex-slaves or their descendants.'[20] For the purpose of the present book an attempt has been made to keep to the original strict definition of the term.

After the earliest manumissions there are some further casual references to freed slaves at the Cape over the next ten or fifteen years, without it always being clear who they were or by whom they had been manumitted, as in the case, for example, of Evert van Guinee who was in 1669 granted a piece of land on the outskirts of the settlement in the Table Valley.[21]

In 1671 the burgher councillor Elbert Dircksz Diemer manumitted Sijbilla, a child of about 5½, who was the daughter of his own slave Catharina by Abraham van Guinee, a slave belonging to the Revd De Voogd, on condition that she would serve him for ten consecutive years, in return for her food and clothing.[22] The following year the freeburgher Thomas Christoffel Muller manumitted the 'little slave girl' Lobbitje, aged about eight, whom he had retained when selling her mother, Gegeima van Guinee, to the Company in 1668,[23] and in 1673 'the honourable Hendrick Barents van der Zee' and 'the honourable Jannetje Geeraerts', his wife, both ill and bedridden, made a will in which they freed Sijmon van Angola if one of them were to die.[24] These three manumissions are the earliest known to have been made by freeburghers as distinct from officials.

In 1673 too, Louis van Bengalen made his first appearance in the Cape muster role, and in 1675 the Governor, Isbrand Goske, sold the slave Louis van Negapatnam, aged thirty, to the freeburgher Theunis Dircx van Schalkwijk 'on condition that he would liberate him after he had served him for 8 years', which was duly done.[25] In 1676 the freeburgher Jochem Marquart manumitted Gerrit van Bengalen,[26] and a visiting skipper freed Sara van Ceylon, leaving her to decide whether she preferred to remain at the Cape or return to the East.[27]

The subsequent history of some of these individuals can be traced in existing records, but on being manumitted they were in principle placed on an equal footing with the white freeburghers. Everyone wishing to farm might request land, while the inhabitants of the Table Valley, where the first free blacks seem to have established themselves, could on request obtain both town or residential plots in the little settlement and garden plots in the immediate vicinity, and might themselves specify the size and situation.[28] No distinction was made in this regard between white and black, so that the races lived intermingled. The free black Anthonij de Later van Japan, for example, had the prominent whites Elbert Dirckx Diemer and Jacob Cornelis van Rosendael as his neighbours,[29] and Louis van Bengalen with his wife Rebecca van Macassar lived next to the sick comforter Albert Coopman and the freeburgher Johannes Pithius.[30] The garden plots were situated largely behind the Castle, to the east and south-east of the settlement and the Company's garden, on the lower mountain slopes and the banks of one of the streams which ran into Table Bay, in the present Mill Street area.[31]

As regards the three most prominent and best documented of the people mentioned thus far, Angela van Bengalen married a white man and became prosperous, as will be described more fully in due course.[32]

Concerning Anthonij van Japan, also known variously as Anthonij van Bengalen, Anthonij de Later and even 'Anthonij de Chinees',[33] there is some confusion, based mainly on his use of the first of these names,[34] and Dr Böeseken distinguishes two individuals of the same name 'who both called themselves Anthony de Later and who probably both originally came from Bengal'.[35]

At the time of the manumission of his 'Japanese slave named Anthonij',[36] Wagenaer referred to his 'ten years of faithful service', which would include Wagenaer's two terms of office in the VOC's Japanese trading post at Nagasaki in 1656–57 and 1658–59. It is therefore possible that the man was a Bengali who had accompanied him there as a boy (he was born in about 1648[37]), and used the soubriquet 'van Japan' to distinguish him from one or more contemporaries at the Cape with the same name. He also signed his name on occasion as 'Anthonij d'Later van Yap[an]'.[38]

Anthonij and his wife Annica must have been baptised already, as they were married according to the Christian rite a few months after their manumission,[39] and shortly afterwards they borrowed 200 guilders from Wagenaer's successor, Cornelis van Quaelberg,[40] both signing the relevant document. Annica seems soon to have died, however, for by 1671 the baptism is recorded of Anthonij's child by Lijsbeth van Bengalen, whom he married two years later.

Anthonij's business dealings, whatever they may have been, do not appear to have been a success, and it was 'Anthonij de Later van Japan' who in 1673 requested the freeburghers W.C. Mostaert and Jan Valckenrijck, two prominent member of the white community, to sell his house in Zeestraat (Strand Street) in the event of his departure, together with certain belongings including a fishing boat and a seine.[41] According to De Wet, however, two burgher councillors were at this time instructed to sell the house and belongings.[42] After this, according to Armstrong, he is no longer recorded in the muster rolls.[43]

The references given above may seem reasonably clear, but the are possibly not as straightforward as they appear, and Hattingh for example doubts whether they all refer to the same individual, drawing attention also to the existence of other contemporaries named Anthonij van Bengalen.[44]

As early as 1666 there is a reference to the property of a person of this name in Zeestraat (Strand Street), who may or may not have been Wagenaer's former slave, although Hattingh disputes this.[45] In 1671 a man of the same name bought two plots of land, a house and 100 sheep from the freeburgher Jacob Cornelis van Rosendael, for which he owed him 2900 guilders, promising to make two payments, 'the first $f1200$ when the second consignment of ships from Batavia in 1672 had left the roadstead, the second $f1700$ the following year when the first [section of the] return fleet had been in the roadstead for 14 days'.[46] Like most other inhabitants of the Cape in his day, he was obviously economically dependent on the arrival of visitors, and especially on the ships of the return fleet. In 1676 he received a plot of ground.[47] In 1673 again Anthony van Bengalen and Catharina van Paliacatte appear in the census returns with two children.[48]

In 1676 Governor Bax, in a rather enigmatic note, 'sold to St. Martin for the use of Anthoni van Bengalen, "free resident here", the slave Baddo of Bali for 50 rixdollars',[49] and in 1678 Anthoni bought the slave Paul from Bax's widow for 300 guilders, 'promising to pay her on her departure for Batavia as much as he was able and the remained when the first consignment of the return fleet left the roadstead. He pledged himself and all his goods.[50] In the same year, Antoni van Bengalen appeared on the list of 'free residents' to whom the Company was at that time distributing monthly rations of rice, being noted for the considerable amount of 150 pounds.[51]

In 1680 'Anthonij van Bangale' was at his own request given permission to leave for Batavia with his family, 'as he is only a burden for the Hon. Company and completely useless to the general citizenry and also for various weighty reasons by no means needed here' as the Council of Policy observed rather waspishly.[52] The following year there is nonetheless a record of the freeburgher Willem van Dieden, after having obtained a *pacht* for 1681, concluding an agreement concerning the supply of brandy and distilled liquors to a man of the same name, which would imply that he ran a taproom.[53]

In addition, there was Anthoni van Bengalen who was sold by a junior merchant of the Company to the Secunde Albert van Breugel in 1673 at the age of ten,[54] and a certain Anthonij Jansz van Bengalen who in 1676 bought Maria van Malabar from a skipper for 35 rixdollars.[55]

To contemporaries, of course, all this was quite unproblematic, and the men concerned were quite well aware of their own identities, as were the other members of the community. The existing confusion has been sketched here at some length in order to show to what extent the world of the slaves and ex-slaves has become impenetrable, based on names noted in cursory and often variant forms by uninvolved officials. A fragmentary record of names and actions has survived, but the identities have largely been lost.

As regards the life of another early free black, Louis van Bengalen, there is more information and greater certainty.[56]

He presumably also accompanied Wagenaer to the Cape in 1662, when according to later evidence he must have been about ten years old, and was sold on Wagenaer's departure in 1666 to the Secunde Hendrick Lacus for 80 rixdollars.[57] After Lacus had been accused of fraud and dismissed, Louis was allowed by Isbrand Goske, in his capacity as visiting Commissioner, to buy his freedom, but as he did not have the required amount, he appears to have been appropriated temporarily by the Company. It was not until 1672, after five years of 'faithful service', that he was manumitted on the payment of 50 rixdollars, with which Lacus's account was duly credited.[58]

Louis himself stated that he was unable to read, but Hattingh remarks that he was one of the few free blacks who had some fixed form of signature. 'The signature took the form of a vertical line for the L, while the V and B were linked together in the shape of a fan.'[59] He was baptised in the Cape church in 1675, his age being given as 23, and further distinguished himself by becoming a professed member in 1697, a long delay of this nature being quite common at the time.

Louis received a garden plot on the outskirts of the Table Valley in 1676, adjoining those of Anthonij van Bengalen and the *mandoor* Sijmon de Arabier,[60] and in 1685 he was to pay 760 guilders in four instalments for a house and plot in the settlement.[61] He is known to have been in possession of the slave Anthonij van Coromandel,[62] while in 1687 he bought Matthijs van Bengalen for 35 rixdollars,[63] and two years later sold Matthijs van Malabar, who may well have been the same individual, for 30 rixdollars. On the latter occasion he was described as a 'black agriculturist'.[64] In 1700 he sold Titus van Macassar for 55 rixdollars.[65]

During the 1680s Louis had various business dealings with Andries Houwer involving wheat, fish and cash, and found himself increasingly in debt of which he was unable to free himself, although he promised on one occasion to repay Houwer before the visit of the return ships, a profitable time commonly used for settling accounts at the Cape.[66] At one stage towards the end of the decade he is known to have been briefly among the free black farmers in the Stellenbosch district,[67] and in 1687 he and his former slave Lijsbeth Jansz, who had been freed by him in 1683 with her two children, formally gave their promise of marriage before the local authorities there. No marriage took place, however, and in 1694 he married Rebecca van Macassar, who had arrived at the Cape the previous year as a professing Christian.[68] It was after this that he himself was confirmed as a member of the church.

Whatever Louis's sources of income may have been, and irrespective of the amounts he may have been owing his creditors, when his possessions were sold by order of the court in 1705 to pay his debts, the furniture included a round table, six high-backed chairs, two mirrors and feather beds and pillows, and his own share of the proceeds amounted to about 2200 guilders.[69] He and his wife had by that time returned to the Table Valley. In 1711 a further compulsory sale took place which produced just over 1000 guilders. In 1715 Louis was still alive, 43 years after his arrival at the Cape as a child with the Wagenaers, but by 1717 his wife was listed in the census returns as a widow.[70]

In addition to these two men, two further interesting figures from this period may be briefly mentioned who occur from time to time in the records and whose lives give some further fragmentary information on the world of the early free blacks.

Grasias van Angola appears in the Cape records for the first time as 'Jacque Jooij',[71] with three other slaves who served as pledge when the free fishermen borrowed 300 guilders from the Commander's wife in 1658.[72] A year later the men exchanged two Angolan slaves, 'Jan Meeu and Jackie Joy, 10 and 12/13 years old respectively', with Van Riebeeck for two Guinean slaves',[73] which implies that Jackje had arrived with the Angolan slaves as a child early in 1658.[74] The names of the two boys appear to have been nicknames, for *meeuw* means 'seagull', while *jak en jooi* is an obsolete Dutch expression approximately equivalent to 'Tom, Dick and Harry'.[75]

Immediately before his departure from the Cape in 1662, Van Riebeeck, in disposing of his slave holdings on a grand scale, sold 'the Angolan slave Jacqje' to the junior merchant Roeloff de Man,[76] and on De Man's sudden death the following year he was presumably among the 'three Angolan male and female slaves' listed in the estate.[77]

With this Jackje disappears from the record until 1678, by which time he had been manumitted and was, in Dr Böeseken's words, 'involved in a civil case with "Anthoni vrij kaffer" against Anthony from Bengale in a claim for the payment of Rds.93, a debt which had fallen in arrears'.[78] As from the same year he appears suddenly as 'the burgher Jackje van Angola' in a number of slave transactions, buying Domingo Apekint van Madagascar, 9 or 10 years old, for 35 rixdollars,[79] Claes van Tuticorijn, aged 15 or 16, for 40 rixdollars,[80] and one Jacob in 1680 for 90 rixdollars.[81] In the last of these transactions, which took place in 1680, he was described as Grasias van Angola, 'freeburgher of this place'.

Likewise in 1678 'Gracias van Angola alias Jackie' was married in a church ceremony to Maria Evertsz, daughter of the free black Evert van Guinee,[82] but the marriage ended in separation of bed and board after two years:[83] according to De Wet he claimed that his wife was planning to kill him. At the same time he manumitted two of his slaves.[84] 'This document,' Hattingh writes about the latter, 'was signed by Grasias of Angola himself with four capital letters: GRVA. This signature makes Grasias van Angola, together with Louis and Anthonij van Bengalen, one of the few free blacks of the time who could write in some fashion, when many of the white freeburghers could barely trace a cross.'[85] With this he disappears finally from the Cape record, aged about 35.

Lastly, something may be said about Joost Ventura whose distinctive name occurs in local documents just often enough to arouse interest, beginning in 1678 with his baptism, his parents, the slaves Ventura and Helena, acting as witnesses, as they had 'adopted our Christian faith'.[86] The same year one finds the enigmatic record: 'Joost, one year, son of Ventura of Bengale and Helena, is manumitted. When old enough, he will be taught a trade.'[87] In 1696 Joost Ventura bought the slave Constantia van Malabar, aged forty, for 80 rixdollars,[88] freeing her two years later, in 1706 he was among the coloured signatories to the testimonial in favour of Governor Van der Stel,[89] in 1710 two plots of ground near the market place (Greenmarket Square) which he had bought at some unspecified date from Mirra Moor and Reba van Macassar respectively, were transferred to him,[90] and in that year and the following he and a fellow free black gave themselves as sureties for a slave who was about to be manumitted.[91] This was already close to the end of his life, however, and in 1714 his widow, Constantia van Bengalen, married Johannes Pretorius, the illegitimate son of a Dutchman by a coloured woman.[92]

If all these references are to the same individual, as they would appear to be, one wonders why and in what circumstances the baby was manumitted and brought up, what trade he was taught, and how he acquired the money not only to buy a slave at what would seem to be a very early age but to free her as well. The history of Cape slavery is filled with insoluble but intriguing problems like these.

These are the earliest free blacks of whom some record has remained, but by the end of the century Isak van Bengale, Maria Hansdochter and Domingo van Bengalen had also been granted plots in the Table Valley,[93] and in addition to the various individuals already mentioned, Jan van Ceylon, Claas Gerritsz van Bengalen, Emanuel Pereira, Jan Fuguerede, Jan de Soeza, Marretje Pietersz van de Caab, Manuel van Macassar, Pieter Claassz (de Groot), Intje Poetje van Malacca, and Mirra Moor van Ceylon are listed by Hattingh as having bought land here over the same period, for prices, where these are given, mostly between 850 and 1400 guilders.[94] This may well be regarded as a more or less complete roll call of members of the free coloured community by this time, including former slaves, and in the circumstances it is surprising how much additional information is available on several of these individuals, even if in disjointed and fragmentary form. So Maria Hansdochter, for example, is known to have had four children baptised between 1688 and 1697 of whom the father was a Dutchman, Dirk Pretorius, stable master to the VOC, who acknowledged them in his will.[95]

Of the three men with Portuguese names, who were presumably Mardijkers from Batavia, Jan Fuguerede was probably identical with Jan Figoredo, the former butler in the house of Commander Van der Stel, who had obtained his freedom in 1686.[96] As regards Emanuel Pereira, there is a reference in a court case to 'Manuel Perera' lying sick in bed in 1690 and in a conversation in Portuguese with Domingo van Bengalen and Francis Perera, leaving half of his boat to the former and the other half to the child of the latter;[97] he was presumably a fisherman, like so many members of the early free coloured population.

In 1695 'the Mardyker Jan de Soisa' was given permission to return to Batavia, and at the end of the following year the Cape authorities reported that this would be put into effect.[98] While this is possibly not an uncommon Mardijker name, however, it is worth mentioning the existence of a probate inventory for 'the free black Jan de Zousa of Calijpatnam' who died towards the end of 1705,[99] owning part of a house, basic household furnishings including a bed, mattress and 3 feather pillows, an equally basic set of kitchen equipment including a rice block and pestle, two chests with odds and ends, and 6 stivers in cash. This example of basic and elementary Westernisation is probably as close to the world of the average free black in the Table Valley around the turn of the century as it is still possible to get.

As regards the individuals in the above list with 'slave names', Isak van Bengalen seems later to have owned land briefly in the Stellenbosch district,[100] and by 1704 to have been living in the house of Jacob van de Cust (Coromandel).[101] Jan van Ceylon who purchased a house plot in the Table Valley must, however, be distinct from the man, also known as Jan Luij, who farmed and worked as carrier in the Stellenbosch district, where he is mentioned up to 1712.[102]

Domingo van Bengalen can likewise not be identified clearly, for this was, like Louis van Bengalen, a very common name among slaves and free blacks, and occurred at the Cape as early as Van Riebeeck's day. The most that can be said without further research is that according to records which may well refer to more than one individual, a person of this name was baptised in 1686, bought his freedom for 100 rixdollars from his owner, Matthijs Greeff, in 1689, and the same year married Maria van Bengalen.[103] In 1689 he was fined 200 rixdollars for boarding a ship within three days of its arrival, which was forbidden to freeburghers,[104] and in 1690 was sentenced to one year's hard labour for having embezzled the inheritance of Manuel van Angola.[105] In 1692 he received a house plot in the Table Valley, which he sold two years later,[106] in 1693 he borrowed 300 guilders from the church fund at 6%, repaying it within eighteen months,[107] and in 1694 removed to Batavia with his wife.[108]

Whoever he may or may not have been, however, the person who departed for Batavia cannot have been the Mardijker of the same name who was sent out from Batavia with his wife four years later.[109] In 1698 two young slaves, Cupido van Negapatnam and Pieter van Malabar, were sold in two separate transactions to 'the Chinaman Domingo' ('den Chinees Domingo'), who, however, signed himself Domingo van Bengalen,[110] and the latter was also among the signatories of the testimonial to Governor Van der Stel in 1706; all of which a further useful warning about the misleading nature of names in the amorphous world of slavery and manumitted slaves.

The antecedents of Claas Gerritsz van Bengalen are unknown,[111] though he is rather unusual in having a patronym. He received a house plot on the harbour side of Zeestraat (Strand Street) in 1683, which on his death in 1697 was, together with the house, valued at 3000 guilders,[112] and in 1686 he married Sara van Solor, by whom he already had a number of children. She came from the Indonesian archipelago, had been baptised as early as 1673 and had also been confirmed as a member of the church, apparently in 1679,[113] and had been a slave of the well-to-do freeburgher Willem van Dieden. In the year of his marriage Claas Gerritsz bought the young slave Pieter van Madagascar from the English slave trader William Deeron for 55 rixdollars.[114]

The relatively full information available on this couple is largely due to the deductions which may be made from the probate inventory compiled on Claas Gerritz's death in 1697.[115] Malan mentions 'ten fish vats, two fish-oil (*traan*) pots, and eight large cooking pots' as 'significant clues to the family's economic base',[116] and there were also two unnamed slaves who were sold for 79 rixdollars each. Quite obviously Claas Gerritsz was a successful man, and it seems likely that he received help at the beginning of his career from the former owner of his wife, Willem van Dieden, a prominent and prosperous freeburgher who during the period 1676–86 owned the official contract for the supply of fish to the Company.[117]

In addition, the couple's house was well furnished, with a mirror, a painting, 2 footstoves, a good deal of porcelain and table and bed linen, and a well-equipped kitchen. More significant, however, are the bedstead, 3 feather beds and 12 feather pillows to which Malan draws attention. A bedstead as an article of furniture was by no means common at the Cape in the early decades, even among whites, while mattresses and pillows stuffed with feathers as opposed to kapok or some cheaper material were also luxury articles. 'A "Dutch" bed in a freeblack family home does not equate to adoption of Dutchness,' remarks Malan; 'it is, rather, a contemporary and locally recognised sign of prestige. This category of consumer item is used by European economic historians as characterising the level of affluence in a household.'[118]

A number of small debts were still outstanding, but after they had been deducted the estate was still worth 4000 guilders. Claas Gerritsz's family must have been one of the most prosperous in the early free black community, with the most comfortable and elegant life style, equal to that of any of the whites.

Finally, 'Intje Poetje van Malacca' in Hattingh's list may well have been 'the exile Intie Poety, (…) a Malay and follower of the rebel Joncker', who was banished to the Cape in 1693: 'Captain Jonker' was a Moslem from the Moluccas (modern Melaku) in Indonesia whom the Dutch authorities had killed in 1689 in an attempt to forestall a coup. 'Ingepouti' is listed among the *bandieten* or convicts employed on public works in 1693,[119] but was described as a free black in 1696, by which time he was able to buy the slave Jacob van Macassar for 400 guilders,[120] and 'Hentje Poetje' likewise bought a young boy, Willem van Bali, three years later for 50 rixdollars, from a fellow free black identified only as Octavio (possibly Octavio of Macassar).[121] He was pardoned by Batavia in 1705 and allowed to return 'at the request of his friends',[122] and duly arrived there at the end of 1707, together with some other returned exiles, 'with their wives and slaves'.[123]

As regards 'Mirra Moor van Ceylon', in 1687 one 'Miramoor' was among six 'old and worn' slaves manumitted by the Company 'after many years of good and faithful service' to earn their own living.[124] By the time Claas Gerritsz van Bengalen died in 1697, he owed 'Mina [*sic*] Moor' 60 guilders.[125]

In 1705 the Cape informed Colombo, 'Two natives, named Mira Moor and Witty Amanja, banished hither 36 and 30 years ago, beg for permission to return. No papers have been received about them, and we refer the matter to you';[126] to which Colombo replied the following year, 'We have had all the old papers examined, but could find no sentence against the exiles Mira Moor and Witty Amanja. As you say they are very old, and unable to earn a living at the Cape, (…) you may send them on to this if you like.'[127]

In 1706 Mira Moor signed the testimonial to the Governor with other 'free burghers' mostly coloured,[128] but two years later the Journal recorded, 'The body of an old black known as Paay Moor found dead in the gardens in a small hut. He was accustomed to beg his food in the town. (…) It is believed that he died of natural disease and great poverty.'[129] This may well have been Mira Moor, *paai* being a term of respect for an older person, as explained, but whether all the information given above relates to the same individual is once more uncertain.

While this chapter deals with the manumission of slaves and the 'free black' community which thus came into being at the Cape, it must be borne in mind that the 'coloured' community as it evolved here during the final decades of the seventeenth century consisted not only of manumitted slaves, but also of convicts (*bandieten*), deportees and political and other exiles sent here from the East since the early years. The despatch of these people to the Cape was often a quite arbitrary matter depending on the convenience of Company authorities in the East, no formal charge having been laid or sentence passed. It is in this context that a note in the published correspondence between the Cape and Batavia such as the following in 1703 is probably to be interpreted, 'Deed by which Rebecca Antonisz cedes a slave to the Company',[130] or the report from the Cape in the same year, 'The slave Bankoe or Moses presented by his mistress to the Company has been "booked" and is doing his work with the others. The slave Alphonso has been sold by public auction and the amount has been remitted to you for the poor fund…'.[131] Or similarly, in 1705: 'Request of the widow Van de Voorde that her slave may be banished to the Cape for her own safety.'[132]

While these examples concern slaves, free people might equally have been involved, as is illustrated graphically by a puzzled query from the Cape to Batavia in 1706: 'The papers received in the cases of the mardyker Abraham Abrahamsz, Intje Sait, a Malay, and Ticon, a shaved [*converted*] Chinaman, who have been exiled to the Cape, but not in irons, for the term of their natural life; please let us know whether they are to serve as convicts, or are to earn their living as freemen.'[133] Where the term '*bandieten*' is used in this chapter, it must be borne in mind that this might in fact refer to deportees rather than condemned criminals or convicts.

According to the statistics compiled in 1709 'there were 51 deportees ['*banditen*'], including 2 girls ['*meyden*'], 18 Europeans on the Robben Island, and 31 natives ['*inlanders*'], being Chinese, Malays, and men from Ceylon and Macassar, who receive the same [rations] as the Company's slaves, but without the pepper'.[134] Not all members of this group were necessarily living on the island, but the enumeration at least gives an indication of its motley nature.

In practice the Company paid no great attention to the distinctions between *bandieten* and ordinary deportees, and was at no great pains to distinguish between *bandieten* and slaves, the persons concerned all merely forming part of its total unfree labour force. The slaves and *bandieten* were enumerated together in censuses, for example, although the halfbreeds, fullbreeds and *bandieten* were recorded in distinct subgroups.[135] Commissioner Van Reede in 1685 was shocked to discover 'the *bandijten* and those sentenced by the court' living in the Lodge with the slaves, and in his subsequent Instruction stipulated: 'The *bandijten* who hitherto have been intermingled in the same quarters with the slaves must henceforth be separated from them, for which a suitable place has been assigned, as they will be able to learn no good from that race.'[136] It is not known how long this separation was subsequently kept up, or where the 'suitable place' was, but in everyday practice there can have been little distinction between members of the two groups.

In many cases convicts and deportees stayed on after serving their sentences, having no means of returning home even if they desired to do so. In 1705, for example, a letter to Batavia declared quite typically: 'Some Chinese exiles sent back. Five others relieved of their chains, and will earn their living here.'[137]

An interesting example of this category is a woman called Anna Codalilla van de Cust Padang (a reference to Sumatra in Indonesia), who was described explicitly as a 'free *bandiet*' when she died at the Cape in 1726. It is interesting too to note that the paltry possessions she left to her 'little daughter named Alime' included a slave, Silon van Nias.[138] By 1749 the Council of Policy was so concerned about the competition to whites offered by the 'Oriental *bandieten* from India' remaining here after serving their sentences and forming a potential danger to the colony 'by their great number' that they asked permission to return them 'to the places from which they may have come'.[139] Deportees, as distinct from condemned criminals, were in many cases left to their own devices once they had arrived and were free to make a living as best they could.

A distinct further category which must be mentioned consisted of individuals who had been formally sentenced to exile at the Cape for political reasons. They were often political or religious leaders, local rulers or members of the Indonesian aristocracy, and were frequently supported by the Company to some extent during their stay, the most famous of them being Sjeich Yusuf from Macassar, who lived here with a group of followers from 1694 until his death in 1699.[140] In some cases members of these exile groups also settled or remained behind at the Cape.

Many people who were not of slave origin or 'free blacks' in the strict sense were thus absorbed into the Cape coloured community in the course of time, as is demonstrated by the diverse origin of the individuals whose lives have been sketched above. The principal members of this community during the formative years have been discussed here in detail, however, irrespective of origin, to give some indication of the wide variety represented. Of the individuals discussed above, there are, as far as this may be ascertained, 4 from Bengal, 2 from Ceylon, 1 each from Macassar and Malacca, 3 who appear to be Mardijkers, 1 each from Angola and Guinea, and 2 women who were locally born, if Maria Hansdochter may be included here. The group includes not only manumitted slaves but also men sentenced to imprisonment or banishment at the Cape, and the latter consist both of those who in due course returned to their homes and those who made a new home for themselves here. It was a very mixed group, but so was the coloured community at the Cape, and so too the world over which the VOC extended its sway.

All this having been said, a few illustrative cases may be quoted of manumissions by the VOC, and of the recorded slave transactions by private persons in the years 1680–1700 in which slaves were in some way manumitted, whether fully, partially or conditionally, for various permutations were possible.

By the 1670s, as a section of the Company's slaves began to grow older and were no longer fit for work, the custom apparently arose for visiting Commissioners to manumit them to earn their own living,[141] though this was formulated in such a way as to make it seem a favour. In 1687, for example, 4 men and 2 women, 'as they are old and worn and unable to serve any longer, and are found to be more of a burden that a benefit to the Hon. Company', received their freedom from the Council of Policy, allegedly at their own request, 'after many years of good and faithful service', with permission 'to support themselves here by acceptable means, and by this example to encourage other bondsmen in due course to be granted the same privilege by their good behaviour'.[142]

At about the same time 9 or 10 elderly manumitted slaves are said to have settled at Het Paradijs behind Table Mountain, possibly with the encouragement of Van der Stel, who was in the process of large-scale tree-planting in the area.[143] The Journal described the area as 'very pleasant', and according to Sleigh it was 'remarkably windless, with a high rainfall and luxurious vegetation',[144] but it was also very cold and damp.

Similar motives may have prompted the early manumission of Maria van Bengalen, who requested her freedom in 1680, which she received on the payment of 40 rixdollars, 'the more so as the Company obtains little or no service from her'.[145]

These people cast adrift in a free society after a lifetime spent in servitude naturally found it difficult to exist. This fact became clear as early as 1682, when the Council remarked on the number of manumitted slaves who still needed to be supported by the Company, and decided that, in future, support would only be given if they once more entered the Company's service.[146]

At the same time the first of the baptised children born at the Cape to slave mothers by white, Christian fathers began to reach adulthood—it will be remembered that the earliest recorded baptism of a slave child took place in 1659.[147] The first of these children who is known to have made use of her moral right to freedom, as it was generally regarded by contemporaries, was Catrina van de Caab in 1680, concerning whom the minutes of the Council of Policy record:

> A certain mestizo or halfcaste woman ['*meijt*'] named Catrina, though procreated here by a female slave of the Company with a European, and likewise incorporated by the most venerable sacrament of holy baptism into the community of Christ and instructed in the Christian religion, having now attained a competent age and hitherto been employed as a slave ['*dienstbare*'] by the Company, and having requested this body that she may, for the abovementioned reasons and also by virtue of the liberty to which she has a legal right on her father's side, be set free and released from her condition as a slave, it has been agreed to grant her the liberty to support herself as a free woman.[148]

Unlike manumissions by freeburghers, those of Company slaves seem not to have been recorded in any readily accessible source, but by 1682 they were sufficient in number for Rijckloff van Goens Jr to issue a warning in his capacity as visiting Commissioner 'that no one should be allowed to set his slaves free excepting those who understand Dutch well and have accepted our customs, having appeared before commissioners and having beforehand been well examined in and admitted to the Reformed religion'.[149]

The question of manumission was to receive much closer attention when Van Reede visited the Cape as Commissioner-General three years later, and more specifically the question of the halfbreed slaves, for he was much concerned at the way in which they had been neglected, particularly as regards the baptism of children.

In his Instruction Van Reede also stipulated that this group were to be taught trades or handiwork which would help them to support themselves, pointing out that 'while the said children of Dutch fathers are not guilty of the transgressions of their parents, besides the fact that the indisputable children of our own nation cannot be enslaved, greater attention will now have to be paid to them'.[150] He furthermore made specific provisions for the halfbreed men to be freed at the age of 25 on the payment of 100 guilders 'for the costs of their education', on condition that they could speak Dutch and had been publicly confirmed in the Christian faith.[151] Halfcaste women could similarly and on similar conditions be set free at the age of 22, although this might be done earlier if a woman was sought in marriage by a Dutchman, who would in that case have to pay the Company 150 guilders and provide a female slave in her place.

De Wet has pointed out the sudden and dramatic rise in the free black population after this, from 26 in 1685, the year of Van Reede's visit, to 47 the next, ascribing it to the use made of the new conditions for manumission.[152]

The manumission of halfcaste slaves was occasionally recorded in the minutes of the Council of Policy, most notably in the case of Maria Schalck, Armozijn van de Caab (Groot Armozijn) and Jannetje Bort, three women who had served in Simon van der Stel's household since he took office in 1679. The Council, possibly at Van der Stel's prompting, was unwilling to send them back to the Slave Lodge in 1686 when their services were no longer needed, 'because of their faithful service, (…) the more so while all three were procreated by Dutch fathers and have received the holy sacrament of baptism, and one of them is moreover already a member of the Reformed congregation, while the others are about to follow her in this'.[153] Groot Armozijn's parentage is unknown, but Maria or Marietje Schalck was the daughter of the Dutchman Willem Schalck van der Merwe,[154] while Jannetje Bort may well have been the offspring of the soldier Jan Bort who died at the Cape in 1666.[155] All three were duly manumitted and in the course of time married white husbands.[156]

The instructions given by Van Reede would also have been instrumental in the manumission in 1689 of Sara van de Caab, described as 'a half-caste female belonging to the Company', who 'promised that upon her death (and after her marriage to Andries Oelsen) she would leave half her possessions to the Company in return for the education she received as a child'.[157] She had been baptised in 1671, and was also known as Sara Leendertsz, Sara Jansz and Sara van Gijselen, which seems to identify her quite clearly as a daughter of Leendert Jansz van Gijselen who arrived at the Cape as a sailor in 1665 and rose to be chief gardener in Company service. He later acquired freeburghership, becoming a reasonably prosperous wine farmer and the owner of 7 slaves.[158] Sara was manumitted on 31 December 1689 and married the Norwegian Andries Oelofsen the following April; a son was baptised four months later by the name of Leendert.[159]

It would appear from the available evidence that fullbreed women might also be manumitted by men who wished to marry them, as in the case of Maria van Bengalen and Catharina van Bengalen in the very early years of the settlement.

It would further appear that where manumitted slave women had small children who were not freed individually, these were allowed to accompany their mothers, but expected to be returned to the Lodge at twelve, the age when children were normally incorporated in the work force. This is at any rate what one deduces from the case of Jan Vosloo, master woodcutter to the Company, who in 1696 purchased the freedom of Helena van Malabar, aged twenty. She was apparently freed together with her two-year-old daughter Jannetje, and in 1707 Vosloo asked permission to keep the latter instead of having her return to the Lodge, pointing out 'that he had supported her for about eleven years at his own expense and was still having her instructed in reading and writing'. This was granted on the payment of 25 rixdollars, and the Council set the condition that he was to support her until her marriage.

Besides the provisions made for the manumission of halfbreed slaves, Van Reede also, somewhat as an afterthought towards the end of his extensive Instruction, regularised the manumission of others, 'so that these people may not sigh under perpetual slavery and be in a worse state than those who have fallen into the hands of private persons who by the favour of their masters may hope for their freedom. Furthermore it will encourage them to virtue and charity, as there is otherwise no hope for them.'[160]

Provision was thus made for freeing slaves brought from elsewhere who had served the Company 'well and truly' for thirty years since their arrival at the Cape, could speak Dutch fluently, had been confirmed in the Reformed faith or were about to be, and could earn their own living. These individuals 'might' be set free at the discretion of the Council of Policy on the payment of 100 guilders 'in reasonable instalments', but it was stipulated that this was granted 'as a favour and not as a right'. Slaves born at the Cape (by which fullbreeds were meant by implication, as opposed to the halfbreeds for whom provision had already been made), could be set free on similar conditions at the age of forty.[161]

In the world of the Cape slaves, Van Reede's visit and his instructions concerning manumissions clearly formed a milestone, and they were still remembered a quarter of a century later. In 1710 the mason Andries Barendse, 'born here in the Lodge of a female slave of the Company', requested his freedom in terms of 'the instructions left behind by the late Commissioner General, the Lord Hendrik Adriaan van Rheede',[162] while in 1713 Pieter van Juwara, 'being a mestizo and slave of the Hon. Company', obviously not locally born but complying with the further conditions, requested in the same terms to be freed and allowed to return to Batavia.[163]

Round about the year 1680, when the question of manumitting both elderly and halfbreed slaves arose, a third motive for manumission also came to the attention of the Company which aroused more interest and received greater official attention.

As has been mentioned, it was the constant concern of both the Gentlemen XVII and the Council of India to cut down the expenses of the establishment at the Cape and especially to make it independent of the supply of rice which had to be sent out annually from Batavia. As early as 1679, when the Company temporarily let its outpost at Hottentots-Holland to freeburghers, two Angolan slaves with their families had been placed there, as Sleigh phrases it, 'to learn farming, in preparation for the time when the Company wished to have farming at the post undertaken by slaves itself'.[164] In March 1681, a year and a half after taking over as Commander, Simon van der Stel wrote to the XVII likewise suggesting that in manumitting slaves preference should be given to Africans such as those from Angola and Guinea. In his words, as paraphrased by Hattingh, 'they were by nature best suited to undertake hard work. As independent farmers they could help develop the colony further. He could also foresee no difficulties with them as manumitted slaves.' A year later the XVII duly replied, accepting the suggestion and authorising the Commander to manumit 'one or two families' for this purpose, 'hoping that the slaves would be more diligent when free'.[165]

The first slaves to receive their freedom and be given land in the newly established colony of Stellenbosch appear to have been Anthonie van Angola and Marquart van Ceylon in 1683, followed some two years later by a few others. Hattingh refers to 'at least five free black families with their children, as well as other "mixed" [*multiracial*] households' along the Eerste River in Jan de Jonkershoek (the present Jonkershoek),[166] and gives the names of 11 men and women from Angola, Guinea, Bengal and Ceylon. These, according to him, were among 'the first group of free blacks in Stellenbosch', who were later joined by further new farmers of Eastern origin and a new generation of locally born free blacks.[167]

Hattingh, however, also points out the main problems facing farmers in the Stellenbosch district, and more particularly the free blacks: the specialised demands of wheat farming, the low price the Company was prepared to pay for wheat, the distance from the market, the difficulties of transport, the size of the farms, which were mostly 60 morgen, and the high price of additional labour,[168] as well as the losses to stock caused by wild animals. Many of the white farmers experienced difficulties as well, and by 1697 the Council of Policy became so concerned at the number of people disposing of their farms at Stellenbosch and Drakenstein in order to make a living in the Table Valley by means of small-scale trading that they set a charge of 50 rixdollars for permission to move, thus further penalising freeburghers who had difficulty in making a living.[169]

Though none of these early free black farmers achieved notable success,[170] this by no means discouraged further attempts, and by 1712 there were, according to Hattingh, 'no fewer than 17 recognisable names of free blacks' in the census returns roll for Stellenbosch, 'although no means all have been identified'.[171]

Thus far then the manumission of Company slaves. As regards the slaves of private owners, the earliest manumissions recorded at the Cape were those by officials in a private capacity, and relatively few private slave owners freed their slaves, who were valuable property and useful possessions.

Some early examples of manumissions of this kind have already been given. In later years the Revd Adrianus de Voogd manumitted Lauwerens van Paliacatte in 1679 on condition that he serve the Secunde Hendrick Crudop for two years, and a skipper gave his slave Alexander van Tuticorijn to the Company on condition that he be manumitted in 1685.[172] Such delayed manumissions, holding out the prospect of future freedom to the slave concerned, were not uncommon at the time, and were presumably intended as an incentive.

As regards freeburghers, to mention a few random examples, in 1687: 'Henning Huijsing (signature Hüsing) manumitted his slave Izak from Ternate on condition that Isak would serve him faithfully for another four years and eight months',[173] while the following year Herman Gresnich sold Jan and Antoni, both from Madagascar, to Hüsing on condition that they would be freed in three years' time.[174] In 1688 one finds 'Petronella from the Cape (23/24) manumitted by orphan-masters according to the wish expressed by Hans Erentraut before his death',[175] and in 1692, 'Jan van Sleijer Macassar freed by Theunis Dirckx van Schalkwijk after 16 years of faithful service.'[176]

Simon van der Stel in 1698 freed Susanna Catharina van Ceylon, aged thirty, and also gave her an unspecified 'liberal gift',[177] which may mean nothing in itself, though one notes that he was not accompanied to the Cape by his wife, and that there were contemporary references to a 'housekeeper' at Constantia who appeared to have had some influence with him.[178]

One notes too the somewhat ambivalent provision in Van der Stel's will, drawn up in 1712 shortly before his death, by which he left the considerable sum of 3000 guilders, with 'half of all my body linen, as well as a bed and its equipment', to 'Francina Grutting van de Caab de Goede Hoop, free woman ["*vrije dogter*"], who has been brought up in my house since birth'.[179] This would seem by its phrasing to refer to a woman of colour. In this connection one has to think of the mysterious woman recorded only as '*nonje* Fransina' and 'Helena Francina' who died in 1713 in the house of Van der Stel's son Frans, who had been recalled to the Netherlands together with his brother the Governor in 1707. She left a bedstead of red ebony, bedding, a painted cupboard, a footstool, a small writing desk, a small mirror, and a good quantity of clothing and trinkets, and the inventory of her possessions was compiled by Johanna Wessels, the wife of Frans van der Stel, who had remained behind at the Cape.[180]

In his own will, drawn up in exile in the Netherlands in 1717, Frans van der Stel left a similar large amount to 'Sophia, born at the Cape and brought up in the house of Simon van der Stel', who at the time was living in his sister's house in Amsterdam.[181] The status of all these women is unclear.

It may be added that while Simon van der Stel bought a large number of slaves for his large-scale farming operations on Constantia, he also manumitted a number towards the end of his life, in several cases on generous terms.[182] He and the chief surgeon of his day, Willem ten Damme, are stated to have had more of their slaves baptised than the average freeburgher,[183] in connection with which one may note that the slaves in private ownership who were manumitted were not necessarily baptised, unlike those of the Company.[184] Maria van Bengalen, who was manumitted with her children by Jan Coenraad Visser in 1696, for example, was not baptised until 1721, when her daughter Susanna Visser and her white son-in-law acted as witnesses.[185]

One further kind of manumission is the rather puzzling and disturbing type in which passengers with the return fleet from Batavia liberated their slaves who had accompanied them as far as the Cape. So one reads, for example, of the following in 1692:

Lovij from Macassar freed with his wife and four children by Jacob Havemeester from Hamburg who worked in the hospital in Batavia and who was now returning to Europe on the *Waterland*. The slave family had to pay Rds.150 for their liberty.—Coridon from the West Coast [*Malabar?*] freed by Jacob Havemeester. For the freedom of his two children he paid Rds.150.—Annika Camelang freed with her four children (Jan, Jacob, Maria and Susanna) by Jacob Havemeester who had worked in the Company's hospital in Batavia.'[186]

According to a Batavian *plakkaat* issued in 1636, as reaffirmed in 1645 and 1657, Company servants returning to Europe were allowed to take no more than a wet nurse with them, 'for whom six months' upkeep had to be provided in advance to the Company Treasury in Batavia for her return voyage',[187] but it is not known what provisions, if any, were made for the return of slaves manumitted en route. These were slaves who had no previous connection with the Cape, and as far as the existing documentation allows any deductions to be made, they seem simply to have been left stranded here. In 1710 Pieter van Macassar, liberated slave of Wouter Valckenier, was permitted to return to Batavia with his wife and child free of charge when occasion offered, but this was probably due to the status of Valckenier, who had visited the Cape as admiral of the return fleet and Commissioner in 1700, probably the occasion on which Pieter had been manumitted. It may be noticed in passing that the Council of Policy in taking this decision used the slightly denigrating '*wijf*' for the woman involved, instead of the more customary '*vrouw*'.[188]

One also notices cases such as that, in 1690, of 'Saterdag from Boeton (30/31) given by skipper Pieter Stippert to Frederick Russouw de Wit for two years. If Stippert did not claim Saterdag back within two years, the slave was to be given his freedom.'[189]

After the regulations limiting the number of slaves who might officially be brought out from Batavia were relaxed in 1713 and 1714,[190] both slave transactions and manumissions at the Cape increased proportionately. The problems caused by the latter are reflected in the *plakkaat* by which the Cape authorities in 1722 attempted to regain and keep control of manumitted slaves. Specific reference is made to manumitted slaves from elsewhere settling here as free blacks without the required permission having been obtained or the necessary sureties given: 'slaves who upon payment of the costs due for transport and keep and having been to Europe, return here with the Company's ships', and 'slaves who have sailed home [*to the Netherlands*], whether from India [*the East Indies*] or this place, and again returned'.[191]

While manumissions were often conditional, as shown by the examples quoted, these conditions are of a relatively straightforward nature, but the transactions in this regard could be complex, and one often has a sense of personal dramas or tragedies hidden between the lines of the official records. In 1679, for example, the Fiscal Tobias Vlasvath sold Pasquaal, aged two, to Hilletje Redox, widow of a prominent freeburgher, Johan Valckenrijck, 'on condition that he would not be sold before he reached the age of 20, when he was to be set free', but the widow died within a year of the transaction, 6 slaves being sold from her estate, and it is not known what became of Pasquaal.[192]

One would also like to know more of the history of Claas van Bengalen who was manumitted by the sick comforter Albert Coopman on 20 October 1692 on condition that he give faithful service up to 1 July 1694. 'This deed was cancelled on 29.4.1693 because Claas behaved badly,' reads a note, but the agreement seems to have been renewed on the same day; 'If the slave did not behave well in the interim, he would be sold to Hendrik Bouman for ƒ400.'[193]

In conclusion it may be noted that slaves were also allowed to buy their freedom under various conditions and for varying prices. In 1685 Willem van Dieden allowed his slave Francisco to do so for 50 rixdollars,[194] and in 1688, 'Jan from Malabar bought his freedom at a public auction for Rds.127. This was in accordance with the will and testament of Barbara Geems'.[195] And the following year a similar note reads, 'Domingo allowed to buy his freedom for Rds.100 by Matthijs Greve (signature Greeff).'[196]

It is a notable fact that the freeburghers who emancipated slaves before 1700 were for much the greater part prominent and wealthy members of the community, such as most notably Van Dieden and Greeff in the immediately preceding examples. Apart from personal considerations in individual cases, it is also possible that the manumission of an individual slave, which only the wealthy could afford, came to be seen as a status symbol just as much as the baptism of a slave child with a child of one's own. In the context of Batavia, Niemeijer refers to families 'exhibiting to the outside world by means of manumissions the fact that it was possible for them to be generous'.[197]

In practice, however, manumission was as often as not a convenient method of disposing of elderly, useless and unwanted slaves. Not only were these people unable to earn their keep, but they were also increasingly worthless as an investment, as is indicated by the probate inventory of the former Secunde Andries de Man, which lists 9 male slaves at 73 rixdollars each, 3 females at 60 rixdollars, 5 unpriced 'small slave children', and '2 old and almost spent slaves' at 30 rixdollars.[198] Similarly the well-to-do farmer Jan Wessels on his death in 1711 left '1 old *jonge* named Claas van Bengale' and '1 old *jonge* mostly sick named Abel', who were both valued at 40 rixdollars each, while the prices of the remaining 8 slaves in the estate were variously given as 50, 70 and 80 rixdollars.[199] In the same year one finds 'a slave *jonge*, cripple', valued at 30 rixdollars in the same context.[200]

A minor tragedy in this context is indicated by a chance reference in a letter from the Council of Policy to Batavia in 1707: 'The female slave sent over by the Balinese lieutenant, Batyan, could find no purchaser, as she is too old.'[201]

This consideration was so generally acknowledged that the Statutes of Batavia, stipulating knowledge of Dutch as a requirement for manumission, had added, 'except in the case of very old people, of which the secretaries are to take account in granting letters of freedom'.[202] They might, in other words, be cast off without further ado, a phenomenon which according to Hattingh was common in all slave societies.[203]

Not only the Company disposed of its elderly and ageing slaves in this way, but so too private owners. In 1706, for example, the wealthy freeburgher Guilliam Heems freed Diana van Macassar when she was forty years old, and the following years she was refused support by the church at Stellenbosch. This was possibly the reason why Commissioner Simons in 1708 felt called upon to point out in his Memorandum that

> when slaves are manumitted here, no corresponding act of guarantee ['*cautie*'] is given according to the Statutes of Batavia that for ten years they will not become a charge on the parish, which must therefore be introduced here as a matter of urgency at the act passed before the secretary and two members of the Council of Justice, as I have learned that families here have already become such a charge.[204]

The requirement was therefore introduced that two sureties were to be given in the letter of manumission, who would undertake to support the person in question where necessary during the first six years after he or she had been freed.[205]

According to Hattingh, documents relating to slave transactions at the Cape are reasonably complete up to 1720, 'after which date they become scarcer'.[206] In the period 1700–20, which is not covered by Dr Böeseken's survey, he found transactions concerning almost 1400 slaves, of whom 143 were manumitted or promised their freedom, bringing the total number of manumissions up to that date to about 257.[207]

These records show that during this later period it was no longer customary to free aged slaves as a matter of convenience. On the contrary, one finds provisions such as those made by Anthonetta Theodora van Schagen, widow of the wealthy farmer Anthonij van der Lith of Koelenhof in the Stellenbosch district, in 1741, stipulating 'that the female slave Silvia van Madagascar being old and worn may not be sold nor removed by anyone, but on account of her long faithful service shall be allowed to live with the said lady's abovementioned son Daniel van der Lith for the remainder of her life'.

In 1753 Daniel van der Lith died in turn, and among the 14 male slaves (including one infant at the breast and one fugitive) and 8 females listed in the probate inventory, was Silvia van Madagascar, by this time some twelve years older, with a note concerning the above stipulation appended to her name, although it is not clear how she was disposed of. Among the gold shirt buttons, diamond eardrops, pearl necklaces, silver spoons and forks and silver snuff boxes now distributed among the children of Daniel van der Lith, there were also, however, 6 slaves. One of the latter went to the eldest son, the 16-year-old Anthonij Gerbrand van der Lith in accordance with an earlier bequest by his grandmother, with the note:

1 slave *jongen* Jonathan, with regard to whom the parents stipulated that he, Anthonij Gerbrand, may have the free

choice of a slave *jongen* from their joint estate in the place of the now aged *jongen* whom his parents took for themselves; in accordance with which the said Anthonij Gerbrand therefore freely chose the slave David van de Caab.[208]

According to the manumission figures available for the later period, most of the slaves concerned were stated to be in their twenties,[209] and the reason given for manumission were usually said to be faithful service, although 'special considerations' were also mentioned frequently. Slaves were also freed on request, allowed to purchase their freedom or freed according to the stipulations in their owner's will, while conditional manumission likewise continued to occur. Knowledge of the Dutch language is mentioned in a number of cases, although the individuals concerned are most often described in guarded terms as 'being reasonably well acquainted with the Dutch language'.[210] The fact that the slave in question had been baptised is mentioned much less often, in only 11 cases out of 32,[211] while only a single individual, the Company slave Pieter van Juwara, was according to Hattingh about to make his profession of faith.[212]

In addition to the above, documents requesting permission to manumit slaves have been preserved for the entire period 1715–91, with only four years missing, and include manumissions both by the VOC and private owners. These have been analysed by Elphick & Shell, and while they fall outside the period covered in this book, it may be interesting to note that they deal with a total of 1075 manumission, of which only 81 involved Company slaves. 'If we turn these manumissions into percentages of the slave force per year,' observe these two writers, 'we find that the manumission rate in South Africa was low and remained so.'[213]

Some further changes seem to have occurred in the pattern of manumission over this period. In the first place, the VOC, in spite of the small number of manumissions, freed twelve times as many slaves in proportion to its total holdings as did private owners.[214]

Privately owned slaves were more frequently manumitted by senior officials than by burghers,[215] while most of the freeburghers who freed their slaves appear to have belonged by then to what the authors concerned call the 'middle-income' rather than the 'wealthy' group.[216] In cases where older slaves (41 years and over) were freed, they were well provided for.[217]

Finally, Elphick & Shell note that manumissions at the Colony during the period examined by them were 'predominantly urban', and very few farmers appear to have been willing to part with valuable labourers.[218] As Hattingh remarks in summing up the slightly earlier period which he himself analysed, 'Manumissions in this period continued to occur in exceptional cases as a personal favour rather than becoming a general humane custom.'[219]

The fledgling free black community at the Cape has already received a good deal of attention, but it deserves to be studied both more fully and more closely than has yet been done.[220] In the present book dealing with the first years of Cape slavery, only a few concluding words can be said concerning the origins and early development of the group which came into being from the local population of ex-slaves, convicts, exiles and deportees.

According to De Wet, the muster rolls list a total of 96 adult male free blacks at the Cape between 1657 and 1707, using the term in the strict sense of manumitted slaves,[221] and by far the greater number had been born in India or the Indonesian archipelago, these two regions contributing 26 and 22,9% of the total respectively.[222] Elphick & Shell add the comment that the people concerned were chiefly Bengalis and Maccasarese/Buginese respectively.[223] Only 14 men had been locally born, in spite of Van Reede's provisions for manumitting this particular group.[224] By 1702 the entire free black population amounted to no more than 46 people: 21 men, 10 women and 15 children, who formed only 3,2% of the total free population.[225]

Making a living at the Cape was difficult enough in the early years, and even more so for people coming from what was in many ways a sheltered environment such as the ex-slaves, while apart from slaves manumitted by the Company, few of them would have received any education. Among the 96 free black males identified by De Wet there were 39 cases in which a signature to a document was called for, and in only 5 of these the man concerned was able to sign his name.[226]

Some training or other form of preparation for freedom was, however, given in certain cases. Angela van Bengalen, manumitted in 1666, was according to her letter of freedom to live in the house of a freeburgher for six months and received unspecified training from him, after which she would be free to continue working for him if she chose, for a monthly wage to be decided by mutual agreement.[227] In 1678 the shoemaker Barent Cornelis Backer similarly undertook to give three years training to Andries Casta (probably from the coast of Coromandel), a slave of the Governor, Joan Bax, and a contract was drawn up specifying the conditions and the wages to be paid.[228] Both these slaves were the property of senior officials, however, and most slave owners were less considerate or had less foresight.

In 1691 Jacob van Malabar, 'who had served Martin Pansjo faithfully for 14 years', was freed by his master 'to earn his living as a farm labourer',[229] but it is not clear what provision was made for him to do so. The following year one reads of 'Isak from Ternate manumitted by Henning Hüsing. As in the case of other liberated slaves, he would be permitted to farm in Stellenbosch as a Free Burgher: "...*om hem neffens andere vrijgelatene slaven als vrijman in Stellenbosch bij den landbouw te erneren*".' The following day Isak undertook to serve Hüsing as a free labourer, 'in return for food and clothes. At the end of the two-year period he was to receive 60 breeding ewes ("*aanteelschapen*").'[230]

In 1694 there is also a record of Jan van Malgassies, aged 40, being manumitted by Claas Leenderts van Houten, 'on condition that he gives satisfaction as a worker to Jan Cotse whom he was to serve for three years', and a contract was drawn up the same day 'in which Jan Cotse promised to pay Jan from Malgassies Rds.45 for his services'.[231] In 1699 there was the case of 'Augustijn from Madagascar, to be given his freedom by Jan Dirckx de Beer when he has served him for three years for a wage of Rds.2 a month',[232] while in 1712, when Simon van der Stel made provision in his will for freeing a number of his slaves, three of them received 10 cows and 20 sheep each, and the fourth a young male slave of his own as well.[233]

Pieter van de Caab, known as Brasman, was manumitted by Christina Does, the wealthy widow of the pioneer freeburgher El- bert Dirckx Diemer, in 1694 at the age of 28, on condition that he serve her son and her son-in-law, Fiscal Blesius, who were business partners, for another six years. 'If he served faithfully during the six year period, he was to receive 150 weaned ewes.'[234] In 1707 Brasman was described as an 'agriculturist in Drakenstein' and was about to buy a farm with house, equipment, cattle and two slaves from Blesi- us for 2600 guilders, extremely favourable terms,[235] when his prom- ising career came to a sudden end.[236]

All of these slave owners in manumitting a slave attempted to prepare him in some way for freedom and cushion the shock of adjusting to a free society. In addition, as Hattingh points out, the proviso often made that a manumitted slave was to continue in his master's service for another year or two, and sometimes for as many as eight or ten years, was not invariably for the latter's benefit, but could also serve as a period in which the slave might adjust to freedom.[237] 'It took some powers of adaptation,' comments Dr Böeseken, 'to change over from a situation in which you are looked after in all respects, to the freedom of deciding on your own resi- dence, food and clothing, work and recreation.'[238] Handling and dealing with money and coping with financial transactions would also have been a new experience to most of the freed slaves.

In practice most of the free blacks seem to have continued the work to which they had become accustomed as slaves and in which they had acquired a certain proficiency, as gardeners or hawkers and peddlers of garden produce and fish. Simon van der Stel wrote as early as 1679 that they sold various kinds of confectionery to patients in hospitals and to visiting ships.[239] They also seem to have run tap houses, or else to have managed them for white owners. Maria Manuelsz, manumitted in 1702 after the death of her mistress, together with her five children, because they all had a white father, was nine years later making a living as the owner of a wine tap-house in the Table Valley 'where sailors spent noisy evenings'.[240]

Free blacks at an early stage became active in the fishing industry, as has already been made clear by various references in this chapter, often in partnership with one another or with whites. A testimonial to the Governor, W.A. van der Stel, by local fishermen in 1706 was signed by both whites and non-whites, the latter forming the majority,[241] and so too a memorial requesting fishing rights in 1722.[242] The former document states that the signatories, 'when the weather was favourable, by day and by night, whenever they had no other work, had gone out fishing in order to earn their food properly and honestly, not only along the shores of this bay [*Table Bay*], but also elsewhere in the neighbourhood and wherever they thought that they could obtain the largest supply of fish'.[243] This illustrates well the part-time, small-scale and co-operative nature of the local fishing industry.

Mentzel goes into some detail concerning the arrangement in his own time: 'Two men provide a boat each, another supplies the net, and various other people the slaves to man the boats. Each boat requires 5 persons. The fish that are caught are divided into 13 lots made up as follows: 1 for each boat, 1 for each of the 10 slaves, and the 13th share for the net.'[244]

The notable success achieved by Claas Gerritsz van Bengalen by fishing has already been described, but there was at least one contemporary who could also make an adequate living in this way. A month before Claas's death at the end of 1697, Jacob van Bengalen lost his wife Neeltjen van Macassar, leaving him with '3 little children', and the 5 fish vats and 'half worn seine' listed in the probate inventory compiled on this occasion give the impression that he too was a fisherman.[245] The household in this case was simpler, but there were also 2 feather beds, in addition to mattresses filled with straw, as well as bedsteads with white and red hangings, table linen, a good deal of porcelain and women's clothing and some silverware.

The total value of this estate was only a little over 500 guilders, but as a standard of comparison it may be mentioned that the estates of two of the French refugees farming in Drakenstein for which inventories were compiled in the same year were worth 689 and 400 guilders respectively, and consisted mainly of land and cattle, the household furniture being scanty and shabby.[246] One might also make a very relevant comparison with Pieter Christiaensz de Jager, a white man as far as is known, who in 1714 owned a house and two plots of land at Salt River, near the shores of Table Bay, together with 12 oxen and a wagon, a boat, a fishing net, and household goods valued at about 100 guilders, a minimal sum. The total value of the estate was 2000 guilders, but 400 guilders were owing to the Orphan Chamber and there were incidental outstanding debts to the value of 700 guilders.[247]

The promising careers of the early years soon proved to be exceptional, however. Increasingly, as Elphick & Ross observe of the free black community in the Table Valley, 'their only means of livelihood were handicrafts and petty retailing, and their fortunes must have oscillated wildly with the presence or absence of ships in the bay'.[248] By 1710, concludes Hattingh in the same vein, 'it had in general become clear that the free blacks of Stellenbosch in general could not succeed in conducting their farming operations on a profitable basis'. One of them, Rangton van Bali, who died in 1720, seems to have supported himself in a modest way as a carpenter,[249] one or two worked as carters, and some of them later became successful cattle farmers.[250] As white farmers moved out of the Liesbeek valley, the smaller and older farms there also became available to free blacks, and there were free black farmers in the area until near the end of the VOC period.[251] 'Freeblacks owned considerable property in the Table Valley from the mid-eighteenth century,' writes Mrs Cairns, 'but a prolonged free-black ownership of farmlands in the Peninsula such as these over a period of some fifty years is perhaps unique.'[252]

Through force of circumstances, the ex-slaves and other coloureds therefore came to be confined to a relatively limited area of the Cape, and Shell, in referring to the 'small and highly urbanized free black community' of the Table Valley, draws attention especially to their 'extensive and persistent family and friendship circles'.[253]

By 1714, report Elphick & Shell, however, 'Even in the Cape district, where thirty-two free blacks lived, most had no property entered on the rolls, except for six who owned slaves and three who had a horse or two',[254] and Hattingh refers in passing to the 'typical senseless series of civil actions in which free blacks were so frequently involved', giving several examples.[255] Litigiousness and increasing poverty seemed increasingly to be their main characteristics,[256] and when Governor De la Fontaine in 1731 sent a detailed report on the inhabitants of the Cape to the Gentlemen XVII, virtually all the individual free blacks were dismissed summarily with the set phrase, 'Free blacks or ex-convicts are poor without exception, many make a living from fishing.'[257]

Of the 253 married white males at the Cape in 1705, only 9 had free black wives, according to Guelke, 3,6% of the whole, after which the figure not only decreased, but showed what he calls a 'marked concentration in Cape Town'.[258] 'A few men married free black women,' is his conclusion, 'but for the vast majority it seems that a woman had to be white to be considered an eligible marriage partner',[259] although it is hard to accept this statement in view of the many marriages between European men and women 'van de Caab' noted in genealogical and other records for the late seventeenth and early eighteenth centuries.[260]

Heese describes the phenomenon of a white man having a number of children by a slave or free black woman and eventually marrying her as increasingly common during the eighteenth century,[261] while he also records a steady increase in the number of marriages between white men and former slaves over the same period.[262] For the woman, he writes, this was 'an escape mechanism from slavery, and enabled her children, if born in wedlock, to reach the highest economic and social rungs in Cape society'.[263] The most notable example is Angela van Bengalen, who married a white man and became prosperous, while her daughter Anna de Koning, born in slavery of an earlier liaison, married Oloff Bergh, a member of the Council of Policy, and died an extremely wealthy woman.[264]

One of the few other examples of racially mixed marriages among senior servants of the Company would appear to have been the Dane K.J. Slotsoo, who as from 1699 held a variety of official positions at the Cape, becoming a member of the Council of Policy in 1708.[265] He was married in 1703 to Anna Regina Hartz, the daughter of a German whose wife is described in a later source as 'Judith Marquardt van de Caab', in other words a locally born coloured woman, though this seems doubtful.[266] Slotsboo's wife died in 1713, leaving him with three children.

Among the freeburgher population there are likewise cases which show that a man's career was not necessarily inhibited by such a marriage. 'In spite of the fact that Arie Cruijtsman [*Arnoldus Kreutzmann*] was married to a woman of slave origin (Maria Vosloo) and sometimes had social contact with other coloureds,' writes Hattingh with reference to the Stellenbosch district, 'he served as *heemraad* for his area and in addition was one of the wealthiest farmers in 1716.'[267] After his death in 1722 his widow married the equally wealthy Arnoldus Willemsz Basson, who had a free black grandmother.[268]

A similar case is that of the German H.O. Eksteen, who arrived at the Cape in 1702 as a cadet in the service of the Company and became a freeburgher two years later.[269] At the same time he married Maria Heyns, a daughter of Maria Schalck, one of the three Company slaves who had been freed by Simon van der Stel in 1686, and a German, Paul Heyns, whom she had subsequently married. By the time of the marriage the bride's mother had died, but her stepmother was likewise a free black woman, Maria Lozee, widow of the Company's master mason Douwe Gerbrandsz Steyn.[270] It was probably in this way that Eksteen established early contacts with the free black community, which would appear to have been close, for in a will made in 1709 the well-to-do Claas Cornelisz van de Caab, former schoolmaster in the Slave Lodge, and his wife, Beatrice van Cochin, left Eksteen's 'little son' Michiel, who was four years old at the time, the sum of 300 guilders.

Eksteen most likely owed his initial success largely to his father-in-law, who was already a wealthy and well-established man and over the period 1708–13 uninterruptedly held one or more parts of the remunerative wine *pacht*. It was probably with Heyns's active help and support that Eksteen himself managed to obtain shares in the brandy and later also wine *pachten* consistently over the period 1708–21, so that by 1715 he could already be described as 'a moderately wealthy man'.[271] The fact that Paul Heyns twice in succession married a free black woman was clearly no impediment to his success as a farmer; but if this interpretation is correct, Eksteen was one of the rare men at the Cape who owed his success directly to his marriage with a free black wife.[272]

In 1715, after the early death of Maria Heyns, Eksteen married a granddaughter of the wealthy Cape businessman Jan Meyndertsz Cruywagen, and continued on the course which was to make him the richest freeburgher at the Cape in his day, the equivalent in his own generation of Henning Hüsing in the previous century.[273] He seems, however, to have kept up his early connections with the free black community, and in 1719, when Eksteen was married for the third time, again to a white wife, Beatrice van Cochin, by now a widow, still appointed him as one of her executors.[274] By this time he was the owner three houses in the Table Valley and four farms.[275]

A more modest but also more representative example of a successful 'mixed' marriage is provided by Jannetje (Johanna) Bort, another of the three Company slaves freed by the Council of Policy in 1686. Two months later it was pointed out to Council that she had already borne four children to Sergeant Dirk van Koningshoven, 'under the assurance of a promise of marriage', but that he had meanwhile acquired a 'concubine' and now refused to acknowledge either her or the children.[276] This was probably no uncommon course of affairs, but Jannetje clearly enjoyed the protection of Commander Van der Stel, in whose house she had served, and Van Koningshoven was ordered to support his children properly and forbidden to marry anyone other than their mother, which he duly did.

Jannetje died a prosperous widow and well-established member of the local community in 1713, 27 years after her manumission. With regard to the probate inventory compiled at her death, Malan observes that it 'epitomises the household of a woman who successfully created a colonial home and future for her family from whatever limited resources she could muster'.

> There were certain items listed in this document in ways that indicate a level of gentility that was absent in many of the previous households [discussed]. There was a tea table, and looking glasses—one with a black frame and the other with brass fluting—the black bed was curtained with muslin and there were chintz curtains and valances in the best room. (…) There was a small glass-fronted cabinet full of ornaments, and a painted linen cupboard with decorative dishes and bowls on top. (…) There were also enough cooking utensils to suggest that more food could be produced and consumed than was necessary just for the family of a widow, four teenage children and a single slave.[277]

This was by no means the home of an average or representative free black woman of the first generation, but it shows nonetheless what was in principle possible at the Cape.

In order to restore some perspective to the picture, however, it may be as well to turn to Sara van de Caab, the putative daughter of Leendert Jan van Gijselen, who in 1690, shortly after her manumission, had married the Norwegian Andries Oelofsen. In 1709 he died on their farm in the Bottelarij district of Stellenbosch, leaving her with eight children, and a house furnished with a table, 2 chairs, 2 benches, 2 chests, 2 sets of shelves, a bedstead, 2 mattresses covered in sailcloth, and a reasonably well equipped kitchen. The farm was stocked with 4 cows, 4 heifers, 8 oxen, a horse, an ox wagon, a plough, a harrow, some pick-axes and spades, and a slave called Cupido, and the estate was valued at 1732 rixdollars.[278] The widow was by no means badly off by the standards of her day, but her putative father was long since dead, and one wonders whether in the isolation of the farm and as a single woman facing the world with her large family there were times when she missed the solidarity, companionship and relative security of life in the Slave Lodge where she had grown up.

A final point which must be made about what may perhaps be called the early black bourgeoisie of the Table Valley is that the former slaves in many cases bought and owned slaves themselves, obviously regarding slavery as a normal institution, whatever their own experience of it may have been.

The curiously mixed or fluid state of Cape society during these early years, the vague feelings about slavery and the ambivalent position of slaves, are illustrated by the fact that a few years after the Dutch freeburgher Arnoldus Willemsz Basson had married the former slave Angela van Bengalen he was successfully sued for a debt of 15 rixdollars by the slave Isaak van Bengalen,[279] while Angela herself would in due course own Bengali slaves herself.[280] 'The one form of registered property which free blacks did possess in increasing numbers was slaves,' observe Elphick & Shell; 'for example, in 1735 the 132 free black adults owned 139 slaves (adults and children).'[281]

On the other hand, Shell makes the point that slaves purchased by free blacks were usually absorbed into the free black community, 'and later manumitted de facto, if not always de jure'.[282] In many cases free blacks were equally willing not only to pay the considerable sums required to purchase a slave but also to buy the freedom of others or to give the required sureties for them. So one reads in the records in 1699, for example: 'Jacob, born at the Cape of Good Hope (14), liberated by his father Jacob from Macassar, who paid the Company Rds.100. Cornelis [Stevensz] Botma signed the deed of liberation.'[283] In 1703 Cesij van Macassar paid 60 rixdollars for the freedom of her daughter, Cornelia van de Caab, and the latter's little girl aged eighteen months, the condition being made that they would support her for the remainder of her life.[284]

Shell gives the interesting and illuminating example of Cecilia van Macassar, who

> not only freed her son, Jan Holdsmidt of the Cape, but also friends. Lena of Bengal and Cecilia had been fellow slaves in the governor's 'establishment' many years ago. On her son's manumission deed, it stipulates that she bought Jan from the agent of Willem Adriaan van der Stel in 1714, and therefore Jan Holdsmidt of the Cape was technically a slave of his own mother for 14 years.[285]

In a footnote he adds, 'Cecilia of Macassar was a slave of Van der Stel's on 29 May 1695, when she had her daughter, Flora of the Cape, baptized. Similarly, Lena, her friend ("Magdalena of the Cape") and her mother, Cecilia of Bengal, appear in the baptismal registers 13 June 1706 as slaves of W.A. van der Stel. Cecilia bought and manumitted them all.'[286]

With similar persistence Claas Jonasz van de Caab pursued the younger Van der Stel after the latter's return to the Netherlands concerning the freedom of his own wife, Dina van Bima, receiving in reply in 1711 a letter in Van der Stel's own hand confirming her manumission and wishing the couple well.[287]

Investigating the manumissions of the period 1715–91, Elphick & Shell further established that 'fully a quarter of manumitting owners were free blacks (if institutional owners like the Company and the Church be ignored)', although it should be noted that their definition of the term 'free black' includes all free coloured people, whether of slave origin or not.[288] They remark likewise, 'A large number (12.2 per cent) were cases of blacks buying their own freedom or that of their children, spouses or parents.'[289] Of the 12 older slaves manumitted over the period 1715–91, 9 were according to the same authors freed through the efforts of members of their own families,[290] while Hattingh points out free blacks offering themselves as sureties for slaves due to be freed.[291]

As further examples of what might be called an ambivalent attitude to slavery, mention may be made of the free black Maria Evertsz, who was sentenced to six months hard labour in 1679 for having harboured a female slave, and the mestizo Jacob Hages, sentenced to ten years in 1694 for trying to help an absconded slave from an English ship escape on a Danish vessel.[292]

'The free blacks had exactly the same, right, privileges and obligations as the freeburghers,' writes De Wet. 'There were no legal limitations which excluded them from full participation in public life',[293] while Heese in this regard agrees with Böeseken. 'The status which a free black enjoyed before 1700 depended largely on the individual and not necessarily on his race or ethnic grouping,' he writes,[294] and points out that at the beginning of the eighteenth century a free person of slave origin enjoyed de facto burgher status, even though this was soon to change.[295]

De Wet writes that 11 free blacks were baptised as adults, and 5 had their children baptised,[296] although Hattingh mentions that they seldom proceeded from baptism to confirmation or profession of faith.[297] By the church they were regarded as members equal in standing to the whites, and it is possible to find an entry such as the following in the church registers: '21 December [1689], transferred to the congregation on profession of faith, S[ieur] Joannes Gulielmus de Grevenbroek, Secretary [to the Council of Policy] at this place, and Claes Cornelisz., schoolmaster in the Company's Lodge.'[298]

Free black men served in the burgher militia together with the whites,[299] and therefore by implication were in possession of the required flintlocks and swords.[300] Pieter Willemsz van de Caab acted as drummer of the Stellenbosch cavalry until 1728, to which he owed the nickname 'Pieter Tambouer',[301] while Jan Jacobsz van de Caab was fined 3 rixdollars for being absent during a parade in 1712.[302]

Free blacks could borrow money from the church, the Orphan Chamber and white burghers on the same terms as whites,[303] and when in want they were as readily assisted as the whites, though possibly not always on the same terms.[304] Free black farmers employed both white and coloured farmhands and were themselves employed by both whites and coloureds in turn, and Hattingh points out that there was 'virtually no difference' in their wages: 'It varied rather from one case to another which was probably determined by factors other than skin colour.'[305]

When two free black farmers in the Stellenbosch district, Jan van Ceylon and Anthony van Angola, together with a white farmer and his *knecht*, in 1692 undertook a hunting expedition of thirteen days beyond the Berg River without official permission, shooting a hippopotamus and an eland, but possibly also trying to barter cattle illegally with the Khoikhoi, all four men were likewise condemned equally to be 'thoroughly whipped'.[306]

In spite of this, however, there seem to have been tacit reservations or built-in limitations, and while Willem Basson, son of the

349

former slave Angela van Bengalen by a European father, was one of the official meat *pachters* in 1705–07,[307] he was very much an exception, demonstrating no more than the fact that this was possible. As far as is known, free blacks held no public office, and it is significant, for example, that Hattingh could find no coloured officers in the Stellenbosch burgher militia during the early years, in spite of the presence of coloured men in the ranks.[308]

Most significant of all in this regard, however, is the limited and hesitant way in which the name 'freeburgher' was applied to free blacks and other free people of colour. In a slave transaction in 1679 Grasias van Angola was referred to as *'vrijborger alhier'* ('freeburgher of this place'),[309] and Jacob Hages appeared in the records of the Council of Justice as 'mestizo and freeburgher', while Anthonie van Bengalen was called a 'free resident' and Jan van Ternaten a 'freeman'.[310] Heese likewise points out that Louis van Bengalen was described as a 'freeburgher' in a number of documents over the years,[311] and Hattingh that the latter and Claas van Guinee appeared as freeburghers of Stellenbosch when they began farming there in partnership.

In noting the fact that Christina van Canarie, a manumitted slave of Simon van der Stel, was described as a *'burgeresse'* in a deed of transfer 1717, Mrs Cairns describes it, however, as 'a term not commonly applied to freeblacks',[312] with which De Wet agrees,[313] though Hattingh qualifies this statement. 'It is true that free blacks were not addressed as freeburghers in all documents,' he remarks, 'but such references occur in more places than Dr De Wet would suggest.'[314] Heese, however, gives the impression that manumission did not automatically confer freeburgher status. 'Usually free blacks possessed a status between those of slave and burgher and it would be possible for the freeborn alone to acquire burgher status.'[315]

The various examples of the use of the term 'freeburgher' quoted above, plentiful as they may seem, are very much in the minority when seen in a wider context. The most commonly used contemporary name in this connection was 'free black', and when a reference to manumitted slaves occurred in contemporary documentation they were in the vast majority of cases identified by means of this term or some equivalent such as 'a manumitted black',[316] or in the case of Africans by some soubriquet. Thus Anthonie van Angola was known as Zwarte Anthonie ('Black Anthonie') and 'Anthonie de Kaffer',[317] while Evert van Guinee appears as 'the free Kaffer Evert',[318] and Maria Evertsz, his daughter, as Zwarte Maria ('Black Maria').

This, however, interesting though it may be, is not the subject of the present book, and the fortunes of manumitted slaves have only been sketched here. As has been mentioned already, the free black and coloured community of the VOC period deserves to be studied both more fully and more closely.

9. Three lives

With the exception of the chapter on early slavery under Van Riebeeck, in which an attempt was made to provide the slaves involved with some individuality and identity, this book had inevitably dealt largely in generalisations, and the slaves and free blacks themselves have been little more than names mentioned in passing.

As the VOC was a business enterprise, however, its records tended to be very full and its bookkeeping meticulous to the point of compulsiveness. By reading widely and assembling fragments of information from a great number of sources, it is therefore often possible to recreate the life of a given individual under its authority to a surprising extent, even if only in outline, and this includes slaves and free blacks. In this final chapter an attempt will be made to compile patchwork biographies of this nature for three individuals, all of them slaves who in due course obtained their freedom. They are two women and a man, one from the East, one from Africa and the third locally born, whose lives jointly span the first seventy or eighty years of colonial history at the Cape.

These lives are of value in the first place for what they can contribute directly to our knowledge of the world of early Cape slavery, relatively little though this may be. In addition, however, they can also provide much information indirectly, for the people concerned were the products of that world and had been shaped by it.

Angela van Bengalen has already been mentioned as one of the slaves who reached the Cape in the very early years of the Dutch presence,[1] having been acquired by Van Riebeeck as a personal slave before the two large consignments of 1658, most likely in 1657. She must have been one of the 'three Batavia female slaves' listed in his household shortly afterwards,[2] meaning that they had been obtained from Batavia.

Insofar as her name may be taken as an indication of origin, she came from the area in what is now the north-east of India and Bangladesh, from which the Dutch in Batavia at that time acquired large numbers of slaves captured by professional slave dealers by means of raiding and kidnapping.

As part of the extensive slave transactions he undertook before leaving the Cape early in 1662, Van Riebeeck sold Angela to the fiscal Abraham Gabbema, who was shortly afterwards promoted to Secunde. No price was mentioned, nor was there any reference on this occasion to children.[3] She therefore continued to live in the Fort in what, in the world of slavery, must be regarded as a privileged position, as personal slave in the family of a senior official. Like the Van Riebeecks, the Gabbemas had small children, and in addition they owned no fewer than 8 slaves, men, women and children, the highest number recorded in that year after Commander Wagenaer and his family, recently arrived from Batavia, who had 10.

When Gabbema was transferred to Batavia with his family early in 1666, he manumitted Angela, this being the earliest recorded manumission at the Cape after the three in the 1650s,[4] and at the same time set free her three children, who are mentioned here for the first time.[5] They had presumably been born at the Cape with white fathers, but if they were baptised the fact was not recorded. One of them must have been the child later known as Anna de Koning, and a François de Koninck from Ghent in the Southern Netherlands (Belgium) is known to have been at the Cape in this time, first as a soldier and later as a free mason,[6] but a name by itself can prove nothing, and the fact is mentioned only to eke out the little information available.

The reason given for setting Angela free were stated to be 'her extremely good and faithful service' and 'pure affection', and it was stipulated that she was to live for six months in the house of the freeburgher Thomas Christoffel Muller, a German who had spent a considerable sum of money on setting himself up as a baker and had married the maidservant of a minister on a ship bound for Batavia. He served as burgher representative on the Council of Policy during the period 1666–68, and was thus clearly among the more respectable members of the still very rough-and-ready little community in the Table Valley.

The arrangement by which Muller would train Angela in return for her food and clothing shows a good deal of consideration on the part of the Gabbemas for their former slave who was now being launched in the unfamiliar world of freedom as a young, single woman with small children. In this too, and in the choice of the Mullers as her mentors, she may be regarded as exceptional in the slave world of her time, and as exceptionally fortunate.

After this Angela is heard of again in February 1667, when at her own request she received a house plot in one of the three streets in the fledgling town in the Table Valley, 'to the north Heere Street, to the east the dwelling of the freeburgher Wouter Cornelis Mostaert, to the south still unbuilt towards Table Mountain, to the west the tail of the Lion Mountain [*Lion's Head*]'.[7] A year later she hired a slave described as 'A Bengali boy called Scipio Africanus from the Malabar Coast' from a passing skipper at 5 guilders a month,[8] which was considerably cheaper than buying a slave, but set her apart from most other residents of the Cape, who at this early stage as yet had no slave labour of any kind.

There is no indication of how Angela was making a living, although she may have continued working for Muller for some time, or have supported herself by means of a garden plot. In later years the Council of Policy, according to Hattingh, referred to such a plot and to her having 'transformed it from a wilderness to a garden with great labour and expense'.[9] She seems, however, to have been doing well as a member of the embryonic free black community which a few years later consisted of only 2 men, 2 women and 2 children. The women would have been Angela herself and Annica van Bengalen, the wife of Anthonij de Later van Japan, the two slaves freed by Commander Wagenaer shortly after Angela herself had obtained her freedom.

A further milestone on the path of Angela's integration in the local free community was reached in 1668, when she and a Company slave called Catharina (possibly Catharina van Paliacatte) were baptised. A few months later she had a son baptised by the name of Pieter, Catharina, 'a slave but a Christian', acting as witness, and in 1669 she in turn acted as witness during the baptism of children of 'Groot Katrijn' (probably the same Catharina) and another slave woman.[10]

Before the end of the same year Angela completed what may be called her process of integration in the white community by her marriage to the 32-year-old Arnoldus Willemsz Basson from the Dutch-German border area, who had originally come to the Cape as a soldier in the service of the VOC and had for a time been employed by a local tavern keeper. He is known to have been involved in sea fishing at Saldanha and to have farmed, possibly on a small scale, and several slave transactions are recorded for him over the years. By 1682 he owned 3 slaves, 2 horses, 43 head of cattle, 500 sheep and 6 pigs, and harvested wheat, rye and barley.[11]

Over the period 1670–95 the Bassons were to have seven children baptised,[12] and the baptism of their first daughter in 1677 was witnessed by Oloff Bergh, a Swede of unclear antecedents in Company employ, who about this time married Anna de Koning, one of the children born to Angela while she was still a slave. A black-and-white copy of a possibly monochrome portrait by an amateur artist, the original of which seems to have disappeared, shows the latter as a beautiful and elegant young Eastern woman in the ringlets and dress fashionable in her day, holding a fan and a piece of fruit.[13] Her husband is portrayed in a companion piece which makes it appear likely that he was, at any rate as far as appearance is concerned, the unidentified 'popeyed hoodlum and king of the thieves' referred to by his colleague, the prickly J.G. de Grevenbroek, secretary to the Council of Policy.[14] Bergh, who had come to the Cape as a soldier, was to have a long and successful career under the VOC, and in 1686 Commander Van der Stel acted as sponsor at the baptism of one of the couple's children.[15]

Arnoldus Basson died in 1698, in possession of house and garden plots in the Table Valley, a farm in Drakenstein, 5 slaves, 73 head of cattle and 260 sheep,[16] and while his wife was afterwards usually referred to as 'the widow Arnoldus Basson',[17] references also occur in the respectful Eastern form '*maai* Angela'. She is known to have undertaken a number of further business transactions, including some involving slaves,[18] and Dr Böeseken praises her 'skilful' administration of his estate.[19]

Angela's son-in-law was by this time captain of the garrison, member of the Council of Policy and a favourite of the Van der Stels, father and son. Under W.A. van der Stel her eldest son, Willem Basson, in 1705–07 was in possession of the lucrative meat *pacht*, while his brothers became well-to-do farmers and his sisters married Dutch husbands.[20]

There is a brief glimpse of Angela during this period in the letters of Johanna Maria van Riebeeck, a granddaughter of the first Commander of the Cape, who stopped here in 1710 on her way back to the Netherlands with her husband, the former Governor-General Joan van Hoorn.

> I was also visited by a black woman who had been a servant ['*mijt*'] of Grandmother and said that she looked after Father and all the other children and also that she spoke to Father when he came here again from the Fatherland [in 1676]. Her name is Ansiela [*sic*], she was married here to a Hollander and her daughter is the wife of Captain B[ergh] here at the Cape who has the paintings of Grandfather and Grandmother, and she seems to think highly of them.[21]

'Anssla van Bengalen' died in 1720 as a well-to-do woman, most probably in her seventies. She was still in possession of her garden plot in the Table Valley, with a small house which, judging by the probate inventory, was not so much comfortable as over-furnished.[22] The contents included seven chairs with loose cushions, a four-poster bed with eight pillows, a mirror with a gilded frame, a teaset, further porcelain, clothing, jewellery, and a portrait of her husband. She was furthermore in possession of 3 male slaves, one of whom was from Bengal like herself, 2 slave women and 2 children, and 39 goats, while a small farm with a further 3 slaves, 63 head of cattle and 300 sheep was also recorded. The not inconsiderable estate of 6495 guilders which she had inherited from her husband had by this time increased to almost 15 000 guilders.[23]

Oloff Bergh eventually retired on half-pay and remained a highly respected member of the local establishment until his death in 1724. His widow Anna de Koning died in 1733 as an extremely wealthy widow owning houses and a garden plot in the Table Valley, the farm Constantia which had formerly belonged to Simon van der Stel, and two farms in the Piketberg area, and no fewer than 24 adult slaves were listed in her house on the Heerengracht (the present Adderley Street) alone.[24] Her descendants were prominent members of the local white community throughout the VOC period.

The life of Evert van Guinee, who arrived at the Cape about a year after Angela van Bengalen, differed in all respects from her privileged existence, except insofar as he was also manumitted and ended his life here as a free black.[25]

Judging by his name, which is so often all the evidence one has to go on in the case of a slave, Evert must have been one of the 271 slaves bought for the VOC at Popo by the *Hasselt* early in 1658, one of the 228 who survived the voyage, and one of the 41, 'including the old and sick', who had remained at the Cape and were still alive by the beginning of the next year.[26] In the course of little more than a year he had therefore not only been removed forcibly from his own country and people, but had lost no fewer than 230 of his companions, whether through death or their having been sent on to Batavia.

As already mentioned, a number Guinean slaves were sold to the freeburghers on credit soon after their arrival at 100 guilders each, and Evert was purchased by Casper Brinckman.[27] In the winter of 1659, during the First Khoi War, Brinckman was stated to have lost 'all his livestock (19 head of cattle and 67 sheep)',[28] and a year later he had 10 morgen under wheat and rye,[29] which makes him one of the bigger farmers in the Liesbeek valley by the pioneering standards of his day.

Within little more than a month of his purchase Brinckman arrived at the Fort 'with tears in his eyes' to report that all four of his Guinean slaves had decamped during the night, but a man and a woman returned voluntarily within a week, while the other two were brought back by Khoikhoi a week later.[30] This gives the impression that his holdings consisted of two slave couples or 'paired slaves', as was so often the case with the members of these early consignments, so that Evert was presumably a young man or an adult at this time.

Whether paired or not, Evert was early in 1659 sold singly by Brinckman, without his age or a price being mentioned, to Van Riebeeck, who had begun farming on his own account at Bosheuvel (Wynberg) and Uitwijk (Mowbray). This was done on a considerably larger scale than was possible for the freeburghers, and shortly before Van Riebeeck left the Cape in 1662 there were 2 white *knechten*, 8 slaves and 22 draught oxen at Bosheuvel, where orchards and vineyards had been laid out, while at Uitwijk, which was closer to the Fort and better situated for personal supervision, there were 3 *knechten*, 5 slaves, 13 ploughing oxen, 18 milch cows and a small number of sheep, and wheat was sown.

On his departure Van Riebeeck sold Uitwijk to a former freeburgher, while Bosheuvel was ultimately taken over by the Company. His slaves, including Angela of Bengalen, were mostly sold as well, and mostly to fellow officials, who had more money at their disposal than the freeburghers, and it is likely that Evert van Guinee was among them. Senior officials were also the most likely to manumit their slaves on leaving the Cape, as subsequently happened in the case of Angela, and this may likewise have happened to Evert, for in 1669, when he re-appears in the available records, it is in connection with a garden plot granted to him as a free black behind the Fort in the Table Valley.[31] He was allowed to use the water of the channelled stream running alongside his property for irrigation purposes.[32]

In the local community Evert was generally known as Zwarte Evert or 'Evert the Kaffir', as was commonly the case with free blacks from Africa. In the muster roll of 1670 he appears with a wife, Anna van Guinee, and two children,[33] which gives the impression of 'paired' slaves who had been cohabiting for some time and had been freed together with their family by a particularly benevolent owner. Their daughter, Maria Evertsz, was later described by Van Riebeeck's granddaughter as 'a daughter of a woman or slave ["*mijd*"] who once worked in Grandfather's house',[34] but Anna van Guinee is not mentioned among Van Riebeeck's slaves, though a the 'female slave from Guinea, Maij', was sold by Evert's former master Brinckman to Van Riebeeck's wife in 1660, two years after the sale of Evert himself.[35]

In 1670 Evert borrowed 200 guilders from the church at 6% interest, and when he signed a bond for the outstanding amount in 1674, he was able to give his newly built house, outbuildings and cultivated land as security.[36] In 1676 he borrowed a further 150 guilders, undertaking to repay it after the visit of the return fleet, as was common at the time,[37] and in 1678 he acquired an adjacent piece of ground for 150 guilders, so that he was in possession of almost two morgen.[38] He owned a young Eastern slave, Claes van Bengalen, whom he sold for 32 rixdollars in 1677 when the child was twelve or thirteen years old.[39]

All in all, Evert van Guinee was leading the life of a reasonably prosperous free resident, not differing essentially from that of a white freeburgher, and Hattingh describes him as 'one of the most successful free blacks'[40] in the Table Valley, but by 1680 everything seems to have changed suddenly and he was ordered by the court to repay his debts.

What other setbacks Evert may have suffered at this time is unknown, but at the time when the manumission of the Company's African slaves was being discussed in official circles with a view to settling them in the Stellenbosch district as farmers, he seems to have requested land there himself, and it was later said that he had been established there by 1682, earlier than any of the other black pioneers.[41]

As has been mentioned, there were a number of slaves from Guinea and Angola in this group, but the scale of their farming was modest, and while a number of them seem to have made progress initially, few managed to keep it up beyond the end of the decade.[42] By the time Anthonie van Angola died in 1696, for example, he was in possession of 'a small clay house thatched with reeds', a bed with a mattress stuffed with kapok and two kapok pillows, 2 tripod stools, an old tea-table, a chest with some tools, 2 iron pots, 1 tin dish, a flintlock, a spade, an old wooden shovel, some further agricultural implements and a slave woman called Susanna with her child.[43] This was most likely the world of Evert and Anna van Guinee as well.

Evert is listed in 1682 as owning 8 head of cattle and 2 pigs and having sown wheat, and six years later he had 12 head of cattle only, but his farming at Stellenbosch does not appear to have been a success either. In 1685 he had sold his farm to the Norwegian Andries Oelofsen, who in due course was to marry the manumitted Company slave Sara van Gijselen, and in 1686 he was sued for debt. By 1688 his wife was stated to be a widow.[44]

While Evert's life ended obscurely, one of his daughters, Maria Evertsz, also known as Zwarte Maria or 'Black Maria' and 'Black Evert's Marij', had a successful career which rivalled that of Angela of Bengalen in the previous generation.[45] At the time when her father was experiencing his first difficulties in the Table Valley, she was married in 1678 to the free black Grasias (Jackje) van Angola, which seems to indicate that she must have been born in the early years after her parents arrived at the Cape, but the marriage ended in legal separation after only two years. During this time she was sentenced to six months hard labour for having harboured an absconded female slave.[46]

After this Maria had a permanent relationship with a Dutchman, Bastiaan Colijn, whom she could not marry as her legal husband Grasias van Angola appears still to have been alive. Their eldest child was baptised in 1684,[47] and by 1689 they were living together openly in her mother's house.[48] Heese draws attention to the fact 'that Colyn apparently possessed nothing, while his "wife", the daughter of black Guinean parents, at that stage owned three male slave and a female'.[49] In 1701 she was promised 60 morgen of land in the present Camps Bay by W.A. van der Stel, which were legally transferred to her in 1711, in addition to which she inherited the land in the Table Valley which had belonged to her parents.

'While the prosperity of Angela van Bengalen was largely determined by her marriage to Arnoldus Willem Basson,' writes Hattingh, '(…) the estate of Maria Evertsz, whose parents had begun as free blacks, was much more impressive.'[50] Her eldest son, Johannes Colijn, did well for himself too, and in 1718 acquired part of the old Constantia estate through his marriage to the coloured widow Elsabe van Hoff who had been left the farm by her first husband, a German.[51]

As far as recorded slave transactions are concerned, Maria bought the young girl Martha van Bengalen in 1698 for 60 rixdollars,[52] and the following year Coridon van Madagascar, whose name was changed to Cupido at her request.[53]

'In 1709 Maria's prosperity had increased to such an extent,' writes Heese, that she disposed over a white farmhand, as well as seven male slaves, two females and a young slave boy. She owned 24 head of cattle and 300 sheep and her 6000 vines produced 2 leaguers of wine, while she also harvested 15 muid of wheat. Colyn still reported no possessions in his census returns apart from the customary flintlock, sword and pistol which each white male possessed.[54]

Maria seems by this time to have been a prominent member of the local community, and Jan van Riebeeck's granddaughter, Johanna Maria, describes in 1710 having received a visit from 'a black woman called Black Mary ["*Swarte Maria*"]', on the strength of her mother having worked in the Commander's house.[55] In 1713 a visiting Englishman, Samuel Briercliffe, seeking accommodation at the Cape, was referred by the acting Governor, Willem Helot, to 'one Black Moll (who is married to a Dutchman)': 'She is a tall woman, very black,' Briercliffe reported in a letter, 'having sparkling eyes which, though frightful in her, yet would be very killing in an English face, but she is a very good hostess, and provides for us very splendidly and neatly withal.'[56]

While Maria herself was the daughter of black parents from Guinea, her halfbreed children were, like the semi-Asiatic descendants of Angela van Bengalen, to be accepted in the white community. After her death, which appears to have occurred in 1724, their prosperity does not seem to have continued, however. In a report compiled in 1730, Governor De la Fontaine described her widower, Bastiaan Colijn, as 'an old, poor man', their son Evert, who had been given his black grandfather's name, as 'an unmarried man who supports himself by gardening and limeburning', and their daughter Johanna as 'an unmarried woman who does not possess much'.[57]

In the case of the former slave Armozijn van de Caab or Armozijn Claasz one is likewise dependent on the information to be derived from circumstantial evidence, although much pioneering research in the archival sources has been done by Margaret Cairns.[58]

Firstly, the toponym 'van de Caab' indicates that she was locally born. In a will drawn up in 1713 she was later described as 'about 54 years old', and in one made in 1721 as 'about sixty,[59] which must be regarded as approximations only, by means of which her birth can be placed vaguely between 1659 and 1661. It therefore seems likely that her mother came from one of the two large batches of slaves brought to the Cape from Angola and Guinea in 1658.

In the muster roll of the Company's slaves compiled in 1693, Armozijn appears among the 'fullbreed women', but examined in its context this would appear to be a clerical error and the list in question is more likely to consist of 'halfbreeds' or children with white fathers. The fact that she later called herself Armozijn Claasz would, given contemporary usage, further suggest that her father was a Dutchman with the extremely common name Claas. The evidence for this remains contradictory.

The fact that Armozijn was only baptised late in life would suggest that she was not born a Company slave, and it is not impossible that her mother belonged to a freeburgher and was only made over to the Company at a later stage with her child, leaving the latter unbaptised. One recalls, for example, many freeburghers returning their slaves to the Company at the end of 1658, after the series of repeated desertions,[60] and the freeburgher Thomas Christoffel Muller selling Gegeima van Guinee to the Company in 1668.[61]

The unusual name Armozijn may possibly have originated as a nickname rather than a personal name, although it was subsequently conferred on her in baptism. It was in fact the name of a light silken stuff from the East, known in English as armosine, which at this time was extremely popular and was used especially for the lining of clothes, bed hangings and banners.[62] She was also known as Klein Armozijn, 'Little Armozijn', to distinguish her from an older contemporary, Groot Armozijn.

As a solution to the various problems concerning Armozijn's

origins, Van Rensburg has suggested that she was the child of the freeburgher Cornelis Claasz by the slave Isabella van Angola who belonged to Jan Reijniersz, and that she had subsequently adopted her father's patronym as a surname.[63] This hypothesis was put forward in an article entitled 'The jigsaw puzzle', which is as good a way as any of describing the irregular, disjointed and scattered fragments of information from which the lives of slaves must be pieced together.[64]

Whatever her antecedents, Armozijn probably grew up as a Company slave in the old slave house which was destroyed by fire in 1679. In 1677 an infant baptised by the name of Frans was entered in the baptismal register as 'the child of a female slave of the Hon. Company, the father an unknown Christian, the mother Armosyn',[65] and though Klein Armozijn, who would have been about sixteen at the time, may well have been the mother, this could equally refer to Groot Armozijn.

Three other children who can be attributed with greater certainty to Klein Armozijn were born in the insalubrious Slave Lodge and baptised in 1685, 1686 and 1692 respectively, but did not survive. Of her four surviving children, the baptisms in three cases are known to have taken place in 1679, 1688 and 1697.[66] The further information on these four children is also in its way revealing.

In the case of the only son, Claas Jonasz, the second part of his name seems to have been regarded definitely as a patronym and a name to be handed on in the family according to the Dutch custom, for his own son was in turn to be called Jonas Jonasz.[67] It seems reasonably certain therefore that his father was a white man with the also not uncommon first name Jonas.

Manda van de Caab, also known as Manda Gratia, who was baptised in 1679 and described as a 'fullbreed',[68] draws attention by her unusual Portuguese name which, as Upham observes, 'could either have Angolan or Asian origins'.[69] One remembers too the presence at the Cape in this time of the free black Grasias van Angola, the former Jackje, whose name was also written Gratias and Gracias, and who was legally separated from his wife Maria Evertsz in 1680.

Armozijn's daughter Marie, named by the former as Maria Stuart in her will, may owe this name to a white father, or it may equally be an unexplained reference to the English princess who in 1677 married the Prince of Orange, William III: they became King and Queen of England in 1688. The name may also well have been a nickname.

Finally, there is Machtelt (Magdalena) Ley, the only one of Armozijn's children clearly described as a halfbreed, with her German first name, and a surname which may possibly identify the German immigrant Michael Ley as her father. He arrived at the Cape as a soldier in 1696, and married a local white woman a few months after Manda was baptised the following year. He would in due course become a prominent member of the white community.[70]

All these children were born as slaves in the Lodge and remained there as such with their mother, and Mrs Cairns points out 'that she had added her own four issue to the tally of the Company's slaves and that these children, in their turn, contributed a further ten'.[71]

Armozijn herself was baptised in 1687,[72] and in the muster roll of 1693 is listed as *matres* (schoolmistress or matron) of the slave children. She appears to have held this position as long as she remained in the Lodge, and thus enjoyed the benefits as regards status, rations of food and clothing, and possibly accommodation as well which were attached to it.[73] This would seem to support her halfbreed status, as fullbreeds were rarely appointed to similar positions in the Lodge.[74]

The level of education demanded for this post is unknown, but Armozijn had at any rate benefited sufficiently from the erratic teaching available to herself to be able to sign her name.[75]

During these years in the Lodge and thereafter, over a period totalling forty years or more, Armozijn seems to have acquired and maintained, in her own right and through her family, a status which might be described as that of Lodge aristocracy. This development may be said to have begun with her brother or halfbrother, Claas

Cornelisz van de Caab, a halfbreed who in 1687 was appointed schoolmaster in the Lodge and was highly commended. He became a member of the local congregation two years later, and was subsequently manumitted.

In 1695 Claas Cornelisz and his wife Beatrice van Cochin were among the small number of free blacks living in Drakenstein, which had recently been opened for settlement,[76] but in 1701 he received what Upham describes as 'a rather sizeable erf in Table Valley',[77] where the couple made 'numerous appearances (…) as baptismal witnesses in the church registers'.[78] The relationship between Claas Cornelisz and Armozijn is revealed in a will drawn up in 1709, to which the same writer has drawn attention, in which Claas left 700 guilders to his sister Armozijn Claasse and 600 guilders 'to his nephew Frans van Leeuwen, being a son of his niece Manda van de Caab'.[79] In 1719 his widow in turn made provisions in her own will for money to be paid out to her late husband's sister Armosijn Claasse.[80]

Some time between 1699 and 1704, by which date her youngest child would have been seven, Armozijn was manumitted,[81] and by 1711 she was described officially as 'Armozijn van de Caap, former *matres* of the children of the Company's female slaves in the Lodge, given her freedom by the Lord Willem Adriaan van der Stel in recompense for her good services'.[82] She would have been in her early forties by this time, which would again seem to argue in favour of her having been a fullbreed, for this was the age laid down by Commissioner Van Reede for the freeing of fullbreed slaves.

In 1704 Armozijn at any rate requested a house plot in the settlement, which was granted four years later. It was situated immediately alongside the Company's garden to the east, in the street which led from the settlement to the gateway of the garden and the Company's stable, and diagonally opposite the Slave Lodge where she had lived for a quarter of a century (modern Parliament Street).[83] Here she spent the remainder of her life as a free woman.

Manda Gratia succeeded her mother as *matres* in the Slave Lodge, but in 1711 applied for her freedom, which was granted during the next few years, and married a white man, Guilliam Frisnet, widow-er of the free black woman Groot Armozijn.[84] Manda had previous-ly had children by various white men, and a son, Johannes Smies-ing, became schoolmaster of the Lodge in turn before also being manumitted, leaving behind a notebook which provides an inter-esting if not particularly revealing record of life in the Lodge and a unique personal record of one of its inmates.[85] Another son, Frans van Leeuwen, entered the service of the Company as a soldier, dying on board ship in 1721.

When Manda herself died in 1719, 'This ex-matron of the lodge slave children (…) had four slaves of her own in her home, two four-poster beds, one made of teak, and the usual household furni-ture. The family had kept out of debt except for a sum of 295 guilders owing to Maije ['*maai*'] Battrice, probably Beatrice of Cochin.'[86]

Armozijn's second daughter Maria Stuart had two children who both bore the surname Cleef,[87] which may possibly refer to the fam-ily of the German freeburgher Nicolaas Cleef who married in 1684 and had eight legitimate children.[88] Armozijn herself requested Maria's manumission in 1711, offering as an alternative to buy her freedom, but this was deferred for three years, and the last known of Maria is that she accompanied the wife of a skipper on a visiting ship to the Netherlands as attendant.[89]

Claas Jonasz had a number of children by Dina van Bima, a slave of W.A. van der Stel who was subsequently manumitted by the lat-ter, and Claas also acquired his freedom, in 1722 becoming sergeant of the newly formed militia for 'free blacks and free Chinese in this Table Valley'.[90] A daughter of this couple, Armozijn Jonasz, and her husband later acquired the farm Coornhoop in the Liesbeek valley, while a son, Claas Jonasz de Jonge, through his marriage to a white widow, Anna Maria Brits, by whom he had already had a child, became the owner of the farms Liesbeek and Raapenburg in the same area. Dina van Bima died as a widow in 1782, only thirteen years before the end of VOC rule at the Cape.[91]

Armozijn's youngest child, Machtelt Ley, was most likely freed

367

together with her mother. In 1720 she married the German barber-surgeon Hermanus Combrink, and their children were all absorbed in the white community.[92]

After Machtelt's marriage, Armozijn transferred her property to Combrinck and remained living with them.[93] Governor De la Fontaine's report in 1730 describes her as 'an old free black woman who lives with her son', which is more attention than is given to the remainder of the free black community.[94] 'Supports himself by shaving,' runs De la Fontaine's note on Combrinck, but he also acted as corporal and sergeant in the burgher militia and as an official of the local fire-fighting brigade.

The last of Armozijn's three wills, that of 1728, was, as Mrs Cairns remarks, 'signed very shakily',[95] and she appears to have died in 1733, when she would have been in her early seventies. Her estate consisted of a big chest with brass clasps containing her clothing, which was bequeathed to her daughter Machtelt, and a slave called Sabina van Malabar, which had been originally been left to one of her granddaughters, 'because of her handicapped condition', but had meanwhile been bought for 50 rixdollars by her grandson Johannes Smiesing, the former schoolmaster in the Lodge. She also left the considerable sum of 330 rixdollars in cash, and a bequest of 15 guilders was made to the poor.[96]

The accounts of the expenses connected with Armozijn's funeral have been preserved,[97] and these include 'a grave in the church-yard', which would have referred to the site of the present Groote Kerk, down the street from the house where Armozijn died, a coffin, 'the use of the pall and bier', and the services of the gravedigger. Money was spent lavishly on the funeral repast, as was also the custom in the Netherlands and Batavia at the time, and Combrink submitted an account for almonds, walnuts, raisins, a bottle of olives, a ham, cakes and cracknels, 10 bottles of white wine and 4 of red, half a gross (72) of pipes, which would have been of the long-stemmed clay type discarded after use, and 2 pounds of tobacco. Armozijn was clearly mourned in the very best style.

Both in her life and in her death Armozijn Claasz demonstrates what was possible for a slave and a free black at the Cape around the turn of the eighteenth century, even though there may have been few individuals who in practice achieved as much as she and the members of her immediate family did. In this regard I would like to repeat what I have written on them before.

> In summarising, one may say that while the members of the family lived modestly they make a collective impression of industry, thrift and above all decency, although decency was by no means easy to maintain in the early colonial world of the Cape, to say nothing of the demoralising Slave Lodge. On the basis of these random details, one is therefore inclined to regard the family as part of the burgeoning bourgeoisie of the Cape in their day, white as well as black, and in the modest terms of the free black and slave community as a kind of local 'gentry'.[98]

The same phenomenon is illustrated more concisely but no less vividly by the probate inventories quoted in the last two chapters, most notably those of Claas Gerritsz van Bengalen and Angela van Bengalen. In fact, however, these individuals were exceptions of a kind which was already becoming increasingly rare at the Cape, for the turn of the eighteenth century, which seemed to hold so much promise for the free blacks, in fact marked a turning point in their affairs and signalled the beginning of a rapid and dramatic reversal.

Coda: the turning point

From the available information it is not clear to what extent colour consciousness in the sense of actual or implicit discrimination was present in the small community at the Cape during the first fifty or sixty years of white settlement. The available evidence takes the form largely of deductions which may be made from a few racially mixed marriages during the early years of settlement when the situation was unfamiliar to most of those concerned, and it inevitably changed as the size of both the slave population and the free black community increased.

It is likely that more information in this regard may be found in the records of the Council of Justice, which have yet to be fully examined, but lacking this, one must for the purpose of the present book make do with a single symbolic incident. It concerns one Daniel Rodrigo, who in the muster roll of Company slaves and *bandieten* compiled in 1693 was listed with the other *bandieten* assigned to public works, but apparently was already acting as schoolmaster to the slave children in the Lodge.[1]

At noon on Boxing Day 1698 Rodrigo arrived at the Castle with the schoolchildren from the Lodge, together with the white schoolmaster Johannes Kleijn with his own class, presumably to attend the church service to be held that day. For lack of a church building, services were at this time still held in the hall of the Governor's residence, in the Kat building of the Castle.[2]

It was the year after the Dutchman Arnoldus Willemsz Basson had died, leaving his wife, the former slave Angela van Bengalen, well off as a widow, the year after the free black Claas Gerritsz van Bengalen and the wife of the free black Jacob van Bengalen had died in their respective well-furnished and comfortable homes in the Table Valley. In a few weeks' time W.A. van der Stel would arrive to succeed his father as Governor, and under him the free black woman Maria Evertsz, daughter of the former slave Evert van Guinee, would receive her grant of land at Camps Bay, and Armozijn van de Caab, *matres* in the Slave Lodge and colleague of Rodrigo, her freedom. For the small free black and coloured population both present and future seemed promising, and if ever some slender hope existed that a multiracial society might be established at the Cape, even if in theory only rather than in practice, it must have been round about this time. But the promise was built on an insecure foundation.

'On Friday 26 December 1698,' writes Wayne Dooling in passing, in an article dealing with the Castle,

> two schoolmasters, Johannes Kleyn and Daniel Rodrigo, had an argument on the Kat balcony, during which Kleyn beat Rodrigo with a cane. Johannes Swellengrebel, a Company official who had arrived on the scene, grabbed Rodrigo by the hair, threw him to the ground and told him: 'you black dog, how dare you lift your hands at a Christian.'[3]

This episode is revealing enough as described here, but the document on which it is based, a statement by a Dutch soldier on guard at the Kat balcony outside the Governor's residence at the time, reveals even more. According to him Kleijn, after an altercation, had beat Rodrigo 'about the ears' with his cane. When Rodrigo tried to react, Swellengrebel had come up, caught him by the hair, struck him in the face and thrown him to the ground with the words quoted, 'allowing him to be well beaten by Monsr. Kleijn'. This was repeated, and after Rodrigo had been flung down by Swellengrebel for the third time, the latter 'had him beaten by Monsr. Kleijn for so long until he lay still'—all this, it may be noted, in a

371

public place, before a church service, and in the presence of Rodrigo's own class and that of the white schoolchildren.

A complaint was apparently lodged with the Secunde and the above statement made, but it does not seem that any further action was taken, and one is left with this single incident on the Kat balcony in the front courtyard of the Castle at twelve o'clock on a summer morning.

Given these facts, it is not possible to do more than to make a few remarks. Swellengrebel was a young man of 27 who had previously spent some five years in the service of the VOC in the East, where his views on the relations between white and non-white would have been formed.[4] He had subsequently been appointed at the Cape with the official rank of Bookkeeper, and earlier that year had become a member of the Council of Policy: it was presumably in this capacity that he had felt called upon or entitled to intervene in the dispute. Kleijn for his part was a German who had been in the service of the Company since 1689, attaining only the junior rank of Assistant, which nonetheless made him a colleague of Swellengrebel, and this was presumably why he was carrying a cane.[5] What is further made clear by Swellengrebel's remark to Rodrigo as quoted, is that the latter was in his opinion a 'black dog' and by implication inferior to Kleijn who was a 'Christian'.

Thus four distinct factors of importance at the time and to those concerned were involved in the incident: the official status of three individuals concerned, the fact that Rodrigo was a convict or former convict, and the distinction between white and black and between Christian and non-Christian. Here, in fact, one has the same considerations that were taken into account by the Council of Policy ten years earlier when the discrepancy in diet between white servants of the Company sentenced to hard labour as *bandieten* and the Company's slaves was being discussed: 'that it would seem like barbaric cruelty to punish Christian and white people, born as free as we, and having served the same Master [*the VOC*] as ourselves, so severely (…).'[6]

What was possibly of the most immediate relevance here was Rodrigo's status as a convicted felon, and it may be illuminating to remember in this regard an incident described by Sleigh in writing of the VOC's transport centre at De Schuur at roughly the same time. In 1686, according to him, Arent Hendrickx, one of the wagon drivers stationed here, was sentenced to flogging and hard labour for his share in plundering a wrecked ship. 'Five years later, when he was postholder at De Schuer and reprimanded a young driver who had driven one of the draught oxen until the animal fell down dead, the driver addressed him as a "whipped dog" and shot him dead without further ado.'[7] Here the positions were reversed, but even though the driver was subordinate to the man regarded dishonoured by his punishment, he still considered himself entitled to look down on Hendrickx because of the latter's loss of honour. The fact that anyone who had been publicly punished on the scaffold (*geschavotteerd*) was thereby rendered permanently dishonoured or 'infamous' was a matter which was taken very seriously in the seventeenth and eighteenth century.

The objections to Rodrigo were stated more fully in the list of grievances enumerated in 1707 by the obstreperous Revd Le Boucq, who had shortly before been transferred from Batavia, by which time Rodrigo seems to have been acting as schoolmaster to white children as well. Among the suggestions made in a letter to the Council of Policy was one 'that the black schoolmaster Daniel, who was sent here from Batavia scourged, branded and as a *bandiet*, may be ordered to cease from teaching school, as it is not fitting for a publicly punished criminal to teach the children of honest people, even though the period of his banishment may have expired and he has satisfied the demands of justice, as the infamy resting upon him remains'.[8] One notices especially the reference to 'honest' people, by which, according to the usage of the time, 'honourable' was in fact meant.

That the question of honour was taken seriously is further illustrated by the case of the slave woman Flora van Bengalen. As far as her story can be pieced together from the available information, she was, in 1718, when she was about twenty years old and the property of the stable master Sybrand Steen, found guilty of desertion and theft, scourged, branded on the right cheek and returned to her owner in chains.[9] The severity of the punishment implies that there must have been aggravating factors.

Shortly after this Flora appears to have been bought by a fellow official of Steen, the provost marshal Bartholomeus Franse or Vos, a well-to-do unmarried man, by whose underlings her punishment would have been administered,[10] and on his death in 1719 he left her her freedom; but to this the Orphan Chamber formally objected, on the grounds

> that the slave Flora van Bengalen not only is not a Christian, but moreover has only recently been publicly scourged and branded on the cheek for scandalous misdeeds, and that it would therefore be completely improper and against the instituted regulations to allow such a person freedom in this colony, thereby giving considerable offence to others.[11]

The Council of Policy agreed, and ordered that the provisions of the will be set aside and Flora sold to a new owner.

In Flora's case the fact of her not being a Christian seems to have been subsidiary to her 'dishonourable' or dishonoured state as a condemned criminal, and was only mentioned incidentally. In the episode concerning Daniel Rodrigo, Swellengrebel's remark about the schoolmaster Kleijn being a Christian must in the circumstances, however, be regarded as no more than a rhetorical exclamation, 'Christian' being used as synonymous with 'white man', as was increasingly to happen at the Cape. Rodrigo had in fact been admitted as a professing member of the local congregation as early as 1691,[12] for his status as *bandiet* would not in itself have been a handicap if he was a baptised Christian, no more than his status as a slave.[13]

Fuller evidence of the way in which relations between members of different groups and races had developed by the turn of the century may be found by close reading of documents relating to the agitation against Governor W.A. van der Stel during the years 1705–07.[14]

Succeeding his father as Governor early in 1699, Van der Stel soon acquired extensive land holdings in Hottentots-Holland, where he began farming on a large scale on his estate Vergelegen, allegedly making illegal use of the Company's artisans and slaves. To simplify a complex matter: by his farming activities, to which he seems to have devoted the greater part of his time and energy, and the scale on which he competed with the freeburghers in his purchase of slaves, who had by this time already become an essential element in the local economy,[15] he soon became a threat to the chief farmers at the Cape. To this was added dissatisfaction with the way in which the wine and meat *pachten* were awarded by the authorities, together with various other grievances, many of a petty and personal nature, against the Governor and a number of senior officials who enjoyed his patronage.

Because of his haughty manner and high-handed style of government, Van der Stel was by no means popular at the Cape, where the normally autocratic VOC by this time had to deal with a sizeable and independently minded free white community. By 1705 organised opposition to his regime had emerged among a section of the freeburgher community, led by the wealthy Henning Hüsing and his nephew Adam Tas, who had sufficient self-confidence to address a formal complaint about his activities directly to the Council of India in Batavia. When the return fleet which arrived at the Cape early in 1706 on its way to the Netherlands brought no response, the disaffected party, undaunted, compiled a petition signed by 63 whites and addressed to the XVII themselves, which was to be smuggled out with the ships.[16]

Hearing of this, Van der Stel and his supporters immediately set about drawing up a testimonial in his favour, and according to his opponents he used force, threats and bribery to obtain signatures:

'He had the said testimonial read to his creatures,' they later declared, 'while serving up a pipe of tobacco, a cup of tea and a glass of strong beer, and thus sought to move them with flattering words to grace it with their signatures'.[17] It is possible that many of the signatories were not so much active supporters of the Governor as indifferent to the preoccupations of his opponents, whose economic interests were at stake, and felt no reason to antagonise him by refusing his request. His testimonial was finally signed by 240 people, including a number of prominent freeburghers and burgher councillors,[18] and also by many lesser members of the community, as well as 15 identifiable free blacks and other persons of colour.[19]

In the flurry of activity by Van der Stel and his supporters during the brief period before the departure of the fleet, a further testimonial was moreover drawn up in which a number of men, 'all free burghers and domiciled here', testified that they had never been prevented by the Governor from fishing in Table Bay or elsewhere.[20] The published texts of this document give the names of 24 individuals, if 'Mosis en Aron' are to be counted as two, but this seems to be an error of transcription, and De Wet, referring to the original, gives this particular signature as 'Moses Aron van Makassar'.[21]

Of the 23 signatories, the first 10 would seem to be white (although Willem Basson was in fact a son of the free black Angela van Bengalen and a white father) and the remainder people of colour. The document itself states that 'the 12 first named, being Europeans [and Christians], each uttered the solemn words, "So truly [help me God almighty]"', whilst the remaining 11 do so by means of their signatures,[22] which implicitly includes the two first-named 'blacks', Domingo van Bengalen and the Chinese Abraham de Vijf, who were both Christians, in the former group.[23]

The result of this conflict was a victory for Van der Stel's opponents, for the Gentlemen XVII early in 1707 recalled the Governor and a number of his supporters. In the Netherlands Van der Stel made an attempt at refuting the charges against him in a publication entitled the *Korte deductie*,[24] and at the Cape, where feelings continued to run high in certain circles, this produced a counter-blast under the title *Contra-deductie*, which, though inevitably biased, is the main source of information on the entire episode.[25]

The *Contra-deductie* was published in 1712 by two leading members of Hüsing's party, Adam Tas and Jacobus van der Heiden, but it has been suggested that it was in fact the work of J.G. de Grevenbroek, a well-educated if pedantic elderly Dutchman who had previously served as secretary to the Council of Policy and was at this time living in retirement on Van der Heiden's farm.[26] Apart from the fact that it contains a full collection of contemporary documents and sworn statements, it is a prolix account running to 300 pages, complete with classical allusions and Latin tags, and appears to contain a good deal of the author's personal prejudices. In spite of this, however, he was also in close contact with the freeburgher party and well aware of the feelings among them, and his text was moreover authorised by them insofar as it was published by their official representatives, so that it may be considered an accurate reflection of their own opinions and feelings.

Dr Böeseken remarks that it is striking how rare references to colour and race are in the struggle against Van der Stel,[27] but this must be ascribed to the fact that it primarily concerned the personal grievances of a section of the white farmers and was largely irrelevant to the free black community of the time. Slaves were likewise not a factor of importance in this context, apart from the extent, tellingly enough, that the Governor was alleged to have made use of the Company's slaves for his own work or to have retained runaway slaves on his estate.

On the other hand Heese writes, concerning the same period: 'With the increase in the number of free blacks after 1700, (…) the tendency arose to see the "black" (colour) in free blacks rather than the "free"',[28] and while it never becomes a significant issue, a marked awareness of colour runs through the freeburghers' official account of the agitation.

What aroused particular wrath on the part of the freeburghers, or at any rate that of the author of the *Contra-deductie*, was the fact that the Governor had obtained the signatures of non-whites for his testimonial. In general an attempt was made to discredit his supporters, but in this particular case questions of race and origin added fuel to the fire.

Adam Tas in Stellenbosch, hearing in 1706 that this document was being circulated, had already reported disapprovingly in his diary, 'that yesterday all the free burghers at the Cape, [even] including some blacks, had been summoned by the officer to the presence of the Governor. Having arrived in the Castle, they were treated with wine, tobacco, etc. The Governor next produced a document, which he made them sign.'[29] The following day he commented further on

the campaign to declare the Governor honest [*honourable*], e.g. that a number of blacks who had been banished and whipped, had signed, and now the Governor is sure an honest man, but a sorrier potentate I have never seen who must recover his lost honour at the hands of rogues.[30]

In a seventeenth-century context of honour and dishonour the word 'rogue' ('*schelm*') was a much stronger term than today and regarded as defamatory.

The *Contra-deductie*, in writing of the signatories of the testimonial, likewise mentions

a number of these (apart from the honest people who had been misled) being of the lowest and most contemptible kind of people resident here, who were to polish up his dirty and stinking affairs; among whom there were not only those who [Van der Stel] rejects in his Deduction as emigrant French and Walloons who cannot read or understand the Dutch language, but fellows ['*knapen*'] who are ninety-nine percent worse, and have been scourged and branded in Macassar,

Ternate, Bengal, Ceylon, Amboina, Banda, Batavia (besides Europeans who have been punished in public) because of their offences; for which Robben Island, the place assigned to them according to their sentences, would have been more suitable than for them to bear the name of freeburghers among honest Hollanders.[31]

Here it is the honour of the individuals concerned which is being attacked, and the fact that they had as condemned criminals been dishonoured and therefore disabled from acting as witnesses on behalf of the Governor, or even from bearing the name of free-burghers among 'honest' people. The specific mention of seven places in the East from which many slaves and subsequently many free blacks as well had come to the Cape, and their being contrasted so explicitly with 'Hollanders' or whites, would seem to suggest that matters of race and colour were involved here too.

In the *Contra-deductie* there is also considerable harping on the detention of one of the freeburgher leaders, Van der Heiden, which could indeed point to the document being the work of his dependent De Grevenbroek if not his own. What seems to have rankled especially is the fact that he was kept confined in the dark 'with a black slave, arsonist and murderer', this being the deserter Ary van Bengalen already referred to elsewhere, 'with whom our fellow burgher had to place himself on an equal footing'.[32] There are no fewer than six references to Ary in these terms in the *Contra-deductie*, although he is nowhere identified by name.[33]

Apart from Van der Heiden's understandable indignation at the fact of his arrest and the treatment he received, the main complaints in this regard would seem to be the fact that Ary was black and a criminal, or at any rate accused of crime and thus potentially 'dishonourable' and no fit companion for a Christian such as Van der Heiden. While there are references to the 'unchristian treatment' the latter received, and his relief at being released and lodged in one of the bastions of the Castle 'among Christians',[34] this must be interpreted in a very general way as a reference to colour. The only reference to the fact that Ary himself was, in contrast, a heathen is to be found in the statement in which Van der Heiden subsequently declared that, 'fearing to be murdered by him, he had called him colleague ["*confrater*"], and always shared his food and drink with him, yea, even became so well acquainted with him that he taught him to pray the Ten Commandments, the Creed and the Our Father'.[35]

Thus far the evidence of the *Contra-deductie*, but there are further contemporary sources which deserve attention.

The German Peter Kolb who lived at the Cape over the period 1705–13 and had close contact with Van der Stel during the early part of his stay, was a witness to the entire conflict, and for the last two years before his departure served as secretary to the Landdrost and Heemraden of Stellenbosch, where he had equally close contact with the leading members of the freeburgher group. He would therefore seem to be as reliable a witness as the author or authors of the *Contra-deductie*, and considerably more likely to be impartial, but he appears to have accepted and shared all the prejudices of the latter.

The *Contra-deductie* contains two uncomplimentary references to 'the country of His Honour's great-grandmother on his father's side',[36] which while not explicitly negative are at least ambivalent, but in Kolb this has become more explicit. Intermingled with a good deal of local Cape gossip and hearsay about the allegedly scandalous private life of the former Governor, was the completely irrelevant, and also quite inaccurate, information that his father, Simon van der Stel, 'as I was assured here', had been born on Mauritius 'of a black heathen slave woman, a concubine ["*byzit*"] of his father, called Maimonica da Costa, without knowing himself in what year he first saw the light of day'.[37] Van der Stel had in fact spent his early youth on Mauritius, where his father, a Dutchman, had been Commander, while his mother had been born in the East and his grandmother, the woman referred to, was Monica da Costa, a Portuguese name which probably indicates that she was a Mardijker.

A racial heritage which had been no handicap to Simon van der

Stel himself, growing up in the East, and which had not prevented him from subsequently marrying into a patrician Amsterdam family or his son from occupying public office in Amsterdam, had in Cape freeburgher circles by the early eighteenth century become, in suitably distorted form, a stick with which the latter might conveniently be beaten. The immigrants from Europe who were the Governor's opponents had clearly developed standards which differed from those obtaining in Batavia.

In much the same style, but even more unedifying both in its implications and its wording, is the allegation likewise made in the *Contra-deductie* that the Revd Kalden had fathered a child by one of his female slaves.[38]

As is made clear by the somewhat random and often emotional reactions to the specific situations quoted above, there seem to have been four chief factors governing the relations between whites and non-whites in the colonial world of the Cape. In the case of slaves, the most important of these was of course the question of freedom.

The distinction between free men and slaves was of the greatest importance at a time when slavery was a daily reality, and one of which freemen living in a slave society were especially aware. It is significant therefore that the Council of Policy, in considering the question of the rations of white *bandieten* or convicts, should have stated, as already quoted above, 'that it would seem like barbaric cruelty to punish Christian and white people, born as free as we, (…) so severely (…).' The fact that these people had been born free was therefore regarded as a distinguishing mark equal to their being Christians or whites.

Slaves, because of their servile and dependent status and their lack of rights, as enshrined in legislation, were beyond society, and one is reminded of the casual reference in a *plakkaat* renewed in 1715, forbidding gambling with 'a male or female slave, *bandiet* of any similar vile person'.[39] The word *veragt* used in the original could also be translated more literally as 'contemptible' or 'despised', and this was the way in which slaves were by virtue of their slave status regarded by the white world in which they lived and worked. In the very first of the 38 articles in their petition to the Gentlemen XVII, Henning Hüsing and his followers declared 'that we are here not only sorely pressed by the haughty rule of the Governor Willem Adriaan van der Stel now in office, but treated worse than slaves, and as we are freeborn people, this outrageous oppression must redouble our suffering'.[40]

The second significant distinction was that between Christians and non-Christians, who were often referred to comprehensively as 'heathens', though 'Moors', 'Mohammedans' or Muslims were often distinguished as a separate group. A slave who was the child of a white and therefore putatively Christian father had by this fact a moral claim on the Christian community, and so too the slave who by baptism had subsequently been incorporated into that community. These characteristics, by means of which they were drawn from the outer darkness of their slavery into the charmed circle of the privileged, made their slave status problematical and were seen as cogent arguments for the manumission of baptised slaves.

A further important distinction, as already mentioned, was that between 'honourable' people and those who were 'dishonoured' or 'infamous' as a result of being sentenced and punished publicly for some misdemeanour, or because of deviant behaviour.

What might seem to a later generation the most essential difference between the groups, that between Europeans or 'whites' on the one hand, and non-Europeans or 'blacks' in the widest sense on the other, was possibly of the least importance to contemporaries at the time under discussion here. Once the shock of the first encounter had been overcome and the strangeness of the experience had worn off, the white immigrants had settled down and a new, locally born generation of Cape whites who had grown up with people of a different colour was establishing itself.

As far as the situation of free blacks or manumitted slaves in Cape society around the turn of the century is concerned—although this is a personal opinion only, not backed by further research, and tentatively impression—it would seem that according to the standards of the day they were, by the fact of being baptised Christians and free, regarded as the equals of whites in the same situation, provided that their 'honour' was untarnished. The overall conclusion is therefore that colour as such was not yet a decisive factor in the relationship between the groups. Yet if this was indeed the case, the promising situation was already about to change even as it was taking shape.

The importance which questions of colour and race were beginning to assume by this time, and the extent to which they were present in the background during the freeburgers' campaign, has already been indicated. It is made even clearer, however, by what Dr Böeseken describes as the 'long torrent of words' in the form of a petition to the XVII signed by Adam Tas and 14 others. While it is undated, internal evidence makes it clear that it must have been compiled immediately after the news of Van der Stel's recall was received at the Cape on 16 April 1707, and before the departure of the return fleet for the Netherlands on the 29th,[41] while the feelings of the colonists were still extremely excited.

In this lengthy text of more than 20 pages the petitioners, among other things, express the explicit fear that the Khoikhoi would, if given the opportunity, 'fall upon all Christians, both good and bad, without distinction, and exterminate us'. Concerning the slaves, they then go on to state that

> not much better was to be expected; and far less from the Caffers, mulattos, mestizos, castizos and all that black brood living amongst us,[42] and related to European and African Christians by marriages and other connections, who have to our utter amazement increased in property, number and pride, and have been allowed to share in the handling of

arms and all manner of military exercises, [who] make it clear to us in no indistinct manner by their haughty behaviour that they would, given the opportunity, be willing and able to place their foot on our necks, for that blood of Ham is not to be trusted.[43]

The Old Testament reference at the end of this quotation is to the curse Noah put upon his son Ham, saying, 'a servant of servants shall he be unto his brethren'.[44] According to the wilful interpretation given to these words at the time, this referred to the black or negro race, and they were often cited as a Scriptural justification for slavery.

It is as well to repeat that this document was signed by only 15 people, and that it did not form part of the campaign against W.A. van der Stel, although it appears to have been an offshoot of it. Voluminous and vehement though it may have been, it therefore expressed the fears and prejudices of what at the time was a concerned minority only, but these fears and prejudices are nonetheless revealing. As Heese remarks of the main signatory: 'What is clear is that Adam Tas seemingly had no faith in the free coloured group; [and] that he saw little difference in status between a slave or a freeborn coloured (…).'[45]

It is furthermore interesting to note that these thoughts were expressed in much the same words by Abraham Bógaert, the ship's surgeon who smuggled out the freeburghers' petition in 1706 and remained their loyal supporter. In his account of his travels in the East which appeared in print in 1711, he described their struggle against the Governor at some length and with a vehemence similar to that of the *Contra-deductie*. What is even more interesting, though its significance is not fully clear, is the fact that he quotes these arguments as part of the reasons which prompted the freeburghers to send their petition to the XVII, as they feared, in the context of the War of the Spanish Succession at that time being waged in Europe, that Khoikhoi, slaves and free blacks might act as a third column in the event of a French invasion.[46] This possibility is not, however, raised in the *Contra-deductie*, which concentrates on the failings, actual or alleged, of the Governor and his supporters, and one wonders what or who inspired Bógaert's interpretation and how much authority it has.

This brief Coda began with the episode involving Daniel Rodrigo in 1698; it can be closed with the no less symbolic episode ten years later involving Pieter Brasman or Pieter van de Caab, the former slave of Christina Does, who had started his career so well with the active encouragement and support of his former mistress and her family.[47] In 1708 he was involved in an argument with a Frenchman about a missing whip in an inn on the road between Stellenbosch and the Cape, and in the course of this he grabbed his adversary by the hair, threw him to the ground and wounded him with a knife 'below the left shoulder behind in the back'. He was sentenced to scourging, a fine of 50 rixdollars, and banishment from the colony for life, which naturally meant the end of his career as a farmer.[48]

It was alleged that Brasman was under the influence of liquor at the time this incident took place. Though nothing is known for certain about what appears to be his surname, it seems in the circumstances likely to have been a nickname, and the possibility must be borne in mind that it was derived from the Dutch *brassen*, meaning 'guzzling', and was given in the sense of 'guzzler' or 'carouser' with its connotations of over-indulgence.[49] He may well have been a somewhat flamboyant character whose conduct on this occasion was felt by the whites to be aggressive or offensive.

It would further appear that all twelve people in the inn at the time were white, and that at least half of them were French, which could have added further tensions to the gathering, and to an interaction between its members not readily visible in the court records. Among these would naturally have been the inherent tension between white and non-white, and for all one knows also that tension between locally born and immigrants which was becoming notice-able within the white community round about the same time.[50]

Similar tensions over a wider field, in colonial society as a whole, must presumably serve to explain what seems a very harsh sentence, especially as it brought to an end a promising career of a free black farmer, and moreover a man who was locally born. The previous year the Frenchman Pieter Cronjé (Pierre Crosnier), who had been found guilty of having shot and killed two Khoi women after an altercation, had been sentenced 'to be sent away from the Cape for 25 years, and to remain banished from this territory. The half of his property shall be confiscated for the use of the Landdrost, &c.'[51] It is hard to believe that Pieter Brasman's sentence was not partially at least determined by the basic fact that in this case a white man had been attacked and injured by a black, regardless of whether the latter was free or not.

To return to the criteria already enumerated: by definition all free blacks were naturally both free and 'black' or coloured, although in the case of halfbreeds the physical difference was not always readily apparent. Insofar as they were manumitted slaves, they were by definition also baptised Christians, and few of them are known to have been punished felons. These last two criteria did not necessarily apply to other members of the local free coloured community, as distinct from free blacks, which might have contained individuals who were both heathen and 'dishonourable'.

It would seem that about the time under discussion here—and this observation too is meant to be tentative only—these various criteria became blurred, and the fact of 'black' origin in itself came gradually to be regarded as 'dishonourable' or at least unacceptable to the core of the white community, which consisted of people who were nominally Christians and mostly more or less 'honourable' according to the standards of their time.

This was a slow process which was to continue throughout the eighteenth century and beyond, but the first signs of this reaction, fed by personal feelings such as envy, resentment or insecurity, were already to be observed in a section of the white community, and also of the white establishment, as the first generation of free blacks and other coloured people began visibly to take their place in Cape society.

While the subsequent pattern of South African society was already discernible by 1714, observes Hattingh, 'it might at that stage still have developed in several directions—directions which would largely be determined by both external and internal circumstances. The most important aspect, however, is that closer examination shows that the community by then might still be described as open.'[52] How this promising situation developed over the remainder of the century, against a background of continuing slavery, and how long the Cape community continued to be 'open', is a subject for another book.

Endnotes

1. Beginnings – *pp.11-49*

1 The East Indies (the present Indonesia) were generally referred to as 'India', as is the case in the documents quoted in this book.

2 See Raben, 'Batavia and Colombo', p.119; Vink, 'World's oldest trade', pp.149–151, 159, and *passim*.

3 Raben, 'Batavia and Colombo', p.119.

4 For slaves in the Portuguese colonial world, see C.R. Boxer, *The Portuguese sea-borne empire, 1415–1825* (London: Hutchinson, 1969), *passim*; Ann M. Pescatello, 'The African presence in Portuguese India', *Journal of Asian History* 11 (1977); Jeanette Pinto, *Slavery in Portuguese India, 1510–1842* (Bombay: Himalaya Publishing House, 1992).

5 The standard history of the VOC is Femme S. Gaastra, *De geschiedenis van de VOC*; 5th ed. (Zutphen: Walburg Pers, 2002). For the legal position of the Company, see Jan A. Somers, *De VOC als volkenrechtelijke actor* (Deventer: Gouda Quint, 2001).

6 Vink, 'World's oldest trade', p.151.

7 Fox, 'For good and sufficient reasons', p.248.

8 The most comprehensive and satisfying single work on the subject seems to be the long article by Vink, 'World's oldest trade'. See also Arasaratnam, 'Slave trade'; Fox, 'For good and sufficient reasons', pp.246–251; Niemeijer, 'Calvinisme', pp.43–54.

9 Vink, 'World's oldest trade' p.132.

10 Arasaratnam, 'Slave trade', p.195; as quoted (in a slightly adapted form) in Vink, 'World's oldest trade', p.131.

11 Quoted in Raben, 'Batavia and Colombo', p.120.

12 Armstrong, 'Madagascar and the slave trade', p.223; van Dam, *Beschryvinge* I:II, 652.

13 Vink, 'World's oldest trade', p.140. Cf. Arasaratnam, 'Slave trade', p.202.

14 Vink, 'World's oldest trade', pp.141–143. Cf. Raben, 'Batavia and Colombo', p.120.

1. Beginnings – *pp.11-49*

15 Raben, 'Batavia and Colombo, p.122.

16 Raben, 'Batavia and Colombo', p.128.

17 Arasaratnam, 'Slave trade', p.207.

18 Raben, 'Batavia and Colombo', pp.122, 123 (table), 124 (graph).

19 Niemeijer, 'Calvinisme', p.44.

20 Raben, 'Batavia and Colombo', p.120.

21 Vink, 'World's oldest trade', pp.163–168.

22 Niemeijer, 'Calvinisme', p.45.

23 Niemeijer, 'Calvinisme', p.45. See also *ibid.*, p.47.

24 Niemeijer, 'Calvinisme', p.47.

25 Niemeijer, 'Calvinisme', p.46 (with tables).

26 Raben, 'Batavia and Colombo', pp.131–132.

27 Valentyn, *Description* II, 213 (slightly emended).

28 Vink, 'World's oldest trade', p.168.

29 See G.J. Schutte, 'Bij het schemerlicht van hun tijd: zeventiende-eeuwse gereformeerden en de slavenhandel', in *Mensen van de nieuwe tijd: een liber amicorum voor A.Th. van Deursen*; ed. M. Bruggeman (Amsterdam: Bert Bakker, 1996).

30 *Oud Batavia* I, 455.

31 *Oud Batavia* I, 461.

32 *Oud Batavia* I, 462.

33 Niemeijer, 'Calvinisme', p.47. See further *ibid.*, pp.47–48; Fox, 'For good and sufficient reasons', pp.251–255.

34 Fox, 'For good and sufficient reasons', p.253.

35 Fox, 'For good and sufficient reasons', p.252.

36 Fox, 'For good and sufficient reasons', p.256. See further *ibid.*, pp.256–258.

37 Fox, 'For good and sufficient reasons', p.256.

38 For the original text, see 'Slaeven ofte lyffeygenen'. See also Fox, 'For good and sufficient reasons'; la Bree, *Rechterlijke organisatie*, p.116.

39 See also La Bree, *Rechterlijke organisatie*, pp.95–96.

40 La Bree, *Rechterlijke organisatie*, p.248.

41 See Niemeijer, 'Calvinisme', pp.47–51; *Oud Batavia* I, pp.451–484.

42 Cf. *Oud Batavia* I, 457–458.

43 Raben, 'Batavia and Colombo', p.120.

44 Figures from Niemeijer, 'Calvinisme', p.50.

45 Raben, 'Batavia and Colombo', p.121 (table).

46 Niemeijer, 'Calvinisme', pp.48–51 *passim* (with tables).

47 Raben, 'Batavia and Colombo', p.122.

48 Raben, 'Batavia and Colombo', p.[307] (table).

49 Niemeijer, 'Calvinisme', p.26 (table).

50 Niemeijer, 'Calvinisme', p.44.

51 Niemeijer, 'Calvinisme', p43.

52 *Oud Batavia* I, 465.

53 Nicolaus de Graaff, *Oost-Indise spiegel*; ed. J.C.M. Warnsinck (The Hague: Martinus Nijhoff, 1930), p.18; bound with *Reisen van Nicolaus de Graaff, gedaan naar alle gewesten des werelds, beginnende 1639 tot 1687 incluis* (separate pagination).

54 Quoted in G.D.J. Schotel, *Het maatschappelijk leven onzer vaderen in de zeventiende eeuw*; 2nd rev. ed., ed. H.C. Rogge (Leiden: A.W. Sijthoff, ca.1900), pp.309–310.

55 See p.47 above.

56 Vink, 'World's oldest trade', p.148.

57 *Oud Batavia* I, 453.

58 *Oud Batavia* I, 454.

59 *Oud Batavia* I, 455.

60 *Oud Batavia* I, 466.

61 *Oud Batavia* I, 456.

62 Schoeman, *Armosyn: voorspel*, pp.177–178.

63 *De opkomst van het Nederlandsche gezag over Java*; ed. J.K.J. de Jonge, III (The Hague: Martinus Nijhoff, 1872) (*De opkomst van het Nederlandsche gezag in Oost-Indië*, VI), pp.5–6. See further Marion Peters, 'VOC-vrouwen op de Kust van Coromandel in India', *Jaarboek van het Centraal Bureau voor Genealogie*, 58 (2004), p.95.

64 Niemeijer, 'Calvinisme', pp.42–43 (with the incorrect division of the columns in the tables on p.42 corrected on a separate sheet). See further *ibid.*, pp.39–43.

65 See Niemeijer, 'Calvinisme', pp.52–55; *Oud Batavia*, pp.512–537.

66 Niemeijer, 'Calvinisme', p.54 (tables).

67 See Niemeijer, 'Calvinisme', pp.72–87.

68 Wagenaer, *Dagregister*, p.xxv.

69 See Fox, 'For good and sufficient reasons', p.250. Also Sybille Pfaff, *Zacharias Wagener (1614–1668)* (Haßfurt: The Author, 2001), pp.181–182.

70 The standard work on the WIC is Henk den Heijer, *De geschiedenis van de WIC*; 2nd rev. ed. (Zutphen: Walburg Pers, 2002).

71 For the slave trade in West Africa, see for example Robin Law, *The Slave Coast of West Africa, 1550–1750* (Oxford: Clarendon pr., 1991); Patrick Manning, *Slavery, colonialism and economic growth in Dahomey, 1640–1960* (Cambridge: CUP, 1982); Oliver Ransford, *The slave trade; the story of Transatlantic slavery* (London: John Murray, 1971).

72 Van Riebeeck, *Journal* I, 33.

73 Van Riebeeck, *Journal* I, 35.

74 Van Riebeeck, *Journal* I, 36.

75 Van Riebeeck, *Journal* I, 36. Cf. *Letters despatched 1652* I, 27, 29.

76 *Letters despatched 1652* I, 44.

77 *Letters received 1649* I, 84.

78 Van Riebeeck, *Journal* I, 224.

79 Van Riebeeck, *Journal* I, 224 n2. Quoted verbatim (in Dutch) in *Daghregister gehouden by den oppercoopman Jan Anthonisz van Riebeeck*, ed. D.B. Bosman & H.B. Thom; vol.1 (1651–1655) (Cape Town: A.A. Balkema, 1952), pp.447–448. See further *Letters despatched 1652* I, 271.

80 *Letters despatched 1652* I, 270.

81 *Letters despatched 1652* I, 146. Cf. *ibid.*, 142. The '*gunees linnen*' in the original Dutch refers to Guinea cloth, a coarse material used in the slave trade on the West Coast of Africa.

82 *Letters despatched 1652* I, 148.

83 *Letters despatched 1652* I, 265/267. Cf. also *ibid.*, 335.

84 *Letters despatched 1652* II, 80.

85 *Letters despatched 1652* II, 76.

86 *Letters despatched 1652* II, 82. The phrase between brackets was left untranslated by Leibbrandt who edited these texts.

87 Van Riebeeck, *Journal* I, 231.

88 The description is from Van Riebeeck, *Journal* I, 232.

89 *Letters despatched 1652* I, 302.

90 Van Riebeeck, *Journal* I, 242.

91 Van Riebeeck, *Journal* I, 245.

92 *Letters despatched 1652* I, 314.

93 Van Riebeeck, *Journal* I, 257–258.

94 Van Riebeeck, *Journal* I, 275. See *ibid.*, 275–277 for Verburgh's report.

95 Cf. Van Riebeeck, *Journal* I, 190.

96 The Journal gives '3 lasts of paddy'; Van Riebeeck, *Journal* I, 276. For the slaves, see below.

97 *Letters despatched 1652* I, 408/410.

98   *Letters despatched 1652* II, 170, 172.

99   *Letters despatched 1652* II, 176. The phrase between brackets has been translated by Leibbrandt as 'some slaves'.

100   Van Riebeeck, *Journal* I, 336.

101   The last referred to here was probably that used in the grain trade; the Amsterdam last measured 3000 litres.

102   Van Riebeeck, *Journal* II, 105. For a fuller account, see *ibid.*, 106–108.

103   *Letters despatched 1652* II, 74.

104   Unless otherwise stated, all the information about the early slaves at the Cape has been obtained from Blommaert, *Invoeren van de slavernij*. Much the same ground is covered in Böeseken, *Slaves and free blacks*, pp.7–9.

105   *Letters despatched 1652* II, 259; Van Riebeeck, *Journal* I, 146.

106   *Letters despatched 1652* II, 259.

107   *Letters despatched 1652* II, 259–260.

108   *Letters despatched 1652* I, 340.

109   Blommaert, *Invoeren van de slavernij*, pp.5–6.

110   For Van Herwerden, see DSAB III, 806. His name is given there as 'Van Harwaerden', but the form he himself used has been followed here; cf. *Resolusies* 1, *passim*.

111   Van Riebeeck, *Journal* I, 300.

112   This always refers to the elder Van Goens. Where his son is mentioned, he will be indicated as 'Rijckloff van Goens Jr.'.

113   *Letters received 1649* I, 211/213 (own translation; that by Leibbrant on pp.210/212 is incomplete). These are probably the '2 slaves and a dog' referred to by Van Riebeeck in a letter of 24 June; *Letters despatched 1652* II, 167.

114   *Letters despatched 1652* III, 427.

115   Böeseken, *Jan van Riebeeck*, p.82.

116   Cf. Van Riebeeck, *Journal* I, 363–368 *passim*.

117   Van Riebeeck, *Journal* II, 93–97 *passim*.

118   See pp.353–357 above.

119   Upham, 'Mooij Ansela' I, 13. For a further example of Domingo being used as a woman's name, see Domingo Elvingh, p.44 above. There is no justification for Dr. Böeseken's reference to 'Domingo and Angela from Bengal and their three children' being bought in 1655; Böeseken, *Slaves and free blacks*, p.9.

120   Cf. Van Riebeeck, *Journal* II, 24–27.

121   Van Riebeeck, *Journal* II, 40.

122   'Artikel-brief van de geoctroyeerde Nederlandsche Oost-Indische Compagnie', in *Nederlandsch-Indisch plakaatboek, 1602–1811; 2, 1642–1677*; ed. J.A. van der Chijs (Batavia: Landsdrukkerij, 1886), p.269 (§50).

123 *Letters received 1649* II, 236. See also *Memoriën*, p.9. In the original document the total is incorrectly given as 10.

124 *Letters despatched 1652* III, 427.

125 *Letters despatched 1652* II, 323; Van Riebeeck, *Journal* II, 131 n1.

126 *Letters despatched 1652* II, 322.

127 Van Riebeeck, *Journal* II, 133.

128 Van Riebeeck, *Journal* II, 251.

129 *Letters despatched 1652* II, 323.

130 Van Riebeeck, *Journal* II, 121 n1.

131 *Letters despatched 1652* III, 290. Blommaert gives the name of the surgeon as Velteman; Blommaert, *Invoering van de slavernij*, p.7; but Vetteman is correct.

132 *Letters despatched 1652* III, 290.

133 *Letters received 1649* II, 56.

134 Van Riebeeck, *Journal* II, 239.

135 Van Riebeeck, *Journal* II, 230.

136 *Letter received 1649* II, 58.

137 Van Riebeeck, *Journal* II, 314.

138 Incorrectly totalled as 10; *Letters received 1649* II, 236.

139 Fox, 'For good and sufficient reasons', p.260.

140 H.J. Olthuis, *De doopspraktijk der Gereformeerde kerken in Nederland, 1568–1816* (Utrecht: G.J.A. Ruys, 1908), pp.127–129.

141 *Letters received 1649* I, 322.

142 *Letters received 1649* I, 301 (retranslated). Leibbrandt's translation is inaccurate.

143 Cf. Armstrong & Worden, 'The slaves', p.116; Fox, 'For good and sufficient reasons', p.260; Visagie, *Regspleging*, p.88. Also *Oud Batavia* I, 456–457.

144 It seems to be implied in the *plakkaat* on freed slaves issued at the Cape in 1722, however; *Kaapse plakkaatboek* II, 94–95.

145 Private information from Gerrit Schutte (23.5.2006), with reference to a *plakkaat* of the Dutch States-General dated 23.5.1776; *Groot placaetboek* IX, 526.

146 Gerrit Schutte, 'Ad fontes. Over Samuel Elsevier, zijn vrouwen en zijn slaven: een voorstel tot herinterpretatie', *Historia* 45,2 (Nov. 2000), p.363.

147 *Letters received 1649* I, 254. The words between brackets ('*de gene die daertoe gerechticht zijn*') have been translated by Leibbrandt as 'their masters'.

148 Cf. also in this regard *Letters received 1649* I, 322.

149 W.M. Ottow, *Rijckloff Volckertsz van Goens; krijgsman, commissaris en regent, dienaar der V.O.C.*; 2nd rev. ed. (1996) (printout), p.14.

150 *Letters despatched 1652* II, 251.

151 This has been deduced from Van Riebeeck, *Journal* II, 28–31 *passim*; *Letters despatched 1652* II, 259; and W. Wijnaendts van Resandt, *De gezaghebbers der Oost-Indische Compagnie* (Amsterdam: Liebaert, 1944), p.243.

152 *Resolusies* 1, 68.

153 Van Riebeeck, *Journal* II, 27.

154 Van Riebeeck, *Journal* II, 35–36.

155 *Resolusies* 1, 68; *Bouwstoffen* I, 8.

156 *Resolusies* 1, 36; Van Riebeeck, *Journal* I, 235.

157 *Uit die Raad van Justisie*, pp.109 (para.19), 111 (para.28),

158 *Resolusies* 1, 69.

159 Van Riebeeck, *Journal* I, 282.

160 *Uit die Raad van Justisie*, p.108 (para.10).

161 *Uit die Raad van Justisie*, p.107 (paras.7 & 8).

162 *Uit die Raad van Justisie*, p.110 (para.22).

163 The chief gardener, Hendrick Boom, and his family had their own home outside the Fort.

164 *Letters despatched 1652* III, 290.

165 *Uit die Raad van Justisie*, p.108 (para.11).

166 For the documents relating to this case, see *Resolusies* 1, 88–89, 95; *Uit die Raad van Justisie*, pp.105–117.

167 *Resolusies* 1, 95–96; Van Riebeeck, *Journal* II, 101–102.

168 Van Riebeeck, *Journal* II, 121.

169 Van Riebeeck, *Journal* II, 167, 229.

170 *Letters despatched 1652* III, 290.

171 See p.35 above.

172 *Letters despatched 1652* II, 323–324. A *mutsje* was 150cc.

173 Van Riebeeck, *Journal* II, 148.

174 Van Riebeeck, *Journal* II, 152.

175 Van Riebeeck, *Journal* II, 243, 250, 251,

176 *Resolusies* 1, 81. The marriage is not recorded in Van Riebeeck's *Journal*.

177 See p.33 above.

178 Böeseken, 'Verhouding', p.12.

179 Hattingh, 'Kaapse notariële stukke' 1, 53.

180 *Letters despatched 1652* III, 264.

181 Van Riebeeck, *Journal* II, 308.

182 Van Riebeeck, *Journal* II, 308.

183 Van Riebeeck, *Journal* II, 303.

184 Van Riebeeck, *Journal* II, 303.

185 *Resolusies* 1, 157 n1.

186 *Resolusies* 1, 157.

187 According to the original Dutch version they hit her ('*item oock geslagen*').

188 Van Riebeeck, *Journal* III, 134.

189 For a plan, see Van Riebeeck, *Journal* I, opp. p.192.

190 Cf. Van Riebeeck, *Journal* III, 53, 68, 93.

191 Van Riebeeck, *Journal* III, 199.

192 See Van Riebeeck, *Journal* III, 257–261.

193 Van Riebeeck, *Journal* III, 309.

194 Van Riebeeck, *Journal* III, 417, 418.

195 Wagenaer, *Dagregister*, p.82.

196 Wagenaer, *Dagregister*, p.93. This may be the child later referred to as 'Jan Bruijn'; see p.151 above.

197 Wagenaer, *Dagregister*, p.82.

198 Wagenaer, *Dagregister*, pp.127, 142, 143, 144, 150, 152, 153.

199 Wagenaer, *Dagregister*, p.199.

200 Wagnaer, *Dagregister*, p.200.

201 Sleigh, *Buiteposte*, p.355.

202 Wagenaer, *Dagregister*, p.200.

203 *Journal* 1662, p.280.

204 *Journal* 1671, p.15.

205 Johann Christian Hoffmann, *Reise nach dem Kaplande, nach Mauritius und nach Java, 1671–1676*; ed. S.P. l'Honoré Naber (The Hague: Martinus Nijhoff, 1931), pp.42–43 (*Reisebeschreibungen von deutschen Beambten*, VII).

206 See the two references on p.53 of an article by Victor de Kock, ''n Liefdesverhaal van lank gelede', *Die Huisgenoot* (24.7.1936).

207 *Uit die Raad van Justisie*, pp.106–107 *passim* ('*genouchsaem volgens spreeckwoort als op een stroowis is comen aendrijven*').

208 *Uit die Raad van Justisie*, p.107 (para.6).

209 *Uit die Raad van Justisie*, p.110 (para.21).

210 See p.343 above.

2. The first slave imports – *pp.50-83*

1 *Letters despatched 1652* I, 26.

2 *Letters received 1649* I, 146.

3 *Letters despatched 1652* II, 66/106.

4 Van Riebeeck, *Journal* II, 89–93. For the freeburghers, see De Wet, *Vryliede*. Also G.C. Olivier, 'Die vestiging van die eerste vryburgers aan die Kaap die Goeie Hoop, I–VII', *Historia* XIII–XV (Sept. 1968–March 1970).

5 See pp.34–35 above.}

6 *Letters received 1649* II, 295.

7 *Letters despatched 1652* II, 94/96.

8 *Letters received 1649* I, 226.

9 *Letters despatched 1652* II, 98/100 (emended).

10 *Letters received 1649* I, 222.

11 *Letters received 1649* I, 226.

12 Cf. *Letters received 1649* I, 286, 324.

13 But see *Letters received 1649* II, 228 (para.21).

14 *Letters received 1649* I, 284/286.

15 *Letters received 1649* I, 290. Cf. *Memoriën*, p.6 (para.23).

16 Van Riebeeck, *Journal* II, 102.

17 *Letters received 1649* II, 230 (para.23).

18 *Letters despatched 1652* II, 307.

19 *Letters received 1649* II, 4/6.

20 See *Letters received 1649* II, 230/232 (para.23); Böeseken, *Slaves and free blacks*, pp.10–12.

21 *Letters received 1649* II, 12, 32/34.

22 Van Riebeeck, *Journal* II, 129.

23 Van Riebeeck, *Journal* II, 143.

24 Van Riebeeck, Journal II, 149.

25 *Resolusies* 1, 128–130; Van Riebeeck, *Journal* II, 216–218.

26 Van Riebeeck, *Journal* II, 225.

27 *Letters despatched 1652* III, 38–40; Van Riebeeck, *Journal* II, 277–278.

28 See Van Riebeeck, *Journal* II, 250–251. War had meanwhile broken out formally between the Dutch Republic and Portugal, as the XVII notified van Riebeeck on 6 December 1657, but the *Amersfoort* would probably not have known this, so that the capture of the slaves was a question of general aggression; cf. *Letters received 1649* II, 46.

2. The first slave imports – *pp.50-83*

29 *Resolusies* 1, 139.

30 Transcription in Van Rensburg, 'Jigsaw puzzle', pp.13–15

31 Van Riebeeck, *Journal* II, 251.

32 *Letters despatched 1652* III, 32.

33 See Schoeman, *Armosyn: voorspel*, pp.54–57.

34 'Paired' slaves were those living together as man and wife.

35 Van Riebeeck, *Journal* II, 258–259.

36 Except where otherwise stated, what follows is taken from Van Dam, *Beschryvinge* II:II, 532–540) ('Secret sealed instruction' and note of trading); and Van Riebeeck, *Journal* II, 265–268.

37 For details, see Schoeman, *Armosyn: voorspel*, pp.48–56.

38 Van Dam, *Beschryvinge* II:II, 497–498.

39 Van Dam, *Beschryvinge* II:II, 498.

40 *Letters dispatched 1652* III, 424–425 (statement by Gysbert van Campen, 1.3.1659). Cf. *ibid.*, 37, 61. For Popo, see Schoeman, *Armosyn: voorspel*, pp.52–53.

41 Elizabeth Claridge, in her introduction to Mary H. Kingsley, *Travels in West Africa*; 5th ed. (London: Virago, 1982).

42 Cf. Schoeman, *Armosyn: voorspel*, p.53.

43 Van Dam, *Beschryvinge* II:II, 499.

44 *Letters despatched 1652* III, 35.

45 The published translation (Van Riebeeck, *Journal*, II, 267) has been slightly emended. In the original, 'cowries' ('*bougijs*') has been translated as 'bric-a-brac'. Cf. for this point *Letters despatched 1652* III, 36, 40.

46 *Letters despatched 1652* III, 60, 61.

47 Van Dam, *Beschryvinge* II:II, 537.

48 Apparently in their private capacity.

49 *Letters received 1649* II, 244.

50 *Letters received 1649* II, 62.

51 *Letters despatched 1652* III, 31.

52 Van Riebeeck, *Journal* II, 269.

53 *Letters despatched 1652* III, 36.

54 *Letters despatched 1652* III, 38.

55 *Letters despatched 1652* III, 55.

56 Van Riebeeck, *Journal* II, 344.

57 Van Riebeeck, *Journal* II, 352, 353.

58 Van Riebeeck, *Journal* II, 279.

59 *Letters despatched 1652* III, 62.

60 *Letters despatched 1652* III, 62.

61 *Letters despatched 1652* III, 62.

62 *Letters despatched 1652* III, 426–427. See also Böeseken, *Jan van Riebeeck*, pp.190, 192–194; Franken, *Taalhistoriese bydraes*, pp.31–33.

63 *Letters despatched 1652* III, 62.

64 *Letters despatched 1652* III, 96.

65 *Letters despatched 1652* III, 82.

66 Van Riebeeck, *Journal* II, 325.

67 Van Riebeeck, *Journal* II, 285.

68 Van Riebeeck, *Journal* II, 287.

69 Van Riebeeck, *Journal* II, 343.

70 *Letters despatched 1652* III, 82.

71 Van Riebeeck, *Journal* II, 281–283 *passim*. They were still recorded as missing by March 1659; *Letters despatched 1652* III, 62.

72 See Böeseken, *Slaves and free blacks*, pp.14–19.

73 Van Riebeeck, *Journal* II, 286.

74 Van Riebeeck, *Journal* II, 355.

75 Van Riebeeck, *Journal* III, 122, where this passage is translated 'even if I knock them senseless' ('*al slae ick se doot*'). The slaves were replaced; *ibid.*, 130.

76 Margaret T. Hodgen, *Early anthropology in the sixteenth and seventeenth centuries* (Philadelphia: Univ. of Philadelphia pr., 1964), pp.421–422. See also *ibid.*, Chapter X, pp.386–430 in general. For the extreme distaste of two well-educated Dutchwomen at being attended by a female slave during their stay at the Cape in 1736, see *Op reis met de VOC;* ed. M.L. Barend-van Haeften (Zutphen: Walburg Pers, 1996), p.99.

77 Van Riebeeck, *Journal* II, 285.

78 Van Riebeeck, *Journal* II, 285

79 *Kaapse plakkaatboek* I, 36–37. For 'domestic correction', see p.19 above.

80 Van Riebeeck, *Journal* II, 293.

81 Van Riebeeck, *Journal* II, 354, 361.

82 Cf. Van Riebeeck, *Journal* II, 291.

83 Van Riebeeck, *Journal* II, 321.

84 Van Riebeeck, *Journal* II, 375.

85 Van Riebeeck, *Journal* II, 341.

86 Van Riebeeck, *Journal* II, 287, 290. Cf. Dutch text (23.6.1658).

87 Van Riebeeck, *Journal* II, 282.

88 Van Riebeeck, *Journal* II, 272.

89 Van Riebeeck, *Journal* II, 291.

90 Van Riebeeck, *Journal* II, 329.

91 *Kaapse plakkaatboek* I, 37–38 (Dutch text); Van Riebeeck, *Journal* II, 329–330.

92 Van Riebeeck, *Journal* II, 334.

93 Van Riebeeck, *Journal* II, 337.

94 *Letters despatched 1652* III, 55.

95 Van Riebeeck, *Journal* II, 334.

96 Van Riebeeck, *Journal* II, 341.

97 Van Riebeeck, *Journal* II, 334.

98 Van Riebeeck, *Journal* II, 337.

99 *Letters despatched 1652* III, 50.

100 Van Riebeeck, *Journal* II, 345.

101 Van Riebeeck, *Journal* II, 354 *passim*.

102 Van Riebeeck, *Journal* II, 348.

103 Van Riebeeck, *Journal* II, 380.

104 Van Riebeeck, *Journal* III, 6.

105 *Letters received 1649* I, 8.

106 *Letters received 1649* II, 218 (paras.1–3).

107 Van Riebeeck, *Journal* II, 147–148.

108 *Letters received 1649* II, 264/266.

109 *Letters received 1649* II, 274.

110 Van Riebeeck, *Journal* II, 24.

111 *Letters despatched 1696*, p.241.

112 *Letters despatched 1652* III, 30–31.

113 Van Riebeeck, *Journal* II, 281–282.

114 *Letters despatched 1652* III, 477.

115 *Letters despatched 1652* III, 30.

116 *Letters despatched 1652* III, 15.

117 *Memoriën*, p.29.

118 Van Riebeeck, *Journal* II, 334.

119 *Letters despatched 1652* III, 85.

120 Van Riebeeck, *Journal* II, 330 ('*'t uytdraegen van der slaven dreckbalys ende ander vuyl, morssigh wercq'* in the original).

121 Van Riebeeck, *Journal* III, 130–131.

2. The first slave imports – *pp.50-83*

122 Van Riebeeck, *Journal* III, 18.

123 *Letters despatched 1652* II, 273.

124 *Letters despatched 1652* III, 51.

125 Van Riebeeck, *Journal* II, 383.

126 See p.68 above.

127 *Resolusies* 1, 152.

128 Van Riebeeck, *Journal* II, 316.

129 Van Riebeeck, *Journal* II, 376.

130 *Kaapse plakkaatboek* I, 64.

131 Cf. Van Riebeeck, *Journal* II, 279.

132 *Memoriën*, p.30.

133 Van Riebeeck, *Journal* II, 260. Incorrectly translated as 'Robben Island'.

134 Van Riebeeck, *Journal* II, 261 ('seal meat, which had been cooked'). See also *ibid.*, 277; *Letters despatched 1652* III, 85.

135 Van Riebeeck, *Journal* II, 278. Translated as 'seal meat and eggs'.

136 Van Riebeeck, *Journal* II, 279, 280.

137 Van Riebeeck, *Journal* III, 131, 141,

138 *Kaapse plakkaatboek* I, 49. See also *Letters despatched 1652* III, 85.

139 Van Riebeeck, *Journal* III, 243.

140 *Letters received 1649* II, 6.

141 *Letters despatched 1652* III, 40.

142 *Letters received 1649* II, 92.

143 *Letters despatched 1652* III, 151.

144 Van Riebeeck, *Journal* III, 262.

145 Wagenaer, *Dagregister*, p.181.

146 *Memoriën*, p.53.

147 *Letters despatched 1652* III, 443.

148 Van Riebeeck, *Journal* II, 341.

149 *Letters despatched 1652* III, 426–427.

150 *Letters despatched 1652* III, 448. For Cornelisz, who appears to have been causing some trouble at this time, see *ibid.*, 447–451 *passim*. He was fined 50 reals for this offence; *Uit die Raad van Justisie*, p.xxiv (no.74).

151 *Letters despatched 1652* III, 446–447.

152 *Letters despatched 1652* III, 452.

153 *Letters despatched 1652* III, 443.

2. The first slave imports – *pp.50-83*

154 *Letters despatched 1652* III, 450. See further p.364 above.

155 Hattingh, 'Kaapse notariële stukke' II, 19 ('Jan Reijmersz').

156 *Letters despatched 1652* III, 478.

157 Böeseken, 'Verhouding', pp.14–15; *Uit die Raad van Justisie*, p.xxxvii (no.296).

158 Böeseken, 'Verhouding', p.15.

159 See p.325 above.

160 Hattingh, 'Kaapse notariële stukke' I, 58.

161 Cf. Böeseken, 'Verhouding', p.14.

162 *Bouwstoffen* I, 12–13.

163 *Bouwstoffen* I, 17.

164 For Caron, see W. Wijnaendts van Resandt, *Gezaghebbers der Oost-Indische Compagnie op hare buiten-comptoiren in Azië* (Amsterdam: Liebaert, 1944), p.128.

165 *Bouwstoffen* I, 20. For further baptisms in the same year, see Wagenaer, *Dagregister*, p.95.

166 *Bouwstoffen* I, 26.

167 Van Riebeeck, *Journal* III, 57 (retranslated).

168 Van Riebeeck, *Journal* III, 48.

169 'would like to eat them' in the original ('*haer wel willende eeten*').

170 Van Riebeeck, *Journal* III, 51.

171 Van Riebeeck, *Journal* III, 52.

172 Van Riebeeck, *Journal* III, 121.

173 See Albert van Dantzig, *Forts and castles of Ghana* (Accra: Sedco Publishing Ltd., 1980), pp.28–29.

174 Van Riebeeck, *Journal* II, 354.

175 Van Riebeeck, *Journal* III, 358.

176 Van Riebeeck, *Journal* III, 124. Cf. *ibid.*, 121.

177 Van Riebeeck, *Journal* III, 172.

178 Van Riebeeck, *Journal* III, 420.

179 Van Riebeeck, *Journal* III, 438.

180 Van Riebeeck, *Journal* III, 429.

181 *Memoriën*, pp.46–47.

182 Van Riebeeck, *Journal* III, 351.

3. The slave trade: Batavia – *pp.84-102*

1   Cf. *Letters despatched 1652* III, 105; *Letters received 1649* II, 76/78, 114.

2   *Letters despatched 1652* III, 59.

3   *Letters received 1649* II, 88/90.

4   *Letters received 1649* II, 90.

5   For the latter, see Van Riebeeck, *Journal* III, 420–429 *passim*.

6   Wagenaer, *Dagregister*, p.382.

7   Böeseken, *Slaves and free blacks*, p.14.

8   Böeseken, *Jan van Riebeeck*, p.193–194; Böeseken, *Slaves and free blacks*, pp.22–23; Hattingh, 'Kaapse notariële stukke' I, 56–57 *passim*.

9   Böeseken, *Jan van Riebeeck*, p.194.

10 Wagenaer, *Dagregister*, p.xxvi.

11 Hattingh, 'Kaapse notariële stukke' I, 59–61.

12 Hattingh, 'Kaapse notariële stukke' I, 60.

13 Kloeke, *Herkomst en groei*, pp.249–250.

14 Hattingh, 'Kaapse notariële stukke' I, 61.

15 *Resolusies* 1, 397. For other transactions by Borghorst, see Hattingh, 'Kaapse notariële stukke' I, 63.

16 Hattingh, 'Kaapse notariële stukke' I, 62.

17 See p.33 above.

18 Hattingh, 'Kaapse notariële stukke' I, 56.

19 Kloeke, *Herkomst en groei*, p.250.

20 See Hattingh, 'Kaapse notariële stukke' II, 18.

21 *Memoriën*, p.98. For Commander Hackius's reaction, see *ibid.*, p.107.

22 Kloeke, *Herkomst en groei*, p.250.

23 Kloeke, *Herkomst en groei*, pp.250, 254–256,

24 Cf. De Wet, *Vryliede*, pp.188–189.

25 Wagenaer, *Dagregister*, p.171.

26 Hattingh, 'Kaapse notariële stukke', *passim*.

27 Hattingh, 'Kaapse notariële stukke' I, 65.

28 Hattingh, 'Kaapse notariële stukke' I, 58.

29 Hattingh, 'Kaapse notariële stukke' I, 56, 61.

30 De Wet, *Vryliede*, p.148.

31 For this development, see Guelke & Shell, 'Early colonial landed gentry'.

32 Van Riebeeck, *Journal* II, 319.

33 See Richard Elphick, *Khoikhoi and the founding of white South Africa* (Johannesburg: Ravan pr., 1985), p.124.

34 See for this Elphick, *Khoikhoi* (see previous note), pp.117–137; Schoeman, *Kinders*, pp.283–308, 560 (sources).

35 Hattingh, 'Kaapse notariële stukke' II, 15.

36 See Böeseken, *Slaves and free blacks*, pp.61–76.

37 For the latter, see Böeseken, *Slaves and free blacks*, pp.137 (31.5.1679); 154 (8.4.1689), etc.

38 Raben, 'Batavia and Colombo', p.122. See further p.21 above.

39 See p.15 above.

40 See p.15 above.

41 Böeseken, *Slaves and free blacks*, p.72.

42 Hattingh, 'Kaapse notariële stukke' II, 18–19.

43 See Groenewald, 'Slawe, Khoekhoen en Nederlandse pidgins', pp.240–241 (tables).

44 Shell, 'Rangton van Bali', p.176 n58, and *passim*.

45 *Briewe van Johanna Maria van Riebeeck*, pp.43–44, 48, 52.

46 Hattingh, 'Kaapse notariële stukke' II, 26, 28–30 *passim*, 35.

47 Hattingh, 'Kaapse notariële stukke' II, 34–35.

48 Böeseken, *Slaves and free blacks*, pp.137–194; with corrections in Hattingh, 'Addendum'.

49 Theal, *History* I, 242–243.

50 *Letters despatched 1696*, p.139.

51 Armstrong & Worden, 'The slaves', p.123.

52 Böeseken, *Slaves and free blacks*, p.73.

53 Hattingh, 'Kaapse notariële stukke' II, 20.

54 Hattingh, 'Kaapse notariële stukke' II, 23.

55 Böeseken, *Slaves and free blacks*, p.151 (26.11.1687).

56 Böeseken, *Slaves and free blacks*, p.163 (28.5.1693); corrected in Hattingh, 'Addendum', p.20.

57 Cf. Groenewald, 'Slawe, Khoekhoen en Nederlandse pidgins', p.241 (table).

58 Böeseken, *Slaves and free blacks*, pp.95–96.

59 Böeseken, *Slaves and free blacks*, p.75.

60 Böeseken, *Slaves and free blacks*, p.75.

61 Armstrong & Worden, 'The slaves', p.140 (table).

62 See Hattingh, 'Kaapse notariële stukke' II, 21 (19.5.1674); 25 (12.3.1676); Böeseken, *Slaves and free blacks*, p.153 (5.5.1688), etc.

63 Hattingh, 'Kaapse notariële stukke' II, 25 (14.3.1676); 34 (19.7.1678); Böeseken, *Slaves and free blacks*, p.137 (30.5.1679); 140 (5.10.1683), etc.

64 Böeseken, *Slaves and free blacks*, pp.152 (16.4.1688); 153 (24.4.1688).

65 Böeseken, *Slaves and free blacks*, p.157 (25.5.1690).

66 Böeseken, *Slaves and free blacks*, p.182 (27.2.1698).

67 Worden, *Slavery*, p.48; with reference to Hattingh, 'Ontleding'. See also *ibid.*, pp.48–51.

68 Hattingh, 'Ontleding', pp.44–46 (tables, also giving prices), and *passim*.

69 Hattingh, 'Ontleding', p.53; see also *ibid.*, p.47.

70 CAD, MOOC 8/1.63.

71 Hattingh, 'Ontleding', pp.42–43 (tables, also giving prices), and *passim*. For Van der Stel, see also Böeseken, *Slaves and free blacks*, pp.138–190 *passim*.

72 Hattingh, 'Klagte', p.40 (tables).

73 Hattingh, 'Klagte', p.41.

74 Hattingh, 'Ontleding', pp.42–43 (tables).

75 Hattingh, 'Kaapse notariële stukke' I, 63.

76 Böeseken, *Slaves and free blacks*, pp.157 (corrected in Hattingh, 'Addendum', p.19), 164, 166, 167, 172, 181, 182, 183.

77 See pp.346–347 above.

78 Böeseken, *Slaves and free blacks*, p.156 (8.2.1690).

79 Böeseken, *Slaves and free blacks*, p.161 (5.8.1692).

80 *Resolusies* 3, 238–239 & 238 n20.

81 *Journal 1671*, p.129.

82 *Journal 1671*, p.199.

83 Cf. Yule & Burnell, *Hobson-Jobson*, pp.678–680 ('pariah, parriah').

84 *Journal 1671*, p.200.

85 *Journal 1671*, p.130.

86 *Journal 1671*, p.197.

87 Arasratnam, 'Slave trade', p.205.

88 *Resolusies* 2, 180, 181.

89 *Resolusies* 2, 259.

90 *Letters received 1695*, p.288. See also *ibid.*, p.314.

91 Fox, 'For good and sufficient reasons', p.260.

4. The slave trade: Madagascar – *pp.103-126*

1 Armstrong, 'Madagascar and the slave trade', p.223.

2 Armstrong, 'Madagascar and the slave trade', p.216.

3 *Letters received 1649* II, 178. See also Armstrong, 'Madagascar and the slave trade', p.224.

4 Raymond K. Kent, *Early kingdoms in Madagascar, 1500–1700* (New York: Holt, Rinehart and Winston, 1970), pp.184–185.

5 *Letters received 1649* II, 178.

6 *Resolusies* 1, 301.

7 *Resolusies* 1, 301–302; Wagenaer, *Dagregister*, p.71.

8 Wagenaer, *Dagregister*, p.75.

9 *Resolusies* 1, 309; Wagenaer, *Dagregister*, pp.110–111.

10 *Resolusies* 1, 317–318; Wagenaer, *Dagregister*, pp.70, 172 n206

11 Wagenaer, *Dagregister*, p.111.

12 Wagenaer, *Dagregister*, p.325.

13 *Resolusies* 1, 317.

14 *Resolusies* 1, 323; Wagenaer, *Dagregister*, pp.172–173.

15 Wagenaer, *Dagregister*, pp.170–171. See also Armstrong, 'Madagascar and the slave trade', p.218.

16 *Memoriën*, p.87; Wagenaer, *Dagregister*, p.268.

17 *Journal 1662*, p.196.

18 Armstrong & Worden, 'The slaves', p.112.

19 Armstrong, 'Madagascar and the slave trade', p.219.

20 Wagenaer, *Dagregister*, p.348.

21 Valentyn, *Description* II, 181.

22 *Memoriën*, p.93.

23 *Journal 1671*, pp.56–57. See also *Resolusies* 2, 91.

24 *Journal 1671*, p.17; *Resolusies* 2, p.66.

25 Armstrong, 'Madagascar and the slave trade', p.225.

26 For Hugo, see Schoeman, *Kinders*, pp.268–276, 559 (sources).

27 *Journal 1671*, p.98.

28 Cf. Armstrong, 'Madagascar and the slave trade', p.226; *Journal 1671*, p.118.

29 *Journal 1671*, p.116.

30 *Journal 1671*, p.135.

31 *Journal 1671*, pp.117–118.

4. The slave trade: Madagascar – *pp.103-126*

32   Armstrong, 'Madagascar and the slave trade', p.226. Cf. *Journal 1671*, p.116.

33   *Journal 1671*, p.118.

34   *Journal 1671*, pp.119, 120.

35   *Journal 1671*, p.135.

36   *Journal 1671*, p.129.

37   Armstrong, 'Madagascar and the slave trade', p.226; *Memoriën*, p.123 n4.

38   Armstrong, 'Madagascar and the slave trade', p.116.

39   *Memoriën*, p.123.

40   *Memoriën*, p.135. For Sijmon, see below. For a survey of the trade with Madagascar, see Armstrong, 'Madagascar and the slave trade'; Armstrong & Worden, 'The slaves', pp.112–115; Böeseken, Slaves and free blacks, pp.64–69, 72.

41   Armstrong, 'Madagascar and the slave trade', p.226. For the *Voorhout*, see *Journal 1671*, pp.228, 252,

42   Barendse, 'Slaving', p.144.

43   Armstrong, 'Madagascar and the slave trade', pp.225–226. For what follows, see *ibid.*; also Armstrong & Worden, 'The slaves', pp.112–116; Barendse, 'Slaving'; Vink, 'World's oldest trade', pp.144–146.

44   Armstrong, 'Madagascar and the slave trade', p.216. For Magelagie, see also Barendse, 'Slaving', pp.149–150.

45   'about 9 (Dutch) miles from each other'; *Journal 1671*, p.301.

46   François Valentyn, *Oud en nieuw Oost-Indiën* (Amsterdam: Gerard onder de Linden, 1724–26), 5(2), 148.

47   Van Dam, *Beschryvinge* I:II, 659.

48   *Resolusies* 3, 386.

49   Barendse, 'Slaving', p.140.

50   See Raymond K. Kent, *Early kingdoms in Madagascar, 1500–1700* (New York: Holt, Rinehart and Winston, 1970), pp.159–204.

51   Barendse, 'Slaving', p.148.

52   Armstrong & Worden, 'The slaves', p.114.

53   *Journal 1671*, p.301.

54   *Briewe van Johanna Maria van Riebeeck*, p.49.

55   *Journal 1671*, p.301.

56   *Journal 1671*, p.302.

57   *Journal 1671*, p.303.

58   Sleigh, *Buiteposte*, p.155.

59   *Resolusies* 2, 181–182, 218.

60   Armstrong, 'Madagascar and the slave trade', pp.227 & 227 n85.

61 *The Record*, p.363. See further Armstrong, 'Madagascar and the slave trade', p.231 (table) (122 slaves traded); *Resolusies* 2, 218.

62 *The Record*, p.363.

63 *Resolusies* 2, 274.

64 *Resolusies* 2, 218–219, 274, 300.

65 *Resolusies* 2, 218–219. See also *ibid.*, p.274.

66 *Resolusies* 2, 300.

67 *The Record*, p.363.

68 Armstrong, 'Madagascar and the slave trade', p.228. See also Armstrong & Worden, 'The slaves', pp.115–116.

69 Hattingh, 'Kaapse notariële stukke' II, 27–29 *passim*. The two transactions on p.28 are duplicated on p.29. For Seurensz, see *Memoriën*, p.135.

70 Hattingh, 'Kaapse notariële stukke' II, 32–33 *passim*.

71 Elphick & Shell, 'Intergroup relations', p.213.

72 Groenewald, 'Slawe, Khoekhoen en Nederlandse pidgins', p.240.

73 For Sijmon, see Schoeman, *Kinders*, pp.347–363, 561 (sources). The chief source of information is Armstrong, 'Madagascar and the slave trade', pp.232–233.

74 *Journal 1671*, p.118; *Memoriën*, p.135.

75 See Boshoff & Nienaber, *Afrikaanse etimologieë*, p.408.

76 Hattingh, 'Grondtoekennings', pp.41, 42 (table)

77 Cf. *Memoriën*, p.135.

78 *Memoriën*, p.135.

79 *Memoriën*, p.135.

80 Van Dam, *Beschryvinge* I:II, 654.

81 Armstrong, 'Madagascar and the slave trade', p.226.

82 Armstrong, 'Madagascar and the slave trade', pp.228–229; Van Dam, *Beschryvinge* I:II, 654–655 (date incorrectly given as 1687).

83 Armstrong, 'Madagascar and the slave trade', p.233.

84 Armstrong, 'Madagascar and the slave trade', p.233; Van Dam, *Beschryvinge* I:II, 655 ('een Madagascarees').

85 Armstrong, 'Madagascar and the slave trade', p.229.

86 Armstrong, 'Madagascar and the slave trade', p.233.

87 Armstrong, 'Madagascar and the slave trade', p.233.

88 Listed in Armstrong, 'Madagascar and the slave trade', pp.230–231 (table). For the voyages between 1678 and 1686, see Van Dam, *Beschryvinge* I:II, 653–665.

89 Armstrong, 'Madagascar and the slave trade', p.227 (table). For the journal of the *Leidsman* (1715), see *Slave trade with Madagascar*.

90 Van Dam, *Beschryvinge* I:II, 659.

91 Van Dam, *Beschryvinge* I:II, 660.

92 Van Dam, *Beschryvinge* I:II, 662–663. See also *ibid.*, 664–665.

93 *Letters despatched 1696*, p.45.

94 *Letters received 1695*, p.236.

95 *Memoriën*, p.154; *Resolusies* 3, 11.

96 For Van Breugel, see DSAB IV, 676; *Resolusies* 3, 11 n37. He is also mentioned in *Memoriën*, pp.154, 222; Van Dam, *Beschryvinge* I:II, 668.

97 *Resolusies* 3, 306.

98 Böeseken, *Slaves and free blacks*, pp.175, 189, 190–192 *passim*; quotation from p.191. 'Adriaan' given as first name on p.192.

99 *Letters despatched 1696*, p.111.

100 *The Record*, p.371 (date of purchase incorrectly given as 1673). Cf. Van Dam, *Beschryvinge* I:II, 655.

101 Armstrong, 'Madagascar and the slave trade', p.232.

102 Hattingh, 'Kaapse notariële stukke' II, 27–28 *passim*.

103 For the following, see Van Dam, *Beschryvinge* I:II, 668–670.

104 Van Dam, *Beschryvinge* I:II, 665.

105 Van Dam, *Beschryvinge* I:II, 658.

106 Van Dam, *Beschryvinge* I:II, 660–661, 667–668.

107 Van Dam, *Beschryvinge* I:II, 666.

108 Armstrong, 'Madagascar and the slave trade', p.229.

109 Van Dam, *Beschryvinge* I:II, 660.

110 *The Record*, p.363.

111 Franken, *Taalhistoriese bydraes*, pp.46, 76; cf. *ibid.*, p.49.

112 Van Reede, *Journaal*, p.238.

113 Van Dam, *Beschryvinge* I:II, 654.

114 Armstrong & Worden, 'The slaves', p.118.

115 Armstrong, 'Madagascar and the slave trade', p.218.

116 Armstrong & Worden, 'The slaves', p.118.

117 Armstrong & Worden, 'The slaves', p.118.

118 Böeseken, *Slaves and free blacks*, p.141. For details of his transactions, see *ibid.*, pp.140–141 (corrected in Hattingh, 'Addendum', p.19).

119 Böeseken, *Slaves and free blacks*, pp.144–146 (corrected in Hattingh, 'Addendum', pp.11, 12, 20–21); 155–156 (Hattingh, 'Addendum', p.17).

120 Böeseken, *Slaves and free blacks*, p.164.

4. The slave trade: Madagascar – *pp.103-126*

121 Böeseken, *Slaves and free blacks*, p.143.

122 Böeseken, *Slaves and free blacks*, p.147.

123 See Böeseken, *Slaves and free blacks*, pp.146–147.

124 Armstrong, 'Madagascar and the slave trade', p.227 (table). Also in Armstrong & Worden, 'The slaves', p.112 (total incorrectly given as 1069).

125 Böeseken, *Slaves and free blacks*, pp.148–150 *passim*. See also transactions by crew members of other ships, *ibid., passim.*

126 Hattingh, 'Klagte', p.30 (table).

127 Groenewald, 'Slawe, Khoekhoen en Nederlandse pidgins', p.240.

128 *Letters despatched 1696*, p.283; *Letters received 1695*, pp.375–378 (with text of charter).

5. The world of the slaves: the Slave Lodge – *pp.127-194*

1 Van Riebeeck, *Journal* II, 130. For Van Goens's recommendation, see *Letters received 1649* II, 222 (para.10).

2 Van Riebeeck, *Journal* I, 27 (letter 't' on the plan). Geyser appears to confuse the accommodation for the slaves planned by Van Riebeeck with the projected redoubt Coornhoop in the Liesbeek Valley; see Geyser, *Old Supreme Court building*, p.21, and the relevant entries in Van Riebeeck's Journal.

3 *Letters received 1649* II, 258.

4 Van Riebeeck, *Journal* II, 350.

5 *Uit die Raad van Justisie*, p.130.

6 Van Riebeeck, *Journal* II, 329.

7 Van Riebeeck, *Journal* II, 334.

8 *Letters despatched 1652* III, 77.

9 Van Riebeeck, *Journal* II, 281–282.

10 Van Riebeeck, *Journal* II, 334.

11 *Resolusies* 1, 285–286.

12 Wagenaer, *Dagregister*, p.320.

13 See pp.25–26 above.

14 Niemeijer, 'Calvinisme', p.46.

15 Wagenaer, *Dagregister*, p.350.

16 Wagenaer, *Dagregister*, p.350.

17 Sleigh, *Buiteposte*, p.119.

18 *Journal 1662*, p.309.

5. The world of the slaves: the Slave Lodge – *pp.127-194*

19 *Journal 1662*, p.311.

20 See p.145n above.

21 *Resolusies* 2, 278.

22 *Resolusies* 2, 285.

23 See Anna C. Ras, *Die Kasteel en ander vroeë Kaapse vestingswerke, 1652–1713* (Cape Town: Tafelberg, 1959), p.80 (no.18 on plan).

24 Quoted in Böeseken, *Simon van der Stel*, p.112.

25 WNT VIII(II), column 2606.

26 'Ou Hoërhof feestelik hernoem', *Die Burger* (25.9.1998), p.4.

27 Van Reede, *Journaal*, p.29.

28 Valentyn, *Description* II, 101.

29 Geyser, *Old Supreme Court building*, pp.26, 84, 89.

30 Kolb, *Beschryving* II, 247b.

31 For the history of the building, see Geyser, *Old Supreme Court building*.

32 See Kolb, *Beschryving*, *passim*; cf. the notes to the quotations in what follows for more exact references to the various passages. This is a contemporary Dutch translation of his original German work, and passages quoted in the present book are therefore retranslations.

33 *Resolusies* 2, 278. For further descriptions of the building, see Kolb, *Beschryving* II, 247b–248a; van Reede, *Journaal*, p.29.

34 Kolb, *Beschryving* I, 397a.

35 *Resolusies* 5, 162.

36 Mentzel, *Description* 1, 116–117.

37 Kolb, *Beschryving* II, 248a.

38 It is reproduced in Valentyn, *Beschryvinge* I, opp. p.130.

39 See also Kolb's detailed description in Kolb, *Beschryving* I, 395.

40 Kolb, *Beschryving* I, 395a; *ibid.* II, 247a.

41 Kolb, *Beschryving* I, 395b.

42 Kolb, *Beschryving* II, 247b.

43 Van Reede, *Journaal*, p.185.

44 Kolb, *Beschryving* I, 395b.

45 Heese, 'Slawegesinne', p.45.

46 Barnard, *Diaries* I, 159–160.

47 CAD, BR 29, pp.8–9 (translated from the French).

48 CAD, BR 29, p.11. See also Geyser, *Old Supreme Court building*, pp.34–35, 76–79.

49 Mentzel, *Description* 1, 116.

5. The world of the slaves: the Slave Lodge – *pp.127-194*

50   Kolb, *Beschryving* I, 396a.

51   Shell, *Children of bondage*, p.173.

52   *Journal 1671*, p.135.

53   Armstrong & Worden, 'The slaves', p.126.

54   Heese, 'Slawegesinne', p.42.

55   Theal, *History* I, 426.

56   Armstrong & Worden, 'The slaves', p.126.

57   Kolb, *Beschryving* II, 268b.

58   Van Hoorn's diary, quoted in Böeseken, *Nederlandsche commissurissen*, p.64.

59   CAD, C2419 pp.14–15. For this report, see further *Resolusies* 4, 157–158. I am grateful to Dr C.G. de Wet for transcribing the indistinct copy of the original manuscript for me in 1999.

60   *Resolusies* 4, 133–134.

61   *Resolusies* 5, 47.

62   *Resolusies* 5, 161, 161–162.

63   *Resolusies* 5, 162.

64   *Resolusies* 5, 47.

65   *Resolusies* 5, 160.

66   *Resolusies* 8, 221.

67   Cook, 'Memorandum', pp.[1]–[2].

68   Cook, 'Memorandum', p.[2].

69   Kolb, *Beschryving* I, 397a.

70   Sleigh, *Buiteposte*, p.424.

71   See C.F.J. Muller, *Die geskiedenis van die vissery aan die Kaap tot aan die middel van die agtiende eeu* (Archives Year Book 1942, II), pp.23–24, 29, 38 (Van der Stel), 52–54 *passim*. For Van der Stel, see also Böeseken, *Simon van der Stel*, p.215.

72   *Journal 1662*, p.293.

73   *Resolusies* 2, 35.

74   *Journal 1671*, p.49.

75   *Resolusies* 2, 77.

76   *Journal 1671*, p.76. See also *ibid.*, p.171.

77   Wagenaer, *Dagregister*, p.253.

78   *Journal 1671*, p.167.

79   *The Record*, p.355.

80   *Resolusies* 3, 167.

81   *Letters despatched* 1696, p.350 (1708); cf. *ibid.*, p.351.

5. The world of the slaves: the Slave Lodge – *pp.127-194*

82 Valentyn, *Description* II, 241 (figure given as 121, corrected from the Dutch text). See also *Journal 1699*, p.139; and H.B. Thom, *Die geskiedenis van die skaapboerdery in Suid-Afrika* (Amsterdam: Swets & Zeitlinger, 1936), p.34 (table).

83 *Journal 1699*, p.188.

84 *Journal 1699*, 88. Cf. *Resolusies* 3, 430; *Letters despatched 1696*, p.329.

85 Mentzel, *Description* 3, 99.

86 Mentzel, *Life at the Cape*, p.46.

87 e.g. *Journal 1699*, pp.17, 66; *Letters despatched 1696*, p.350.

88 *Defence*, p.38 (paras.801 & 802).

89 *Contra-deductie*, p.146. See also *ibid.*, p.251.

90 Sleigh, *Buiteposte*, p.432.

91 Sleigh, *Buiteposte*, p.433.

92 *Memoriën*, p.148.

93 *Resolusies* 3, 26.

94 *Memoriën*, p.148.

95 *Resolusies* 3, 4.

96 Van Reede, *Journaal*, p.239.

97 Quoted in Böeseken, *Nederlandsche commissarissen*, p.67.

98 *Resolusies* 3, 188.

99 *Letters despatched 1696*, p.102.

100 *Journal 1699*, p.116. Cf. *Letters despatched 1696*, p.321.

101 Valentyn, *Description* II, 243.

102 CAD, C2419 p.14.

103 *Resolusies* 2, 324.

104 *Letters despatched 1696*, 304.

105 *Resolusies* 4, 158.

106 *Resolusies* 2, 220.

107 Kolb, *Beschryving* I, 396a–b.

108 Sleigh, *Buiteposte*, p.120.

109 Kolb, *Beschryving* I, 396b.

110 *Kaapse plakkaatboek* I, 107–108.

111 Mentzel, *Description* 3, 30.

112 *Journal 1671*, p.176.

113 Cf. *Resolusies* 2, 259.

114 *Resolusies* 3, 135.

115 Cf. *Resolusies* 5, 66.

116 Jacobus Cruse, in *Reports of Chavonnes*, p.35.

117 Valentyn, *Description* II, 243.

118 *Journal 1671*, p.167.

119 *Resolusies* 3, 292–293.

120 *Uit die Raad van Justisie*, p.217 (para.12)

121 CAD, C2419 p.15.

122 CAD, C338 p.25 (winter, undated); C339 p.83 (winter, 1721); *ibid.* p.95 (summer, 1720).

123 *Journal 1662*, p.319.

124 *Resolusies* 2, 77.

125 *Resolusies* 2, 324.

126 See below.

127 Van Reede, *Jounaal*, pp.183–184.

128 *Resolusies* 2, 237; *ibid.* 5, 66.

129 Reproduced, for example, in Karel Schoeman, *Dogter van Sion* (Cape Town: Human & Rousseau, 1997) (illus. nos.11 & 12).

130 Mentzel, *Description* 2, 124.

131 Mentzel, *Description* 1, 169.

132 Reproduced on the front cover of this book. See, however, the remarks by De Haan in *Oud Batavia* I, 467–468.

133 Van Riebeeck, *Journal* III, 308.

134 *The Khoikhoi at the Cape of Good Hope: seventeenth-century drawings in the South African Library*; text Andrew B. Smith (Cape Town: S.A. Library, 1993), p.43.

135 Mentzel, *Description* 1, 169.

136 This was originally a kind of cloak, but may be intended here to indicate a long, loose jacket or coat as opposed to a short working jacket.

137 Van Reede, *Journaal*, pp.194–195. See also *Memoriën*, p.207.

138 Mentzel, *Description* 1, 169.

139 *Journal 1671*, p.49.

140 *Resolusies* 4, 157.

141 *Memoriën*, p.218.

142 Kolb, *Beschryving* II, 389B.

143 *Resolusies* 2, 202.

144 *Journal 1699*, p.46.

145 Kolb, *Beschryving* II, 233. See also *Resolusies* 6, 82.

146 *Resolusies* 4, 157.

147 *Resolusies* 4, 157.

148 *Resolusies* 4, 214.

149 *Resolusies* 6, 83.

150 *Resolusies* 6, 81–82.

151 See the letter from the Council of India to Zacharias Wagenaer (22.3.1666), *Bouwstoffen* I, 29–31; *Resolusies* 1, 340–341. For baptismal practice at the Cape in general, see Hattingh, 'Beleid en praktyk'.

152 Quoted in *Resolusies* 1, 340.

153 Böeseken, *Slaves and free blacks*, p.25.

154 *Resolusies* 1, 340; Böeseken, *Slaves and free blacks*, p.27.

155 Wagenaer, *Dagregister*, p.214.

156 For Baldaeus, see Schoeman, *Kinders*, pp.188–203, 555–556 (sources).

157 *Resolusies* 1, 340–341.

158 Bouwstoffen II, 256–257. For a survey of the situation, see also Hattingh, 'Beleid en praktyk'; A. Moorrees, *Die Nederduitse Gereformeerde Kerk in Suid-Afrika, 1652–1873* (Cape Town: S.A. Bible Society, 1939), pp.33–36; J.D. Vorster, *Die kerkregtelike ontwikkeling van die Kaapse Kerk onder die Kompanjie, 1652–1792* (Potchefstroom: Pro Rege, 1956), pp.124–125.

159 *Bouwstoffen* II, 270.

160 *Bouwstoffen* II, 269–270 *passim*.

161 Van Reede, *Journaal*, pp.209–210. See also *Memoriën*, p.208.

162 Van Reede, *Journaal*, p.211. See also *Memoriën*, pp.207, 217.

163 Van Reede, *Journaal*, p.206.

164 *Bouwstoffen* I, 62–73; *Resolusies* 4, 12–13,

165 Kolb, *Beschryving* II, 322b–323a.

166 *Bouwstoffen* II, 257.

167 *Memoriën*, p.101.

168 *Resolusies* 2, 160.

169 *Memoriën*, p.101.

170 Van Reede, *Journaal*, p.207.

171 *Memoriën*, p.205.

172 *Memoriën*, pp.204–205.

173 Yule & Burnell, *Hobson-Jobson*, pp.604–605 ('Mustees, Mestiz, &c.').

174 For examples of the use of the term at the Cape, see Böeseken, 'Verhouding', p.17; and p.383 above.

175 Shell, *Children of bondage*, p.71.

5. The world of the slaves: the Slave Lodge – *pp.127-194*

176 Petrus Kalden, *Afgeperste verweering en nodige verantwoording tegen twee nu onlangs uytgekomene laster-schriften* (Utrecht: gedrukt voor den Autheur by Willem Broedelet, 1713), p.48 ('*gy kunt wel denken, hoedanig het op het Schip zal toegaan*'). See further *ibid.*, pp.48–50. For the original accusation, see *Contra-deductie*, p.174.

177 De Wet, *Vryliede*, pp.149–150 (table).

178 *Memoriën*, p.127.

179 Wagenaer, *Dagregister*, p.197.

180 *Memoriën*, p.104; *Resolusies* 2, 61–62.

181 See Femme S. Gaastra, *De geschiedenis van de VOC*, 5th ed. (Zutphen: Walburg pers, 2002) pp.82, 115 (tables).

182 Shell, *Children of bondage*, pp.173, 174 (charts).

183 For Crudop, see DSAB III, 188; Schoeman, *Kinders*, pp.241, 254–256 *passim*.

184 *Resolusies* 2, 270.

185 *Kaapse plakkaatboek* I, 151–152.

186 Böeseken, *Simon van der Stel*, pp.43–44.

187 *Resolusies* 3, 28.

188 *Kaapse plakkaatboek* I, 179–180.

189 Van Reede, *Journaal*, p.185.

190 Van Reede, *Journaal*, p.212.

191 Van Reede, *Journaal*, p.213. Cf. *Memoriën*, p.206 n75.

192 Petrus Kalden, *Afgeperste verweering*, p.49 (see n156 above).

193 *Kaapse plakkaatboek* II, 41 (para.9).

194 *Resolusies* 5, 114.

195 *Resolusies* 5, 115 (art.3).

196 Mentzel, *Description* 2, 125.

197 See Armstrong & Worden, 'The slaves', pp.125–126 (Company slaves), 133–134.

198 Heese, 'Slawegesinne', pp.40–41.

199 See the reference in n122 above.

200 For births among Company slaves, see Armstrong & Worden, 'The slaves', pp.125–126.

201 Kolb, *Beschryving* II, 268a.

202 Wagenaer, *Dagregister*, pp.109, 339.

203 Wagenaer, *Dagregister*, pp.353–354 (name not given).

204 *Bouwstoffen* II, 257.

205 *Memoriën*, pp.100–101.

5. The world of the slaves: the Slave Lodge – *pp.127-194*

206 *Resolusies* 2, 77–78.

207 *Memoriën*, p.126.

208 *Resolusies* 2, 160.

209 *Memoriën*, p.205.

210 Van Reede, *Journaal*, p.207. See also *Memoriën*, p.207.

211 *Memoriën*, p.189 (original Dutch text); De Kock, *Those in bondage*, p.103 (English translation). The admonition to the children is described as illegible in the Dutch, and is taken from the earlier English version.

212 Van Reede, *Journaal*, p.234.

213 *Memoriën*, p.205.

214 Van Reede, *Journaal*, p.208. See also *Memoriën*, pp.205–206.

215 Quoted in Böeseken, *Nederlandsche Commissarissen*, p.73.

216 *Resolusies* 4, 150 (para.8).

217 *Resolusies* 3, 179.

218 *Resolusies* 3, 171.

219 Franken, *Taalhistoriese opstelle*, p.48.

220 See p.178.

221 The punctuation in this part of the text is not clear in the source quoted.

222 *Letters despatched 1696*, p.29.

223 Kolb, *Beschryving* I, 71.

224 *Letters received 1649* II, 250 (para.46).

225 Cf. Groenewald, 'Konvergensieteorie', p.215.

226 See Franken, 'Vertolking', p.43.

227 See Franken, 'Vertolking', pp.46–47 & *passim*.

228 *Memoriën*, p.46.

229 Van Reede, *Journaal*, p.184.

230 Cf. Franken, *Taalhistoriese bydraes*, p.26 n6.

231 CAD, C2419 p.14.

232 *Journal 1671*, pp.204–205.

233 *Memoriën*, p.153.

234 A.M. Hugo, *Die kerk van Stellenbosch* (Cape Town: Tafelberg, 1963), p.7.

235 *Resolusies* 6, 261.

236 *Resolusies* 2, 376.

237 Kolb, *Beschryving* II, 262.

238 *Journal 1699*, p.74.

239 Kolb, *Beschryving* II, 262.

240 *Letters received 1649* II, 220/222 (para.8).

241 Valentyn, *Description* II, 221.

242 Sleigh, *Buiteposte*, pp.122–123, with comment.

243 *Journal 1699*, p.255; Theal, *History* I, 426.

244 Van Dam, *Beschryvinge* III, 223–224.

245 *Reports of Chavonnes*, p.107.

246 *Resolusies* 4, 214.

247 Kolb, *Beschryving* II, 228b.

248 *Reports of Chavonnes*, p.107.

249 *Resolusies* 5, 160.

250 See p.325 above.

251 *Resolusies* 3, 136.

252 Valentyn, *Description* II, 251.

253 *Defence*, p.11 (paras.215–216). 'Company's dominion' ('*Compagnies regiment*') is possibly meant here in the sense of running an official residence of the Company.

254 CAD, C2419 p.15.

255 CAD, C2419 p.15.

256 For the outposts, see Sleigh, *Buiteposte*.

257 Sleigh, *Buiteposte*, p.177.

258 Sleigh, *Buiteposte*, p.177.

259 Sleigh, *Buiteposte*, pp.117, 230.

260 Sleigh, *Buiteposte*, p.178.

261 Sleigh, *Buiteposte*, p.237.

262 Sleigh, *Buiteposte*, p.250.

263 Sleigh, *Buiteposte*, p.180.

264 Sleigh, *Buiteposte*, pp.178, 181.

265 Sleigh, *Buiteposte*, p.181.

266 Mentzel, *Description* 2, 91. See also *ibid*. 3, 40–41.

267 Sleigh, *Buiteposte*, p.257.

268 Sleigh, *Buiteposte*, p.231.

269 Sleigh, *Buiteposte*, p.259.

270 Sleigh, *Buiteposte*, p.267.

271 Sleigh, *Buiteposte*, p.269.

5. The world of the slaves: the Slave Lodge – *pp.127-194*

272 Sleigh, *Buiteposte*, pp.154–155.

273 Sleigh, *Buiteposte*, p.157.

274 Sleigh, *Buiteposte*, p.162.

275 Van Reede, *Journaal*, p.118, 119.

276 Sleigh, *Buiteposte*, p.199, 200.

277 Van Reede, *Journaal*, pp.133–134.

278 Sleigh, *Buiteposte*, p.201. The date 1697 in the text seems to be an error; cf. *ibid.*, 120, 201 n244.

279 Van Reede, *Journaal*, p.116.

280 Sleigh, *Buiteposte*, pp.165–166.

281 Van Dam, *Beschryvinge* II:III, 546–547.

282 Sleigh, *Buiteposte*, p.425.

283 Sleigh, *Buiteposte*, p.450.

284 Sleigh, *Buiteposte*, p.122, with comment. See also p.194 above.

285 Cf. *Kaapse plakkaatboek* I, 224.

286 Sleigh, *Buiteposte*, pp.117, 201.

287 Sleigh, *Buiteposte*, p.201.

288 Sleigh, *Buiteposte*, p.162.

289 Sleigh, *Buiteposte*, p.200.

290 Valentyn, *Beschryvinge* II, 215 ('*die ambagstlieden*').

291 *Resolusies* 6, 261.

292 *Memoriën*, p.207. See also Van Reede, *Journaal*, p.204.

293 *Contra-deductie*, pp.147, 154.

294 *Resolusies* 4, 170.

295 Valentyn, *Description* II, 213.

296 *Letters received 1695*, p.105. Cf. *ibid.*, p.102.

297 *Letters despatched 1696*, 31; *Letters received 1695*, p.128. The argument is not clear, and there is possibly some error in the English translation.

298 *Briewe J.M. van Riebeeck*, pp.107–108, 113.

299 *Resolusies* 3, 205.

300 *Journal 1699*, 121.

301 *Resolusies* 4, 207. See also *Journal 1699*, p.246 (3 & 7 April, with incorrect translations).

302 *Resolusies* 4, 207. See also *Journal 1699*, p.246 (3 & 7 April, with incorrect translations). For Maria Stuart, see further pp.365, 367 above.

303 *Resolusies* 5, 164.

5. The world of the slaves: the Slave Lodge – *pp.127-194*

304 *Resolusies* 6, 45.

305 *Memoriën*, p.133.

306 *Journal 1699*, p.188.

307 Valentyn, *Description* I, 107.

308 *Kaapse plakkaatboek* I, 148–149; *ibid*. II, 11–12; *Resolusies* 3, 372–373. See also the reference in *Kaapse plakkaatboek* I, 320.

309 See pp.230–231 above.

310 See Armstrong & Worden, 'The slaves', p.127.

311 Kolb, *Beschryving* II, 247b.

312 Shell, *Children of bondage*, pp.177–178. Cf. CAD, C2419.

313 Van Reede, *Journaal*, p.208. See also *Memoriën*, pp.205–206.

314 DSAB II, 666–667; *Resolusies* 4, 145..

315 Hattingh, 'Kaapse notariële stukke' II, 31, 36.

316 *Memoriën*, p.135.

317 Nationaal Archief, The Hague, VOC 4953 pp.851–885 *passim*. I am indebted to Dr Robert Shell for a printout.

318 *Letters despatched 1696*, p.381.

319 CAD, MOOC8/2,42.

320 *Resolusies* 3, 171.

321 For the hospital, see *Resolusies* 3, 167; *ibid*. 4, 131.

322 Hoge, *Personalia*, p.43 (under 'Brand, Burchard').

323 *Resolusies* 4, 158.

324 See the references in n122 above.

325 Shell, *Children of bondage*, p.188.

326 CAD, C2419.

327 Cf. Shell, *Children of bondage*, pp.180, 188.

328 *Resolusies* 4, 164.

329 *Letters despatched 1696*, pp.108, 224.

330 *Resolusies* 4, 164.

331 Böeseken, *Nederlandsche commissarissen*, pp.70–71.

332 Upham, 'Armosyn revisited', p.24.

333 Cf. Franken, *Taalhistoriese bydraes*, p.26 n6.

334 Original document quoted in Upham, 'Armosyn revisited', p.24 n30.

335 *Resolusies* 3, 170 n64.

336 *Resolusies* 3, 170–171.

5. The world of the slaves: the Slave Lodge – *pp.127-194*

337 Upham, 'Armosyn revisited', p.25 & n32.

338 For Rodrigo, see pp.370–373 above.

339 For Armosyn, see pp.362–369 above.

340 Cf. WNT IX, column 316.

341 *Resolusies* 5, 162.

342 CAD, C2419 pp.14–15.

343 Kolb, *Beschryving* I, 395b.

344 *Reports of Chavonnes*, p.105.

345 CAD, C2419 p.14.

346 *Kaapse plakkaatboek* 2, 65 *Resolusies* 5, 115–116.

347 Shell, *Children of bondage*, p.185.

348 *Resolusies* 3, 129.

349 *Resolusies* 3, 127.

350 *Resolusies* 3, 154.

351 *Defence*, p.11 (paras. 217–220) (slightly amended). Cf. Mentzel, *Description* 1, 140.

352 Mentzel, *Description* 2, 129.

353 Shell, *Children of bondage*, p.188.

354 Mentzel, *Description* 2, 130.

355 See for this paragraph La Bree, *Rechterlijke organisatie*, pp.32, 87–88; *Oud Batavia* I, 462–463.

356 *Oud Batavia* I, 463–464.

357 *Journal 1662*, p.215.

358 *Journal 1662*, p.240.

359 See Shell, *Children of bondage*, pp.189–194.

360 Shell, *Children of bondage*, p.191.

361 *Kaapse plakkaatboek* I, 221.

362 Heese, *Reg en onreg*, p.213.

363 Cf. WNT XIII, column 1400.

364 Cf. Van Riebeeck, *Journal* II, 60 (entry dated 1656).

365 Heese, *Reg en onreg*, pp.47–48.

366 Franken, 'Vertolking', pp.49, 53, 62, 76.

367 Franken, 'Vertolking', pp.52, 53,

368 Franken, 'Vertolking', p.70.

369 Franken, 'Vertolking', p.76.

5. The world of the slaves: the Slave Lodge – *pp.127-194*

370 Franken, 'Vertolking', p.72; also 71, 75–77 *passim*.

371 Heese, *Reg en onreg*, pp.240, 252.

372 *Almanak voor de Kaap de Goede Hoop* (1804); repr. (Cape Town, South African Library, 1973), p.[4].

373 Tas, *Diary*, p.69.

374 Mentzel, *Description* 2, 124.

375 La Bree, *Rechterlijke organisatie*, p.87.

376 *Memoriën*, p.100. See also *ibid.*, p.113.

377 *Memoriën*, p.144.

378 *Memoriën*, p.208, 217.

379 Journal, quoted in *Kaapse plakkaatboek* I, 224.

380 In Valentyn, *Description* II, 213. In the published text '*by de naaste opneming*' has been translated as 'with those next received'.

381 *Journal 1699*, p.279. This information is included in his transcriptions over the period November 1730–December 1732; *ibid.*, pp.319–341 *passim*.

382 *Resolusies* 7, 16.

383 *Resolusies* 5, 129.

384 Shell, *Children of bondage*, p.178. See also the statistical tables 'Slaves in possession of the Company (1702–1796)', in Van Duin & Ross, *Economy*, p.113.

385 Armstrong & Worden, 'The slaves', p.123. For statistics (1661–1793), see *ibid.*, p.124 (table).

386 Van Reede, *Journaal*, p.213.

387 *Memoriën*, p.206.

388 Generale opneming 1693.

389 CAD, C2419 p.14.

390 Valentyn, *Description* II, 243.

391 Kolb, *Beschryving* II, 267b.

392 *Letters despatched 1696*, p.320.

393 Valentyn, *Description* II, 243.

394 *Reports of Chavonnes*, pp.87–88.

395 *Reports of Chavonnes*, pp.97–98.

396 *Reports of Chavonnes*, p.105.

397 Sleigh, *Buiteposte*, pp.121–122, with comment.

398 Armstrong & Worden, 'The slaves', p.129. See also Geyser, *Old Supreme Court building*, p.57.

6. The world of the slaves: the slaves of private owners – *pp.195-265*

1 'South rising' (book review), *Times Literary Supplement* (23.7.1999), p.28.

2 Armstrong & Worden, 'The slaves', p.123.

3 Armstrong & Worden, 'The slaves', p.132.

4 Coenraad Beyers, *Die Kaapse Patriotte gedurende die laaste kwart van die agtiende eeu* (Pretoria: Van Schaik, 1967), p.340 (table).

5 Guelke, 'Anatomy', p.459 (table).

6 Guelke & Shell, 'Early colonial landed gentry', p.276.

7 See *Reports of Chavonnes*, pp.86–128. The exception was D.M. Pasques de Chavonnes; see *ibid.*, pp.103–110.

8 See for example *Reports of Chavonnes*, pp.87, 98.

9 *Reports of Chavonnes*, p.101.

10 *Reports of Chavonnes*, p.116.

11 *Reports of Chavonnes*, p.121.

12 *Reports of Chavonnes*, p.112.

13 *Reports of Chavonnes*, p.126.

14 *Reports of Chavonnes*, p.126.

15 *Reports of Chavonnes*, pp.104–105.

16 See DSAB II, 167–168.

17 Böeseken, *Slaves and free blacks*, p.49.

18 Heese, *Groep*, p.24 (table). This is the figure for a 'white farmer married to a white wife'. Other tables with correspondingly lower averages are given for other permutations, *ibid.*, pp.24–25.

19 Biewenga, *Kaap de Goede Hoop*, pp.90–93; Groenewald, 'Slawe, Khoekhoen en Nederlandse pidgins', p.188–189.

20 Shell, *Children of bondage*, p.153.

21 Guelke & Shell, 'Early colonial landed gentry', pp.267–268.

22 Shell, *Children of bondage*, p.154.

23 Shell, *Children of bondage*, p.154. See also CAD, MOOC 8/1.69.

24 *Boedelinventarisse* I, 39.

25 Heese, *Groep sonder grense*, p.20 (table).

26 Hattingh, 'Klagte', p.40 (table), & *passim*.

27 *Contra-deductie*, p.129.

28 Heese, *Groep*, p.24 (table).

29 See Franken, *Taalhistoriese bydraes*, pp.113–114.

6. The world of the slaves: the slaves of private owners – *pp.195-265*

30 Böeseken, *Slaves and free blacks*, pp.161, 164 ('Didlof Bibou').

31 CAD, MOOC 8/1.14 ('Ditloff Bibout').

32 Böeseken, *Slaves and free blacks*, p.50.

33 *Boedelinventarisse* I, 8.

34 *Boedelinventarisse* I, 14.

35 *Boedelinventarisse* I, 27.

36 *Boedelinventarisse* I, 11.

37 *Boedelinventarisse* I, 12.

38 C.S. Woodward, 'The interior of the Cape house, 1670–1714' (thesis; University of Pretoria, 1982), p.3.

39 *Boedelinventarisse* I, 5.

40 *Boedelinventarisse* I, 56–60.

41 Shell, *Children of bondage*, p.14. For the probate inventory of Greeff's estate (1712), see *Boedelinventarisse* I, 122–128.

42 *Boedelinventarisse* I, 102–104 ('Claas').

43 *Boedelinventarisse* I, 122–128.

44 *Reports of Chavonnes*, p.93.

45 *De la Fontaine report*.

46 Cf. *Shaping*, pp.258–259.

47 Cf. Heese, *Reg en onreg*, p.23.

48 For Mentzel, see DSAB I, 530–532.

49 See Armstrong, 'Malagasy slave names', p.44; Armstrong & Worden, 'The slaves', p.122.

50 See Böeseken, *Slaves and free blacks*, pp.73–74; Hattingh, 'Naamgewing'.

51 See Hattingh, 'Naamgewing'; statistical list on pp.14–20.

52 Böeseken, *Slaves and free blacks*, p.184.

53 Böeseken, *Slaves and free blacks*, p.141 (12.5.1684).

54 Böeseken, *Slaves and free blacks*, p.189 (9.6.1699).

55 Armstrong, 'Malagasy slave names', p.44.

56 *Trials of slavery*, p.8.

57 Cairns, 'Freeblack landowners', p.24.

58 Hattingh, *Eerste vryswartes*, p.38.

59 Hattingh, 'Kaapse notariële stukke' II, 26.

60 *Trials of slavery*, p.8.

61 *Resolusies* 4, 371.

6. The world of the slaves: the slaves of private owners – *pp.195-265*

62 Quoted in Franken, *Taalhistoriese bydraes*, p.114.

63 Quoted in Franken, 'Vertolking', p.47. For an imaginative attempt to re-create the background of an individual slave, see Shell, 'Rangton van Bali'.

64 For an exception, see for example Hattingh, 'Kaapse notariële stukke' II, 36 (8.12.1678); though Rijckloff van Goens Jr is not known to have been at the Cape in this year.

65 Cairns, 'Slave transfers', p.21. For the first two transactions, see also Böeseken, *Slaves and free blacks*; pp.140, 142. Early in the following century there was a farm known as *'de zo genaamde hoffstede van Piet Snap'* and *'de post van Piet Snap'* in Hottentots-Holland; *Contra-deductie*, pp.132, 134.

66 Cairns, 'Slave transfers', p.29.

67 See Böeseken, *Slaves and free blacks*, p.30; Cairns, 'Slave transfers'; Hattingh, 'Kaapse notariële stukke' I, 44–49.

68 Cairns, 'Slave transfers', pp.22–24.

69 The intermediary seems to have been to the French Refugee Gilles Sollier, 'who understood English'; M. Boucher, *French speakers at the Cape of Good Hope* (Pretoria: University of South Africa, 1981), p.164 n80.

70 *Journal 1699*, p.267.

71 Joubert Papers (unsorted).

72 CAD, MOOC 8/1.63.

73 CAD, MOOC 14/19, vol.3, 124 folio 8 (double page). I am grateful to Gerald Groenewald for help in transcribing this text.

74 Böeseken, *Slaves and free blacks*, p.171. Van Schalkwyk's first name is transcribed here as 'Thomas'.

75 Hattingh, *Kaapse notariële stukke* II, 16.

76 Böeseken, *Slaves and free blacks*, p.147.

77 Böeseken, *Slaves and free blacks*, p.154.

78 CAD, MOOC 8/3.47.

79 CAD, MOOC 8/3.20.

80 Cairns, 'Slave transfers', p.25. For auctions, see also De Kock, *Those in bondage*, pp.45–47.

81 Kolb, *Beschryving* II, 429.

82 CAD, MOOC 8/3.15.

83 Böeseken, *Slaves and free blacks*, p.152 (22.2.1688).

84 Böeseken, *Slaves and free blacks*, p.152 (17.4.1688).

85 Böeseken, *Slaves and free blacks*, p.151.

86 *Trials of slavery*, p.92.

87 Quoted in De Kock, *Those in bondage*, p.42.

88 Böeseken, *Slaves and free blacks*, p.178.

89 See CAD, MOOC 8/1.44.

90 See CAD, MOOC 8/1.44.

91 CAD, CJ 781 pp.103–112. I am grateful to Gerald Groenewald for tracing and transcribing this document for me.

92 I owe the background information on the case to Gerald Groenewald.

93 Barnard, *Diaries* I, 72.

94 For a contemporary account of an auction in Batavia by a German who was in the East in the service of the VOC during 1671–76, see Johann Christian Hoffmann, *Reise nach dem Kaplande, nach Mauritius und nach Java, 1671–1676*; ed. S.P. l'Honoré Naber (The Hague: Martinus Nijhoff, 1931), pp.59–60 (*Reisebeschreibungen von Deutschen Beamten* VII).

95 Hattingh, 'Kaapse notariële stukke' II, 37 (26.2.1679);

96 Quoted in Shell, *Children of bondage*, p.121.

97 Böeseken, *Slaves and free blacks*, p.152.

98 Hattingh, 'Klagte', pp.38–39.

99 Tas, *Diary*, p.155.

100 CAD, MOOC 8/1.63.

101 See p.368 above.

102 Hattingh, 'Kaapse notariële stukke' II, 18.

103 See Hattingh, 'Kaapse notariële stukke' II, 23 (1.9.1674); 34 (7.4.1678); Böeseken, *Slaves and free blacks*, p.139 (4.5.1681), etc.

104 *Journal 1699*, p.164.

105 *Contra-deductie*, pp.130, 142, 251–254 *passim*.

106 *Contra-deductie*, p.165.

107 *Kaapse plakkaatboek* I, 175.

108 Mentzel, *Description* 3, 110.

109 Mentzel, *Description* 3, 108.

110 Mentzel, *Description* 2, 54.

111 Mentzel, *Description* 1, 84–85.

112 Mentzel, *Description* 2, 80.

113 CAD, MOOC 8/2.43 ('*een streepte astemine rok—an de meijd geschenk*'). The reference is to a type of textile known as *estamijn* or *stamijn*.

114 CAD, C369 ref.95 pp.80–83.

115 J.L.M. Franken, *'n Kaapse huishoue in die 18de eeu* (Archives Year Book 1940, I), pp.11, 18. See further *ibid.*, pp.60–67.

116 *Journal 1699*, p.198.

6. The world of the slaves: the slaves of private owners – *pp.195-265*

117 e.g., in CAD, MOOC 8/3/40.

118 *Reports of Chavonnes*, p.126.

119 *Boedelinventarisse* 1, 122.

120 *Boedelinventarisse* 2, 506, 509.

121 *Contra-deductie*, p.165.

122 See for example Hattingh:Eerste vryswartes, p.54; CAD, MOOC 8/2.5; CAD, MOOC 8/2.20.

123 'Slaeven ofte lyffeygenen', p.575.

124 CAD, C369 ref.95 pp.80–83.

125 Cf. Barnard, *Journals*, p.157. For Batavia by mid-century, see *Oud Batavia* I, 467.

126 O.F. Mentzel (quotation not further identified), quoted in De Kock, *Those in bondage*, p.49.

127 Pascoe Thomas, *A true and impartial journal of a voyage to the South-Seas and round the globe* (…) (London: S. Birt, 1745), p.344. I am grateful to Gerald Groenewald for verifying this quotation for me.

128 Denyssen, 'Statement', p.159 (para.75).

129 Cf. *Trials of slavery*, pp.57 (art.9), 92 (art.5).

130 *Reports of Chavonnes*, p.112.

131 Cf. Scholtz, *Afrikaans-Hollands*, pp.136–137 ('kombers').

132 *Trials of slavery*, p.663 (index entry under 'possessions (of slaves)'. For a chest, see also p.241 above.

133 Böeseken, *Slaves and free blacks*, p.72.

134 CAD, MOOC 8/4.23.

135 See Kolb, *Beschryving* II, 324a–b; Mentzel, *Description* 3, 110; *Reports of Chavonnes*, p.105.

136 For an anecdote about Commissioner Van Hoorn tipping a female slave 10 cents during his visit in 1710, see Kolb, *Beschryving* II, 433b.

137 *Kaapse plakkaatboek* I, 46.

138 *Kaapse plakkaatboek* II, 41 (para.7).

139 Heese, *Reg en onreg*, p.265.

140 Hattingh, *Eerste vryswartes*, p.58.

141 Quoted in Heese, *Reg en onreg*, pp.114–115 *passim*.

142 Barnard, Journals, pp.158–159.

143 *Kaapse plakkaatboek* II, 10.

144 Mentzel, *Description* 1, 117.

145 H.N. Vos, 'An historical and archaeological perspective of colonial Stellenbosch, 1680–1960' (thesis; Stellenbosch, 1993), p.198.

6. The world of the slaves: the slaves of private owners – *pp.195-265*

146 Vos, 'Historical perspective' (see previous note), p.249.

147 Mentzel, *Life*, p.40.

148 Yvonne Brink, 'Places of discourse and dialogue: a study of the material culture of the Cape during the rule of the Dutch East India Company, 1652–1795' (thesis; Cape Town, 1992), p.116 (examples in parentheses omitted).

149 CAD, MOOC 8/3.81.

150 CAD, MOOC 8/3.21.

151 CAD, MOOC 8/3.92.

152 *Trials of slavery*, pp.104–106 *passim*.

153 Biewenga, *Kaap de Goede Hoop*, p.111.

154 Armstrong & Worden, 'The slaves', p.145.

155 Woodward. This item is omitted in the transcription given in *Inventories*, but appears in the original document (CAD, MOOC 8/2.28). I am grateful to Gerald Groenewald for checking this for me.

156 *Boedelinventarisse* I, 125–126.

157 *Boedelinventarisse* I, 134–135.

158 CAD, MOOC 8/3.21.

159 *Boedelinventarisse* I, 201–202. See also CAD, MOOC 8/3.41 & 42,

160 *Boedelinventarisse* II, 365–366.

161 See Ann B. Markell, 'Building on the past; the architecture and archaeology of Vergelegen', *SA Archaeological Society: Godwin Series* 7 (1993), pp.74–76.

162 *Boedelinventarisse* I, 134.

163 Biewenga, *Kaap de Goede Hoop*, p.114.

164 *Boedelinventarisse* I, 267–268

165 Valentyn, Beschryvinge II, 239.

166 Quoted in Heese, *Reg en onreg*, pp.118–119 *passim*.

167 Mentzel, *Description* 1, 118; cf. *ibid.*, 133, and the folded plan between pp.86/87 (no.36).

168 *Kaapse plakkaatboek* 2, 9.

169 Ross, 'Occupations', p.8.

170 Mentzel, *Description* 1, 90–91; *ibid.* 2, 91; Ross, 'Occupations', pp.8–9. See also *The Cape journals of Lady Anne Barnard, 1797–1798*; ed. A.M. Lewin Robinson (Cape Town: Van Riebeeck Society, 1994), p.157; John Barrow, *An account of travels into the interior of southern Africa…*, vol.I (London: T. Cadell Jr. & W. Davies, 1801), p.20.

171 *Memoriën*, p.84.

172 For *koeliegeld*, see Franken, *Taalhistoriese bydraes*, pp.105–107.

173 Mentzel, *Description* 1, 88.

174 *Kaapse plakkaatboek* I, 130–131.

175 *Resolusies* 3, 438–439. Cf. *Letters despatched 1696*, pp.296, 353.

176 Quoted in Ross, 'Occupations', p.10.

177 See Karel Schoeman, *'n Duitser aan die Kaap* (Pretoria: Protea, 2004), p.134.

178 Mentzel, *Description* 2, 91.

179 Mentzel, *Description* 2, 98.

180 Quoted in Schoeman, *Armosyn: wêreld*, p.585.

181 Mentzel, *Description* 2, 89–90.

182 Ross, 'Occupations', p.10.

183 A.M. Hugo, *Die kerk van Stellenbosch, 1686–1963* (Cape Town: Tafelberg, 1963), p.69 n3.

184 Theal, *History* II, 54.

185 Mentzel, *Description* 2, 90.

186 Mentzel, *Description* 1, 90.

187 CAD, MOOC 8/3.69.

188 Joubert Papers (unsorted).

189 Mentzel, *Description* 2, 86.

190 Ross, 'Occupations', p.10.

191 Ross, *'Occupations'*, p.9.

192 Kolb, *Beschryving* II, 306b.

193 *Kaapse plakkaatboek* II, 90. Cf. *ibid.*, 92.

194 Ross, *Cape of torments*, p.7. For the Chinese in this connection, see also Heese, *Reg en onreg*, pp.19, 85.

195 Ross, *Cape of torments*, p.8.

196 *Kaapse plakkaatboek* I, 320–321.

197 Ross, *Cape of torments*, pp.262 ('Tamtanko'), 263 ('Theepesio').

198 Heese, *Reg en onreg*, pp.85, 179, 244, 264.

199 Heese, *Reg en onreg*, pp.183 ('Chioe Ahoeko'), 187, 253 ('Santico').

200 Denyssen, 'Statement', p.156 (para.60).

201 *Uit die Raad van Justisie*, p.200 par.6.

202 For the comments of two female Dutch visitors in 1736, see *Op reis met de VOC;* ed. M.L. Barend-van Haeften (Zutphen: Walburg Pers, 1996), p.98.

203 *Reports of Chavonnes*, p.109.

204 *Reports of Chavonnes*, p.118.

205 Mentzel, *Life*, p.136. See also Mentzel, *Description* 2, 125–126.

206 *Contra-deductie*, p.132.

6. The world of the slaves: the slaves of private owners – *pp.195-265*

207 *Contra-deductie*, p.137.

208 Tas, *Diary, passim*.

209 Armstrong & Worden, 'The slaves', pp.143–145; extensively quoted with the kind permission of the authors. See also Worden, *Slavery*, pp.20–22; and Mentzel, *Description* 3, 108–109, for a contemporary account of the daily routine on a farm.

210 Mentzel, *Description* 3, 105–106.

211 *Contra-deductie*, p.205.

212 Biewenga, *Kaap de Goede Hoop*, p.111; Valentyn, *Beschryvinge* II, 217.

213 *Trials of slavery*, p.19.

214 CAD, MOOC 8/2,75.

215 Mentzel, *Description* 2, 90.

216 Armstrong & Worden, 'The slaves', pp.144–145.

217 *Contra-deductie*, p.205.

218 *Reports of Chavonnes*, p.104.

219 CAD, MOOC 8/3.40.

220 Armstrong & Worden, 'The slaves', p.145.

221 Tas, *Diary, passim*.

222 Cf. Groenewald, 'Slawe, Khoekhoen en Nederlandse pidgins', pp.188–192.

223 *Journal 1662*, p.319. See also *Kaapse plakkaatboek* I, 114; Mentzel *Description* 3, 15.

224 *Journal 1662*, p.319. See also *Kaapse plakkaatboek* I, 114.

225 *Journal 1671*, p.175.

226 Tas, *Diary*, pp.103, 127.

227 Biewenga, *Kaap de Goede Hoop*, pp.207–208.

228 Mentzel, *Description* 3, 15.

229 A primitive stringed instrument.

230 Mentzel, *Description* 3, 109.

231 Mentzel, *Description* 3, 15. See also *ibid.*, p.121.

232 Barnard, *Diaries* I, 283.

233 Kolb, *Beschryving* II, 323b.

234 Mentzel, *Description* 3, 110.

235 Kolb, *Beschryving* II, 324a.

236 Kolb, *Beschryving* II, 324b.

237 Kolb, *Beschryving* II, 324b *passim*.

238 *Kaapse plakkaatboek* I, 297.

239 *Journal 1699*, p.97. Cf. *Resolusies* 3, p.446. The original Dutch is also quoted in Franken, *Hugenote*, p.92.

240 *Kaapse plakkaatboek* I, 297–298. Cf. *Resolusies* 3, 302–303.

241 *Kaapse plakkaatboek* I, 215.

242 *Kaapse plakkaatboek* I, 299–300. Cf. *Resolusies* 3, 312–313.

243 *Kaapse plakkaatboek* II, 10–11.

244 In Franken, *Taalhistoriese bydraes*, p.107.

245 *Kaapse plakkaatboek* I, 219.

246 *Kaapse plakkaatboek* I, 246–247.

247 Quoted in Biewenga, *Kaap de Goede Hoop*, p.112.

248 Biewenga, *Kaap de Goede Hoop*, p.112; Hattingh, 'Slawevrystellings', p.36

249 CAD, CJ780 pp.914–915; see *ibid.*, pp.914–919 for the entire document. I am grateful to Gerald Groenewald for the transcription of the original.

250 Böeseken, *Slaves and free blacks*, p.72.

251 Hattingh, *Eerste vryswartes*, p.65.

252 Cf. Heese, *Reg en onreg*, p.104.

253 CAD, VC12 pp.701–708. I owe these Journal entries relating to this case to Gerald Groenewald as well.

254 Biewenga, *Kaap de Goede Hoop*, p.111.

255 CAD, MOOC 8/3.15.

256 Tas, *Diary*, p.75.

257 *Boedelinventarisse* I, 274, 275.

258 Heese/Lombard 1, 160.

259 De Villiers, *Genealogies*, pp.443, 1082–1083 ('Martha'); Hattingh, *Eerste vryswartes*, p.74; Hoge, Personalia, pp.220 (Kreutzmann), 442 (Vosloo).

260 See Biewenga, *Kaap de Goede Hoop*, p.109; Franken, *Hugenote*, pp.150, 154–156 *passim*.

261 See Heese, 'Slawegesinne', p.38; Shell, *Children of bondage*, pp.345–346 (including graph).

262 Hattingh, 'Slawevrystellings', p.29 (with examples).

263 Böeseken, *Slaves and free blacks*, pp.58–59; Hattingh, 'Slawevrystellings', p.29.

264 See for this development Karel Schoeman, *Dogter van Sion* (Cape Town: Human & Rousseau, 1997), pp.273–339; Karel Schoeman, *The early mission in South Africa, 1799–1819* (Pretoria: Protea, 2005), pp.20–41.

265 Kolb, *Beschryving* II, 326a.

266 Biewenga, *Kaap de Goede Hoop*, p.260.

267 Biewenga, *Kaap de Goede Hoop*, p.261.

6. The world of the slaves: the slaves of private owners – *pp.195-265*

268 *Resolusies* 5, 72.

269 *Bouwstoffen* I, 276.

270 *Trials of slavery*, p.19.

271 Biewenga, *Kaap de Goede Hoop*, p.111.

272 *Trials of slavery*, pp.44–45.

273 *Resolusies* 7, 224.

274 Heese, *Reg en onreg*, pp.47–48, 134 ('Hendriksz'), 181. It is not clear whether Hendriksz's surname was Van Reenen, or he came from the town of Rhenen in the Netherlands. He is also referred to as 'Joost Hendriksz van Dort', which would refer to the Dutch town of Dordrecht; *ibid.*, p.48 n.51.

275 Franken, *Taalhistoriese bydraes*, pp.114–115. For both forms, see also Boshoff & Nienaber, *Afrikaanse etimologieë*, p.573 ('*seur* II'); Scholtz, *Afrikaans uit die vroeë tyd*, pp.153, 190–191; Scholtz, *Afrikaans-Hollands*, p.113; *Trials of slavery*, pp.620, 623.

276 See Boshoff & Nienaber, *Afrikaanse etimologieë*, p.147 ('*baas*').

277 Boshoff & Nienaber, *Afrikaanse etimologieë*, pp.449 ('*nôi*'); *Trials of slavery*, p.622. See for example 'nonje Elisabeth', in CAD, MOOC 8/2.29 (1709).

278 *Trials of slavery*, p.621.

279 *Trials of slavery*, pp.82–83. Original text, *ibid.*, pp.78.

280 Boshoff & Nienaber, *Afrikaanse etimologieë*, pp.312 ('*jong* II'), 398 ('*maagd*'), 418 ('*meid*'); *Trials of slavery*, pp.621, 622.

281 See Boshoff & Nienaber, *Afrikaanse etimologieë*, pp.399 ('*maai* III'), 475 ('*paai* I'); Scholtz, *Afrikaans-Hollands*, p.153 ('*paai*').

282 Franken, 'Vertolking', p.41 (emphasis in the original).

283 See Franken, *Taalhistoriese bydraes*, pp.211–213 (lists of names in the Index under the heading '*Portugees en Maleis*').

284 *Trials of slavery*, p.406 *passim*.

285 Gerald Groenewald, in *Trials of slavery*, p.5.

286 Edith H. Raidt, *Historiese taalkunde* (Johannesburg: Witwatersrand Univ. pr., 1994, pp.213–214; in an article previously published as 'Vrouetaal en taalverandering', *Tydskrif vir Geesteswetenskappe* 24,4 (Dec. 1984), pp.256–286. See also Edith H. Raidt, 'Women in the history of Afrikaans', *Language and social change*; ed. Rajend Mesthrie (Cape Town: David Philip, 1995), pp.129–139.

287 See De Wet, *Vryliede*, pp.100–102.

288 *Kaapse plakkaatboek* I, 115.

289 *Kaapse plakkaatboek* I, 276.

290 De Wet, *Vryliede*, p.101.

291 Jan de la Fontaine, in *Reports of Chavonnes*, p.116.

292 Heese, *Groep sonder grense*, p.20 (table).

293 See pp.94 & 114.

6. The world of the slaves: the slaves of private owners – *pp.195-265*

294 Valentyn, *Beschryvinge* II, 231.

295 De Wet, *Vryliede*, p.102.

296 De Wet, *Vryliede*, p.119.

297 De Wet, *Vryliede*, p.121.

298 De Wet, *Vryliede*, o,119.

299 Biewenga, *Kaap de Goede Hoop*, p.268.

300 Biewenga, *Kaap de Goede Hoop*, pp.104–105.

301 See Worden, Slavery, pp.89–90

302 Mentzel, *Description* 3, 99.

303 Mentzel, *Description* 3, 99–100.

304 Biewenga, *Kaap de Goede Hoop*, p.114.

305 *Trials of slavery*, p.14.

306 The quotations which follow are all from CAD, CJ780 pp.1265–1279. I have to thank Gerald Groenewald for the transcription of this document.

307 See p.296 above.

308 *Boedelinventarisse* I, 20–21 (Kouthoff).

309 *Kaapse plakkaatboek* 2, 149–150,

310 *Resolusies* 3, 146.

311 Heese, *Reg en onreg*, p.167.

312 Armstrong & Worden, 'The slaves', p.153.

313 Shell, *Children of bondage*, p.72.

314 Böeseken, *Slaves and free blacks*, pp.33–34.

315 Kolb, *Beschryving* II, 438B–439A.

316 Heese, *Reg en onreg*, p.161.

317 Heese, *Reg en onreg*, p.167.

318 *Trials of slavery*, p.90.

319 *Trials of slavery*, pp.93–94 ('dog wanneer hij gesien heeft dat se bij een andere lag, doe doen mijn hart seer').

320 Gerald Groenewald, in *Trials of slavery*, p.84.

321 See Heese, *Reg en onreg*, pp.94–96 & *passim* (entries under 'passiemoorde' in the Internet index); *Trials of slavery*, *passim* (entries under 'crimes of passion' in the Index).

322 Kolb, *Beschryving* II, 324b–325a.

323 Botha, 'Slavery', p.89.

324 See De Klerk, 'Verhaal van Susanna Biebow'; Heese/Lombard 1, 275–276; *ibid.*, 7, 21.

6. The world of the slaves: the slaves of private owners – *pp.195-265*

325 CAD, MOOC 8/2.87 ('Maria Bibou'); CAD, MOOC 8/2.106 ('Zusanna Bebout').

326 Hoge, 'Miscegenation', p.108 n36.

327 Hoge, 'Miscegenation', p.108 n35. Given as 'Andries Pretorius' in Heese/Lombard 8, 357.

328 Heese, *Groep*, p.6; Heese/Lombard 1, 583.

329 *Resolusies* 2, 68; Sleigh, *Buiteposte*, p.178. Cf. Heese/Lombard 1, 583.

330 Sleigh, *Buiteposte*, p.120.

331 *Resolusies* 6, 128.

332 Botha, 'Slavery', p.89. See also the summary of existing slave legislation in Denyssen, 'Statement'.

333 For the text, see *Records of the Cape Colony* XV, 336–342.

334 Denyssen, 'Statement', pp.147–148 & marginal note.

335 Armstrong & Worden, 'The slaves', p.155.

336 'Letter' (1796), p.307.

337 Cf. Ross, *Cape of torments*, p.13.

338 Cf. Worden, Slavery, p.86.

339 Quoted in Mossop, 'Three slaves who ran away'.

340 *Boedelinventarisse* I, 256 *passim*.

341 Tas, *Diary*, p.181.

342 Ross, *Cape of torments*, p.34.

343 Ross, *Cape of torments*, pp.12, 128 n13; the latter referring to Böeseken, *Slaves and free blacks*, p.147 (6.6.1686). For Francis van Batavia, see further p.275 above.

344 Quoted in Mossop, 'Three slaves who ran away'.

345 Worden, *Slavery*, p.124.

346 *Trials of slavery*, p.3.

347 *Trials of slavery*, p.8. For Ary, see further Franken, 'Van der Heiden en die swart slaaf'.

348 *Trials of slavery*, p.58.

349 Quoted in Franken, *Hugenote*, p.64 n25.

350 Biewenga, *Kaap de Goede Hoop*, pp.112–113.

351 *Journal 1699*, p.68. This is probably also the case referred to in Franken, *Hugenote*, p.139.

352 Quoted in Biewenga, *Kaap de Goede Hoop*, p.113.

353 A.M. Hugo, *Die Kerk van Stellenbosch* (Cape Town: Tafelberg, 1963), p.96.

354 Heese, *Reg en onreg*, pp.104–105.

7. Resistance and control – *pp.266-304*

1   For crime and punishment, though mainly in the eighteenth century, see Heese, *Reg en onreg*.

2   For these sources, see Trials of slavery, 'Introduction', pp.xi–xxxi. Also Ross, *Cape of torments*, p.7.

3   Ross, *Cape of torments*, p.3; referring in an endnote (p.127) to H. Aptheker.

4   Heese, *Reg en onreg*, p.72.

5   Heese, *Reg en onreg*, p.23. See also *ibid.*, pp.72–83, for the eighteenth century.

6   Heese, *Reg en onreg*, p.73.

7   The Independent Fiscal, Cornelis van Beaumont, in *Resolusies* 4, 452.

8   See chapter 1 above.

9   *Journal 1671*, p.82.

10 *Kaapse plakkaatboek* I, 121.

11 *Journal 1671*, pp.156, 158, 159.

12 *Journal 1671*, pp.222–224.

13 *Resolusies* 3, 140. Cf. *Kaapse plakkaatboek* I, 216.

14 *Resolusies* 3, 188–189.

15 Quoted in Hendrik Carel Vos Leibbrandt, *Rambles through the archives of the Cape of Good Hope*; 1st series (Cape Town: J.C. Juta, pp.31–32. See also De Kock, *Those in bondage*, pp.72–73; Ross, *Cape of torments*, p.12.

16 Quoted in De Kock, *Those in bondage*, p.23 (1695).

17 Böeseken, *Slaves and free blacks*, p.51 & n79.

18 Böeseken, *Slaves and free blacks*, p.52.

19 Böeseken, *Slaves and free blacks*, p.52.

20 *Kaapse plakkaatboek* 1, 258–259.

21 See *Journal 1699*, 198–199.

22 *Boedelinventarisse* I, 169.

23 *Boedelinventarisse* I, 214.

24 Armstrong & Worden, 'The slaves', p.123 n(*).

25 Sleigh, *Buiteposte*, p.257.

26 *Journal 1699*, p.68.

27 For the similar wanderings of Ary van Bengalen, see Franken, 'Van der Heiden en die swart slaaf'; *Trials of slavery*, pp.5–9.

28 Heese, *Reg en onreg*, p.234.

29 *Journal 1699*, p.70.

7. Resistance and control – *pp.266-304*

30 Heese, *Reg en onreg*, pp.84, 188, 206, 234.

31 Sleigh, *Buiteposte*, p.201. See also Böeseken, *Slaves and free blacks*, pp.50–52.

32 *Journal 1699*, p.106. See also *ibid.*, p.108.

33 *Journal 1699*, p.56.

34 *Letters despatched 1696*, pp.212–213.

35 Valentyn, *Description* II, 3.

36 For another reference to the river, see p.262 above.

37 In Valentyn, *Description* II, 228. In this context, *'verstekelingen'* might perhaps better be translated as 'deserters' than 'stowaways'.

38 In Valentyn, *Description* II, 231.

39 *Kaapse plakkaatboek* I, 291–295; *Resolusies* 3, 299–300.

40 *Kaapse plakkaatboek* II, 95–97.

41 See Ross, *Cape of torments*, pp.54–72.

42 Ross, *Cape of torments*, p.4.

43 Mossop, 'Three slaves who ran away'.

44 See p.65 above.

45 Heese, *Reg en onreg*, p.24. See also Sleigh, *Buiteposte*, p.430.

46 *Journal 1699*, p.141.

47 Cf. Mentzel, *Description* 3, 300. See also the chapter 'The slaves and the Khoisan', in Ross, *Cape of torments*, pp.38–53.

48 Cf. Sleigh, *Buiteposte*, p.424.

49 Quoted in Böeseken, *Slaves and free blacks*, p.40 & n2 (Dutch text).

50 *Resolusies* 2, 309.

51 *Journal 1671*, p.139.

52 Sleigh, *Buiteposte*, p.422.

53 Sleigh, *Buiteposte*, p.423.

54 Sleigh, *Buiteposte*, p.426.

55 *The journals of Bergh and Schrijver*, ed. E.E. Mossop (Cape Town: Van Riebeeck Society, 1931), p.197.

56 *Journals of Bergh and Schrijver* (see previous note), p.171.

57 See Sleigh, *Buiteposte*, p.430.

58 *Journal 1699*, p.142. See also *ibid.*, pp.144–146.

59 *Letters despatched 1696*, pp.46–47. Cf. *Resolusies* 3, 307–308, 311

60 *Letters despatched 1696*, p.47.

61 Heese, *Reg en onreg*, pp.24–25.

62 *Defence*, p.133.

63 *Journal 1699*, p.198.

64 *Resolusies* 4, 289.

65 Mentzel, *Description* 3, p.300. For the fugitive slaves under Baatjoe van Sambowa who tried to reach 'Caffirsland' by sea in 1746, see Heese, *Reg en onreg*, pp.25–26, 176.

66 *Resolusies* 3, 112–113.

67 *Letters despatched 1696*, p.263.

68 *Letters despatched 1696*, pp.267–268.

69 Ross, *Cape of torments*, pp.76–77.

70 *Boomwachter*, the official responsible for the boom with which a river or canal was closed off at night.

71 *Contra-deductie*, pp.231–232.

72 See Heese, *Reg en onreg*, pp.102–104.

73 *Trials of slavery*, p.8.

74 *Kaapse plakkaatboek* 1, 62–63.

75 Heese, *Reg en onreg*, p.88.

76 Kolb, *Beschryving* II, 325a–326a.

77 See 'Letter' (1796), from which the following quotations are taken.

78 'Letter' (1796), p.304.

79 Van Riebeeck, *Journal* II, 292.

80 *Uit die Raad van Justisie*, p.131.

81 In this regard, see also Böeseken, *Slaves and free blacks*, pp.32–34, 40–44.

82 *Journal 1671*, p.204.

83 *Journal 1671*, p.259.

84 *The Record*, p.384.

85 *The Record*, p.384.

86 *The Record*, p.384.

87 Heese, *Reg en onreg*, p.229. See also *ibid.*, p.91.

88 *Journal 1699*, p.64.

89 *Letters despatched 1696*, p.240.

90 Heese, *Reg en onreg*, pp.172–173.

91 Heese, *Reg en onreg*, p.186.

92 Cf. Heese, *Reg en onreg*, p.121.

93 Quoted in Franken, *Taalhistoriese bydraes*, p.111 (1727).

7. Resistance and control – *pp.266-304*

94 *Contra-deductie*, p.9 (para.25).

95 Mentzel, *Description* 3, 109.

96 Denyssen, 'Statement', p.148 (para.15).

97 Denyssen, 'Statement', p.143 (para.14).

98 Van Reede, *Journaal*, p.97.

99 *Memoriën*, p.217.

100 Van Reede, *Journaal*, p.97. See also *Memoriën*, p.217.

101 Quoted in Biewenga, *Kaap de Goede Hoop*, p.113.

102 Mentzel, *Description* 2, 132.

103 Kolb, *Beschryving* II, 323b–324a.

104 Cf. Franken, *Taalhistoriese bydraes*, pp.109–112; *Trials of slavery*, p.267 n4.

105 Mentzel, *Description* 2, 132.

106 *Journal 1699*, p.67. Cf. *Letters received 1695*, p.327.

107 Kolb, *Beschryving* II, 325b.

108 *Journal 1699*, p.69.

109 Heese, *Reg en onreg*, p.204.

110 *Kaapse plakkaatboek* 2, 150.

111 *Trials of slavery*, p.5 n5.

112 *Letters received 1695*, p.474 (2 letters); *Letters despatched 1696*, p.396.

113 Heese, *Reg en onreg*, p.82.

114 Heese, *Reg en onreg*, p.261 ('Springveld').

115 *Journal 1699*, p.251. Cf. *Resolusies* 4, 226–228.

116 *Resolusies* 4, 452.

117 *Resolusies* 7, 333.

118 Cf. *Journal 1699*, pp. 77, 78, 91, 92, 167–8, 173.

119 *Journal 1671*, p.158.

120 For their early use (1668), see Böeseken, *Slaves and free blacks*, p.31.

121 Mentzel, *Description* 2, 133.

122 *Journal 1699*, p.120.

123 Mentzel, *Description* 2, 133.

124 Heese, *Reg en onreg*, p.121.

125 Heese, *Reg en onreg*, pp.39–40, 142; *Journal 1699*, p.260.

126 Mentzel, *Description* 2, 133.

127 Quoted in Heese, *Reg en onreg*, p.91 (1707).

7. Resistance and control – *pp.266-304*

128 *Journal 1699*, p.92.

129 See Heese, *Reg en onreg*, pp.161, 186, 206, 222, 223, 231, 262.

130 Heese, *Reg en onreg*, pp.98–99, 168; *Journal 1699*, p.256.

131 Heese, *Reg en onreg*, p.102.

132 Kolb, *Beschryving* II, 439a. For Moses, see also Heese, *Reg en onreg*, pp.102, 237.

133 Letter (1796), p.303.

134 Yule & Burnell, *Hobson-Jobson*, p.149 ('caluete, caloete'). See also *ibid.*, pp.432–433 ('impale').

135 See the description in Anders Sparrman, *A voyage to the Cape of Good Hope (…), 1772–1776*; ed. V.S. Forbes (Cape Town: Van Riebeeck Society, 1975–77), vol.II, p.257; and that quoted in *In dienst van de Compagnie*; ed. Vibeke Roeper & Roelof van Gelder (Amsterdam: Athenaeum-Polak & Van Gennep, 2002), pp.138–139.

136 Mentzel, *Description* 2, 133.

137 Heese, *Reg en onreg*, pp.39–40, 265.

138 Heese, *Reg en onreg*, p.267; *Journal 1699*, p.258.

139 See Heese, *Reg en onreg*, pp.210, 258, 259.

140 *Journal 1699*, p.171. Cf. *Resolusies* 4, 67.

141 See La Bree, *Rechterlijke organisatie*, pp.95–96.

142 See Lucien Peytraud, *L'esclavage aux Antilles françaises avant 1789*; [repr.] (Paris: Émile Désormeaux, 1973), pp.140–211. The text of the document is given on pp.154–163.

143 Peytraud, *L'esclavage* (see previous note), articles 33–41 *passim*.

144 Mentzel, *Life*, p.94.

145 Mentzel, *Description* 2, 133.

146 'Letter' (1796), p.303 *passim*.

147 Denyssen, 'Statement', p.153 (para.38).

148 Denyssen, 'Statement', p.153 (para.39).

149 Heese, *Reg en onreg*, pp.109–110. Cf. *ibid.*, pp.108–112.

150 Gerald Groenewald, in *Trials of slavery*, pp.9–10.

151 For this case, see *Trials of slavery*, pp.9–17.

8. Uncertain freedom: the first free blacks – *pp.305-351*

1 De Kock, *Those in bondage*, p.37.

2 Figure from Shell, *Children of bondage*, p.448. For his estimates of annual slave statistics for the period 1656–1835, see *ibid.*, pp.445–448. Similar statistics are given in Van Duin & Ross, Economy, pp.113 (Company slaves, 1702–95), and 114–155 (total population, including slaves divided by gender and age, 1701–95).

3 *Kaapse plakkaatboek* III, 1–6; *ibid.* 4, 244–250. See further Denyssen, 'Statement'; Letter (1796).

4 Armstrong & Worden, 'The slaves', p.120.

5 Armstrong & Worden, 'The slaves', p.120; Shell, *Children of bondage*, pp.146–148.

6 For the text, see *Records of the Cape Colony* XV, 336–342.

7 Armstrong & Worden, 'The slaves', p.167.

8 Armstrong & Worden, 'The slaves', p.109. Shell gives 36 278; Shell, *Children of bondage*, p.448.

9 For a survey of manumission at the Cape, see Cairns, 'Slave transfers'; Elphick & Shell, 'Intergroup relations', pp.204–214; Hattingh, 'Slawe-vrystellings'.

10 'Slaeven ofte lyffeygenen', pp.575–576.

11 For these two women, see pp.39–49 above.

12 For Angela, see pp.353–357 above.

13 Cf. Hattingh, 'Kaapse notariële stukke' I, 61. For this man, see further p.309 above.

14 Hattingh, 'Kaapse notariële stukke' I, 60.

15 Elphick & Shell, 'Intergroup relations', p.184 n(†).

16 Heese, *Groep*, p.21.

17 *Kaapse plakkaatboek* II, 93 (para.9).

18 Heese, *Groep*, p.29.

19 Cf. the definition given in Elphick & Shell, 'Intergroup relations', p.184(†); and the remarks on this in Heese, *Groep*, p.21 & n21.

20 Elphick & Shell, 'Intergroup relations', p.216.

21 For Evert, see pp.357–362 above.

22 Hattingh, 'Kaapse notariële stukke' II, 14.

23 Hattingh, 'Kaapse notariële stukke' II, 18. For Lobbitje, see also *ibid.*, 17; Hattingh, *Eerste vryswartes*, p.42.

24 Hattingh, 'Kaapse notariële stukke' II, 20.

8. Uncertain freedom: the first free blacks – *pp.305-351*

25 Böeseken, *Slaves and free blacks*, p.140.

26 Hattingh, 'Kaapse notariële stukke' II, 27.

27 Hattingh, 'Kaapse notariële stukke' II, 26.

28 See Hattingh, 'Grondbesit'.

29 Böeseken, 'Verhouding', p.16.

30 Böeseken, *Slaves and free blacks*, p.91. Coopman's name is given as 'Johannes' in the original.

31 See Hattingh, 'Grondbesit', p.33 (plan).

32 See pp.353–357 above.

33 *Uit die Raad van Justisie*, p.203.

34 For a summary of the most readily available information, see Armstrong, 'Japanese slave'.

35 Böeseken, *Slave and free blacks*, pp.93–95.

36 Quoted in Böeseken, *Slave and free blacks*, p.93.

37 *Uit die Raad van Justisie*, p.203.

38 See the documents reproduced and transcribed in Böeseken, *Slaves and free blacks*, pp.,100–101, 108–109.

39 See the documents reproduced and transcribed in Böeseken, *Slaves and free blacks*, pp.100–101, 108–109.

40 Hattingh, 'Kaapse notariële stukke' II, 61.

41 Hattingh, 'Kaapse notariële stukke' II, 20. See also Hattingh, 'Grondbesit', p.36.

42 De Wet, *Vryliede*, p.208.

43 Armstrong, 'Japanese slave'.

44 See Hattingh, 'Grondbesit', pp.36–37.

45 Hattingh, 'Grondbesit', pp.36–37.

46 Hattingh, 'Kaapse notariële stukke' II, 16.

47 Hattingh, 'Grondbesit', p.41.

48 Böeseken, *Slave and free blacks*, p.93.

49 Hattingh, 'Kaapse notariële stukke' II, 26.

50 Hattingh, 'Kaapse notariële stukke' II, 35 (2 entries).

51 *Resolusies* 2, 232.

52 *Resolusies* 2, 324.

53 Hattingh, 'Grondbesit, p.37.

54 Hattingh, 'Kaapse notariële stukke' II, 20.

55 Hattingh, 'Kaapse notariële stukke' II, 25.

56 See Böeseken, *Slaves and free blacks*, pp.89–91 (corrected by Hattingh in *Eerste vryswartes*); Hattingh, 'Blanke nageslag'; Hattingh, *Eerste vryswartes*, pp.21–30.

57 Hattingh, 'Kaapse notariële stukke' I, 61. Repeated references to Louis's Khoi wife Zara during this time by various modern writers seem to rest on a misreading of the original Dutch text (*Resolusies* 1, 363); see Schoeman, *Armosyn: Wêreld*, p.781 n157.

58 *Resolusies* 2, 82.

59 Hattingh, *Eerste vryswartes*, p.22.

60 Hattingh, 'Grondbesit', p.41.

61 Böeseken, *Slaves and free blacks*, p.142.

62 Hattingh, *Eerste vryswartes*, p.22.

63 Böeseken, *Slaves and free blacks*, p.150.

64 Böeseken, *Slaves and free blacks*, p.154.

65 Böeseken, *Slaves and free blacks*, p.193.

66 Hattingh, *Eerste vryswartes*, p.23.

67 See for this Hattingh, *Eerste vryswartes*, pp.21–31.

68 Böeseken, *Slaves and free blacks*, p.91; Hattingh, *Eerste vryswartes*, p.22.

69 Hattingh, *Eerste vryswartes*, p.28.

70 Hattingh, *Eerste vryswartes*, p.29.

71 For a brief biography, see Böeseken, *Slaves and free blacks*, pp.91–92.

72 Hattingh, 'Kaapse notariële stukke' I, 53.

73 Hattingh, 'Kaapse notariële stukke' I, 55.

74 Böeseken, *Slaves and free blacks*, pp.91–92.

75 Cf. WNT VII, column 149,

76 Hattingh, 'Kaapse notariële stukke' I, 57.

77 CAD, ZK 8/1/10 p.66.

78 Böeseken, *Slaves and free blacks*, p.91. See also *ibid.*, p.94.

79 Hattingh, 'Kaapse notariële stukke' II, 34.

80 Hattingh, 'Kaapse notariële stukke' II, 37.

81 Böeseken, *Slaves and free blacks*, p.138.

82 Böeseken, *Slaves and free blacks*, p.92.

83 Böeseken, *Slaves and free blacks*, p.92.

84 Böeseken, *Slaves and free blacks*, p.138; as corrected in Hattingh, 'Addendum', pp.18–19.

85 Hattingh, 'Addendum', p.19.

8. Uncertain freedom: the first free blacks – *pp.305-351*

86   Biewenga, *Kaap de Goede Hoop*, p.184.

87   Hattingh, 'Kaapse notariële stukke' II, 36.

88   Böeseken, *Slaves and free blacks*, p.173.

89   Böeseken, *Slaves and free blacks*, p.185.

90   Hattingh, 'Grondbesit', p.47.

91   Hattingh, 'Slawevrystellings', p.27 n10.

92   C.C. de Villiers, *Genealogies of old South African families*; ed. C. Pama (Cape Town: A.A. Balkema, 1981), p.738; Heese/Lombard 8, 357.

93   Hattingh, 'Grondbesit', p.45 (table).

94   Hattingh, 'Grondbesit', p.47 (table).

95   See p.257 above.

96   *Resolusies* 3, 136.

97   Franken, 'Vertolking', p.45.

98   *Letters received 1695*, p.7; *Letters despatched 1696*, p.33.

99   CAD, MOOC 8/2.1.

100 Hattingh, *Eerste vryswartes*, p.49.

101 Franken, 'Vertolking', pp.45–46.

102 Hattingh, *Eerste vryswartes*, pp.31–40. See also Kolb, *Beschryving* I, 106a–b.

103 Böeseken, *Slaves and free blacks*, pp.85, 154. The dates given here do not seem to have been interpreted correctly.

104 De Wet, *Vryliede*, p.213.

105 De Wet, *Vryliede*, p.213.

106 Hattingh, 'Grondbesit', p.45.

107 Böeseken, *Slaves and free blacks*, p.162.

108 De Wet, *Vryliede*, p.216.

109 *Letters received 1695*, p.142.

110 Böeseken, *Slaves and free blacks*, p.185.

111 For Claas Gerritsz and his wife, see Böeseken, *Slaves and free blacks*, p.96; Malan, 'Chattels or colonists?', pp.54–55, 68–69.

112 De Wet, *Vryliede*, p.214.

113 De Wet, *Vryliede*, p.212 & n47.

114 Böeseken, *Slaves and free blacks*, p.145.

115 CAD, MOOC 8/1.28.

116 Malan, 'Chattels or colonists?', p.54.

117 De Wet, *Vryliede*, p.59.

118 Malan, 'Chattels or colonists?', p.55.

119 Generale opneming.

120 Böeseken, *Slaves and free blacks*, p.174.

121 Böeseken, *Slaves and free blacks*, p.190.

122 *Letters received 1695*, p.361.

123 *Letters received 1695*, p.456. See also *Letters despatched 1696*, p.271, 335.

124 *Resolusies* 3, 153.

125 CAD, MOOC 8/1.28; rendered thus in the transcription.

126 *Letters despatched 1696*, p.272.

127 *Letters received 1695*, p.415.

128 *Defence*, p.180.

129 *Journal 1699*, p.159.

130 *Letters received 1695*, p.319.

131 *Letters despatched 1696*, p.231.

132 *Letters received 1695*, p.342.

133 *Letters despatched 1696*, p.277.

134 In Valentyn, *Description* II, 243.

135 Cf. Generale opneming.

136 *Memoriën*, p.207. Cf. Van Reede, *Journaal*, p.208.

137 *Letters despatched* 1696, p.253.

138 CAD, MOOC 8/4.79.

139 Resolutions of the Political Council (16.9.1749); available on Internet at <http://www.tanap.net>.

140 See DSAB I, 893–894.

141 Cf. *Kaapse plakkaatboek* I, 184; *Resolusies* 3, 40.

142 *Resolusies* 3, 153.

143 Sleigh, *Buiteposte*, p.257.

144 Sleigh, *Buiteposte*, p.257.

145 *Resolusies* 3, 323.

146 *Kaapse plakkaatboek* I, 184; *Resolusies* 3, 40.

147 See pp.79–80 above.

148 *Resolusies* 3, 322–323.

149 *Memoriën*, p.158.

150 *Memoriën*, p.206.

151 *Memoriën*, p.206.

152 De Wet, Vryliede, p.206. Cf. Böeseken, *Slaves and free blacks*, p.81.

153 *Resolusies* 3, 127–128 *passim*.

154 See p.78 above.

155 Wagenaer, *Dagregister*, p.273.

156 See for them also Schoeman, *Wêreld*, pp.123–124, 560–561.

157 Böeseken, *Slaves and free blacks*, p.155.

158 For Van Gijselen, see Schoeman, *Kinders*, pp.437–450, 564 (sources).

159 See Heese/Lombard 7, 40; and the biographical note on Sara in *Capensis* 4/99, p.35 n9.

160 *Memoriën*, p.217.

161 *Memoriën*, p.217.

162 *Resolusies* 4, 170.

163 *Resolutions* 4, 337.

164 Sleigh, *Buiteposte*, p.159.

165 Hattingh, *Eerste vryswartes*, p.10.

166 Hattingh, *Eerste vryswartes*, p.31.

167 Hattingh, *Eerste vryswartes*, p.11.

168 Hattingh, 'Grondbesit', p.41.

169 *Resolusies* 3, 320.

170 See Hattingh, *Eerste vryswartes*.

171 Hattingh, *Eerste vryswartes*, p.48.

172 Böeseken, *Slaves and free blacks*, pp.137.

173 Böeseken, *Slaves and free blacks*, p.150.

174 Böeseken, *Slaves and free blacks*, p.152.

175 Böeseken, *Slaves and free blacks*, p.153.

176 Böeseken, *Slaves and free blacks*, p.161.

177 Böeseken, *Slaves and free blacks*, p.185.

178 *Contra-deductie*, pp.195–196.

179 Böeseken, *Simon van der Stel*, p.219.

180 CAD, MOOC 8/3.17. The death notice has been misfiled in the probate inventory of P.A. van Schagerbergh; CAD, MOOC 8/3.9.

181 Böeseken, *Simon van der Stel*, p.235.

182 See Böeseken, *Slaves and free blacks*, pp.59–60; Böeseken, *Simon van der Stel*, p.220.

183 Heese, *Groep*, p.18.

8. Uncertain freedom: the first free blacks – *pp.305-351*

184 Hattingh, 'Slawevrystellings', pp.29, 37 (statistical table).

185 Böeseken, *Slaves and free blacks*, p.72; Hattingh, *Eerste vryswartes*, p.65.

186 Böeseken, *Slaves and free blacks*, pp.159–160.

187 Fox, 'For good and sufficient reasons', p.260.

188 *Resolusies* 4, 157.

189 Böeseken, *Slaves and free blacks*, p.157. See also the two slaves left at the Cape 'to be set free in 1685', *ibid.*, p.137 (30.5.1679).

190 See p.102 above.

191 *Kaapse plakkaatboek* II, 94.

192 Böeseken, *Slaves and free blacks*, p.138 *passim*.

193 Böeseken, *Slaves and free blacks*, p.162.

194 Böeseken, *Slaves and free blacks*, 142.

195 Böeseken, *Slaves and free blacks*, p.153 (1688).

196 Böeseken, *Slaves and free blacks*, p.154 (1688).

197 Niemeijer, Calvinisme, p.52.

198 CAD, MOOC 8/1.20.

199 CAD, MOOC 8/2.50.

200 CAD, MOOC 8/2.68.

201 *Letters despatched 1696*, p.327.

202 'Slaeven ofte lyffeigenen', p.575.

203 Hattingh, 'Slawevrystellings', p.26.

204 *Collectanea*, pp.46–47. An abbreviated version appears in Valentyn, *Description* II, 235. This proviso is not to be found in the original version of the Statutes of Batavia; cf. 'Slaeven offte lyfeygenen'.

205 Hattingh, 'Slawevrystellings', p.27/

206 Hattingh, 'Slawevrystellings', pp.24–25.

207 Hattingh, 'Slawevrystellings', p.25.

208 *Boedelinventarisse* III, 652–654 *passim*. For a further incidental reference to Silvia van Madagascar, see *Trials of slavery*, p.200.

209 Hattingh, 'Slawevrystellings', p.25.

210 Hattingh, 'Slawevrystellings', p.28

211 Hattingh, 'Slawevrystellings', pp.29, 37 (statistical table).

212 Hattingh, 'Slawevrystellings', pp.28–29.

213 Elphick & Shell, 'Intergroup relations', p.206.

214 Elphick & Shell, 'Intergroup relations', p.211.

215 Elphick & Shell, 'Intergroup relations', p.211.

216 Elphick & Shell, 'Intergroup relations', p.210 (table).

217 Elphick & Shell, 'Intergroup relations', p.206.

218 Elphick & Shell, 'Intergroup relations', pp.212–213.

219 Hattingh, 'Slawevrystellings', p.36.

220 See Böeseken, *Slaves and free blacks*, pp.77–97; Cairns, 'Free black landowners'; De Wet, *Vryliede*, pp.204–216; Elphick & Shell, 'Intergroup relations', pp.214–224; Hattingh, *Eerste vryswartes*; Hattingh, 'Grondbesit'; Heese, *Groep sonder grense*; Malan, 'Chattels or colonists?'.

221 De Wet, *Vryliede*, p.206 (table).

222 De Wet, *Vryliede*, p.209 (table).

223 Elphick & Shell, 'Intergroup relations', p.219.

224 De Wet, *Vryliede*, p.209 (table).

225 De Wet, *Vryliede*, p.206. See also the figures in Elphick & Shell, 'Intergroup relations', p.218 (tables).

226 De Wet, *Vryliede*, p.211.

227 Hattingh, 'Kaapse notariële stukke' I, 60.

228 Hattingh, 'Kaapse notariële stukke' II, 33.

229 Böeseken, *Slaves and free blacks*, p.158.

230 Böeseken, *Slaves and free blacks*, p.161.

231 Böeseken, *Slaves and free blacks*, p.166.

232 Böeseken, *Slaves and free blacks*, p.189.

233 Böeseken, *Simon van der Stel*, p.220.

234 Böeseken, *Slaves and free blacks*, p.165.

235 Hattingh, *Eerste vryswartes*, p.49.

236 See pp.385–386 above.

237 Hattingh, 'Slawevrystellings', pp.26–27.

238 Böeseken, 'Verhouding', p.15.

239 De Wet, *Vryliede*, p.208.

240 Hattingh, 'Slawevrystellings', p.32.

241 *Defence*, p.180.

242 Elphick & Shell, 'Intergroup relations', p.223.

243 *Defence*, p.180. Cf. *Korte deductie*, p.158.

244 Mentzel, *Description* 2, 88–89.

245 CAD, MOOC 8/1.26.

246 *Boedelinventarisse* I, 24 (Votie), 26 (Lekkerwijn).

247 CAD, MOOC 8/2.101. But see also CAD, MOOC 8/3.34 (1715).

248 Elphick & Shell, 'Intergroup relations', p.224. The original reads 'pretty retailing'.

249 See Shell:Rangton van Bali.

250 Hattingh, *Eerste vryswartes*, p.72.

251 Cairns, 'Freeblack landowners'. See also Cairns, 'Armosyn Claasz', pp.93–97.

252 Cairns, 'Armosyn Claasz', p.97.

253 Shell, *Children of bondage*, p.119.

254 Elphick & Shell, 'Intergroup relationships', p.221.

255 Hattingh, *Eerste vryswartes*, pp.52–53, & *passim*.

256 For litigiousness, see Hattingh, *Eerste vryswartes*, pp.52–53. For free blacks supported by the church, see Schoeman, *Armosyn: wêreld*, pp.666–668 (with sources).

257 *De la Fontaine report.*

258 Guelke, 'Anatomy', p.464 (table), 470.

259 Guelke, 'Anatomy', p.472.

260 e.g. Heese/Lombard; Hoge, *Personalia*; both *passim*. See also Heese, *Herkoms*.

261 Heese, *Groep*, p.6.

262 Heese, *Groep*, p.7.

263 Heese, *Groep*, p.8. Cf. *ibid.*, p.33.

264 See pp.353–357 above.

265 For Slotsboo, see DSAB II, 684–685.

266 Heese/Lombard 3, 111.

267 Hattingh, *Eerste vryswartes*, p.74.

268 See p.243 above.

269 Heese/Lombard 2, 174; Hoge, *Personalia*, p.86.

270 See Heese/Lombard 3, 384; Hoge, *Personalia*, p.161.

271 Guelke & Shell, 'Early colonial landed gentry', p.277.

272 Information on the liquor leases obtained from Gerald Groenewald's 'Database of alcohol pachters at the Cape of Good Hope, 1680–1795'; printout (2003).

273 For Eksteen, see Guelke & Shell, 'Early colonial landed gentry', pp.277–278; Schoeman, *Wêreld*, p.688 (with sources).

274 *Resolusies* 6, 79; Upham, 'Armosyn revisited', p.26.

275 CAD, MOOC 8/3.93.

276 *Resolusies* 3, 137–138.

277 Malan, 'Chattels or colonists', p.64. See also *ibid.*, pp.63–64, 69–70.

278 CAD, MOOC 8/2.19.

8. Uncertain freedom: the first free blacks – *pp.305-351*

279 Böeseken, *Slaves and free blacks*, p.32.

280 See further Chapter 8 above.

281 Elphick & Shell, 'Intergroup relations', p.221.

282 Shell, *Children of bondage*, p.119.

283 Böeseken, *Slaves and free blacks*, p.190.

284 Hattingh, 'Slawevrystellings', p.30.

285 Shell, *Children of bondage*, p.120. Jan Holsmit was the name of a successful freeburgher who in 1684 married the widow of the pioneer W.C. Mostaert and in 1698 returned to Europe.

286 Shell, *Children of bondage*, p.120 n143.

287 Quoted in Cairns, 'Armosyn Claasz', p.93 (Dutch text).

288 See p.307 above.

289 Elphick & Shell, 'Intergroup relations', pp.212, 213 (fig.).

290 Elphick & Shell, 'Intergroup relations', p.206.

291 Hattingh, 'Slawevrystellings', p.27

292 Böeseken, *Slaves and free blacks*, p.92; De Wet, *Vryliede*, p.213.

293 De Wet, *Vryliede*, p.215.

294 Heese, *Groep*, p.28; with reference to Böeseken, *Slaves and free blacks*, p.97.

295 Heese, *Reg en onreg*, p.36.

296 De Wet, *Vryliede*, pp.212–213,

297 Hattingh, *Eerste vryswartes*, p.22.

298 Original documents quoted in Upham, 'Armosyn revisited', p.25.

399 Hattingh, *Eerste vryswartes*, p.48. See also *ibid.*, pp.73, 74.

300 Hattingh, *Eerste vryswartes*, p.74.

301 Hattingh, *Eerste vryswartes*, pp.48, 74.

302 Hattingh, *Eerste vryswartes*, p.61.

303 Hattingh, *Eerste vryswartes*, p.70. Cf. Elphick & Shell, 'Intergroup relations', p.224.

304 See, for a somewhat later period, Maria M. Marais, *Armesorg aan die Kaap onder die Kompanjie, 1652–1795* (Archives Year Book, 1943).

305 Hattingh, *Eerste vryswartes*, p.53,

306 Hattingh, *Eerste vryswartes*, p.33.

307 Hattingh, *Eerste vryswartes*, p.70.

308 Hattingh, *Eerste vryswartes*, p.74.

309 Böeseken, *Slaves and free blacks*, p.138.

310 De Wet, *Vryliede*, p.204.

8. Uncertain freedom: the first free blacks – *pp.305-351*

311 Heese, *Groep*, p.28.

312 Cairns, 'Freeblack landowners', p.24.

313 De Wet, *Vryliede*, p.204.

314 Hattingh, 'Eerste vryswartes', p.44.

315 Heese, *Groep sonder grense*, p.22.

316 Cf. Böeseken, *Slaves and free blacks*, p.77; De Wet, *Vryliede*, p.204.

317 Hattingh, *Eerste vryswartes*, p.20.

318 Hattingh, 'Grondbesit', p.41.

9. Three lives – *pp.352-369*

1 For Angela, see Böeseken, *Slaves and free blacks*, pp.79–81; Malan, 'Chattels or colonists?', pp.64–65, 70; Schoeman, *Kinders*, pp.176–187, 554 (sources); Upham, 'Mooij Ansela'.

2 *Letters despatched 1652* III, 290.

3 Hattingh, 'Kaapse notariële stukke' I, 56.

4 See pp.306–307 above.

5 Hattingh, 'Kaapse notariële stukke' I, 60.

6 Monsterrolle.

7 Hattingh, 'Kaapse notariële stukke' I, 61. See further Hattingh, 'Grondbesit', p.43.

8 Hattingh, 'Kaapse notariële stukke' I, 62.

9 Hattingh, 'Grondbesit', p.43.

10 Böeseken, *Slaves and free blacks*, p.80 *passim*.

11 For Basson, see Böeseken, *Slaves and free blacks*, p.139; De Wet, *Vryliede, passim*.

12 Heese/Lombard 1, 160–164 *passim*.

13 For a reproduction, see Schoeman, *Armosyn: wêreld*, illus. no.32.

14 Quoted in A.V. van Stekelenburg, 'Een intellectueel in de vroege Kaapkolonie', *Tydskrif vir Nederlands & Afrikaans* 8 (2001), 21, 33 n22. The portrait in question is reproduced in *The journals of Bergh and Schrijver*; ed. E.E. Mossop (Cape Town: Van Riebeeck Society, 1931), frontispiece.

15 For Bergh and his family, see DSAB I; Heese/Lombard 1, 232–235.

16 Boedelinventarisse I, 31.

17 Hattingh, 'Addendum', p.17.

18 Böeseken, *Slaves and free blacks*, pp.185, 193; Malan, 'Chattels or colonists?', p.65.

9. Three lives – *pp.352-369*

19 Böeseken, *Slaves and free blacks*, p.80.

20 For Angela's children, see Heese, 'Identiteitsprobleme', p.30.

21 *Briewe van Johanna Maria van Riebeeck*, p.104. Bergh's name was omitted in this published version.

22 CAD, MOOC 8/4.15. I must thank Dr Antonia Malan for a transcription of this document.

23 Böeseken, *Slaves and free blacks*, p.81.

24 CAD, MOOC 8/5.118. See further Malan, 'Chattels or colonists?', p.65; Schoeman, *Armosyn: wêreld*, pp.645–646.

25 For Evert, see Hattingh, *Eerste vryswartes*, pp.41–43; Hattingh, 'Grondbesit', pp.39–41; Schoeman, *Kinders*, pp.393–402, 562 (sources).

26 *Letters despatched 1652* III, 62.

27 Hattingh, 'Kaapse notariële stukke' I, 54.

28 Van Riebeeck, *Journal* III, 63.

29 Van Riebeeck, *Journal* III, 216.

30 Van Riebeeck, *Journal* II, 285, 291, 292.

31 Hattingh, 'Kaapse notariële stukke' I, 62.

32 Hattingh, 'Grondbesit', p.39.

33 Hattingh, *Eerste vryswartes*, p.41.

34 *Briewe van Johanna Maria van Riebeeck*, p.88.

35 Hattingh, 'Kaapse notariële stukke' I, 55.

36 Hattingh, 'Kaapse notariële stukke' II, 21.

37 Hattingh, 'Kaapse notariële stukke' II, 26.

38 Hattingh, 'Grondbesit', pp.40, 41.

39 Hattingh, 'Kaapse notariële stukke' II, 27.

40 Hattingh, 'Grondbesit', p.39.

41 Hattingh, *Eerste vryswartes*, p.41.

42 See Hattingh, *Eerste vryswartes*, pp.16, 26, 34 (tables).

43 *Boedelinventarisse* I, 15.

44 See Hattingh, *Eerste vryswartes*, op.41–43.

45 See *Schoeman, Armosyn: wêreld*, pp.651–654.

46 De Wet, *Vryliede*, p.213.

47 Schoeman, *Armosyn: wêreld*, p.652.

48 De Wet, *Vryliede*, pp.124, 176.

49 Heese, *Groep*, p.7,

50 Hattingh, 'Grondbesit', p.41.

51 See Heese/Lombard 1, 640 ('Colyn'); *ibid.* 2, 419 ('Van Hoff').

52 Böeseken, *Slaves and free blacks*, p.184.

53 Böeseken, *Slaves and free blacks*, p.189.

54 Heese, *Groep*, pp.7–8.

55 *Briewe van Johanna Maria van Riebeeck*, p.88.

56 Samuel Briercliff, letter to 'My Lord' (17.5.1713); typescript copy, National Library, Cape Town, MSB 1006,1(4).

57 *De la Fontaine report*.

58 See Cairns, 'Armosyn Claasz'; Heese, *Groep*, pp.13–14; Schoeman, *Armosyn: wêreld*, *passim*; Upham, 'Armosyn revisited'; Van Rensburg, 'Jigsaw puzzle'.

59 Quoted in Upham, 'Armosyn revisited', pp.26, 27.

60 See pp.69–70 above.

61 Hattingh, 'Kaapse notariële stukke' II, 18. For Lobbitje, see also *ibid.*, 17.

62 Schoeman, *Armosyn: wêreld*, pp.124–128.

63 Van Rensburg, 'Jigsaw puzzle'. See also Upham, 'Armosyn revisited', pp.30–31.

64 Van Rensburg, 'Jigsaw puzzle', referring to Cairns, 'Armosyn Claasz', p.97 (closing sentence).

65 Cairns, 'Armosyn Claasz', p.87.

66 Cairns, 'Armosyn Claasz', p.88–97 *passim*; Heese, *Groep*, p.13; Heese/Lombard 1, 82.

67 Cairns, 'Armosyn Claasz', p.94.

68 Generale opneming 1693; Heese, *Groep*, p.13.

69 Upham, 'Armosyn revisited', p.24 n26.

70 Hoge, *Personalia*, p.483.

71 Cairns, 'Armosyn Claasz', p.86.

72 Cairns, 'Armosyn Claasz', p.84.

73 For the office of *matres*, see p.184 above.

74 See p.187 above.

75 Upham, 'Armosyn revisited', p.27 (reproduction).

76 *Paarl Valley, 1687–1987*; ed. A.G. Oberholster (Pretoria: HSRC, 1987), p.20.

77 Upham, 'Armosyn revisited', p.25. Cf. Hattingh, 'Grondbesit', pp.44, 45.

78 Upham, 'Armosyn revisited', p.25.

79 Upham, 'Armosyn revisited', p.26.

80 Upham, 'Armosyn revisited', p.26.

81 Cairns, 'Armosyn Claasz', p.86.

82 *Resolusies* 4, 203.

83 Cairns, 'Armosyn Claasz', p.86; Hattingh, 'Grondbesit', pp.35 (plan), 45.

84 For Groot Armosyn, see p.325 above; and Heese/Lombard 2, 375–376 (Frisnet).

85 'Johannes Smiesing, schrif en leer meester in dienst der E. Oostindische Comp' (1727–32); MS, CAD, A1414(56)(d). See also Schoeman, *Armosyn: wêreld*, pp.658–659.

86 Cairns, 'Armosyn Claasz', pp.88–89 *passim*. For the probate inventory of her estate, see CAD, MOOC8/3.96.

87 Cairns, 'Armosyn Claasz', pp.89–90; Heese, *Groep*, 13–14. See also Heese, *Groep*, p.13.

88 Heese/Lombard 1, 587; Hoge, *Personalia*, p.61.

89 See Upham, 'Armosyn revisited', pp.28–29; and p.179 above.

90 *Resolusies* 6, 211.

91 Cairns, 'Armosyn Claasz', pp.92–97; Cairns, 'Freeblack landowners', pp.27–30; Heese, *Groep*, p.13; Heese/Lombard 4, 100.

92 Cairns, 'Armosyn Claasz', p.97; Heese, *Groep*, p.14; Heese/Lombard 1, 641; Hoge, *Personalia*, p.62.

93 Cairns, 'Armosyn Claasz', p.86' Hattingh, 'Grondbesit', p.45.

94 *De la Fontaine report*.

95 Cairns, 'Armosyn Claasz', pp.86–87.

96 CAD, CJ 2604 no.25.

97 CAD, MOOC 14/5 no.76. My attention was drawn to them by Loretha du Plessis, at that time (2002) a member of the Archives staff.

98 Schoeman, *Armosyn: wêreld*, p.663.

Coda: the turning point – *pp.371-388*

1 Generale opneming.

2 For church services on Boxing Day, see *Journal 1671*, pp.175 (26.12.1673), 307 (26, 27.12.1676).

3 Wayne Dooling, 'The Castle; its place in the history of Cape Town in the VOC period', *Studies in the History of Cape Town* 7 (1994), p.23.

4 See DSAB II, 726–727.

5 Hoge, *Personalia*, p.204.

6 *Resolusies* 3, 188.

7 Sleigh, *Buiteposte*, p.179.

8 *Bouwstoffen* I, 69.

9 Hattingh, *Reg en onreg*, p.198.

10 See for him CAD, MOOC 8/4.23; *Resolusies* 5, 215 n243.

11 *Resolusies* 5, 384.

12 Upham, 'Armosyn revisited', p.25 n33.

13 For slaves as members of the congregation, see Catrina van de Caab (p.324 above); and a passing reference in Biewenga, *Kaap de Goede Hoop*, p.183.

14 For various accounts, mostly from the freeburghers' point of view, see Leo Fouché in Tas, *Diary*, pp.206–391 (Dutch and English); Böeseken, *Simon van der Stel*, pp.170–205; A.J. Böeseken in DSAB II, 780–783 ('Van der Stel, Wilhem Adriaen'); Theal, *History* 1, 395–415. For Van der Stel's attempted justification, see *Defence*. See also the brief but more balanced account by Gerrit Schutte in *Shaping*, pp.303–307.

15 See Hattingh, 'Klagte'.

16 For the text of this document, see *Contra-deductie*, pp.4–14; *Defence*, pp.52–65 (English translation).

17 *Contra-deductie*, 'Voorreden' p.[8].

18 See Franken, *Hugenote*, pp.115–122

19 *Korte deductie*, pp.56–58; *Defence*, pp.68–72 (English translation). The signatures referred to occur on pp.57 & 71 respectively.

20 *Korte deductie*, p.158; *Defence*, pp.180–181 (English translation).

21 De Wet, *Vryliede*, p.208.

22 *Defence*, pp.180–181 (emended).

23 Franken, *Hugenote*, p.119.

24 See *Defence*.

25 See *Contra-deductie*.

26 His authorship is suggested in Franken, *Hugenote*, p.114. For De Grevenbroeck, see DSAB III, 200–201, and the article listed on p.452 n14.

27 Böeseken, *Simon van der Stel*, p.182.

28 Heese, *Groep*, p.28.

29 Tas, *Diary*, p.197 (amended) ('*tot Zwarten in cluijs*').

30 Tas, *Diary*, p.199.

31 *Contra-deductie*, 'Voorreden' p.[8].

32 *Contra-deductie*, pp.39, 44.

33 *Contra-deductie*, pp.27, 39, 44, 48, 49, 55–56. See further Franken, 'Van der Heiden en die swart slaaf'.

34 *Contra-deductie*, pp.55–56 & 49 respectively.

35 *Contra-deductie*, p.44.

36 *Contra-deductie*, pp.189, 256.

37 Kolb, *Beschryving* II, 181a–b.

38 *Contra-deductie*, p.174.

39 *Kaapse plakkaatboek* II, 41 (para.7).

40 *Contra-deductie*, p.4. An English translation of the entire document is given in *Defence*, pp.52–59.

41 Cf. *Journal 1699*, pp.121, 122. I am grateful to René Janssen of the Nationaal Archief, The Hague, for the information regarding the document concerned, and to Ena Jansen, Amsterdam, for her help.

42 *Castiço* was used by the Portuguese for a child of Europeans born in the East, but the Dutch appear to have used *kasties* in the sense of a 'quarter-breed'.—Dr Böeseken in quoting this passage omits the phrase '*dat swart gebroeijdsel*'; Böeseken, *Simon van der Stel*, p.183. Heese quotes more fully, with a number of apparent errors of transcription, and points out that the phrase was not necessarily pejorative at the time, though given the emotional nature of the document as a whole, this seems to be the more likely interpretation; cf. Heese, *Groep*, p.28.

43 Quoted (in Dutch) in Heese, *Groep*, p.28. See also Böeseken, Simon van der Stel, p.183. The original document is in the Nationaal Archief, The Hague, VOC 4057 (1.04.02) pp.1030–1050.

44 Genesis 9:25.

45 Heese, *Groep*. p.28.

46 *A. Bógaerts historische reizen door d'oostersche deelen van Asia* (Amsterdam: Nicolaas ten Hoorn, 1711), pp.493–495.

47 See p.339 above.

48 Franken, *Hugenote*, pp.143–144; Hattingh, *Eerste vryswartes*, p.49.

49 Cf. WNT III(1), columns 1148–1151 ('*brassen*'); also *ibid.*, column 1154 ('*brasser*').

50 See Biewenga, *Kaap de Goede Hoop*, p.270; Schoeman, *Kinders*, pp.527–534, 568 (sources); Schoeman, *Armosyn: wêreld*, pp.495–500.

51 *Journal 1699*, p.120. See also Franken, *Taalhistoriese bydraes*, pp.31, 39–40; Schoeman, *Armosyn: wêreld*, p.337.

52 Hattingh, *Eerste vryswartes*, p.67; with reference to the conclusions in *Shaping* (1st ed., 1979), pp. 150 & 154.

Sources

Armstrong, James C.: 'A Japanese slave and free burgher at the Cape' [Anthonij de Later van Japan]. Printout (1999).

——: 'Madagascar and the slave trade in the seventeenth century', *Omaly sy Anio* (Antananarivo) 17–20 (1983–84), pp.211–233.

——: 'Malagsy slave names in the seventeenth century', *Omaly sy Anio* (Antananarivo) 17–20 (1983–84), pp.43–59.

——, & Nigel A. Worden: 'The slaves, 1652–1832', in *The shaping of South African society* (see below), pp.108–183.

Arasaratnam, S.: 'Slave trade in the Indian Ocean in the seventeenth century', in *Mariners, merchants and oceans*; ed. K.S. Mathew (New Delhi: Manohar, 1995), pp.195–208.

Barendse, R.J.: 'Slaving on the Malagasy coast, 1640–1700', in *Cultures of Madagascar*; ed. Sandra Evers & Marc Spindler (Leiden: International Institute for Asian Studies, 1995), pp.137–155. Also in R.J. Barendse, *The Arabian seas; the Indian Ocean world of the seventeenth century* (Armonk, NY: M.E. Sharpe, 2002), pp.259–274.

Barnard, Anne: *The Cape diaries of Lady Anne Barnard, 1799–1800*; ed. Margaret Lenta & Basil le Cordeur (Cape Town: Van Riebeeck Society, 1998–1999).

——: *The Cape journals of Lady Anne Barnard, 1797–1798*; ed. A.M. Lewin Robinson, with Margaret Lenta & Dorothy Driver (Cape Town: Van Riebeeck Society, 1994).

Biewenga, Arend Willem: *De Kaap de Goede Hoop; een Nederlandse vestigingskolonie, 1680–1730* (Amsterdam: Bert Bakker, 1999). Index of personal names available on the Internet at <http://www.gendata.co.za>.

Blommaert, W.: *Het invoeren van de slavernij aan de Kaap* (Archives Yearbook 1938, I).

Boedelinventarisse (Die) van erflaters in die distrik Stellenbosch, 1679–1806; transcribed by Annemarie Krzesinski-de Widt (Stellenbosch: Stellenbosch Museum, 2002). *See also the note under* Inventories of deceased persons *below.*

Böeseken, A.J.: *Jan van Riebeeck en sy gesin* (Kaapstad: Tafelberg, 1974).

——: *Nederlandsche commissarissen aan de Kaap, 1657–1700* ('s-Gravenhage: Martinus Nijhoff, 1938).

——: *Simon van der Stel en sy kinders* (Kaapstad: Nasou, 1964).

——: *Slaves and free blacks at the Cape*, 1658–1700 (Cape Town: Tafelberg, 1977; with corrections by J.L. Hattingh in *Kronos* 9 (1984). *Index available on the Internet at* <http://www.gendata.co.za>.

——: 'Die verhouding tussen blank en nie-blank in Suid-Afrika aan die hand van die vroegste dokumente', *South African Historical Journal* 2 (Nov.1970), pp.3–18.

Boshoff, S.P.E., & G.S. Nienaber: *Afrikaanse etimologieë* ([Pretoria]: Suid-Afrikaanse Akademie vir Wetenskap en Kuns, 1967).

Botha, C. Graham: 'Slavery'; 'Legal administration at the Cape, 1652–1828', Chapter 30. Typescript; National Library, Cape Town; pp.87–95.

Bouwstoffen voor de geschiedenis der Nederduitsch-Gereformeerde Kerken in Zuid-Afrika; ed. C. Spoelstra (Amsterdam: H.A.U.M., 1906–07).

Bradlow, Frank R.: 'The origins of the early Cape Muslims', in Frank R. Bradlow & Margaret Cairns, *The early Cape Muslims; a study of their mosques, genealogy and origins* (Cape Town: A.A. Balkema, 1978), pp.80–132.

Briewe van Johanna Maria van Riebeeck, en ander Riebeeckiana; ed. D.B. Bosman (Amsterdam: D.B. Bosman, 1952).

CAD—Cape Town Archives Depository. *See also the note under* MOOC *below.*

Cairns, Margaret: 'Armosyn Claasz of the Cape and her family, 1661–1783', *Familia* XVI,4 (1979), pp.84–99.

——: 'Slave transfers, 1658–1795; a preliminary survey', *Kronos* 6 (1983), pp.21–32

Cook, Mary A.: 'Memorandum on the Old Supreme Court Building'. Duplicated (1953?); National Library, Cape Town, AF 913 Cap.

Contra-deductie, ofte Grondige demonstratie van de valsheit der uitgegevene Deductie, by den Ed. Heer Willem Adriaan van der Stel… (Amsterdam: Nicolaas ten Hoorn, 1712).

de Haan, F., *see* Oud Batavia

de Klerk, E.: 'Die verhaal van Susanna Bibouw', *Familia* XXIII,4 (1986), pp.70–72.

de Kock, Victor: *Those in bondage; an account of the life of the slaves at the Cape in the days of the Dutch East India Company* (Cape Town: Howard B. Timmins, 1950).

De la Fontaine Report (The); ed. Leonard Guelke, Robert Shell & Anthony Whyte (New Haven: Opgaaf Project, 1990).

de Villiers, C.C.: *Genealogies of old South African families*; ed. C. Pama (Cape Town: A.A. Balkema, 1981).

de Wet , C.G.: *Die vryliede en vryswartes in die Kaapse nedersetting, 1657–1707* (Cape Town: Historical Publications Society, 1981).

Defence (The) of W.A. van der Stel; ed. H.C.V. Leibbrandt (Cape Town: W.A. Richards, 1897). Translation of van der Stel's *Korte deductie.*

Denyssen, D.: 'Statement of the laws of the Colony of the Cape of Good Hope regarding slavery' (16.3.1813), in *Records of the Cape Colony* IX (1901), pp.146–161.

DSAB—*Dictionary of South African biography*; ed. W.J. de Kock a.o. (1968–87).

Elphick, Richard, & Robert Shell: 'Intergroup relations: Khoikhoi, settlers, slaves and free blacks, 1652–1795', in *Shaping (The) of South African society* (see below), pp.108–183.

Fox, J.: '"For good and sufficient reasons"; an examination of early Dutch East India Company ordinances on slaves and slavery', in *Slavery, bondage and dependency in Southeast Asia*; ed. Anthony Reid (St. Lucia: Univ. of Queensland pr., 1983), pp.246–262.

Franken, J.L.M.: *Die Hugenote aan die Kaap* (Archives Year Book, 1978).

——: 'Die slawe van Jan van Riebeeck', in his *Taalhistoriese bydraes* (see below), pp.31–33.

——: *Taalhistoriese bydraes* (Amsterdam: A.A. Balkema, 1953).

——: 'Van der Heiden en die swart slaaf' I, in his *Taalhistoriese bydraes* (see above), pp.87–97.

——: 'Vertolking aan die Kaap in Maleis en Portugees', in his *Taalhistoriese bydraes* (see above), pp.41–79.

Generale opneming 1693—'Generale opneming en monster rolle van s'Comp. soo slaven als bandieten' (1.1.1693); Nationaal Archief, The Hague, VOC 4030 pp.359–368. Transcription by H.F. Heese (photocopy).

Geyser, O.: *The history of the old Supreme Court building*; [tr. Desmond Windell] (Johannesburg: Africana pr., 1982).

Godée Molsbergen, E.C.: *De stichter van Hollands Zuid-Afrika; Jan van Riebeeck, 1618–1677* (Amsterdam: S.L. van Looy, 1912).

Groenewald, Gerald: 'Slawe, Khoekhoen en Nederlandse pidgins aan die Kaap, ca. 1590–1720; 'n kritiese ondersoek na die sosiohistoriese grondslae van die Konvergensieteorie oor die ontstaan van Afrikaans'. Thesis, Cape Town (2002).

Guelke, Leonard: 'The anatomy of a colonial settler population: Cape Colony, 1657–1750', *International Journal of African Historical Studies*, 21,3 (1988), pp.453–473.

——, & Robert Shell: 'An early colonial landed gentry; land and wealth in the Cape Colony, 1682–1731', *Journal of Historical Geography* 9,3 (1983), pp.265–286.

Hattingh, J.L. 'Beleid en praktyk; die doop van slawekinders en die sluit van gemengde verhoudings aan die Kaap voor 1720', *Kronos* 5 (1982), pp.25–42.

——: 'Die blanke nageslag van Louis van Bengale en Lijsbeth van die Kaap', *Kronos* 3 (1980), pp.5–15.

——: *Die eerste vryswartes van Stellenbosch, 1679–1720* (Bellville: Institute for Historical Research, UWC, 1981).

——: 'Grondbesit in die Tafelvallei; deel 1, Die eksperiment: vryswartes as grond-eienaars, 1652–1719'. *Kronos* 10 (1985), pp.32–48.

——: 'Kaapse notariële stukke waarin slawe van vryburgers en amptenare vermeld word', *Kronos* 14 (1988), pp.43–65; *ibid.* 15 (1989), pp.3–48. Index available on the Internet at <http://www. gen data . co. za>.

——: 'Die klagte oor Goewerneur W.A. van der Stel se slawebesit; 'n beoordeling met behulp van kwantitatiewe data', *Kronos* 7 (1983), pp.13–41.

——: 'Naamgewing aan slawe, vryswartes en ander gekleurdes', *Kronos* 6 (1983), pp.5–20.

——: ''n Ontleding van sekere aspekte van slawerny aan die Kaap in die sewentiende eeu', *Kronos* 1 (1979), pp.34–78.

——: 'Slawevrystellings aan die Kaap tussen 1700 en 1720', *Kronos* 4 (1981), pp.24–36.

Hattingh, *Addendum*—J.L. Hattingh: 'A.J. Böeseken se addendum van Kaapse slawe-verkooptransaksies: foute en regstellings', *Kronos* 9 (1984), pp.3–23.

Heese, H.F.: *Groep sonder grense; die rol en status van die gemengde bevolking aan die Kaap, 1652–1795* (Bellville: Institute for Historical Research UWC, 1984).

——: 'Identiteitsprobleme gedurende die 17de eeu', *Kronos* 1 (1979), pp.27–33.

——: *Reg en onreg; Kaapse regspraak in die agtiende eeu* (Bellville: Institute for Historical Instituut Research UWC, 1994). Index available on the Internet at <http://www.gendata.co.za>.

——: 'Slawe-gesinne in die Wes-Kaap, 1655–1795', *Kronos* 4 (1981), pp.38–48.

Heese/Lombard: J.A. Heese, *South African geneaologies*; ed. R.T. J. Lombard and GISA (Pretoria: HSRC, 1986–92; Stellenbosch: Genealogical Institute of South Africa, 1999–). In progress.

Hoge, J.: 'Miscegenation in South Africa in the seventeenth and eighteenth centuries'; [tr. from the German]; in Marius F. Valkhoff, *New light on Afrikaans and 'Malayo-Portuguese'* (Louvain: Editions Peeters, 1972).

——: *Personalia of Germans at the Cape (1652–1806)* (Archives Year Book, 1946)

Inventories of the Orphan Chamber of the Cape of Good Hope. Transcriptions of documents in the archival series MOOC (see below), available on the Internet at <http://www.tanap.net/content/activities/documents/Orphan_Chamber Cape_of_Good_Hope/index.htm>. Also partly transcribed in *Boedelinventarisse (Die) van erflaters in die distrik Stellenbosch, 1679–1806* (see above).

Joubert Papers; MSS, CAD MOOC14/5.71

Journal, 1662–1670; ed. H.C.V. Leibbrandt (Cape Town: W.A. Richards, 1901) (Precis of the Archives of the Cape of Good Hope). Index for 1666–70 available on the Internet at <http://www. gendata.co.za>.

Journal, 1671–1674 & 1676; ed. H.C.V. Leibbrandt (Cape Town: W.A. Richards, 1902) (Precis of the Archives of the Cape of Good Hope). Index available on the Internet at <http://www.gendata.co.za>.

Journal, 1699–1732; ed.H.C.V. Leibbrandt (1896) (Precis of the Archives of the Cape of Good Hope). Index (up to and including 1708) available on the Internet at <http://www.gendata.co.za>.

Kaapse plakkaatboek, 1652–1806; ed. M.K. Jeffreys & S.D. Naudé (1944–48).

Kloeke, G.G.: *Herkomst en groei van het Afrikaans* (Leiden: Universitaire pers Leiden, 1950).

Kolb, Peter: *Naaukeurige en uitvoerige beschryving van de Kaap de Goede Hoop*; [tr. from the German] (Amsterdam: Balthazar Lakeman, 1727).

Korte deductie, see *Defence (The) of W.A. van der Stel* above

la Bree, J.: *De rechterlijke organisatie en rechtsbedeling te Batavia in de XVIIe eeuw* (Rotterdam: Nijgh & Van Ditmar, 1951).

'Letter from the Court [=*Council*] of Justice to Major General Craig' (Cape Town, 14.1.1796); [translated], in *Records of the Cape Colony* I (1897), pp.302–309.

Letters despatched 1652—*Letters despatched from the Cape, 1652–1662*; ed H.C.V. Leibbrandt (Cape Town: W.A. Richards, 1900) (Precis of the Archives of the Cape of Good Hope). I, 1652–54; II, 1655–77; III, 1658–62.

Letters despatched 1696—*Letters despatched [from the Cape], 1696–1708*; ed. H.C.V. Leibbrandt (1896) (Precis of the Archives of the Cape of Good Hope). Index available on the Internet at <http://www. gendata.co.za>.

Letters received 1649—*Letters and documents received, 1649–1662*; ed. H.C.V. Leibbrandt (1898–99) (Precis of the Archives of the Cape of Good Hope). I, 1649–56; II, 1657–61.

Letters received 1695—*Letters received, 1695–1708*; ed. H.C.V. Leibbrandt (Cape Town: W.A. Richards, 1896) (Precis of the Archives of the Cape of Good Hope). Index available on the Internet at <http://www.gendata.co.za>.

Malan, Antonia: 'Chattels of colonists? "Freeblack" women and their households', *Kronos* 25 (1998/99), pp.50–71.

Memoriën en instructiën, 1657–1699; ed. A.J. Böeseken (S.A. Argiefstukke: Belangrike Kaapse dokumente I).

Mentzel, *Description*—Mentzel, O.F.: *A geographical and topographical description of the Cape of Good Hope*; tr. H.J. Mandelbrote, G.V. Marais & J. Hoge (Cape Town: Van Riebeeck Society, 1921, 1925, 1944).

Mentzel, *Life*:—O.F. Mentzel, *Life at the Cape in the mid-eighteenth century: being the biography of Rudolph Siegfried Allemann*; tr. Margaret Greenlees (Cape Town: Van Riebeeck Society, 1919).

MOOC—this refers to the sequence 'Master of the Orphan Chamber' in the Cape Town Archives Depository. For a transcription available on the Internet, see *Inventories of the Orphan Chamber of the Cape of Good Hope* (above). Also partly transcribed in *Boedelinventarisse (Die) van erflaters in die distrik Stellenbosch, 1679–1806* (see above).

Mossop, E.E.: 'Three slaves who ran away in 1683; an unpublished page from the history of the Cape', *Cape Times* (8.8.1929).

Niemeijer, H.E.: 'Calvinisme en koloniale stadscultuur; Batavia, 1619–1725'. Thesis, VU Amsterdam (1996).

Oud Batavia; gedenkboek uitgegeven door het Bataviaasch Genootschap voor Kunsten en Wetenschappen naar aanleiding van het driehonderdjarig bestaan der stad in 1919 (Batavia: G. Kolff, 1922). Compiled by F. de Haan.

Raben, Remco: 'Batavia and Colombo; the ethnic and spatial order of two colonial cities, 1600–1800'. *Thesis, Leiden (1996)*.

Record (The), or A series of official papers relative to the condition and treatment of the native tribes of South Africa; ed. Donald Moodie; [facs. repr.] (Cape Town: A.A. Balkema, 1960).

Reports (The) of Chavonnes and his Council, and of Van Imhoff, on the Cape, with incidental correspondence (Cape Town: Van Riebeeck Society, 1918).

Resolusies van die Politieke Raad, I–8; ed. A.J. Böeseken & C.G. de Wet (Suid-Afrikaanse argiefstukke, 1957–75).

Ross, Robert: *Cape of torments; slavery and resistance in South Africa* (London: Routledge & Kegan Paul, 1983).

——: 'The occupations of slaves in eighteenth century Cape Town', in *Studies in the history of Cape Town*, II; ed. C. Saunders and H. Philips (Cape Town: History Dept. UCT, 1980), pp.1–14.

Schoeman, *Armosyn: voorspel*—Karel Schoeman: *Armosyn van die Kaap; voorspel tot vestiging, 1415–1561*; 2nd ed. (Cape Town: Human & Rousseau, 2005).

Schoeman, *Armosyn: wêreld*—Karel Schoeman: *Armosyn van die Kaap; die wêreld van 'n slavin, 1652–1733*; 2nd ed. (Cape Town: Human & Rousseau, 2005).

Schoeman, *Kinders*—Karel Schoeman: *Kinders van die Kompanjie*. (Pretoria: Protea Boekhuis, 2006).

Scholtz, J. du P.: *Afrikaans uit die vroeë tyd; studies oor die Afrikaanse taal en literêre volkskultuur van voor 1875* (Kaapstad: Nasou, [1965?]).

——: *Afrikaans-Hollands in die agtiende eeu; verdere voorstudies tot 'n geskiedenis van Afrikaans* (Cape Town: Nasou, pref.1970).

Shaping (The) of South African society, 1652–1840; ed. Richard Elphick & Hermann Giliomee; 2nd ed. (Cape Town: Maskew Miller Longman, 1989).

Shell, Robert C.-H.: *Children of bondage; a social history of the slave society at the Cape of Good Hope, 1652–1838* (Johannesburg: Witwatersrand Univ. pr., 1994).

——: 'Rangton van Bali (1673–1720); roots and resurrection', *Kronos* 19 (Nov. 1992), pp.167–199.

'Slaeven ofte lyffeygenen', in *Nederlandsch-Indisch plakaatboek, 1602–1811*; vol.1; red. J.A. van der Chijs (Batavia: Landsdrukkerij, 1885), pp.572–576. Section of the Statutes of Batavia dealing with slaves.

Slave trade with Madagascar: the journals of the Cape slaver Leijdsman, 1715; ed. Piet Westra & James C. Armstrong (Cape Town: Africana Publishers, 2006).

Sleigh, D.: *Die buiteposte; VOC-buiteposte onder Kaapse bestuur, 1652–1795* (Cape Town: HAUM, 1993); with separate index. The 2nd printing (Pretoria: Protea Boekhuis, 2004) includes the index.

Statutes of Batavia, see 'Slaeven ofte lyffeygenen'

Tas, Adam: *The diary of Adam Tas, 1705–1706*; ed. Leo Fouché; rev. A.J. Böeseken; tr. J. Smuts (Cape Town: Van Riebeeck Society, 1970).

Theal, George McCall: *History of South Africa under the administration of the Dutch East India Company (1652–1795)*, vol.I; 2nd ed., rev. & enl. (London: Swan Sonnenschein, 1897).

——: *ibid.*, vol.II (London: Swan Sonnenschein, 1897).

Trials of slavery; selected documents concerning slaves from the criminal records of the Council of Justice at the Cape of Good Hope, 1705–1794; ed. Nigel Worden & Gerald Groenewald (Cape Town: Van Riebeeck Society, 2005).

Uit die Raad van Justisie, 1652–1672; ed. A.J. Böeseken (1986) (S.A. Argiefstukke: Belangrike Kaapse dokumente, III).

Upham, Mansell: 'Armosyn revisited', *Capensis* 2/2000, pp.19–33.

——: 'Mooij [*sic*] Ansela and the black sheep of the family' I–VII, *Capensis* 4/1997–2/1999.

Valentyn, François: *Description of the Cape of Good Hope with the matters concerning it, Amsterdam 1726*; ed. E.H. Raidt; Eng. tr. R. Raven-Hart (Cape Town: Van Riebeeck Society, 1971–73).

van Dam, Pieter: *Beschryvinge van de Oostindische Compagnie*; ed. F.W. Stapel a.o. (The Hague: Marthinus Nijhoff, 1927–54).

van Duin, Pieter, & Robert Ross: *The economy of the Cape Colony in the eighteenth century* (Leiden: Centre for the History of European Expansion, 1987).

van Reede, *Journaal*—'H.A. van Reede tot Drakenstein: Journaal van zijn verblijf aan de Kaap'; ed. A. Hulshoff, *Bijdragen en Mededelingen van het Historisch Genootschap (gevestigd te Utrecht)* 62 (1941).

van Rensburg, A.M.: 'The jigsaw puzzle: Isabella van Angola, Cornelis Claasen and Armosyn', *Capensis* 2/2000, pp.9–19.

van Riebeeck, Jan: *Journal*; [tr. W.P.L. van Zyl, C.K. Johnman & A. Ravenscroft]; ed. H.B. Thom (Cape Town: A.A. Balkema, 1952–58).

Vink, Markus: '"The world's oldest trade": Dutch slavery and slave trade in the Indian Ocean in the seventeenth century', *Journal of World History* 14 (2003), pp.131–177.

Visagie, G.G.: *Regspleging en reg aan die Kaap van 1652 tot 1806; met 'n bespreking van die historiese agtergrond* (Cape Town: Juta,1969).

Wagenaer, Zacharias: *Die dagregister en briewe van Zacharias Wagenaer, 1662–1666;* ed. A.J. Böeseken (Pretoria: Government Printer, 1973).

WNT—*Woordenboek der Nederlandsche taal* (1882–1998).

Worden, Nigel: *Slavery in Dutch South Africa* (Cambridge: Cambridge Univ. pr., 1985).

Yule, Henry, & A.C. Burnell: *Hobson-Jobson; a glossary of colloquial Anglo-Indian words and phrases, and of kindred terms, etymological, historical, geographical and discursive*; new ed., ed. William Crooke (London: Routledge & Kegan Paul, 1903); repr. (Ware, Herts.: Wordsworth Editions, 1996).

1. Index of personal names

Borns, Bartolomeus, 89
Bort, Jannetje (Johanna), 325
Botma, Cornelis Stevensz, 222, 224, 250, 264, 347
Botma, Jan Stevensz, 263, 281–282, 283; widow, 225
Botma, Steven Jansz, 76, 78, 83, 200, 225
Bouman, Hendrik, 279, 333
Brand, Burchard Heinrich, 182
Brasman, Pieter, 339, 385–386
Breda, Engela, 222
Briercliffe, Samuel, 362
Brinckman, Casper, 64, 358, 359
Brits, Anna Maria, 367
Broer, Anna Pieters, 215
Broertje, Jan Pietersz (Jan Pietersz Louw), 212, 215
Brommert (farmer, Drakenstein district), 279
Brons (Broens), Jan Albertsz, 182
Bruijn/Bruyn, Jan (slave children), *see* Jan Bruijn/Bruyn
Bygeval (slave), 207

Caatje (slave), 211, 212
Caatje van de Caab, 231
Caesar van Madagascar, 209
Caffer (Khoi), 252, 304
Caffer, Jan, van Madagascar (slave), *see* Jan Caffer van Madagscar
Caffer, Matthys, van Nova Guinee (slave), *see* Matthys Caffer van Nova Guinee
Calafora (slave woman), 254
Camelang, Annika, 331
Carel van Bengalen (slave in Stellenbosch), 245
Carel van Bengalen (slave in Table Valley), 226
Caron, François, 80
Carpius, Alexander, 164
Cat, Claes (slave), *see* Claes Cat
Catarijn (manumitted slave woman), 159
Cathalisa (slave child), 151
Catharijn (slave child), 152
Catharina (slave of E. Diemer), 308

Catharina (slave of VOC), 355
Catharina Anthonisz van Bengalen (wife of J. Woutersz), 35, 39–43, 56–57; status in community, 41, 48, 306
Catharina van Bengalen (pregnant slave woman), 79
Catharina van Ceylon, 330
Catharina van de Caab (slave child), 215
Catharina van Macassar, 180
Catharina van Madagascar (slave of G. van Wijnegum), 95
Catharina van Madagascar (sold to D. Potter), 213
Catharina van Paliacatte, 36, 42, 311, 355
Catrina van de Caab (Company slave), 324
Catryn van Bengalen, 258
Catryn van Coromandel, 79
Cattibou (Guinean slave), 83
Cecilia van Bengalen, 347
Ceij van Macassar, 347
Chaihantima (Khoi), 68
Chioe Ahoeko (Chinese), 429 n199
Christina van Canarie, 208, 350
Cingala van Madagascar, 186
Cinna (slave), 263–264
Claas Cornelisz van de Caab, *see* Cornelisz, Claas, van de Caab
Claas Gerritsz van Bengalen (free black), *see* Gerritsz, Claas, van Bengalen
Claas van Bengalen, 333–334
Claas van Guinee, 350
Claas van Malabar, 242
Claasz, Armozijn (Klein Armozijn), 183–184, 216, 362–369
Claasz, Cornelis, 78, 79, 258, 364
Claasz, Pieter, de Groot (free black), 315
Claes (slave), 128
Claes van Bengalen, 359
Claes van Malabar, 240–242
Claes van Tuticorijn, 314
Claes Cat (slave), 33
Clapperdop (slave), 207

Geens (Geems), Barbara, 213
Geeraerts, Jannetje, 308
Gegeima (slave woman from
    Guinea), 87, 308, 363
Gerrit ('Indiaan'), 88
Gerrit van Bengalen, 308
Gerritsz, Claas, van Bengalen (free
    black), 315, 317–319, 340, 369
Gideon van Guinea, 207
Gillis, Hermina, 246–247
Goske, Isbrand: restoration of
    discipline (1672), 266, 269; and
    slave population, 88, 99–100,
    153, 163–164, 180, 190, 312; and
    projected slave trade with
    Madagascar, 110, 116, 182;
    personal slaves, 308
Gracias van Angola ('Jackje Joy'), *see*
    Grasias van Angola
Granaet, Jacob, 105
Grasias van Angola ('Jackje Joy'),
    313–314, 361, 364–365
Greeff, Matthijs, 204, 218, 223, 249,
    333
Gresnich, Herman, 215, 329
'Grietje Grof', *see* Visser, Margaretha
    Gerritsz
Groenewald, Christoffel, 195
'Grof, Grietje', *see* Visser, Margaretha
    Gerritsz
Groot Armozijn (slave woman), see
    Armozijn van de Caab (Groot
    Armozijn), 325
'Groot Katrijn' (slave woman), 355
Grutting, Francina, van de Caab, 330
Gulix, Helena, 222–223

Hackius, Pieter, 139, 266
Hages, Jacob, 348, 350
Ham (Scriptural), 385
Hannibal van Macassar, 278–279
Hannibal van Tuticorijn, 240
Hansdochter, Maria, 257, 315, 316
Harmen the thatcher (white
    artisan), 228
Hartz, Anna Regina, 343
Hasewinkel, Christoffel, 277–279
    passim

Havemeester, Jacob, 331
Hector (slave), 186
Heems, Guilliam, *see* Eems, Guilliam
Heindrick (slave child), 79–80, 151
Helena (slave woman) 315
Helena van Malabar, 326
Helot, Willem, 217, 362
Hendricks (employer of slave
    worker, 1735), 229
Hendricksz, Jacobus, van de Cust
    (free black), 231
Hendricksz, Joost, 245; name
    432 n274
Hendrickx, Arent, 373
Hentje Poetje (free black), *see* Intje
    Poetje van Malacca
Heuning, Christoffel, 214
Heusden, Arnoldus, 38
Heyns, Maria, 343–344
Heyns, Paul, 344
Hoeks, Anna, 262
Hoffers, Catharina, 99
Hoffmann, J.C., 47
Holdsmidt, Jan (free black), 347
Holsmit, Jan (freeburgher), 96, 242
Honsaar (slave), 212
Houwer, Andries, 312–313
Hubert, Pieter, *see* Imbert, Pieter
Hugo, Hubert, 47–48, 107, 111
Hüsing, Henning, 91, 226, 232, 249,
    264, 344, 375, 382; widow, 179;
    slaves, 329, 338

Ibrahim van Batavia, 189
Imbert, Pieter, 278
Indien (Madagascan slave), 210
Ingepouti (free black), *see* Intje
    Poetje van Malacca
Ingora (Madagascan slave), 121
Inserwole (Madagscan slave and
    interpreter), 120
Intje Poetje van Malacca (free
    black), 315, 319
Intje Sait (deportee), 320
Isaacq (slave boy), 212
Isabella van Angola, 78, 364
Isak van Bengalen (free black), 315,
    316–317, 346

468

Isak van Bengalen (slave of Z. Wagenaer), 87
Isak van Ceylon, 253
Isak van Ternate, 329, 338

'Jackje Joy': possible origin of name, 314. *See further* Grasias van Angola ('Jackje Joy').
Jacob (*knecht*), 242
Jacob (manumitted slave child), 331
Jacob (slave boy bought in 1680), 314
Jacob (slave children baptised), 80, 151
'Jacob de Smid', *see* Jacob van Ceylon
Jacob van Bengalen, 277–278
Jacob van Bocum van Ceylon (slave), 220
Jacob van Ceylon ('De Smid'), 284, 285
Jacob van de Caab, 347
Jacob van de Cust (Coromandel), 316–317
Jacob van Macassar (free black), 340–341
Jacob van Macassar (slave child), 347
Jacob van Macassar (slave of Intje Poetje), 319
Jacob van Malabar, 338
Jacob van Siam, 263, 282, 283
Jacobus Hendricksz van de Cust (free black), *see* Hendricksz, Jacobus, van de Cust
Jan ('Indian slave'), 88
Jan (Madagascan slave), 120
Jan (manumitted slave child), 331
Jan van Bali, 211
Jan van Batavia, 91
Jan van Ceylon (Stellenbosch) ('Jan Luij'), 317
Jan van Ceylon (Table Valley), 315, 317
Jan van Cochin, 297
Jan van Madagascar, 329. *See also* Jan van Malgassies.
Jan van Malabar, 333

Jan van Malgassies, 338–339. *See also* Jan van Madagascar.
Jan van Sleijer Macassar, 330
Jan van Ternaten, 350
Jan van Tuticorijn, 95
'Jan Bombam', *see* Cornelisz, Jan
Jan Bruijn (Cape-born slave child), 151, 396 n196
Jan Bruyn (slave child from Madagascar), 32–33
Jan Caffer van Madagscar, 242
Jan de Zousa van Calijpatnam (free black), *see* de Zousa, Jan, van Calijpatnam
Jan Luij (free black), *see* Jan van Ceylon (Stellenbosch)
Jan Meeuw, 313–314
Jan Roscam (slave), 189
Jan Vos (slave), 89
Janever (slave), 189
Jannetie (slave woman), 255
Jannetje (slave child), 326
Jansz, Ariaantje, 292
Jansz, Lambert, 182
Jansz, Lijsbeth (free black), 313
Jansz, Sara (free black), *see* van Gijselen, Sara
Jansz, Willem, 212, 215
January van Malabar, 254
Jochumssen, Maerten, 64
Johannes (slave child), 152
Jommat van Batavia, 242
Jonas van Manado, 246–247
Jonasz, Armozijn, 367
Jonasz, Claas, 347, 364, 367
Jonasz, Claas, de jonge, 367
Jonasz, Jonas, 364
Jonathan (slave), 335
Jongman van Bali, 166, 178
Jonker, Captain (Moluccas), 319
Josep (slave), 33
Joseph (shepherd), 292
Joseph de la Gracia (Portuguese priest), 125
Joseph van Batavia, 242
Joubert, Elisabeth, 229
Joubert, Pieter, 210
Joy, Jackje, *see* 'Jackje Joy'

2. General index

1. *This index contains the names of countries, regions, towns, farms, ships, etc., as well as general subjects relating to slaves and slavery. For personal names, see Index 1.*
2. *All general entries in this index, unless otherwise qualified, refer by implication to slaves (e.g. 'children', 'clothes', 'prices', 'punishments', 'rations', 'transactions'), and those relating to free blacks and to the white population have mainly been concentrated under these headings. Entries beginning with the word 'slave' or 'slaves' have in principle therefore been kept to a minimum and used largely for references.*

and resentment

Angola (West Africa): slave trade, 26; as possible source of slaves for Cape, 36, 53–54, 84, 106, 109, 126; as goal of deserters, 270, 282. *See also* Amersfoort (ship): capture of Portuguese slave ship (1658).

Angolan slaves: reputation, 62l; deserters among early Angolan slaves (1658–59), 62–71 *passim*, 82, 84, 128, 269; as potential farmers, 328

Annabom (Guinea): attempted slave trade, 106–107

antagonisms between population groups, *see references under* enmity

Antilles (West Indies), 302

Antongil (Madagascar), 30, 31, 34, 103, 104–106 *passim*, 111

Apa (Guinea), 58

appearance of slaves, *see* clothing; descriptions of slaves; pictorial records of slaves

appraisals of slavery (official), *see* reports on slavery and slaves: 'De Chavonnes report' (1717)

apprenticeship of slaves and ex-slaves, 305, 306

'Arabian' slave trade, *see* Muslim slave trade

'Arabian' slaves, 34, 63

Arabic language, 116

Aracan (Bangladesh), 14, 15, 84

Arder, Ardra (Guinea), 55, 57–58 *passim*

armed bands, *see* deserters:armed bands

armosine (textile), 363

arms and ammunition: arming of Khoikhoi, 279; of slaves, 81, 202, 239; of *caffers*, 190; of free blacks, 384; theft of arms, 67, 70, 175, 268, 292. *See also* deserters:armed bands; Madagascar:firearms in slave trade.

arson, 255, 264, 287–288, 297; unintentional arson, 291; punishment, 300

artisans (slaves), *see* training of slaves (genl.)

assault, *see entries beginning with* violence…, *and accompanying references*

Atlantic slave trade, 17, 26, 56; irrelevance for Cape slavery, 27, 205

attacks (physical), *see entries beginning with* violence…, *and accompanying references*

auctions: sale of slaves, 213–214, 255–256, 320, 333

Australia, 178

authority: of slave owners, 256, 258–269; of *caffers* over whites, 189–190; corrupting effect of power, 253. *See also* discipline; modes of address; personal relationships (between masters and slaves); terminology of slavery; violence against slaves. *See also references under* defiance by slaves.

autobiographical statements of slaves, 208–209. *See also* personal statements by slaves (genl.).

'average household', 199, 200, 201, 242

baaierd (word), 130, 134

baas (term), 246, 250

babies, *see* children

badges of slavery: clothing, 219; passes (documents), 239

Bali (Indonesia), 15, 21, 92

bandieten (term), 320; 'free *bandiet*', 321. *See further* convicts and deportees.

banditry, *see* deserters

bands (musical), *see* music and musicians

Banghoek, 99, 171

Bangladesh, 40, 353. *See also* Aracan.

banishment: from Cape, 385, 386. *See also* convicts and deportees;

boats, 65

Boegies (Indonesia), *see* Bugis

Boina Bay (Madagascar), 111

Bokkeveld, 254

Boland, 90. *See further* Berg River; Darling; Drakenstein; Four-and-Twenty Rivers; Franschhoek; Groenkloof; Hottentots-Holland; Hottentots-Holland mountains; Klapmuts (outpost); Malmesbury; Paarl valley; Piketberg; Riebeek-Kasteel; Stellenbosch.

Bombetoka (Madagascar), 111

Bommelshoek (outpost), 175

bondage, *see* slavery (Cape)

bookkeeping (VOC), *see* Company slaves:records

boomwachter (term), 437 n70

borrowing (financial), see credit facilities

Bosheuvel (farm), 68, 77, 81, 139, 358–359

Bottelarij (Stellenbosch), 346

Bougies (Indonesia), *see* Bugis

bourgeoisie (black), *see* free blacks: free black bourgeoisie

Bouwa (Indonesia), *see* Sumbawa

Boxing Day, 370

branding (punishment), 67, 214, 253–254, 254, 255, 270–292 *passim*, 297—*no further indexing of passing references done*; of deserting Company slaves (legislation, 1711–27), 298; of whites, 188; specifications, 189, 273, 276, 279, 292, 298, 374

breaking on wheel (punishment), 241–242, 292, 299

Breede River, 229, 276, 285

bribery by slaves, 180

brigands, *see* deserters

British administration (after 1796): and slavery, 133, 135, 194, 219, 305–306. *See also* 'bill of rights' (1823); reports on slavery and slaves:Council of Justice (1796); emancipation of slaves; reports

on slavery and slaves: Fiscal (1813).

brothels, 159. *See also* Slave Lodge (Table Valley):as brothel.

Bugis (Indonesia): 337; as toponym, 189(*2x*)

building trade, 176, 177, 198, 227–228, 228

buitenmoeders (Slave Lodge), 182

burgher militia, 349, 350, 367

burial, *see* cemeteries; deaths and burial; funerals

burning at stake (death penalty), 300

Bushmen, 273, 280

buttons, *see under* clothing

buying of slaves, *see* transactions (genl.)

caffers (officials), 150, 188–190; as executioners, 188, 299, 301; authority over whites, 189–190; at Stellenbosch, 189, 245. *See also* 'domestic correction': administered by *caffers*.

'caffir' (term), 12, 17, 28, 29, 120, 383; as personal name or nickname, 242, 252, 264, 277–278, 314, 351, 359

'Caffirs' (Eastern Cape), *see* Xhosa tribes

'Caffirsland', *see* Transkei

caluete (term), 300

Camps Bay, 361

Canara (Malabar), 101, 208, 252

cane (official), *see* staff of office (VOC officials)

cane matting, 31

Cape Agulhas, 125

Cape Flats, 173, 175, 228

Cape Lopez (Guinea), 122

Cape Town, 52. *See further* Table Valley.

Cape Verde: as toponym, 89, 207

Cape Verde islands, 274

capital punishment, 299–301 *passim*; justified by Council of Justice (1796), 260–261; exposure of corpses, 277, 299 *passim*; fees due for executions, 301; sentencing of Europeans, 302, 304. *See also* breaking on wheel; burning at stake; hanging; impalement; pinching with red-hot pincers; scorching; strangling.

Caribbean, *see* Antilles; Barbados; Curaçao; West Indies (genl.)

cash, *see* money

castigation (punishment), *see* scourging

castizos (term), 383, 455 n42

casual relationships (sexual), *see* interracial relationships; prostitution

catechetical instruction, *see* religious instruction

cattle herding (by slaves), *see* farm work

cattle posts, 262–263

cattle raiding, 281, 285

cattle theft, *see* theft:theft of cattle

cautie (manumission), 334

Celebes (Indonesia), 15. *See also* Mandar.

cemeteries, 149–150, 244. *See also* deaths and burial.

census of slaves, *see* Company slaves:census

census returns for freeburgher slaves, *see under* statistics (slaves and slave trade): private slaves

Ceylon (Sri Lanka), 38, 50, 93(2x), 99, 100, 157; slave trade, 208; slavery, 16, 17, 23, 100. *See also* Colombo.

chaining (punishment), 69, 82, 189, 231, 245, 270–292 *passim*, 296—*no further indexing of passing references done*; chained slaves mentioned, 69, 70, 275, 278; return to owners in chains, 70, 255, 278, 289, 291, 292, 374; cost to owner, 296; chaining in pairs, 67, 128, 273, 298; chaining to ball, block or log, 69, 296 *passim*; further specifications, 214, 292;

recycling of chains, 297; legislation, 297. *See also* horning (punishment).

challenges to authority of slave owners, *see references under* defiance by slaves

chastisement (punishment), *see* scourging

children, 69, 154, 162–163, 187, 194; of slave mothers, 256–257, 365; of slave women and Khoikhoi, 258; halfbreeds, 135, 187, 256–258 *passim*; in Slave Lodge, 135, 146, 154, 162–163, 194, 305; suggested upkeep, 161; separation from mothers forbidden (1823), 259; transactions, 85, 87, 95, 99, 114, 120, 311–314 *passim*, 332, 359; as gifts, 215; work, 168, 235, 326; crimes and misdemeanours, 214. *See also* baptism; church attendance (slave children); family life of slaves; fatherhood; illegitimacy; infanticide; manumission:of children; schooling of slave children.

China, 12. *See also* Macao.

Chinese: in Batavia, 21, 25; as possible colonists, 27–28; deportees, 42, 99, 189; repatriation, 321; settled at Cape, 220, 227, 230, 231, 307, 367, 376, 376; 'Chinaman Domingo', 317; 'shaved Chinese', 320

christening, *see* baptism

Christianity: and slavery, 17–18, 275; as factor in discrimination, 372, 374, 381–382, 382. *See also see* baptism; church attendance (slave children); church membership; religious instruction; *and references under* Reformed Church.

Christmas, 165

church attendance (slave children), 165, 370

church fund, 317, 334, 359

church membership, 259, 313, 315,

318, 336, 355, 374; of free blacks, 312, 349, 355, 366; as factor in discrimination, 372, 374. *See also* baptism:and manumission.

classical slave names, 207

clothing, 54, 57, 60, 75–76, 115, 143, 143–148, 161, 180, 197, 217–219, 259, 263–264; lists (1720–21), 145, 163, 182; making of clothes, 108–109, 146, 217; cost, 193; complaints, 131, 139, 145–146; ornamentation, 237; buttons, 145(2*x*), 147; Eastern dress, 147, 217, 218; leather clothing, 219; discarded clothes of soldiers and sailors, 146; barter of clothing, 181; of women, 145; of infants, 163; of *caffers*, 190; of *mandoors*, 182; 'slave clothes', 218. *See also* blankets; head coverings; shoes.

Cochin (Malabar), 95

Code Noir (Antilles), 302

Colombo (Sri Lanka), 319; slave trade, 157; slavery, 23

colonisation (Cape), 11, 27, 51–42

colonists (Cape), *see* white population

colour consciousness, *see* 'caffir' (term):as personal name or nickname; equality of races (social and legal); free blacks: discrimination

coloured population, *see* free blacks; halfbreeds; Mardijkers (Batavia)

communication, *see* interpreters and interpreting. *See also references under* languages.

Comoros, *see* Mayotte islands

Company outposts, *see* outposts (VOC)

Company servants (VOC), *see* officials (VOC)

Company slaves (Cape), 61–62, 87–88, 99–102, 127–194 *passim*; acquired from private owners, 87–88, 308, 363; donated to Company, 320, 329; hired from colonists, 88, 176; tariff, 176; hired out to colonists, 114–115, 174, 176; sold to private owners, 98–99, 190, 209; distributed to freeburghers, 102; assigned to officials, 170–171, 185–187 *passim*, 194;

obligations towards slaves, 154–155; policy on baptism, 150–152; birth rate, 136, 162–163; mortality rate, 136; clothing (genl.), 143–148; cost of upkeep, 137, 186, 187, 193, 193–194, 196–198 *passim*; names, 120–121, 206; rations (genl.), 138–143; census, 190–191; records, 190–191, 206, 267, 352; records of deserters, 276; reputation, 186–87; right of complaint, 149; specific complaints, 131, 138–139 *passim*, 145–145, 149.

See also accommodation of slaves (VOC); clothing; exchange of slaves; manumission (genl.); rations; slave officials; statistics (slaves and slave trade).

Company's Garden (Table Valley), 72–3, 129, 130, 168, 169, 180, 194, 226; gardener's house, 128

complaints by slaves, 131, 138–139 *passim*, 145–146, 146, 251, 261–264; of maltreatment, 251, 253–254; right of complaint (Company slaves), 149; British legislation (1823), 260. *See also* violence against slaves:alleged murder.

compulsory sale of slaves, 253

concubinage, *see* illegitimacy; interracial relationships

conditional manumission, *see* manumission:conditional

conditional sale of slaves, 332

confessions (interrogation), *see* interrogation

confinements, *see* maternity leave; midwives; pregnancy

Congo, 84

congregating of slaves: as potential threat, *see* social tensions (slavery) conspiracies, *see* social tensions (slavery)

Constantia (farm), 98, 170, 171, 244, 357, 361

conversion (religious), *see* Christianity; church membership

convicts and deportees, 17, 25, 36, 42, 183(2*x*), 275, 288, 320–322 *passim*, 370; local sentences, 270, 276, 291, 317; in Slave Lodge, 183(2*x*), 305, 321; on outposts, 175; statistics, 42, 192, 321; potential danger to colony, 321–322; rations, 142, 372, 381; blankets, 144; deserters, 285; status, 220, 372, 373, 374; discrimination on grounds of colour, 372, 381; 'free *bandiet*', 321. *See also* bandiet (term); political exiles; repatriation to the East (manumitted slaves, exiles and convicts); Robben Island:detainees.

cooking, *see* rations:preparation of food

cooking equipment, 203

'coolie money', *see* koeliegeld

coolies (name), 16, 20, 26

Coon Carnival, 237

co-operation of slaves with system, 197–198, 245, 275

Coornhoop (farm), 367

Coornhoop (redoubt), 410 n2

Coromandel (India), 36, 95, 126; slave trade, 14–15, 16, 21. *See also* Madras; Paliacatte; São Tomé (Coromandel); Tranquebar; Tuticorin.

corporal punishment, *see* punishment

correction, domestic, *see* 'domestic correction'

cost of upkeep (genl.), 196–198 *passim. See also under* Company slaves.

Council of Justice: and slave transactions, 209; transfer of slaves to Council, 215; fees for

executions, 301; report (1796), 260–261, 289–290, 303

Council of Policy: and slave transactions, 209–210

countries of origin, *see references under entries beginning with* origin(s)…

cowrie shells, 58, 59–60, 398 n45

craftsmen (slaves), *see* training

credit facilities, 90, 205, 310, 317, 341, 359

creoles (term), *see under* castizos

crimes and misdemeanours, 128; aiding escape from prison, 189; immorality with schoolgirls, 183; infanticide, 299; killing of Khoi, 301; knife fighting, 385; rape, 268. *See also* arson; crimes of passion; desertion; harbouring deserters; theft; violence against slave owners; violence against slaves.

crimes of passion, 255–256

criminal records of slaves (genl.), 267–268

criminals (slaves): as representative group, 267–268

cripple slaves, 334

'crucifixion' (punishment), *see* impalement

cruelty, *see* violence against slaves

Curaçao, 122

curfew, 74, 239, 288; conduct in streets at night, 231

dancing, 236–237 *passim*

Danish ships, 92, 285, 348

Darling, 233

Dassen Island, 40

'De Chavonnes report' (1717), *see* reports on slavery and slaves: 'De Chavonnes report' (1717)

De Kuilen (outpost), 175(2*x*), 275

De Margriet (ship), 125

De Schuur (outpost), *see* Groote Schuur

death sentences, *see* capital punishment

deaths and burial, 149–150, 191, 244,

483

253; official records, 191; inconvenience for Company, 109. *See also* cemeteries; Company slaves:mortality rate; funerals; sickness and health; suicide; *and entries beginning with* violence…

debt, *see* free blacks:debt

deeds of sale: inclusion of slaves, 216

deference, *see* modes of address; terminology of slavery

defiance by slaves, *see* arson; desertion; sabotage by slaves; suicide; violence against slave owners

delayed manumission, *see* manumission:conditional

Delft (Netherlands), 38

dependence on slave labour, *see under* white population

deportees, *see* convicts and deportees; political exiles

depression, *see under* emotions of slaves

derogatory slave names, *see* nicknames

descriptions of slaves, 125; of free black woman, 362. *See also* pictorial records of slaves.

deserters, 173, 214, 245, 254, 262, 263–264, 268–288 *passim*, 374; among early slaves (1658–59), 64–71 *passim*, 82, 84, 128, 269, 358; from Batavia, 32, 33; from ships, 35, 348; during expeditions to Madagascar, 104, 105; habitual deserters, 268, 298; records, 276; destinations, 65, 270, 271, 282, 286–287; theft of boat, 65; escape to Europe, 285–286;
armed bands, 175, 263, 268–280 *passim*, 271, 279–284 *passim*; incidental crimes, 284; flag used as signal, 275; pursuit, 64, 66, 239–240, 270–272 *passim*, 274, 279–280, 284; capture by fellow slaves, 275; rewards for capture, 274, 282–283, 289; selfdefence

authorised, 269; wounding of deserters authorised, 280, 281; white deserters, 269, 280–281.
See also harbouring deserters; Khoikhoi:and deserters; stowaways.

desertion, 194, 197, 268–269; most common misdemeanour, 268; aggravating factors, 268; as means of sabotage, 268, 289; as unpremeditated reaction, 268; hamstringing as deterrent, 298

despair, *see* helplessness of slaves; suicide

detainees, *see* Robben Island: detainees

dichotomy of slave system, 17–18, 275. *See also* co-operation of slaves with system; free blacks: as slave owners.

diet, *see* rations

disabilities of slaves, *see* helplessness of slaves; legal position of slaves; legislation; restrictions on slaves

disapproval of maltreatment, 253

discipline, 187, 288–291, 302–304; under I. Goske (1672–76), 266, 269; under L. van Assenburgh (1708–11), 279. *See also* punishment; slave ships: revolts; uprisings.

discrimination (racial), *see* caffir (term):as personal name or nickname; equality of races (social and legal); free blacks: discrimination

dishonour, *see* punishment:dishonouring effect

disobedience of slaves, *see* personal relationships (between masters and slaves):tensions

disparity of races, *see under* equality of races (social and legal)

disparity of sentences and punishments, 302–304

displaying of corpses (capital punishment), *see* capital punishment:exposure of corpses displaying of offenders (punishment), *see* public exhibition of offenders

disposal of slaves, *see* auctions; compulsory sale of slaves; Company slaves:donation to VOC; conditional sale of slaves; exchange of slaves; farming out of slaves (VOC); hiring of slaves (from owners); lending of slaves; letting out of slaves (for self-employment); testamentary dispositions; transactions (genl.); transfer of slaves

dissensions among slaves, 265, 276. *See also* violence among slaves.

distribution of slaves (by place of work), *see* outposts (VOC)

distribution of slaves (disposal), *see* Company slaves: distribution to freeburghers; testamentary dispositions: slaves as heritable property

diversity of population, *see* farm communities; free blacks: origins; origins of slaves; white population:origins

divisions among slaves, *see* dissensions among slaves

domestic arrangements, *see* free blacks:living conditions; white population:living conditions

'domestic correction', 19, 67, 251–252 *passim*, 293–296; instruments, 67, 294–296 *passim*; duration, 293; administered by *caffers*, 274, 294–296, 301; description, 295–296; criticised, 294–295; moderation recommended, 293; 'undue' flogging not advisable, 293; defined (1813), 294, (1823), 260. *See further* scourging (punishment).

domestic units, *see* 'average household'; farm communities

domestic work, 226, 231–232. *See also* laundry work.

donation of slaves to VOC, *see* Company slaves:donation of slaves

Drakenstein, 69, 90, 202, 237–238, 329, 341, 356; slaves, 243, 278; free blacks, 339, 366. *See also* Paarl valley.

drawings of slaves, *see* pictorial records of slaves

dress, *see* clothing

drinking, *see* alcohol; free time and recreation

drug addiction, *see* opium

drunkenness, 143, 294

Duinhoop (fort), 45

duration of scourging, 293

Dutch East India Company, *see* V.O.C.

Dutch language, 34, 45, 82, 83, 120, 135, 154, 166–167, 219, 248, 275; and manumission, 306, 324, 325, 327, 334, 336; restructuring at Cape, 248. *See also* modes of address; terminology of slavery.

Dutch Reformed Church, *see* Reformed Church

Dutch slave names, 57, 206–207

Dutch West India Company (WIC), *see* West India Company

earnings, *see* money

East (genl.): slavery, 12. *See further entries and references under* Ceylon; India; Indonesian archipelago; Japan; Persia; Siam.

East Africa, 12, 17, 28–29, 116, 119, 125. *See also* Mombasa; Mozambique; Sofala.

East Indies (Indonesia), *see* Indonesian archipelago

Eastern dress, 147, 217, 218

Eastern slavery, 11–27 *passim*

Eastern textiles, 14, 143–145, 218

economy, *see* credit facilities; *pacht*; white population:economic progress

education, *see* literacy; schooling of slave children; training of slaves (genl.)

Eemland (ship), 118, 118–119
elderly slaves, 59, 62, 69, 145, 194, 305, 333–334, 335–336; diminished value, 333–334; tendency to pine away, 123; mode of address, 247; Cinna (deserter) 263–264. *See also* manumission: of elderly slaves.
Elisabeth (ship), 117–118
Elmina (Guinea), 58
emancipation of slaves: on arrival in Netherlands, 38, 102; under British administration (1827), 194; (1834), 198, 306; in Batavia (1860), 23. *See also* manumission.
embroidery, *see* needlework
emotions of slaves: anger and resentment, 268; depression, 264 *passim*; homesickness, 123; grief, 123; loneliness, 261–263. *See also* crimes of passion; helplessness of slaves; suicide; *and references and entries under* personal relationships.
empalement (punishment), *see* impalement
employment of slaves, *see* work of slaves (genl.)
English ships, 286–297, 348. *See also* slave ships.
enmity between slave groups, *see* dissensions among slaves; violence among slaves
enmity between slaves and Khoikhoi, *see* Khoikhoi:and slaves
enmity of slaves towards masters, *see* social tensions (slavery)
epidemics, *see* sickness and health
equality of races (social and legal), 308–309, 349; prospects for a multiracial society, 383, 387; reservations, 349–351; disparity of sentences and punishments, 302–304; growing colour consciousness, 41, 48, 370–387 *passim*; Christianity as factor, 372, 374, 381–382; baptism as factor, 382; colour as factor, 382,

383, 386; free status as factor, 381–382; honour as factor, 373–374, 378–379. *See also references under* interracial tensions.
escape bids, *see* desertion
estamijn (textile), 426 n113
ethics of slavery, *see* morality of slavery
Ethiopia, 34
ethnic divisions, *see entries beginning with* origins…
ethnic tensions, *see entries beginning with* origins…
evangelisation, *see* baptism; church attendance (slave children); church membership; religious instruction
evening prayers (Slave Lodge), *see* religious instruction
excessive punishment, *see* domestic correction; violence against slaves
exchange of slaves: for goods, 212; for other slaves, 178–179 *passim*, 190, 212, 313, 325
executioners, *see* caffers (officials); hangman
executions, *see* capital punishment
exhibition of corpses (capital punishment), *see* capital punishment:exposure of corpses
exhibition of offenders (punishment), *see* public exhibition
exiles, *see* convicts and deportees; Mauritius:as place of banishment; political exiles
expense of slaves, *see* Company's slaves:cost of upkeep; upkeep of slaves (genl.)
exposure of corpses (capital punishment), *see* capital punishment:exposure of corpses
exposure of offenders (punishment), *see* public exhibition of offenders

False Bay, 138, 140, 216, 281
families (slaves), 331, 331–332. *See also* fatherhood.

first recorded use (1671), 307; avoidance of term 'freeburgher', 350–351; social status, 308–309, 348–350, 383, 384, 386; interracial marriages, 342–346; origins, 322, 337, 378–379; incomers from elsewhere, 332; women, 330, 340;

work, 311, 338, 339–342; as employers, 349; as farmers, 313, 328–329, 338, 339, 341–342, 349, 360, 385–386 *passim*; as *knechten* and employers of *knechten*, 349, 362; as slave owners, 216, 243, 244, 264, 291, 312, 314, 315, 318 *passim*, 319, 339, 346–347, 354, 357, 359, 361–362, 368, (statistics), 347; as sureties (manumission), 315;

and testimonals to W.A. van der Stel (1706), 376, 378–379; burgher militia, 367, 384; arms and ammunition, 384; land ownership: Camps Bay, 361; Liesbeek valley, 341–342, 367; Stellenbosch, 316, 328–329, 360; Table Valley, 307–309 *passim*, 312, 315, 315–316 (list of names), 317, 354–355, 359 *passim*, 361, 366;

cohesiveness as group, 342, 347–348; church membership, 312, 349, 355, 366; literacy, 338; debt, 313 *passim*, 342, 360(2*x*); litigiousness, 342;

living conditions, 313, 316, 318, 330, 341, 345, 346, 357, 360, 367; free black bourgeoisie, 365–369, 370–371;

individual examples, 313, 316, 318, 330, 341, 345, 357, 367, 369; rice rations (1678), 311; discrimination (legal), 303–304; promising prospects, 306–309, 359, 369, 371, 383, 397; change, 369, 370–387 *passim*; growing awareness of colour, 377, 386–387; discrimination (social), 370–387 *passim*; assaults on free blacks, 370–372 *passim*, 385–386.

See also baptism:of free blacks; church membership:of free blacks; equality of races (social and legal); freeburgher agitation (1705–07); manumission:by free blacks; manumission:preparation of slaves for manumission; statistics: free blacks; Stellenbosch:free blacks; Table Valley:free blacks.

free status: as factor in discrimination, 381–382

free time and recreation, 143, 159–160, 180–181, 217, 236–238, 244. *See also* social tensions (slavery).

'freeborn' (term), 307

freeburgher agitation (1705–07), 279, 286, 293, 375–384 *passim*; testimonials signed by free blacks, 315, 317, 319, 340, 375–376, 378–379; element of colour discrimination, 376, 378–379

freeburghers: avoidance of term for free blacks, 350–351. *See further* burgher militia; white population.

freeburghership, 50–52, 250. *See further* colonisation; freeburghers.

freedom of movement (slaves), *see* curfew; free time and recreation; social tensions (slavery)

freeing of slaves, *see* emancipation of slaves; manumission

French Hoek, *see* Franschhoek

French Refugees (Huguenots), 202, 341, 378, 385, 385–386

French ships, 34, 144, 285; fugitive slave, 35

French: and slavery, 302

fuel, *see* firewood

fugitives (slaves), *see* deserters; stowaways

fullbreed (term), 156

funeral expenses (free black), 368. *See further* deaths and burial.

Gabon, 122

Galen (Sri Lanka), *see* Galle

Galle (Sri Lanka), 93(2*x*), 208

Indonesian archipelago: slave trade, 15, 20–21, 91–92, 95; slavery, 12; slaves, 261–262. *See also* Ambon; Bali; Batavia (Jakarta); Bugis; Celebes; Lombok; Macassar; Moluccas; Nias; 'Nova Guinee'; Roti; Sumatra; Sumbawa; Timor.

Indonesian languages and dialects, 166, 246

inequality of races (social and legal), *see under* equality

infanticide, 299

infants, *see* children

infidelity, *see* crimes of passion

informal slave transactions, 209–210

information on slaves (genl.), 214–215, 267; toponyms as source of information, 207–208. *See also* autobiographical statements by slaves; biographies of slaves (reconstructed); legal records; personal statements by slaves (genl.); pictorial records of slaves.

inheritance by slaves, *see* testamentary dispositions: bequests to slaves

inheritance of slaves, *see* testamentary dispositions:slaves as heritable property

insecurity of slave owners, *see* social tensions (slavery)

insecurity of slaves, *see* helplessness of slaves

insolvency: and disposal of slaves, 213

institutional slave-holding (VOC), 13

instruction of slaves, *see* literacy; religious instruction; schooling of slave children; training of slaves (genl.)

interpretation of historical evidence, 245

interpreters and interpreting, 107 *passim*, 119–120, 123, 166, 167, 178, 189, 208. *See also* Sijmon de Arabier, *in Index 1.*

interracial marriages, 24, 39–49 *passim*, 79, 151, 241, 258, 309, 325, 342–346, 355, 367, 370; statistics, 342; status of wives (early years), 41, 48, 49; social standing of husbands, 343–344; slave ownership, 423 n18; relegation of couples to Robben Island, 48, 306. *See also* manumission:for marriage purposes.

interracial relationships, 23–24, 77–79, 113, 154, 158–160, 257, 343, 345, 361; legislation, 159, 160; punishments, 79, 159, 160, 161; allegations against P. Kalden, 381; stable unions, 257–258. *See also* children; halfbreeds; illegitimacy; prostitution.

interracial tensions, *see* equality of races (social and legal); free blacks:discrimination; Khoi-khoi:and slaves; social tensions (slavery)

interrogation: use of torture, 270, 298–299

intestacy: and disposal of slaves, 213

inventories, *see* probate inventories

investment in slavery, *see* elderly slaves:diminished value; prices of slaves:profits; private slaves:as investment

Iran, *see* Persia

Islam, *see* Muslim slave trade; Muslims

isolation, *see* emotions of slaves: loneliness

jails, *see* imprisonment (punishment)

jak en jooi (expression), 314

Jakarta (Indonesia), *see* Batavia

Jambi (ship), 118, 122

Jan de Jonkershoek, 262, 328

Japan, 85–86; as toponym, 309

jealousy, *see* crimes of passion

'jigsaw puzzle' of slavery, 364

Johanna Catharina (slave ship), 108, 111, 116, 136

John and Mary (ship), 124

jongen (term), 23, 247

Jonkershoek, *see* Jan de Jonkershoek

Joubert Papers (Cape Town Archives Depository), 210, 229

judicial punishments, *see* punishments

justification of slavery, 17–18

'Kaffirland', *see* Transkei

'kaffirs' (name) *see* 'caffirs'

kasties (term), *see* castizos

'Khoi sketches', 147

Khoi tribes, *see* Grigriqua; Namaqua

Khoi War (1659–60), 45, 68–69, 81

Khoi War (1673–77), 90, 266, 358

Khoikhoi, 66; and slaves, 33, 45, 68–69, 80–81, 81–82, 265; relationships with slave women, 258; slave with alleged Khoi wife, 442 n57; and nickname 'Zwartemans', 68; and deserters, 64, 271–272, 279, 282–282, 289, 358; arming of Khoikhoi, 279; killing of Khoi by slave, 301; in white employment, 202, 217, 226, 242, 248, 258, 265; as threat to whites, 269, 383, 384–384. *See also* tobacco:and Khoikhoi.

killing of Khoikhoi, *see* violence against Khoikhoi

killing of slave owners, *see* violence against slave owners: murder

killing of slaves, *see* violence against slaves:murder

kinship, *see* family life of slaves; family relationships

kitchen equipment, 203

kitchens, *see* slave kitchens (on farms)

Klapmuts (outpost), 174–176 *passim*, 279

Kloof Nek (Table Valley), 27

knechten, 52, 70, 88, 93, 204, 222–223, 242, 249–251, 280–281, 328; in Company service, 168, 174–175; as overseers, 249–251 *passim*; hiring out of *knechten*, 250; statistics, 249; free blacks as employers and employees, 349, 362

knife fighting, 385

Koelenhof (farm), 335

koeliegeld, 227 *passim*, 229

Kuils River, 175

Kwartel (ship), 114

kwartslag (term), 156

labour, *see* hard labour (punishment); work of slaves (genl.)

labourers (white), *see* knechten; white labour

laksman (term), 301

Lambert's Bay, 282

land ownership (free blacks), *see under* free blacks

Land van Waveren (Tulbagh valley), 263, 279

languages: in Slave Lodge, 166–168. *See also* Afrikaans language; Arabic language; Dutch language; Indonesian languages and dialects; *lingua franca*; Malagasy language; Portuguese language. *See further* interpreters and interpreting.

laundry work, 73, 169

laws, *see* legislation; Statutes of Batavia

leasing system, *see* pacht

leather clothing, 219

legal framework, *see* legislation

legal position of slaves, 258, 258–261, 381–382. *See also* legislation; protection against maltreatment; restrictions on slaves.

legal records, 267–268

legal right to freedom (halfbreed slaves), *see* manumission of halfbreeds:right to freedom

legal separations: and disposal of slaves, 213

legislation: barter (1677, 1700, 1709), 181; barter with slaves (1700), 230; beachcombing (1722), 230; burial of slaves (1731), 253; chaining (1731), 297; clothing (no date), 219; curfew (1686, 1687), 239; deserters (1672), 269, (1696),

influence, 103; projected VOC residency (1663), 103–104; slave trade, 14, 28, 29–33 *passim*, 37, 52, 88, 102, 110–112, 210; expeditions from the Cape, 32–33, 103–126 *passim*, 129, 131, 136, 156, 174, 275; first successful slaving expedition (1676), 110; list of slave ships, 118;

    prices, 105–106, 112, 120–121, 124; use of Mexican rixdollars, 112–113, 114, 118; trade goods, 110, 117; firearms in slave trade, 112, 119; profits on sales, 121; private transactions by crew members, 115–116, 119; statistics, 125–126; freeburghers ask to trade here, 124; as goal of deserters, 282; imports from Madagascar, 142.

    See also Antongil; Boina Bay; Bombetoka; Magelagie; Manigaar; Nosy Antsoheribory; St Augustine's Bay.

Madras (Coromandel), 95

Magelagie (Madagascar), 105, 111–113 *passim*, 114, 118, 124

maize cultivation, 74, 217

Malabar (India), 93, 95, 173; slave trade, 15, 16, 21; reputation of slaves, 241. *See also* Canara; Cochin; Porca; Quilon; Vengurla.

'Malabar' (term of abuse), 241

Malacca (Malaysia), 14–15, 100

Malagasy language, 116, 123, 167, 167–168, 182

Malaka (Malaysia), *see* Malacca

'Malay' (term), 86, 166, 167, 248, 320

Malay language, *see* Indonesian languages and dialects

Malmesbury, 279

maltreatment of slaves, *see* violence against slaves

Mandar (Indonesia): as toponym, 243

mandoors (officials), 114, 117, 184; origin of name, 117; of female slaves on Vergelegen, 200–201; Europeans, 116, 181–182 *passim*;

slave *maandoors*, 149, 182–183, 185; rations, 142. *See also* oppermandoor (Slave Lodge).

Manigaar (Madagascar), 111–113 *passim*, 118

manioc root, 106

manumission (genl.), 85, 99, 257, 306, 326–327; at Batavia, 21, 306; in the Netherlands, 38, 102; early manumissions at Cape, 306–307, 353;

    by Company officials, 337, 359; by free blacks, 313, 314, 315, 347–348; by visitors to Cape, 308; of children, 186, 307, 308, 315, 331, 347; of children of manumitted mothers, 326; of Company slaves, 177, 185–186, 209, 323–329, 336–337; of elderly slaves, 244, 319, 323, 333, 334, 335, 337; of fullbreeds, 366; of Madagascan slaves, 116; of private slaves, 308, 329–337; of slaves from Batavia at the Cape, 39, 331–332; 446 n189;

    conditional, 220, 240, 241, 308, 326, 327, 329–330, 333, 334–335, 336, 338–339, 347, 446 n189; on request, 336; purchase of freedom, 312, 317, 323, 325, 327, 333, 336, 347, 367; price, 312, 323;

    reasons: old age, 328, 330, 336, 354; as status symbol, 333; for marriage purposes, 306, 325, 326;

    records, 323, 325, 336; for Company slaves, 323, 325; statistics, 335, 336; ages, 336; low manumission rate at Cape, 336;

    preparation of slaves for manumission, 338–339, 354; adaptation to free state, 339; sureties, 315, 334–335, 348; support of manumitted slaves,

323, 334–335; obligations of former slaves, 306.
    See also baptism:and manumission; Dutch language:and manumission; letters of freedom; religious instruction:as condition for manumission.
manumission of halfbreeds, 154, 159, 163–164, 324, 340; right to freedom, 156, 324–325, 327, 382; conditions of manumission, 325. *See also entries under* manumission (genl.).
manumitted slaves, *see* free blacks; repatriation to East (manumitted slaves, exiles and convicts)
Mardijkers (Batavia), 24–25, 27, 38, 73, 307, 316(2*x*), 317, 320, 322
Margaret, Margriet (ship), 125
Maria (ship), 54–56 *passim*, 84
Maringaan (Madagascar), *see* Manigaar
Marken (ship), 106
marriage between slaves: legalised (1823), 259. *See further* 'paired slaves'.
marriages (interracial), *see* interracial marriages
masons, *see* building trades
mass escapes of slaves, *see* deserters:armed bands
Massailly (Madagascar), *see* Magelagie
maternity leave, 149
matres (term), 184
matrons (Slave Lodge), 182, 184, 365, 366–367
matting (furniture), 31
Mauritius, 24, 30, 47–48, 105, 380; as place of banishment, 43, 183; slave trade, 103, 107; slaves, 32, 297; tobacco, 143, 191.
Mayotte islands (Comoros), 107, 109, 111, 116
meals, *see* rations
medical care, 138, 149, 193, 243
Meerlust (farm), 262
meid (term), 23, 247

Melaku (Indonesia), *see* Moluccas
menial work, *see* white population:and servile work
mesties, mestizo (term), 155, 383
Mexican rixdollars: in Madagascan slave trade, 112–113, 114, 118
middle class (black), *see* free blacks: bourgeoisie
middlemen (slave trade), *see* slave dealers (Cape)
midwives, 149, 184, 194
migration: from country districts to Table Valley, 329; of free blacks from elsewhere, 332
military service, *see* burgher militia
militia, *see* burgher militia
ministers of religion: as slave owners, 86, 92, 98–99, 157, 277–278 *passim*; allegations against P. Kalden, 381
miscegenation, *see* castizos (term); halfbreeds; interracial marriages; interracial relationships; prostitution
misdemeanours, *see* crimes and misdemeanours
missionary activity, *see* baptism; religious instruction
mistreatment of slaves, *see* violence against slaves
'mixed marriages', *see* interracial marriages
'mixed relationships', *see* illegitimacy; interracial relationships
'mixed-bloods', *see* halfbreeds
'mixed-breeds', *see* halfbreeds
mockadon (term), 117
modes of address, 245–247
moeders (term), 182
Moluccas (Indonesia), 319
Mombasa (East Africa), 125
money, 339; bribes, 180; gifts, 143, 180; independent earnings, 166, 180, 219–220, 228–229, 237–238; savings, 212. *See also* gambling.
Monomotapa, 119
'Moors', *see* Muslims
moral right to freedom (halfbreed slaves), *see* manumission of

495

halfbreeds:right to freedom
morality of slavery, 17–18
mortality rate, *see* Company
    slaves:mortality rate. *See also*
    sickness and health.
Moslem slave trade, *see* Muslim slave
    trade
Moslems, *see* Muslims
motherhood, *see* children; mater-
    nity leave; pregnancy
Mouille Point, 27, 128
Mowbray, 359
Mozambique (East Africa), 104,
    110–111, 114, 125; as goal of
    deserters, 271; 'prize negroes', 305
mulattos (term), 383. *See further*
    halfbreeds.
multiracial society, *see under* equal-
    ity of races (social and legal)
murder, *see under* violence against
    slave owners; violence against
    slaves; violence among slaves
Muscat, 110, 111
music and musicians, 22, 94, 230. *See*
    also dancing; singing.
musical instruments, 236–237 *passim*
Muslim slave trade, 12, 110, 111,
    113, 116, 117
Muslims, 18, 319, 382
muster roll, *see* statistics
mutilation (punishment), 297; loss
    of ears, 270, 273, 274, 283, 291;
    nose, 279; ears and nose, 276,
    298; hand, 247, 292; fingers,
    291–292; mutilation of deserting
    Company slaves (legislation,
    1711–27), 298. *See also* ham-
    stringing.

Namaqua (Khoi tribe), 83
Namaqualand, 283
names, 57(2*x*), 61, 83, 191, 206–208;
    'actualizing power', 207;
    changes of name, 207, 361;
    confusion caused by common
    names, 36, 309–312, 317; most
    common names, 206–207; of
    baptismal candidates, 151–152

passim; of *caffers*, 189; of inter-
    preters, 189 *passim*; Madagascan
    names, 120–121. *See also*
    toponyms.
narcotics, *see* alcohol; opium; tobacco
needlework, 23, 165, 166, 180, 232
Netherlands: impartiality of justice,
    303–304; status of slaves, 38, 102.
    See also transportation of slaves
    (between Batavia, Cape and
    Europe).
New Guinea, *see* 'Nova Guinee'
New Year's Day, 143
Newlands, 172
Nias (Indonesia), 15
nicknames, 57, 207, 313–314, 360–361,
    365, 385; of free blacks, 351. *See*
    also 'caffir' (term):as personal
    name or nickname
night soil, *see* privies
nonje (term), 246, 330
North America, 110, 122, 205
Nossa Senhora de los Milagros (ship), 125
Nosy Antsoheribory
    (Madagascar), 111
'Nova Guinee': as toponym, 278
Nova Mazalagem (Madagascar),
    see Magelagie

obligations of manumitted slaves,
    see under manumission
officials (slaves), *see* slave officials
officials (VOC), 204; fees due for
    executions, 301; in Slave Lodge,
    116, 117, 160; as slave owners,
    85–87, 93–94, 98–99, 127; and
    manumission of slaves, 337, 359;
    wives of officials, 86, 182.
        See also Company
    slaves:assigned to officials;
    mandoors (officials); *opperman-*
    door (Slave Lodge); private
    slaves:holdings of individual
    slave owners; staff of office
    (VOC officials). *See further the*
    subheading personal slaves *under*
    the names of the following in Index
    1: van der Stel, Simon; van der

Stel, W.A.; van Riebeeck, Jan; Wagenaer, Zacharias.

officiers (term), 182

Oirschot (Netherlands), 38

old people, *see* elderly slaves

Olifants River, 282, 283, 284

Olifantspas (Franschhoek), 285

Oman, 110, 111

onderhandse slave transactions (term), 210

Onrust (farm), 223

opgaaf (census), *see* statistics

opium, 230

oppermandoor (Slave Lodge), 137, 181

orchestras, *see* music and musicians

origins of colonists, *see* white population:origins

origins of free blacks *see* free blacks:origins

origins of slaves: random examples, 37, 86–89 *passim*, 91–92 *passim*, 98, 125, 242–243, 262; statistical analyses, 87, 95, 126; of VOC slaves in the East, 14, 21. *See also* 'caffir' (term): as personal name or nickname; toponyms.

Orphan Chamber, 90, 329–330, 341, 349, 374

outposts (VOC), 114, 171–176, 280. *See further* Bommelshoek; De Kuilen; Groote Schuur; Het Paradijs; Hottentots-Holland: outpost; Klapmuts; Rietvallei; Saldanha Bay:outpost; Vissershok.

Overberg, 177

overseers (slaves), *see* mandoors (officials)

overseers (whites), *see* knechten:as overseers; *oppermandoor* (Slave Lodge)

paai (term of respect), 247, 320

Paarl valley, 90, 279

pacht, 90–91, 311, 344, 350, 356, 375

Padang (Sumatra): as toponym, 321

'paired slaves', 57, 76–77, 156, 213–214, 358; attachment of men to women, 81; benefits of stable

unions, 256; instability of unions, 256; legalisation of slave marriages (1823), 259. *See also* crimes of passion; families; family life.

palempores (quilts), 144, 145, 219

Paliacatte (Coromandel), 36

panics among slave owners, *see* social tensions (slavery)

Paradijs (outpost), *see* Het Paradijs

Paradise (Table Mountain), 173

passes (documents), 239

passive resistance of slaves, *see* *references under* defiance by slaves

paternity, *see* fatherhood

patrols, *see* deserters:pursuit

payment, *see* exchange of slaves:for goods

pedak (word), 130

penguin meat and eggs, *see under* rations

pepper, *see under* rations

Persia (Iran), 208

personal accounts by slaves, *see* personal statements by slaves (genl.)

personal details of slaves, *see* descriptions of slaves

personal hygiene, 76, 121, 130

personal names, *see* names

personal property of slaves, 212, 219–220, 224, 241, 264; ownership and acquisition permitted (1823), 259. *See also* bedding; blankets; money.

personal relationships (genl.), *see* crimes of passion; interracial marriages; interracial relationships; 'paired slaves'

personal relationships (between masters and slaves), 244–247 *passim*; gentleness recommended, 289; gentleness inadequate, 290; 'undue' flogging not advisable, 293; co-operation of slaves with system, 197–198, 245, 275; loyalty and affection, 244–245; tensions, 263–264, 266, 268,

290, 294. *See also* complaints; emotions of slaves; *and references under* defiance by slaves.

personal slaves of officials, *see under* officials (VOC)

personal statements by slaves (genl.), 32, 208–209, 240–241, 251, 255–256, 262, 287–288, 433 n319; letter written for slave, 246–247

Peter en Paul (ship), 118

physical punishment, *see* punishment

pictorial records of slaves, 147

Piketberg, 243, 282, 283, 357

pillory (instrument for punishment), 292–293. *See further* public exhibition of offenders (punishment).

pinching with red-hot pincers (punishment), 292, 299

piracy, 111, 121, 122, 220

place names, *see* toponyms

plakkaten, *see* legislation

plantation slavery (Americas), 124, 205

Plattekloof (farm), 97, 98

plotting by slaves, *see* social tensions (slavery)

police force, *see* caffers (officials)

political exiles, 320, 322

pondok (word), 130

Poolse bok (form of punishment), 252, 296

poor fund, *see* church fund

Popo (Guinea), 58–60, 122, 357

population figures, *see* statistics

Porca (Malabar), 95

Port Gentil (Gabon), 122

porters, 227

Portugal, 103, 397 n28

Portuguese: and slave trade, 12, 53, 55, 56; and slavery, 14, 16, 20

Portuguese language, 34, 66, 83, 166–167 *passim*, 247, 300, 316; as *lingua franca*, 237; interpreters, 120; modes of address, 246, 247

Portuguese ships, 55, 56, 125; captured slave woman, 46. *See also* Amersfoort (ship):capture of Portuguese slave ship (1658).

Portuguese slave names, 57, 216, 207, 364

possessions of slaves, *see* personal property of slaves

post-mortem inspections, 253

posts, *see* cattle posts; outposts (VOC)

potestas (legal), *see under* fatherhood

poverty, *see* church fund; free blacks:debt; manumission: sureties

power of slave owners, *see* authority:of slave owners

powerlessness of slaves, *see* helplessness of slaves

prayer services (Slave Lodge), *see* religious instruction

pregnancy, 62, 149, 194, 254

prejudice (racial), *see* equality of races (social and legal); free blacks:discrimination

price of manumission, *see entries under* manumission

prices of slaves (not indexed exhaustively), 61, 83, 86, 88, 91, 95–96, 98–99 *passim*, 120, 124, 125, 210, 213, 286, 311, 314, 318, 319, 333–334; averages, 96; charged by visiting slave ships, 105, 124–125; for experienced slaves, 198, 235; profits, 121, 124; rixdollar as unit of calculation, 95. *See also* elderly slaves: diminished value; *and under* Guinea; Madagascar; São Tomé (Guinea).

prisoners, *see* convicts and deportees

private earnings of slaves, *see under* money

private slaves, 73–74, 88–89, 195–265 *passim*; first sales (1658), 61 *passim*; as investment, 243; slave children, 256–257, 365; elderly, 333; records, 276; holdings, 205; of individual slave owners (examples), 63–64, 86, 97, 98, 198–205 *passim*, 262; spread over several properties, 199–200;

sexual imbalance, 254;
rapid changes of owner-
ship, 209; reputation, 187;
letting out of slaves (for self-
employment), 228; lending of
slaves, 262; slaves received from
Company, 102; clothing (genl.),
217–219; rations (general), 216.
*See also entries and references
under the following:* 'average
household'; clothing; disposal
of slaves; farm communities;
hiring of slaves (from owners);
koeliegeld; manumission; rations;
records of deserters; slave
ownership; statistics.
privies, 73, 133, 224
'prize negroes', 305
prizes (booty), 46, 56, 305
probate inventories: listing of
slaves, 213
profession of faith (Christianity),
see church membership
profits, *see* prices of slaves:profits
promiscuity, *see* interracial relationships; prostitution;
pronken (punishment), *see* public
exhibition of offenders
prostitution, 160–161. *See also* Slave
Lodge:as brothel; venereal
diseases.
protection against maltreatment, 67,
253(2x), 294–295. *See also* 'bill of
rights' (1823).
protest by slaves, *see* arson; complaints; desertion; sabotage;
suicide; violence against slave
owners
public auctions, *see* auctions
public conduct of slaves, 226, 231, 303
public exhibition of corpses (capital
punishment), *see* capital
punishment:exposure of corpses
public exhibition of offenders
(punishment), 291, 292–293
Pulicat (India), *see* Paliacatte
(Coromandel)
punishment (genl.), 35, 65, 191,

289–291; by fellow slaves, 197–
198; dishonouring effect, 373,
378, 378–380, 382; disparity of
punishments between races,
302–304; legislation, 67; severity
justified by Council of Justice
(1796), 260–261, 289–290, 303;
British legislation (1823), 260. *See
also* caffers (officials).
punishments (specific): Antilles,
302; Batavia, 301–302; random
examples (1674–1708), 291–292;
of deserting Company slaves
(legislation, 1711–27), 298. *See
also* branding; chaining;
'domestic correction'; hamstringing; hard labour; horning; imprisonment; mutilation;
scourging; symbolic punishment (of whites). *See further the
references under* capital punishment.
Purakkad (India), *see* Porca (Malabar)
purchase of freedom, *see under*
manumission
pursuit of deserters, *see* deserters:
pursuit; Khoikhoi:and pursuit
of deserters

Quartel (ship), see *Kwartel*
quarterbreeds (term), *see* castizos
Quilon (Malabar), 208
quilts, *see* palempores
quotations from slave testimonies,
see personal statements by slaves
(genl.)

Raapenburg (farm), 367
race relations, *see* interracial marriages; equality of races (social
and legal); interracial relations;
personal relationships
racial tensions, *see* interracial tensions
racially mixed marriages, *see* interracial marriages
racially mixed relationships, *see*
illegitimacy; interracial relationships

rack (instrument of torture), 298–299
raiding, *see* cattle raiding
rape, 268
Rapenburg (farm), *see* Raapenburg
ration money, 184
rations, 28, 43, 53, 55, 108, 138–143,
187, 216–217, 259, 289; bread, 141;
fish, 28, 75, 138–141 *passim*, 216;
game, 139, 216–217; horse meat,
278; meat, 139–140 *passim*;
penguin meat and eggs, 43, 74–
75; pepper, 142, 321; rice, 28, 74,
83, 114, 138–139, 141, 176, 178;
seal meat, 74, 138; turmeric, 142;
vegetables, 142, 217;
preparation of food, 75, 142,
184; morning meal, 217; of
mandoors, 182; of sick, 140, 149;
on slave ships, 60, 121; complaints, 138–139 *passim*, 149, 251;
discrimination on grounds of
colour, 372. *See also* alcohol;
tobacco.
reading and writing, *see* literacy
rebellions, *see* social tensions
(slavery); slave ships:revolts;
uprisings
receiving, *see* theft
records (private slaves), *see* legal
records; probate inventories:
listing of slaves; statistics
records (VOC), *see* Company
slaves:census; Company slaves:
records; statistics
recreation, *see* free time and
recreation; gambling
Red Sea, 17, 111
Reformed Church, *see* baptism;
church attendance (slave
children); church fund; church
membership; ministers of
religion; religious instruction;
sick comforters
religious instruction, 19, 57, 153–154,
155, 163–165 *passim*, 167, 325; as
condition for manumission, 45,
324, 325, 327; of Ary van
Bengalen by J. van der Heiden,

380. *See also* church attendance
(slave children).
renegades, *see* deserters
repatriation to the East (manumitted slaves, exiles and convicts),
308, 311, 316, 317, 319 *passim*, 321,
327, 331–332; forcible repatriation suggested (1749), 321–322
replacement of slaves, *see* exchange
of slaves
reports on slavery and slaves: K.J.
Slotsboo (1710), 137, 141–142,
144–145, 171, 183, 184, 197; 'De
Chavonnes report' (1717), 5, 170,
193–194, 196–198; Council of
Justice (1796), 260–261, 289–290,
303; Fiscal (1813), 219, 231
reputation (genl.), *see* honour
reputation of slaves, *see under the
following:* Angolan slaves;
Company slaves; Guinean
slaves; Madagascan slaves;
Malabar (India); private slaves
research, *see* historical research
resentment, *see* emotions of slaves:
anger and resentment
resistance to slavery, *see references
under* defiance by slaves
respect, *see* modes of address; personal relationships (between
masters and slaves); terminology of slavery
respectability, *see* honour
restrictions on slaves: clothing, 219.
See also helplessness of slaves;
legal position of slaves; legislation.
return fleet (VOC), 26, 39, 310, 311,
313, 331
revenge of slaves, *see references under*
defiance by slaves
revolts, *see* social tensions (slavery);
slave ships:revolts; uprisings
rewards: for killing of wild animals,
237; for return of deserters, 274,
282–283, 289
rice, *see under* rations
rice rations (1678), 311
Riebeek-Kasteel, 218, 244, 280

sexual imbalance in slave population, 37, 179, 254
sexual relationships, *see* interracial marriages; interracial relationships; 'paired slaves'
'shaved Chinese' (term), 320
sheltering deserters, *see* harbouring deserters
shepherds, *see* farm work
ships and shipping, 341. *See also* Danish ships; English ships; French ships; Portuguese ships. *See also* manumission: by visitors; prizes (booty); return fleet (VOC); stow-aways; transactions:with passing ships; transportation of slaves (between Batavia, Cape and Europe). *See also the entries and references under* slave ships.
shoemaker's trade, 338
shoes, 219
Siam, 125; as toponym, 282
sick comforters, 150, 152, 163–164 *passim*, 309; as slave owners, 35, 36, 44, 333
sickness and health, 135, 136, 138, 142 *passim*, 145, 146; epidemics, 85, 140; rations of sick, 140, 149; instructions to slave dealers, 60; sickness among new arrivals, 56, 62, 64, 108, 108, 114.
    See also acclimatisation; Company slaves:mortality rate; deaths and burial; medical care; smallpox; venereal diseases.
signatures, *see* literacy:signatures of free blacks
signs and signals, 275
Sillada (Sumatra), 117
Sillida (ship), 118
Simon's Bay, 138
singing, 165; in the streets, 231
Sirganj (Bangladesh), 40
size of slave holdings, *see references under* slave holdings
skippers (in slave transactions), *see* transactions:with passing ships

slave children, *see* children
Slave Coast (West Africa) *see* Guinea
slave code: Antilles, 302. *See also* 'bill of rights' (1823).
slave dealers (Cape), 88, 96–97, 211. *See further under* slave ships.
'slave experience', 195
slave families, *see* family life of slaves; family relationships
slave holdings, *see* private slaves: slave holdings; statistics (slaves and slave trade)
slave house (VOC, Table Valley), *see under* accommodation of slaves (VOC). *See also* Slave Lodge (Table Valley).
'Slave House' (name), 132
slave houses (on farms), 222–224
slave kitchens (on farms), 224–225
slave labour (genl.), 193–198 *passim*
Slave Lodge (Table Valley), 131–168 *passim*; name, 132; plan, 134; administration, 181–183; regulations (1716), 162, 184–185; population figures, 192, 205; description, 132–136, 181; alterations, 133, 135, 137; routine, 162, 168, 184–185; female population, 156; children, 135, 163, 305; as brothel, 156, 156, 158, 160 *passim*, 161–162; violent incidents, 185. *See also* officials (VOC):in Slave Lodge; slave officials.
slave marriages, *see* 'paired slaves'
slave officials, 82, 144–145, 182–184, 194; preference for halfbreeds, 187. *See also* caffers (officials); *mandoors* (officials): slaves; schoolmaster (Slave Lodge); schoolmistress (Slave Lodge).
slave ownership: corrupting effect, 253. *See further* authority of slave owners; Company slaves (Cape); free blacks:as slave owners; ministers of religion:as slave owners; officials (VOC):as slave owners; private slaves:

slave holdings (individuals); sick comforters:as slave owners; social tensions (slavery).

slave ships, 15–16, 56, 113, 114, 118–119; in slave trade with Madagascar, 29–31 *passim*, 103–106 *passim*, 110–126 *passim*, 118 (list of names); instructions, 121; revolts, 118–119, 121–122; visits to Cape, 88, 105–106 *passim*, 124–125. *See also* Hasselt; Johanna Catharina; Voorhout.

slave society, *see* slave ownership; social tensions (slavery); white population:and servile work

slave women, *see* female slaves

slave trade, *see under* Angola; Annabom; Batavia (Jakarta); Ceylon; Colombo; Coromandel (India); Guinea; Indonesian archipelago; Macassar (Indonesia); Madagascar; Malabar (India); Mauritius; São Tomé (Guinea); Sumatra (Indonesia); V.O.C.; West India Company (WIC).

> *See also* Atlantic slave trade; Muslim slave trade; Portuguese:and slave trade; Saharan slave trade. *See also* slave dealers (Cape); slave ships; trade goods; transactions (genl.).

slavers (dealers), *see* slave dealers (Cape)

slavers (ships), *see* slave ships

slavery (Cape): as unfamiliar phenomenon to colonists, 12, 65–66, 245, 295; changes in system over time, 6, 148; danger of generalisations, 127, 195; distinctive character, 205; irrelevance of information on Atlantic slave trade, 27, 205; uneconomical nature, 198; 'slave experience', 195; 'world of the slaves' (Cape), 205;

> need for slaves first expressed (1652), 28; first recorded slave (1653); first

slaving expedition (1654), 32; first manumission (1656), 39–40, 306; first manumission of Cape slave (1658), 44, 306; first batch of slaves received (1658), 56; first recorded slave transaction (1658), 44; first slave sales (1658), 61; first slave child baptised (1659), 79–80; first successful expedition to Madagascar (1676), 110.

> *See also* discipline; emancipation of slaves; legislation; manumission; morality of slavery; punishment (genl.); punishments (specific); reports:'De Chavonnes report' (1717); social tensions (slavery).

slavery (East), 11–27 *passim*

sleeping arrangements of slaves, *see* accommodation of slaves; bedding; beds; hammocks; palempores

smallpox, 136, 169, 221

smoking: as measurement of time (scourging), 293. *See further* tobacco.

social life, *see* free time and recreation

social position of slaves, 381–382

social tensions (slavery), 65–66; fear of violence, 143, 202, 231, 238–240, 260–261, 266–267, 275, 288, 290 *passim*, 295; articulated (1707), 383–385, 386–387. *See also* deserters: armed bands; uprisings; *references under* defiance by slaves; *and entries beginning with* violence…

Sofala (East Africa), 119

Soldaat (ship), 118, 119, 136

solidarity, *see* co-operation of slaves with system; family relationships; free blacks: cohesiveness as group; harbouring deserters; personal relationships (between masters and slaves):loyalty and affection

'Sonqua Hottentoos', *see* Bushmen
'South Land' (Australia), 178
Southern Netherlands (Belgium), 353
Spaanse bok (form of punishment), 296
spiritual welfare, *see* baptism; church attendance (slave children); church membership; religious instruction
sponsors (baptism), *see under* baptism
Sri Lanka, *see* Ceylon
St Augustine's Bay (Madagascar), 103–106 *passim*, 111, 114, 124
St Helena: capture (1673), 108, 109
staff of office (VOC officials), 371–372 *passim*
stake (instrument of punishment), *see* burning at stake (death penalty)
stamijn (textile), 426 n113
Standvastigheid (ship), 118
statements, *see* autobiographical statements by slaves; personal statements by slaves (genl.)
statistics (genl.): population, 52, 63, 195–196; freeburghers, 88, 199, 269; free blacks, 307, 325, 337, 355; 'average households', 199, 200, 201, 242; *knechten*, 249, 280–281; garrison, 71–72 *passim*, 157–158; 175, 176. *See also under further specific subjects.*
statistics (slaves and slave trade), 34–37 *passim*, 63, 85, 305, 306; Company slaves, 130, 140, 168, 192–193, 194; slaves from Angola and Guinea (1658), 63; from Madagascar, 125–126; private slaves, 85, 94, 195–196, 199; convicts, 321; British period, 194. *See also under further specific subjects.*
status of slaves, *see entries and references under* helplessness of slaves; legal position of slaves; legislation; restrictions on slaves;

social position of slaves; *and references under* defiance by slaves
status symbols (slave owners), *see under* baptism; manumission
Statutes of Batavia, 18–19, 25, 219, 251, 306, 334, 334
Stellenbosch, 90, 202, 328–329; 'average' household, 199, 200, 242; free blacks, 183, 313, 316, 334, 338, 341, 346, 349, 350, 360; establishment as farmers, 114, 328–329; numbers, 328, 329; slaves, 168, 171, 176, 189, 199, 228, 237–238, 292, 295–296 *passim*; *caffers*, 189, 245; deserters, 277–278; P. Kolb here, 380. *See also* free blacks: land ownership (Stellenbosch).
stimulants, *see* alcohol; opium; tobacco
stocks (instrument of punishment), 292–293. *See further* public exhibition (punishment).
stolen goods, *see* theft
stowaways, 32, 33; escape to Batavia, 286–287; escape to Europe, 285–286
strangling (death penalty), 299
street vendors, 227
streets, *see* public conduct of slaves
strictness, *see* discipline
subservience, *see* modes of address; personal relationships (between masters and slaves); terminology of slavery
substitution of slaves, *see* exchange of slaves
suicide, 255, 264, 301; punishment, 264–265
Sulawesi (Indonesia), *see* Celebes
Sumatra (Indonesia), 26; slave trade, 15; slavery, 117–119 *passim*, 122; gold mines, 117–118, 122
Sumbawa (Indonesia), 15
'Sunday clothes' (slaves), 237
Sunday labour, 217, 236, 260

335; earliest transaction recorded (1658), 44; administration, 209; private records of transactions, 210, 211–212; statistics, 92, 94; reactions of slaves concerned, 213–214, 255, 263, 300.

See also auctions; Batavia: private slave trade with Cape; children:transactions; free blacks:slave ownership; illegal transactions; prices; slave dealers (Cape). *See also references under* disposal of slaves.

transfer of slaves: as gifts, 215, 329, 332; to Council of Justice, 215. *See further references under* disposal of slaves.

Transkei, 285, 437 n65

transportation of slaves (between Batavia, Cape and Europe), 37–39, 91, 102, 178–180, 190, 208–209, 331, 332, 367. *See also* transactions:with passing ships.

treatment of slaves, *see* personal relations (between masters and slaves); violence against slaves

tree planting, 173, 174, 202

truancy, *see* desertion

Tulbagh valley, 262, 279

Tulp (ship), 29–31 *passim*

turmeric, *see under* rations

Tuticorin (Coromandel), 16, 95, 101, 101–102

Tygerberg, 63, 67–68, 69, 97, 200, 223, 242, 273

Uitwijk (farm), 358–359

uneconomical nature of slavery, 198

uniforms: of *caffers*, 190

'unpaired slaves', *see* 'paired slaves'

upkeep of halfbreed children, *see* children:suggested upkeep

upkeep of manumitted slaves, *see* manumission:support of manumitted slaves

upkeep of slaves, *see* cost of upkeep (genl.); Company's slaves:cost of upkeep

uprisings: Roggeveld (1772), 298. *See also* social tensions (slavery).

urine: as sterilising agent, 296

V.O.C. (Dutch East India Company), 11; and slavery, 13–27 *passim*; and institutional slaveholding, 13; slave trade, 12–27 *passim*. *See also* Batavia (Jakarta); Company slaves (Cape); Gentlemen XVII; officials (VOC); outposts (VOC); return fleet; Statutes of Batavia.

vagabonds, *see* deserters

vagrants, *see* deserters

value of slaves, *see* prices

vendors (hawkers), 227

venereal diseases, 162

Vengurla (Malabar), 75, 101

verbal statements, *see* autobiographical statements by slaves; personal statements by slaves (genl.)

Vergelegen (farm), 98, 140, 232, 293, 375; slave house, 224. *See also* van der Stel, W.A.: personal slaves, *in Index 1*.

Verlorevlei, 282

violence against free blacks, 370–372 *passim*, 385–386

violence against Khoikhoi, 68, 252, 271, 301, 304, 386

violence against slave owners, 240–242, 247, 288, 289, 292, 299

violence against slaves, 66–67, 251–254, 268; unsavoury reputation of Bokkeveld and Roggeveld, 254; disapproval of maltreatment, 253; legal situation, 253–254; murder, 251–253, 304; alleged murder, 253–254. *See also* protection against maltreatment.

violence among slaves, 185, 292; murder, 277, 292. *See also* crimes of passion.

Vishoek (Gordon's Bay), 140, 216

visiting ships, 26; statistics, 158. *See also* return fleet (VOC); ships and shipping (genl.).

visitors to the Cape: statistics, 158; barter, 227
Vissershok (outpost), 175
visual information on slaves, *see* pictorial records of slaves
vocabulary of slavery, *see* terminology of slavery
Voëlvlei (Vogelvalley), 279
Vogelvalley, see Voëlvlei
Voorhout (ship), 110, 112–114, 116, 117, 120–121 *passim*, 123, 136, 156
vrijgeboren (term), 307
vrijzwart (term), 307

W.I.C., *see* West India Company
wagon drivers, 177(2*x*), 198, 235, 242
washerwomen, *see* laundry work
washing, *see* personal hygiene
Waterhoen (ship), 104–105, 107
weapons, *see* arms and ammunition
werkmeiden (term), 182
West Africa, *see* Angola; Guinea
West India Company (WIC), 26, 50–51, 53, 54, 58, 59; charter territory, 53, 126; slave trade, 17, 55, 122
West Indies (genl.), 105, 110, 124, 205, 296; as possible source of slaves for Cape, 126. *See also* Antilles; Barbados; Curaçao.
Westerwijk (ship), 118, 122
wet nurses, 232, 331
whipping (punishment), *see* scourging
whipping posts, 134, 274, 292; improvised, 239
whistling in streets, 231
white labour, 61, 71–72, 85, 168, 169, 170, 174, 193, 196
white population, 11, 65–66; origins, 242, 247–248, 295; previous experience of slavery, 12, 65–66, 245, 295; social divisions, 250; unmarried men, 157; women, 73, 89; and servile work, 73, 84, 196, 197; dependence on slave labour, 5, 110, 170, 196, 193–194, 196–198; economic

progress, 89–91, 198–199, 202, 204, 266, 333; life style, 94; living conditions, 201, 203–205 *passim*, 252–253, 266–267.
    See also equality of races (social and legal); farming; interracial marriages; interracial relationships; *knechten*; private slaves;white labour; *and references under* interracial tensions.
wijf (term), 332
Wijnberg (Liesbeek valley), *see* Wynberg
wills and testaments, *see* testamentary dispositions
witnesses (baptism), *see* baptism: sponsors
women: death penalty, 299. *See further* female slaves; officials (VOC):wives of officials; sexual imbalance in slave population; white population:women.
work of slaves (genl.), 28, 35, 61, 71–73, 82–83, 168–180 *passim*, 226–232. *See also* free blacks: work; *and specific types of work, e.g.* farm work (by slaves); fishing industry; wagon drivers. *See further under* children; female slaves.
working hours, 168, 259–260
'world of slaves' (Cape), 205
writing, *see* literacy
'writing off', *see* death and burial: official records
written texts, *see under* literacy
Wynberg (Liesbeek valley), 272, 358

Xhosa tribes, 285

young people, *see* age of slaves

Zambesi, 119
Zandloper (ship), 107
Zimbabwe, 119
Zwaag (ship), 166, 178
Zwarte River, 280
'Zwartemans' (nickname), 68